The Practice of Cloud System Administration

Volume 2

The Practice of Cloud System Administration

DevOps and SRE Practices for Web Services

Volume 2

Thomas A. Limoncelli
Strata R. Chalup
Christina J. Hogan

♦Addison-Wesley

Upper Saddle River, NJ • Boston • Indianapolis • San Francisco
New York • Toronto • Montreal • London • Munich • Paris • Madrid
Capetown • Sydney • Tokyo • Singapore • Mexico City

Many of the designations used by manufacturers and sellers to distinguish their products are claimed as trademarks. Where those designations appear in this book, and the publisher was aware of a trademark claim, the designations have been printed with initial capital letters or in all capitals.

The authors and publisher have taken care in the preparation of this book, but make no expressed or implied warranty of any kind and assume no responsibility for errors or omissions. No liability is assumed for incidental or consequential damages in connection with or arising out of the use of the information or programs contained herein.

For information about buying this title in bulk quantities, or for special sales opportunities (which may include electronic versions; custom cover designs; and content particular to your business, training goals, marketing focus, or branding interests), please contact our corporate sales department at corpsales@pearsoned.com or (800) 382-3419.

For government sales inquiries, please contact governmentsales@pearsoned.com.

For questions about sales outside the United States, please contact intlcs@pearsoned.com.

Visit us on the Web: informit.com/aw

Library of Congress Cataloging-in-Publication Data
Limoncelli, Tom.
   The practice of cloud system administration : designing and operating large distributed systems /
Thomas A. Limoncelli, Strata R. Chalup, Christina J. Hogan.
      volumes   cm
   Includes bibliographical references and index.
   ISBN-13: 978-0-321-94318-7 (volume 2 : paperback)
   ISBN-10: 0-321-94318-X (volume 2 : paperback)
  1. Computer networks—Management. 2. Computer systems. 3. Cloud computing. 4. Electronic data processing—Distributed processing. I. Chalup, Strata R. II. Hogan, Christina J. III. Title.
   TK5105.5.L529 2015
   004.67'82068—dc23   2014024033

ISBN-13: 978-0-321-94318-7
ISBN-10: 0-321-94318-X
3   17

Contents at a Glance

Contents

Part II   Operations: Running It

7   Operations in a Distributed World

Preface

Which of the following statements are true?

1. The most reliable systems are built using cheap, unreliable components.
2. The techniques that Google uses to scale to billions of users follow the same patterns you can use to scale a system that handles hundreds of users.
3. The more risky a procedure is, the more you should do it.
4. Some of the most important software features are the ones that users never see.
5. You should pick random machines and power them off.
6. The code for every feature Facebook will announce in the next six months is probably in your browser already.
7. Updating software multiple times a day requires little human effort.
8. Being oncall doesn't have to be a stressful, painful experience.
9. You shouldn't monitor whether machines are up.
10. Operations and management can be conducted using the scientific principles of experimentation and evidence.
11. Google has rehearsed what it would do in case of a zombie attack.

All of these statements are true. By the time you finish reading this book, you'll know why.

This is a book about building and running cloud-based services on a large scale: internet-based services for millions or billions of users. That said, every day more and more enterprises are adopting these techniques. Therefore, this is a book for everyone.

The intended audience is system administrators and their managers. We do not assume a background in computer science, but we do assume experience with UNIX/Linux system administration, networking, and operating system concepts.

Our focus is on building and operating the services that make up the cloud, not a guide to using cloud-based services.

Cloud services must be available, fast, and secure. At cloud scale, this is a unique engineering feat. Therefore cloud-scale services are engineered differently than your typical enterprise service. Being available is important because the Internet is open 24 × 7 and has users in every time zone. Being fast is important because users are frustrated by slow services, so slow services lose out to faster rivals. Being secure is important because, as caretakers of other people's data, we are duty-bound (and legally responsible) to protect people's data.

These requirements are intermixed. If a site is not secure, by definition, it cannot be made reliable. If a site is not fast, it is not sufficiently available. If a site is down, by definition, it is not fast.

The most visible cloud-scale services are web sites. However, there is a huge ecosystem of invisible internet-accessible services that are not accessed with a browser. For example, smartphone apps use API calls to access cloud-based services.

For the remainder of this book we will tend to use the term "distributed computing" rather than "cloud computing." *Cloud computing* is a marketing term that means different things to different people. *Distributed computing* describes an architecture where applications and services are provided using many machines rather than one.

This is a book of fundamental principles and practices that are timeless. Therefore we don't make recommendations about which specific products or technologies to use. We could provide a comparison of the top five most popular web servers or NoSQL databases or continuous build systems. If we did, then this book would be out of date the moment it is published. Instead, we discuss the qualities one should look for when selecting such things. We provide a model to work from. This approach is intended to prepare you for a long career where technology changes over time but you are always prepared. We will, of course, illustrate our points with specific technologies and products, but not as an endorsement of those products and services.

This book is, at times, idealistic. This is deliberate. We set out to give the reader a vision of how things can be, what to strive for. We are here to raise the bar.

About This Book

The book is structured in two parts, Design and Operations.

Part I captures our thinking on the design of large, complex, cloud-based distributed computing systems. After the Introduction, we tackle each element of design from the bottom layers to the top. We cover distributed systems from the point of view of a system administrator, not a computer scientist. To operate a system, one must be able to understand its internals.

Part II describes how to run such systems. The first chapters cover the most fundamental issues. Later chapters delve into more esoteric technical activities, then high-level planning and strategy that tie together all of the above.

At the end is extra material including an assessment system for operations teams, a highly biased history of distributed computing, templates for forms mentioned in the text, recommended reading, and other reference material.

We're excited to present a new feature of our book series: our operational assessment system. This system consists of a series of assessments you can use to evaluate your operations and find areas of improvement. The assessment questions and "Look For" recommendations are found in Appendix A. Chapter 20 is the instruction manual.

Acknowledgments

This book wouldn't have been possible without the help and feedback we received from our community and people all over the world. The DevOps community was generous in its assistance.

First, we'd like to thank our spouses and families: Christine Polk, Mike Chalup, and Eliot and Joanna Lear. Your love and patience make all this possible.

If we have seen further, it is by standing on the shoulders of giants. Certain chapters relied heavily on support and advice from particular people: John Looney and Cian Synnott (Chapter 1); Marty Abbott and Michael Fisher (Chapter 5); Damon Edwards, Alex Honor, and Jez Humble (Chapters 9 and 10); John Allspaw (Chapter 12); Brent Chapman (Chapter 15); Caskey Dickson and Theo Schlossnagle (Chapters 16 and 17); Arun Kejariwal and Bruce Yan (Chapter 18); Benjamin Treynor Sloss (Chapter 19); and Geoff Halprin (Chapter 20 and Appendix A).

Thanks to Gene Kim for the "strategic" inspiration and encouragement.

Dozens of people helped us—some by supplying anecdotes, some by reviewing parts of or the entire book. The only fair way to thank them all is alphabetically and to apologize in advance to anyone we left out: Thomas Baden, George Beech, Raymond Blum, Kyle Brandt, Mark Burgess, Nick Craver, Geoff Dalgas, Robert P. J. Day, Patrick Debois, Bill Duane, Paul Evans, David Fullerton, Tom Geller, Peter Grace, Elizabeth Hamon Reid, Jim Hickstein, Zachary Hueras, Matt Jones, Jennifer Joy, Jimmy Kaplowitz, Daniel V. Klein, Steven Levine, Cory Lueninghoener, Shane Madden, Jim Maurer, Stephen McHenry, Dinah McNutt, Scott Hazen Mueller, Steve Murawski, Mohit Muthanna, Lenny Rachitsky, Amy Rich, Adele Shakal, Bart Silverstrim, Josh Simon, Joel Spolsky, Desiree Sylvester, Win Treese, Todd Underwood, Nicole Forsgren Velasquez, and Dave Zwieback.

Last but not least, thanks to everyone from Addison-Wesley. In particular, thanks to Debra Williams Cauley, for guiding us to Addison-Wesley and steering us the entire way; Michael Thurston, for editing our earliest drafts and reshaping them to be much, much better; Kim Boedigheimer, who coordinated and assisted us calmly even when we were panicking; Lori Hughes, our LaTeX wizard; Julie Nahil, our production manager; Jill Hobbs, our copyeditor; and John Fuller and Mark Taub, for putting up with all our special requests!

Part I   Design: Building It

Chapter 1: Designing in a Distributed World
Overview of how distributed systems are designed.

Chapter 2: Designing for Operations
Features software should have to enable smooth operations.

Chapter 3: Selecting a Service Platform
Physical and virtual machines, private and public clouds.

Chapter 4: Application Architectures
Building blocks for creating web and other applications.

Chapter 5: Design Patterns for Scaling
Building blocks for growing a service.

Chapter 6: Design Patterns for Resiliency
Building blocks for creating systems that survive failure.

Part II   Operations: Running It

Chapter 7: Operations in a Distributed World
Overview of how distributed systems are run.

Chapter 8: DevOps Culture
Introduction to DevOps culture, its history and practices.

Chapter 9: Service Delivery: The Build Phase
How a service gets built and prepared for production.

Chapter 10: Service Delivery: The Deployment Phase
How a service is tested, approved, and put into production.

Chapter 11: Upgrading Live Services
How to upgrade services without downtime.

Chapter 12: Automation
Creating tools and automating operational work.

Chapter 13: Design Documents
Communicating designs and intentions in writing.

Chapter 14: Oncall
Handling exceptions.

Chapter 15: Disaster Preparedness
Making systems stronger through planning and practice.

Chapter 16: Monitoring Fundamentals
Monitoring terminology and strategy.

Chapter 17: Monitoring Architecture and Practice
The components and practice of monitoring.

Chapter 18: Capacity Planning
Planning for and providing additional resources before we need them.

Chapter 19: Creating KPIs
Driving behavior scientifically through measurement and reflection.

Chapter 20: Operational Excellence
Strategies for constant improvement.

Epilogue
Some final thoughts.

Part III Appendices

Appendix A: Assessments
Appendix B: The Origins and Future of Distributed Computing and Clouds
Appendix C: Scaling Terminology and Concepts
Appendix D: Templates and Examples
Appendix E: Recommended Reading
Bibliography
Index

About the Authors

Thomas A. Limoncelli is an internationally recognized author, speaker, and system administrator. During his seven years at Google NYC, he was an SRE for projects such as Blog Search, Ganeti, and various internal enterprise IT services. He now works as an SRE at Stack Exchange, Inc., home of ServerFault.com and Stack-Overflow.com. His first paid system administration job was as a student at Drew University in 1987, and he has since worked at small and large companies, including AT&T/Lucent Bell Labs. His best-known books include *Time Management for System Administrators* (O'Reilly) and *The Practice of System and Network Administration, Second Edition* (Addison-Wesley). His hobbies include grassroots activism, for which his work has been recognized at state and national levels. He lives in New Jersey.

Strata R. Chalup has been leading and managing complex IT projects for many years, serving in roles ranging from project manager to director of operations. Strata has authored numerous articles on management and working with teams and has applied her management skills on various volunteer boards, including BayLISA and SAGE. She started administering VAX Ultrix and Unisys UNIX in 1983 at MIT in Boston, and spent the dot-com years in Silicon Valley building internet services for clients like iPlanet and Palm. In 2007, she joined Tom and Christina to create the second edition of *The Practice of System and Network Administration* (Addison-Wesley). Her hobbies include working with new technologies, including Arduino and various 2D CAD/CAM devices, as well as being a master gardener. She lives in Santa Clara County, California.

Christina J. Hogan has twenty years of experience in system administration and network engineering, from Silicon Valley to Italy and Switzerland. She has gained experience in small startups, mid-sized tech companies, and large global corporations. She worked as a security consultant for many years and her customers included eBay, Silicon Graphics, and SystemExperts. In 2005 she and Tom shared the SAGE Outstanding Achievement Award for their book *The Practice of System and Network Administration* (Addison-Wesley). She has a bachelor's degree in mathematics, a master's degree in computer science, a doctorate in aeronautical engineering, and a diploma in law. She also worked for six years as an aerodynamicist in a Formula 1 racing team and represented Ireland in the 1988 Chess Olympiad. She lives in Switzerland.

Introduction

The goal of this book is to help you build and run the best cloud-scale service possible. What is the ideal environment that we seek to create?

Business Objectives

Simply stated, the end result of our ideal environment is that business objectives are met. That may sound a little boring but actually it is quite exciting to work where the entire company is focused and working together on the same goals.

To achieve this, we must understand the business objectives and work backward to arrive at the system we should build.

Meeting business objectives means knowing what those objectives are, having a plan to achieve them, and working through the roadblocks along the way.

Well-defined business objectives are measurable, and such measurements can be collected in an automated fashion. A dashboard is automatically generated so everyone is aware of progress. This transparency enhances trust.

Here are some sample business objectives:

- Sell our products via a web site
- Provide service 99.99 percent of the time
- Process x million purchases per month, growing 10 percent monthly
- Introduce new features twice a week
- Fix major bugs within 24 hours

In our ideal environment, business and technical teams meet their objectives and project goals predictably and reliably. Because of this, both types of teams trust that other teams will meet their future objectives. As a result, teams can plan better. They can make more aggressive plans because there is confidence that external dependencies will not fail. This permits even more aggressive planning. Such an approach creates an upward spiral that accelerates progress throughout the company, benefiting everyone.

Ideal System Architecture

The ideal service is built on a solid architecture. It meets the requirements of the service today and provides an obvious path for growth as the system becomes more popular and receives more traffic. The system is resilient to failure. Rather than being surprised by failures and treating them as exceptions, the architecture accepts that hardware and software failures are a part of the physics of information technology (IT). As a result, the architecture includes redundancy and resiliency features that work around failures. Components fail but the system survives.

Each subsystem that makes up our service is itself a service. All subsystems are programmable via an application programming interface (API). Thus, the entire system is an ecosystem of interconnected subservices. This is called a service-oriented architecture (SOA). Because all these systems communicate over the same underlying protocol, there is uniformity in how they are managed. Because each subservice is loosely coupled to the others, all of these services can be independently scaled, upgraded, or replaced.

The geometry of the infrastructure is described electronically. This electronic description is read by IT automation systems, which then build the production environment without human intervention. Because of this automation, the entire infrastructure can be re-created elsewhere. Software engineers use the automation to make micro-versions of the environment for their personal use. Quality and test engineers use the automation to create environments for system tests.

This "infrastructure as code" can be achieved whether we use physical machines or virtual machines, and whether they are in datacenters we run or are hosted by a cloud provider. With virtual machines there is an obvious API available for spinning up a new machine. However, even with physical machines, the entire flow from bare metal to working system can be automated. In our ideal world the automation makes it possible to create environments using combinations of physical and virtual machines. Developers may build the environment out of virtual machines. The production environment might consist of a mixture of physical and virtual machines. The temporary and unexpected need for additional capacity may require extending the production environment into one or more cloud providers for some period of time.

Ideal Release Process

Our ideal environment has a smooth flow of code from development to operations.

Traditionally (not in our ideal environment) the sequence looks like this:

1. Developers check code into a repository.
2. Test engineers put the code through a number of tests.

3. If all the tests pass, the a release engineer builds the packages that will be used to deploy the software. Most of the files come from the source code repository, but some files may be needed from other sources such as a graphics department or documentation writers.

4. A test environment is created; without an "infrastructure as code" model, this may take weeks.

5. The packages are deployed into a test environment.

6. Test engineers perform further tests, focusing on the interaction between subsystems.

7. If all these tests succeed, the code is put into production.

8. System administrators upgrade systems while looking for failures.

9. If there are failures, the software is rolled back.

Doing these steps manually incurs a lot of risk, owing to the assumptions that the right people are available, that the steps are done the same way every time, that nobody makes mistakes, and that all the tasks are completed in time.

Mistakes, bugs, and errors happen, of course—and as a result defects are passed down the line to the next stage. When a mistake is discovered the flow of progress is reversed as the team members who were responsible for the previous stage are told to fix their problem. This means progress is halted and time is lost.

A typical response to a risky process is to do it as rarely as possible. Thus there is a temptation to do as few releases as possible. The result is "mega-releases" launched only a few times a year.

However, by batching up so many changes at once, we actually create more risk. How can we be sure thousands of changes, released simultaneously, will all work on the first try? We can't. Therefore we become even more recalcitrant toward and fearful of making changes. Soon change becomes nearly impossible and innovation comes to a halt.

Not so in our ideal environment.

In our ideal environment, we find automation that eliminates all manual steps in the software build, test, release, and deployment processes. The automation accurately and consistently performs tests that prevent defects from being passed to the next step. As a consequence, the flow of progress is in one direction: forward.

Rather than mega-releases, our ideal environment creates micro-releases. We reduce risk by doing many deployments, each with a few small changes. In fact, we might do 100 deployments per day.

1. When the developers check in code, a system detects this fact and triggers a series of automated tests. These tests verify basic code functionality.

2. If these tests pass, the process of building the packages is kicked off and runs in a completely automated fashion.

3. The successful creation of new packages triggers the creation of a test environment. Building a test environment used to be a long week of connecting cables and installing machines. But with infrastructure as code, the entire environment is created quickly with no human intervention.

4. When the test environment is complete, a series of automated tests are run.

5. On successful completion the new packages are rolled out to production. The roll-out is also automated but orderly and cautious.

6. Certain systems are upgraded first and the system watches for failures. Since the test environment was built with the same automation that built the production environment, there should be very few differences.

7. Seeing no failures, the new packages are rolled out to more and more systems until the entire production environment is upgraded.

In our ideal environment all problems are caught before they reach production. That is, roll-out is not a form of testing. Failure during a roll-out to production is essentially eliminated. However, if a failure does happen, it would be considered a serious issue warranting pausing new releases from going into production until a root causes analysis is completed. Tests are added to detect and prevent future occurrences of this failure. Thus, the system gets stronger over time.

Because of this automation, the traditional roles of release engineering, quality assurance, and deployment are practically unrecognizable from their roles at a traditional company. Hours of laborious manual toil are eliminated, leaving more time for improving the packaging system, improving the software quality, and refining the deployment process. In other words, people spend more time making improvements in how work is done rather than doing work itself.

A similar process is used for third-party software. Not all systems are home-grown or come with source code. Deploying third-party services and products follows a similar pattern of release, testing, deployment. However, because these products and services are developed externally, they require a slightly different process. New releases are likely to occur less frequently and we have less control over what is in each new release. The kind of testing these components require is usually related to features, compatibility, and integration.

Ideal Operations

Once the code is in production, operational objectives take precedence. The software is instrumented so that it can be monitored. Data is collected about how long it takes to process transactions from external users as well as from internal APIs. Other indicators such as memory usage are also monitored. This data is collected so that operational decisions can be made based on data, not guesses, luck, or hope. The data is stored for many years so it may be used to predict the future capacity needs.

Measurements are used to detect internal problems while they are small, long before they result in a user-visible outage. We fix problems before they become outages. An actual outage is rare and would be investigated with great diligence. When problems are detected there is a process in place to make sure they are identified, worked on, and resolved quickly.

An automated system detects problems and alerts whoever is oncall. Our oncall schedule is a rotation constructed so that each shift typically receives a manageable number of alerts. At any given time one person is the primary oncall person and is first to receive any alerts. If that individual does not respond in time, a secondary person is alerted. The oncall schedule is prepared far enough in advance that people can plan vacations, recreational activities, and personal time.

There is a "playbook" of instructions on how to handle every alert that can be generated. Each type of alert is documented with a technical description of what is wrong, what the business impact is, and how to fix the issue. The playbook is continually improved. Whoever is oncall uses the playbook to fix the problem. If it proves insufficient, there is a well-defined escalation path, usually to the oncall person for the related subsystem. Developers also participate in the oncall rotation so they understand the operational pain points of the system they are building.

All failures have a corresponding countermeasure, whether it is manually or automatically activated. Countermeasures that are activated frequently are always automated. Our monitoring system detects overuse, as this may indicate a larger problem. The monitoring system collects internal indicator data used by engineers to reduce the failure rate as well as improve the countermeasure.

The less frequently a countermeasure is activated, the less confident we are that it will work the next time it is needed. Therefore infrequently activated countermeasures are periodically and automatically exercised by intentionally causing failures. Just as we require school children to practice fire drills so that everyone knows what to do in an emergency, so we practice fire drills with our operational practices. This way our team becomes experienced at implementing the countermeasures and is confident that they work. If a database failover process doesn't work due to an unexpected dependency, it is better to learn this during a live drill on Monday at 10 AM rather than during an outage at 4 AM on a Sunday morning. Again, we reduce risk by increasing repetition rather than shying away from it. The technical term for improving something through repetition is called "practice." We strongly believe that practice makes perfect.

Our ideal environment scales automatically. As more capacity is needed, additional capacity comes from internal or external cloud providers. Our dashboards indicate when re-architecting will be a better solution than simply allocating more RAM, disk, or CPU.

Scaling down is also automatic. When the system is overloaded or degraded, we never turn users away with a "503—Service Unavailable" error. Instead, the system automatically switches to algorithms that use less resources. Bandwidth fully utilized? Low-bandwidth versions of the service kick in, displaying fewer graphics or a more simplified user interface. Databases become corrupted? A read-only version of the service keeps most users satisfied.

Each feature of our service can be individually enabled or disabled. If a feature turns out to have negative consequences, such as security holes or unexpectedly bad performance, it can be disabled without deploying a different software release.

When a feature is revised, the new code does not eliminate the old functionality. The new behavior can be disabled to reveal the old behavior. This is particularly useful when rolling out a new user interface. If a release can produce both the old and new user interface, it can be enabled on a per-user basis. This enables us to get feedback from "early access" users. On the official release date, the new feature is enabled for successively larger and larger groups. If performance problems are found, the feature can easily be reverted or switched off entirely.

In our ideal environment there is excellent operational hygiene. Like brushing our teeth, we regularly do the things that preserve good operational health. We maintain clear and updated documentation for how to handle every counter-measure, process, and alert. Overactive alerts are fine-tuned, not ignored. Open bug counts are kept to a minimum. Outages are followed by the publication of a postmortem report with recommendations on how to improve the system in the future. Any "quick fix" is followed by a root causes analysis and the implementation of a long-term fix.

Most importantly, the developers and operations people do not think of themselves as two distinct teams. They are simply specializations within one large team. Some people write more code than others; some people do more operational projects than others. All share responsibility for maintaining high uptime. To that end, all members participate in the oncall (pager) rotation. Developers are most motivated to improve code that affects operations when they feel the pain of operations, too. Operations must understand the development process if they are to be able to constructively collaborate.

Now you know our vision of an ideal environment. The remainder of this book will explain how to create and run it.

Part I

Design: Building It

Chapter 1

Designing in a Distributed World

> There are two ways of constructing
> a software design: One way is to
> make it so simple that there are
> obviously no deficiencies and the
> other way is to make it so
> complicated that there are no
> obvious deficiencies.
>
> —C.A.R. Hoare, The 1980 ACM
> Turing Award Lecture

How does Google Search work? How does your Facebook Timeline stay updated around the clock? How does Amazon scan an ever-growing catalog of items to tell you that people who bought this item also bought socks?

Is it magic? No, it's distributed computing.

This chapter is an overview of what is involved in designing services that use distributed computing techniques. These are the techniques all large web sites use to achieve their size, scale, speed, and reliability.

Distributed computing is the art of building large systems that divide the work over many machines. Contrast this with traditional computing systems where a single computer runs software that provides a service, or client–server computing where many machines remotely access a centralized service. In distributed computing there are typically hundreds or thousands of machines working together to provide a large service.

Distributed computing is different from traditional computing in many ways. Most of these differences are due to the sheer size of the system itself. Hundreds or thousands of computers may be involved. Millions of users may be served. Billions and sometimes trillions of queries may be processed.

> ### *Terms to Know*
>
> **Server:** Software that provides a function or application program interface (API). (Not a piece of hardware.)
>
> **Service:** A user-visible system or product composed of many servers.
>
> **Machine:** A virtual or physical machine.
>
> **QPS:** Queries per second. Usually how many web hits or API calls received per second.
>
> **Traffic:** A generic term for queries, API calls, or other requests sent to a server.
>
> **Performant:** A system whose performance conforms to (meets or exceeds) the design requirements. A neologism from merging "performance" and "conformant."
>
> **Application Programming Interface (API):** A protocol that governs how one server talks to another.

Speed is important. It is a competitive advantage for a service to be fast and responsive. Users consider a web site sluggish if replies do not come back in 200 ms or less. Network latency eats up most of that time, leaving little time for the service to compose the page itself.

In distributed systems, failure is normal. Hardware failures that are rare, when multiplied by thousands of machines, become common. Therefore failures are assumed, designs work around them, and software anticipates them. Failure is an expected part of the landscape.

Due to the sheer size of distributed systems, operations must be automated. It is inconceivable to manually do tasks that involve hundreds or thousands of machines. Automation becomes critical for preparation and deployment of software, regular operations, and handling failures.

1.1 Visibility at Scale

To manage a large distributed system, one must have visibility into the system. The ability to examine internal state—called **introspection**—is required to operate, debug, tune, and repair large systems.

In a traditional system, one could imagine an engineer who knows enough about the system to keep an eye on all the critical components or "just knows" what is wrong based on experience. In a large system, that level of visibility must be actively created by designing systems that draw out the information and make it visible. No person or team can manually keep tabs on all the parts.

Distributed systems, therefore, require components to generate copious logs that detail what happened in the system. These logs are then aggregated to a central location for collection, storage, and analysis. Systems may log information that is very high level, such as whenever a user makes a purchase, for each web query, or for every API call. Systems may log low-level information as well, such as the parameters of every function call in a critical piece of code.

Systems should export metrics. They should count interesting events, such as how many times a particular API was called, and make these counters accessible.

In many cases, special URLs can be used to view this internal state. For example, the Apache HTTP Web Server has a "server-status" page (`http://www.example.com/server-status/`).

In addition, components of distributed systems often appraise their own health and make this information visible. For example, a component may have a URL that outputs whether the system is ready (OK) to receive new requests. Receiving as output anything other than the byte "O" followed by the byte "K" (including no response at all) indicates that the system does not want to receive new requests. This information is used by load balancers to determine if the server is healthy and ready to receive traffic. The server sends negative replies when the server is starting up and is still initializing, and when it is shutting down and is no longer accepting new requests but is processing any requests that are still in flight.

1.2 The Importance of Simplicity

It is important that a design remain as simple as possible while still being able to meet the needs of the service. Systems grow and become more complex over time. Starting with a system that is already complex means starting at a disadvantage.

Providing competent operations requires holding a mental model of the system in one's head. As we work we imagine the system operating and use this mental model to track how it works and to debug it when it doesn't. The more complex the system, the more difficult it is to have an accurate mental model. An overly complex system results in a situation where no single person understands it all at any one time.

In *The Elements of Programming Style*, Kernighan and Plauger (1978) wrote:

> Debugging is twice as hard as writing the code in the first place. Therefore, if you write the code as cleverly as possible, you are, by definition, not smart enough to debug it.

The same is true for distributed systems. Every minute spent simplifying a design pays off time and time again when the system is in operation.

1.3 Composition

Distributed systems are composed of many smaller systems. In this section, we explore three fundamental composition patterns in detail:

- Load balancer with multiple backend replicas
- Server with multiple backends
- Server tree

1.3.1 Load Balancer with Multiple Backend Replicas

The first composition pattern is the load balancer with multiple backend replicas. As depicted in Figure 1.1, requests are sent to the load balancer server. For each request, it selects one **backend** and forwards the request there. The response comes back to the load balancer server, which in turn relays it to the original requester.

The backends are called **replicas** because they are all clones or replications of each other. A request sent to any replica should produce the same response.

The load balancer must always know which backends are alive and ready to accept requests. Load balancers send **health check** queries dozens of times each second and stop sending traffic to that backend if the health check fails. A health check is a simple query that should execute quickly and return whether the system should receive traffic.

Picking which backend to send a query to can be simple or complex. A simple method would be to alternate among the backends in a loop—a practice called **round-robin**. Some backends may be more powerful than others, however,

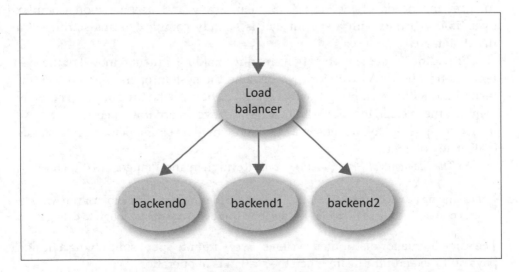

Figure 1.1: A load balancer with many replicas

and may be selected more often using a proportional round-robin scheme. More complex solutions include the **least loaded** scheme. In this approach, a load balancer tracks how loaded each backend is and always selects the least loaded one.

Selecting the least loaded backend sounds reasonable but a naive implementation can be a disaster. A backend may not show signs of being overloaded until long after it has actually become overloaded. This problem arises because it can be difficult to accurately measure how loaded a system is. If the load is a measurement of the number of connections recently sent to the server, this definition is blind to the fact that some connections may be long lasting while others may be quick. If the measurement is based on CPU utilization, this definition is blind to input/output (I/O) overload. Often a trailing average of the last 5 minutes of load is used. Trailing averages have a problem in that, as an average, they reflect the past, not the present. As a consequence, a sharp, sudden increase in load will not be reflected in the average for a while.

Imagine a load balancer with 10 backends. Each one is running at 80 percent load. A new backend is added. Because it is new, it has no load and, therefore, is the least loaded backend. A naive least loaded algorithm would send all traffic to this new backend; no traffic would be sent to the other 10 backends. All too quickly, the new backend would become absolutely swamped. There is no way a single backend could process the traffic previously handled by 10 backends. The use of trailing averages would mean the older backends would continue reporting artificially high loads for a few minutes while the new backend would be reporting an artificially low load.

With this scheme, the load balancer will believe that the new machine is less loaded than all the other machines for quite some time. In such a situation the machine may become so overloaded that it would crash and reboot, or a system administrator trying to rectify the situation might reboot it. When it returns to service, the cycle would start over again.

Such situations make the round-robin approach look pretty good. A less naive least loaded implementation would have some kind of control in place that would never send more than a certain number of requests to the same machine in a row. This is called a **slow start** algorithm.

Trouble with a Naive Least Loaded Algorithm

Without slow start, load balancers have been known to cause many problems. One famous example is what happened to the CNN.com web site on the day of the September 11, 2001, terrorist attacks. So many people tried to access CNN.com that the backends became overloaded. One crashed, and then crashed again after it came back up, because the naive least loaded algorithm sent all traffic to it. When it was down, the other backends became overloaded and crashed. One at a time, each backend would get overloaded, crash, and become overloaded from again receiving all the traffic and crash again.

As a result the service was essentially unavailable as the system administrators rushed to figure out what was going on. In their defense, the web was new enough that no one had experience with handling sudden traffic surges like the one encountered on September 11.

The solution CNN used was to halt all the backends and boot them at the same time so they would all show zero load and receive equal amounts of traffic.

The CNN team later discovered that a few days prior, a software upgrade for their load balancer had arrived but had not yet been installed. The upgrade added a slow start mechanism.

1.3.2 Server with Multiple Backends

The next composition pattern is a server with multiple backends. The server receives a request, sends queries to many backend servers, and composes the final reply by combining those answers. This approach is typically used when the original query can easily be deconstructed into a number of independent queries that can be combined to form the final answer.

Figure 1.2a illustrates how a simple search engine processes a query with the help of multiple backends. The frontend receives the request. It relays the query to many backend servers. The spell checker replies with information so the search engine may suggest alternate spellings. The web and image search backends reply with a list of web sites and images related to the query. The advertisement server

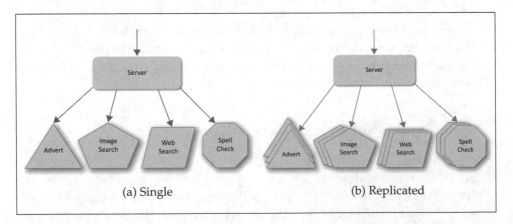

Figure 1.2: This service is composed of a server and many backends.

replies with advertisements relevant to the query. Once the replies are received, the frontend uses this information to construct the HTML that makes up the search results page for the user, which is then sent as the reply.

Figure 1.2b illustrates the same architecture with replicated, load-balanced, backends. The same principle applies but the system is able to scale and survive failures better.

This kind of composition has many advantages. The backends do their work in parallel. The reply does not have to wait for one backend process to complete before the next begins. The system is loosely coupled. One backend can fail and the page can still be constructed by filling in some default information or by leaving that area blank.

This pattern also permits some rather sophisticated latency management. Suppose this system is expected to return a result in 200 ms or less. If one of the backends is slow for some reason, the frontend doesn't have to wait for it. If it takes 10 ms to compose and send the resulting HTML, at 190 ms the frontend can give up on the slow backends and generate the page with the information it has. The ability to manage a latency time budget like that can be very powerful. For example, if the advertisement system is slow, search results can be displayed without any ads.

To be clear, the terms "frontend" and "backend" are a matter of perspective. The frontend sends requests to backends, which reply with a result. A server can be both a frontend and a backend. In the previous example, the server is the backend to the web browser but a frontend to the spell check server.

There are many variations on this pattern. Each backend can be replicated for increased capacity or resiliency. Caching may be done at various levels.

The term **fan out** refers to the fact that one query results in many new queries, one to each backend. The queries "fan out" to the individual backends and the replies **fan in** as they are set up to the frontend and combined into the final result.

Any fan in situation is at risk of having congestion problems. Often small queries may result in large responses. Therefore a small amount of bandwidth is used to fan out but there may not be enough bandwidth to sustain the fan in. This may result in congested network links and overloaded servers. It is easy to engineer the system to have the right amount of network and server capacity if the sizes of the queries and replies are consistent, or if there is an occasional large reply. The difficult situation is engineering the system when there are sudden, unpredictable bursts of large replies. Some network equipment is engineered specifically to deal with this situation by dynamically provisioning more buffer space to such bursts. Likewise, the backends can rate-limit themselves to avoid creating the situation in the first place. Lastly, the frontends can manage the congestion themselves by controlling the new queries they send out, by notifying the backends to slow down, or by implementing emergency measures to handle the flood better. The last option is discussed in Chapter 5.

1.3.3 Server Tree

The other fundamental composition pattern is the **server tree**. As Figure 1.3 illustrates, in this scheme a number of servers work cooperatively with one as the root of the tree, parent servers below it, and leaf servers at the bottom of the tree. (In computer science, trees are drawn upside-down.) Typically this pattern is used to access a large dataset or **corpus**. The corpus is larger than any one machine can hold; thus each leaf stores one fraction or **shard** of the whole.

To query the entire dataset, the root receives the original query and forwards it to the parents. The parents forward the query to the leaf servers, which search their parts of the corpus. Each leaf sends its findings to the parents, which sort and filter the results before forwarding them up to the root. The root then takes the response from all the parents, combines the results, and replies with the full answer.

Imagine you wanted to find out how many times George Washington was mentioned in an encyclopedia. You could read each volume in sequence and arrive at the answer. Alternatively, you could give each volume to a different person and have the various individuals search their volumes in parallel. The latter approach would complete the task much faster.

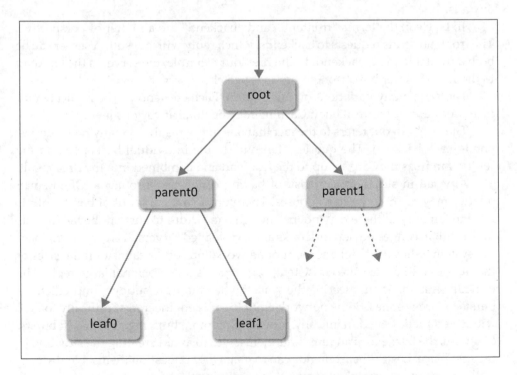

Figure 1.3: A server tree

The primary benefit of this pattern is that it permits parallel searching of a large corpus. Not only are the leaves searching their share of the corpus in parallel, but the sorting and ranking performed by the parents are also done in parallel.

For example, imagine a corpus of the text extracted from every book in the U.S. Library of Congress. This cannot fit in one computer, so instead the information is spread over hundreds or thousands of leaf machines. In addition to the leaf machines are the parents and the root. A search query would go to a root server, which in turn relays the query to all parents. Each parent repeats the query to all leaf nodes below it. Once the leaves have replied, the parent ranks and sorts the results by relevancy.

For example, a leaf may reply that all the words of the query exist in the same paragraph in one book, but for another book only some of the words exist (less relevant), or they exist but not in the same paragraph or page (even less relevant). If the query is for the best 50 answers, the parent can send the top 50 results to the root and drop the rest. The root then receives results from each parent and selects the best 50 of those to construct the reply.

This scheme also permits developers to work within a latency budget. If fast answers are more important than perfect answers, parents and roots do not have to wait for slow replies if the latency deadline is near.

Many variations of this pattern are possible. Redundant servers may exist with a load-balancing scheme to divide the work among them and route around failed servers. Expanding the number of leaf servers can give each leaf a smaller portion of the corpus to search, or each shard of corpus can be placed on multiple leaf servers to improve availability. Expanding the number of parents at each level increases the capacity to sort and rank results. There may be additional levels of parent servers, making the tree taller. The additional levels permit a wider fan-out, which is important for an extremely large corpus. The parents may provide a caching function to relieve pressure on the leaf servers; in this case more levels of parents may improve cache effectiveness. These techniques can also help mitigate congestion problems related to fan-in, as discussed in the previous section.

1.4 Distributed State

Large systems often store or process large amounts of state. State consists of data, such as a database, that is frequently updated. Contrast this with a corpus, which is relatively static or is updated only periodically when a new edition is published. For example, a system that searches the U.S. Library of Congress may receive a new corpus each week. By comparison, an email system is in constant churn with new data arriving constantly, current data being updated (email messages being marked as "read" or moved between folders), and data being deleted.

Distributed computing systems have many ways to deal with state. However, they all involve some kind of replication and sharding, which brings about problems of consistency, availability, and partitioning.

The easiest way to store state is to put it on one machine, as depicted in Figure 1.4. Unfortunately, that method reaches its limit quite quickly: an individual machine can store only a limited amount of state and if the one machine dies we lose access to 100 percent of the state. The machine has only a certain amount of processing power, which means the number of simultaneous reads and writes it can process is limited.

In distributed computing we store state by storing fractions or shards of the whole on individual machines. This way the amount of state we can store is limited only by the number of machines we can acquire. In addition, each shard is stored on multiple machines; thus a single machine failure does not lose access to any state. Each replica can process a certain number of queries per second, so we can design the system to process any number of simultaneous read and write requests by increasing the number of replicas. This is illustrated in Figure 1.5, where N QPS are received and distributed among three shards, each replicated three ways. As a result, on average one ninth of all queries reach a particular replica server.

Writes or requests that update state require all replicas to be updated. While this update process is happening, it is possible that some clients will read from stale replicas that have not yet been updated. Figure 1.6 illustrates how a write can be confounded by reads to an out-of-date cache. This will be discussed further in the next section.

In the most simple pattern, a root server receives requests to store or retrieve state. It determines which shard contains that part of the state and forwards the request to the appropriate leaf server. The reply then flows up the tree. This looks similar to the server tree pattern described in the previous section but there are two

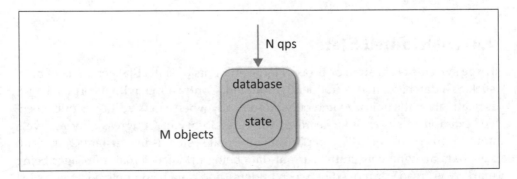

Figure 1.4: State kept in one location; not distributed computing

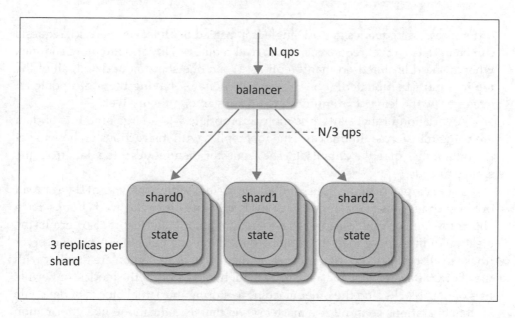

Figure 1.5: This distributed state is sharded and replicated.

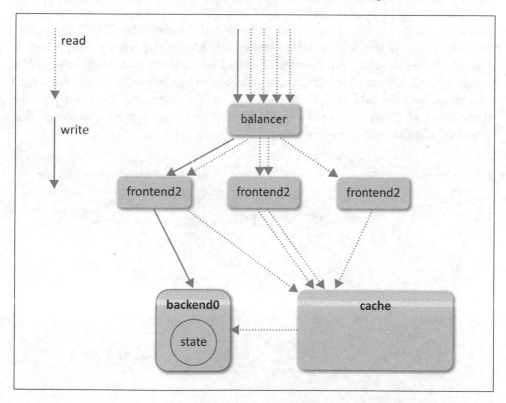

Figure 1.6: State updates using cached data lead to an inconsistent view.

differences. First, queries go to a single leaf instead of all leaves. Second, requests can be update (write) requests, not just read requests. Updates are more complex when a shard is stored on many replicas. When one shard is updated, all of the replicas must be updated, too. This may be done by having the root update all leaves or by the leaves communicating updates among themselves.

A variation of that pattern is more appropriate when large amounts of data are being transferred. In this case, the root replies with instructions on how to get the data rather than the data itself. The requestor then requests the data from the source directly.

For example, imagine a distributed file system with petabytes of data spread out over thousands of machines. Each file is split into gigabyte-sized chunks. Each chunk is stored on multiple machines for redundancy. This scheme also permits the creation of files larger than those that would fit on one machine. A master server tracks the list of files and identifies where their chunks are. If you are familiar with the UNIX file system, the master can be thought of as storing the inodes, or per-file lists of data blocks, and the other machine as storing the actual blocks of data. File system operations go through a master server that uses the inode-like information to determine which machines to involve in the operation.

Imagine that a large read request comes in. The master determines that the file has a few terabytes stored on one machine and a few terabytes stored on another machine. It could request the data from each machine and relay it to the system that made the request, but the master would quickly become overloaded while receiving and relaying huge chunks of data. Instead, it replies with a list of which machines have the data, and the requestor contacts those machines directly for the data. This way the master is not the middle man for those large data transfers. This situation is illustrated in Figure 1.7.

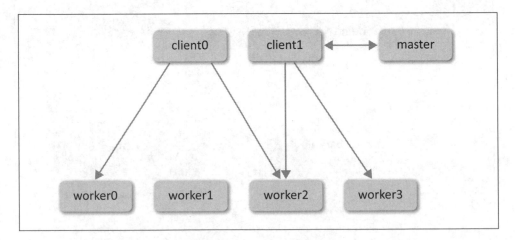

Figure 1.7: This master server delegates replies to other servers.

1.5 The CAP Principle

CAP stands for consistency, availability, and partition resistance. The CAP Principle states that it is not possible to build a distributed system that guarantees consistency, availability, and resistance to partitioning. Any one or two can be achieved but not all three simultaneously. When using such systems you must be aware of which are guaranteed.

1.5.1 Consistency

Consistency means that all nodes see the same data at the same time. If there are multiple replicas and there is an update being processed, all users see the update go live at the same time even if they are reading from different replicas. Systems that do not guarantee consistency may provide **eventual consistency**. For example, they may guarantee that any update will propagate to all replicas in a certain amount of time. Until that deadline is reached, some queries may receive the new data while others will receive older, out-of-date answers.

Perfect consistency is not always important. Imagine a social network that awards reputation points to users for positive actions. Your reputation point total is displayed anywhere your name is shown. The reputation database is replicated in the United States, Europe, and Asia. A user in Europe is awarded points and that change might take minutes to propagate to the United States and Asia replicas. This may be sufficient for such a system because an absolutely accurate reputation score is not essential. If a user in the United States and one in Asia were talking on the phone as one was awarded points, the other user would see the update seconds later and that would be okay. If the update took minutes due to network congestion or hours due to a network outage, the delay would still not be a terrible thing.

Now imagine a banking application built on this system. A person in the United States and another in Europe could coordinate their actions to withdraw money from the same account at the same time. The ATM that each person uses would query its nearest database replica, which would claim the money is available and may be withdrawn. If the updates propagated slowly enough, both people would have the cash before the bank realized the money was already gone.[1]

1.5.2 Availability

Availability is a guarantee that every request receives a response about whether it was successful or failed. In other words, it means that the system is up. For

---

1. The truth is that the global ATM system does not require database consistency. It can be defeated by leveraging network delays and outages. It is less expensive for banks to give out a limited amount of money when the ATM network is down than to have an unhappy customer stranded without cash. Fraudulent transactions are dealt with after the fact. Daily withdrawal limits prevent major fraud. Assessing overage fees is easier than implementing a globally consistent database.

example, using many replicas to store data such that clients always have access to at least one working replica guarantees availability.

The CAP Principle states that availability also guarantees that the system is able to report failure. For example, a system may detect that it is overloaded and reply to requests with an error code that means "try again later." Being told this immediately is more favorable than having to wait minutes or hours before one gives up.

1.5.3 Partition Tolerance

Partition tolerance means the system continues to operate despite arbitrary message loss or failure of part of the system. The simplest example of partition tolerance is when the system continues to operate even if the machines involved in providing the service lose the ability to communicate with each other due to a network link going down (see Figure 1.8).

Returning to our example of replicas, if the system is read-only it is easy to make the system partition tolerant, as the replicas do not need to communicate with each other. But consider the example of replicas containing state that is updated on one replica first, then copied to other replicas. If the replicas are unable to communicate with each other, the system fails to be able to guarantee updates will propagate within a certain amount of time, thus becoming a failed system.

Now consider a situation where two servers cooperate in a master–slave relationship. Both maintain a complete copy of the state and the slave takes over the master's role if the master fails, which is determined by a loss of heartbeat—that is,

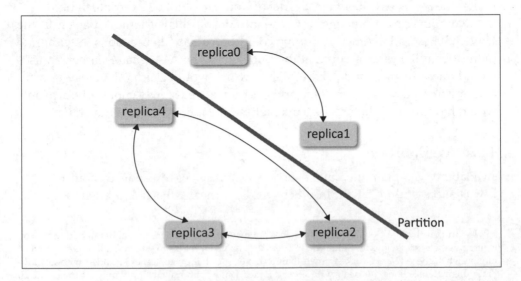

Figure 1.8: Nodes partitioned from each other

a periodic health check between two servers often done via a dedicated network. If the heartbeat network between the two is partitioned, the slave will promote itself to being the master, not knowing that the original master is up but unable to communicate on the heartbeat network. At this point there are two masters and the system breaks. This situation is called **split brain.**

Some special cases of partitioning exist. Packet loss is considered a temporary partitioning of the system as it applies to the CAP Principle. Another special case is the complete network outage. Even the most partition-tolerant system is unable to work in that situation.

The CAP Principle says that any one or two of the attributes are achievable in combination, but not all three. In 2002, Gilbert and Lynch published a formal proof of the original conjecture, rendering it a theorem. One can think of this as the third attribute being sacrificed to achieve the other two.

The CAP Principle is illustrated by the triangle in Figure 1.9. Traditional relational databases like Oracle, MySQL, and PostgreSQL are consistent and available (CA). They use transactions and other database techniques to assure that updates are atomic; they propagate completely or not at all. Thus they guarantee all users will see the same state at the same time. Newer storage systems such as Hbase,

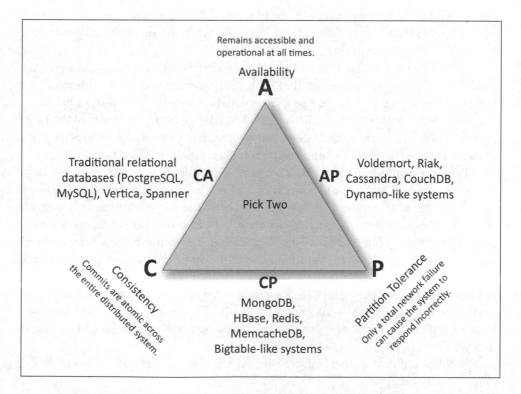

Figure 1.9: The CAP Principle

Redis, and Bigtable focus on consistency and partition tolerance (CP). When partitioned, they become read-only or refuse to respond to any requests rather than be inconsistent and permit some users to see old data while others see fresh data. Finally, systems such as Cassandra, Riak, and Dynamo focus on availability and partition tolerance (AP). They emphasize always being able to serve requests even if it means some clients receive outdated results. Such systems are often used in globally distributed networks where each replica talks to the others by less reliable media such as the Internet.

SQL and other relational databases use the term **ACID** to describe their side of the CAP triangle. ACID stands for Atomicity (transactions are "all or nothing"), Consistency (after each transaction the database is in a valid state), Isolation (concurrent transactions give the same results as if they were executed serially), and Durability (a committed transaction's data will not be lost in the event of a crash or other problem). Databases that provide weaker consistency models often refer to themselves as NoSQL and describe themselves as **BASE**: Basically Available Soft-state services with Eventual consistency.

1.6 Loosely Coupled Systems

Distributed systems are expected to be highly available, to last a long time, and to evolve and change without disruption. Entire subsystems are often replaced while the system is up and running.

To achieve this a distributed system uses **abstraction** to build a loosely coupled system. Abstraction means that each component provides an interface that is defined in a way that hides the implementation details. The system is loosely coupled if each component has little or no knowledge of the internals of the other components. As a result a subsystem can be replaced by one that provides the same abstract interface even if its implementation is completely different.

Take, for example, a spell check service. A good level of abstraction would be to take in text and return a description of which words are misspelled and a list of possible corrections for each one. A bad level of abstraction would simply provide access to a lexicon of words that the frontends could query for similar words. The reason the latter is not a good abstraction is that if an entirely new way to check spelling was invented, every frontend using the spell check service would need to be rewritten. Suppose this new version does not rely on a lexicon but instead applies an artificial intelligence technique called machine learning. With the good abstraction, no frontend would need to change; it would simply send the same kind of request to the new server. Users of the bad abstraction would not be so lucky.

For this and many other reasons, loosely coupled systems are easier to evolve and change over time.

Continuing our example, in preparation for the launch of the new spell check service both versions could be run in parallel. The load balancer that sits in front of the spell check system could be programmed to send all requests to both the old and new systems. Results from the old system would be sent to the users, but results from the new system would be collected and compared for quality control. At first the new system might not produce results that were as good, but over time it would be enhanced until its results were quantifiably better. At that point the new system would be put into production. To be cautious, perhaps only 1 percent of all queries would come through the new system—if no users complained, the new system would take a larger fraction. Eventually all responses would come from the new system and the old system could be decommissioned.

Other systems require more precision and accuracy than a spell check system. For example, there may be requirements that the new system be bug-for-bug compatible with the old system before it can offer new functionality. That is, the new system must reproduce not only the features but also the bugs from the old system. In this case the ability to send requests to both systems and compare results becomes critical to the operational task of deploying it.

Case Study: Emulation before Improvements

When Tom was at Cibernet, he was involved in a project to replace an older system. Because it was a financial system, the new system had to prove it was bug-for-bug compatible before it could be deployed.

The old system was built on obsolete, pre-web technology and had become so complex and calcified that it was impossible to add new features. The new system was built on newer, better technology and, being a cleaner design, was more easily able to accommodate new functionality. The systems were run in parallel and results were compared.

At that point engineers found a bug in the old system. Currency conversion was being done in a way that was non-standard and the results were slightly off. To make the results between the two systems comparable, the developers reverse-engineered the bug and emulated it in the new system.

Now the results in the old and new systems matched down to the penny. With the company having gained confidence in the new system's ability to be bug-for-bug compatible, it was activated as the primary system and the old system was disabled.

At this point, new features and improvements could be made to the system. The first improvement, unsurprisingly, was to remove the code that emulated the currency conversion bug.

1.7 Speed

So far we have elaborated on many of the considerations involved in designing large distributed systems. For web and other interactive services, one item may be the most important: speed. It takes time to get information, store information, compute and transform information, and transmit information. Nothing happens instantly.

An interactive system requires fast response times. Users tend to perceive anything faster than 200 ms to be instant. They also prefer fast over slow. Studies have documented sharp drops in revenue when delays as little as 50 ms were artificially added to web sites. Time is also important in batch and non-interactive systems where the total throughput must meet or exceed the incoming flow of work.

The general strategy for designing a system that is performant is to design a system using our best estimates of how quickly it will be able to process a request and then to build prototypes to test our assumptions. If we are wrong, we go back to step one; at least the next iteration will be informed by what we have learned. As we build the system, we are able to remeasure and adjust the design if we discover our estimates and prototypes have not guided us as well as we had hoped.

At the start of the design process we often create many designs, estimate how fast each will be, and eliminate the ones that are not fast enough. We do not automatically select the fastest design. The fastest design may be considerably more expensive than one that is sufficient.

How do we determine if a design is worth pursuing? Building a prototype is very time consuming. Much can be deduced with some simple estimating exercises. Pick a few common transactions and break them down into smaller steps, and then estimate how long each step will take.

Two of the biggest consumers of time are disk access and network delays.

Disk accesses are slow because they involve mechanical operations. To read a block of data from a disk requires the read arm to move to the right track; the platter must then spin until the desired block is under the read head. This process typically takes 10 ms. Compare this to reading the same amount of information from RAM, which takes 0.002 ms, which is 5,000 times faster. The arm and platters (known as a **spindle**) can process only one request at a time. However, once the head is on the right track, it can read many sequential blocks. Therefore reading two blocks is often nearly as fast as reading one block if the two blocks are adjacent. Solid-state drives (SSDs) do not have mechanical spinning platters and are much faster, though more expensive.

Network access is slow because it is limited by the speed of light. It takes approximately 75 ms for a packet to get from California to the Netherlands. About half of that journey time is due to the speed of light. Additional delays may be attributable to processing time on each router, the electronics that convert from wired to fiber-optic communication and back, the time it takes to assemble and disassemble the packet on each end, and so on.

Two computers on the same network segment might seem as if they communicate instantly, but that is not really the case. Here the time scale is so small that other delays have a bigger factor. For example, when transmitting data over a local network, the first byte arrives quickly but the program receiving the data usually does not process it until the entire packet is received.

In many systems computation takes little time compared to the delays from network and disk operation. As a result you can often estimate how long a transaction will take if you simply know the distance from the user to the datacenter and the number of disk seeks required. Your estimate will often be good enough to throw away obviously bad designs.

To illustrate this, imagine you are building an email system that needs to be able to retrieve a message from the message storage system and display it within 300 ms. We will use the time approximations listed in Figure 1.10 to help us engineer the solution.

Jeff Dean, a Google Fellow, has popularized this chart of common numbers to aid in architectural and scaling decisions. As you can see, there are many orders of magnitude difference between certain options. These numbers improve every year. Updates can be found online.

Action	Typical Time	
L1 cache reference	0.5 ns	
Branch mispredict	5 ns	
L2 cache reference	7 ns	
Mutex lock/unlock	100 ns	
Main memory reference	100 ns	
Compress 1K bytes with Zippy	10,000 ns	(0.01 ms)
Send 2K bytes over 1 Gbps network	20,000 ns	(0.02 ms)
Read 1 MB sequentially from memory	250,000 ns	(0.25 ms)
Round trip within same datacenter	500,000 ns	(0.5 ms)
Read 1 MB from SSD	1,000,000 ns	(3 ms)
Disk seek	10,000,000 ns	(10 ms)
Read 1 MB sequentially from network	10,000,000 ns	(10 ms)
Read 1 MB sequentially from disk	30,000,000 ns	(30 ms)
Send packet from California to Netherlands to California	150,000,000 ns	(150 ms)

Figure 1.10: Numbers every engineer should know

First we follow the transaction from beginning to end. The request comes from a web browser that may be on another continent. The request must be authenticated, the database index is consulted to determine where to get the message text, the message text is retrieved, and finally the response is formatted and transmitted back to the user.

Now let's budget for the items we can't control. To send a packet between California and Europe typically takes 75 ms, and until physics lets us change the speed of light that won't change. Our 300 ms budget is reduced by 150 ms since we have to account for not only the time it takes for the request to be transmitted but also the reply. That's half our budget consumed by something we don't control.

We talk with the team that operates our authentication system and they recommend budgeting 3 ms for authentication.

Formatting the data takes very little time—less than the slop in our other estimates—so we can ignore it.

This leaves 147 ms for the message to be retrieved from storage. If a typical index lookup requires 3 disk seeks (10 ms each) and reads about 1 megabyte of information (30 ms), that is 60 ms. Reading the message itself might require 4 disk seeks and reading about 2 megabytes of information (100 ms). The total is 160 ms, which is more than our 147 ms remaining budget.

How Did We Know That?

How did we know that it will take 3 disk seeks to read the index? It requires knowledge of the inner workings of the UNIX file system: how files are looked up in a directory to find an inode and how inodes are used to look up the data blocks. This is why understanding the internals of the operating system you use is key to being able to design and operate distributed systems. The internals of UNIX and UNIX-like operating systems are well documented, thus giving them an advantage over other systems.

While disappointed that our design did not meet the design parameters, we are happy that disaster has been averted. Better to know now than to find out when it is too late.

It seems like 60 ms for an index lookup is a long time. We could improve that considerably. What if the index was held in RAM? Is this possible? Some quick calculations estimate that the lookup tree would have to be 3 levels deep to fan out to enough machines to span this much data. To go up and down the tree is 5 packets, or about 2.5 ms if they are all within the same datacenter. The new total (150 ms + 3 ms + 2.5 ms + 100 ms = 255.5 ms) is less than our total 300 ms budget.

We would repeat this process for other requests that are time sensitive. For example, we send email messages less frequently than we read them, so the time to send an email message may not be considered time critical. In contrast, deleting a message happens almost as often reading messages. We might repeat this calculation for a few deletion methods to compare their efficiency.

One design might contact the server and delete the message from the storage system and the index. Another design might have the storage system simply mark the message as deleted in the index. This would be considerably faster but would require a new element that would reap messages marked for deletion and occasionally compact the index, removing any items marked as deleted.

Even faster response time can be achieved with an asynchronous design. That means the client sends requests to the server and quickly returns control to the user without waiting for the request to complete. The user perceives this system as faster even though the actual work is lagging. Asynchronous designs are more complex to implement. The server might queue the request rather than actually performing the action. Another process reads requests from the queue and performs them in the background. Alternatively, the client could simply send the request and check for the reply later, or allocate a thread or subprocess to wait for the reply.

All of these designs are viable but each offers different speed and complexity of implementation. With speed and cost estimates, backed by prototypes, the business decision of which to implement can be made.

1.8 Summary

Distributed computing is different from traditional computing in many ways. The scale is larger; there are many machines, each doing specialized tasks. Services are replicated to increase capacity. Hardware failure is not treated as an emergency or exception but as an expected part of the system. Thus the system works around failure.

Large systems are built through composition of smaller parts. We discussed three ways this composition is typically done: load balancer for many backend replicas, frontend with many different backends, and a server tree.

The load balancer divides traffic among many duplicate systems. The frontend with many different backends uses different backends in parallel, with each performing different processes. The server tree uses a tree configuration, with each tree level serving a different purpose.

Maintaining state in a distributed system is complex, whether it is a large database of constantly updated information or a few key bits to which many systems need constant access. The CAP Principle states that it is not possible to build a distributed system that guarantees consistency, availability, and resistance to partitioning simultaneously. At most two of the three can be achieved.

Systems are expected to evolve over time. To make this easier, the components are loosely coupled. Each embodies an abstraction of the service it provides, such that the internals can be replaced or improved without changing the abstraction. Thus, dependencies on the service do not need to change other than to benefit from new features.

Designing distributed systems requires an understanding of the time it takes various operations to run so that time-sensitive processes can be designed to meet their latency budget.

Exercises

1. What is distributed computing?
2. Describe the three major composition patterns in distributed computing.
3. What are the three patterns discussed for storing state?
4. Sometimes a master server does not reply with an answer but instead replies with where the answer can be found. What are the benefits of this method?
5. Section 1.4 describes a distributed file system, including an example of how reading terabytes of data would work. How would writing terabytes of data work?
6. Explain the CAP Principle. (If you think the CAP Principle is awesome, read "The Part-Time Parliament" (Lamport & Marzullo 1998) and "Paxos Made Simple" (Lamport 2001).)
7. What does it mean when a system is loosely coupled? What is the advantage of these systems?
8. Give examples of loosely and tightly coupled systems you have experience with. What makes them loosely or tightly coupled?
9. How do we estimate how fast a system will be able to process a request such as retrieving an email message?
10. In Section 1.7 three design ideas are presented for how to process email deletion requests. Estimate how long the request will take for deleting an email message for each of the three designs. First outline the steps each would take, then break each one into individual operations until estimates can be created.

Chapter 2

Designing for Operations

Your job is to design
systems that operate.

—Theo Schlossnagle

This chapter catalogs the most common operations tasks and discusses how to design for them. It also discusses how to rework an existing architecture that was not designed with operations in mind.

Designing for operations means making sure all the normal operational functions can be done well. Normal operational functions include tasks such as periodic maintenance, updates, and monitoring. These issues must be kept in mind in early stages of planning.

When you consider the full life cycle of a given service, only a small portion of that life cycle is spent building the features of the service. The vast majority of the life cycle is spent operating the service. Yet traditionally the operational functions of software are considered lower priority than features, if they are considered at all.

The best strategy for providing a highly available service is to build features into the software that enhance one's ability to perform and automate operational tasks. This is in contrast to strategies where operations is an after-thought and operations engineers are forced into a position of "running what other people build." That's the outdated way.

2.1 Operational Requirements

Software is usually designed based on requirements related to what the ultimate user will see and do. The functionality required for smooth operations is rarely considered. As a consequence, systems administrators find themselves lacking control points for key interactions. When we design for operations, we take into account the normal functions of an infrastructure life cycle. They include, but are not necessarily limited to, the following:

- Configuration
- Startup and shutdown
- Queue draining
- Software upgrades
- Backups and restores
- Redundancy
- Replicated databases
- Hot swaps
- Toggles for individual features
- Graceful degradation
- Access controls and rate limits
- Data import controls
- Monitoring
- Auditing
- Debug instrumentation
- Exception collection

Features like configuration and backups/restores make typical operational tasks possible. Features like queue draining and toggles for individual features allow such tasks to be done seamlessly. Many of these features create the introspection required to debug, tune, and repair large systems, as previously discussed in Section 1.1.

Typically, developers and managers don't think of these issues and they are often left off of lists of requirements. At best, they are after-thoughts or it is assumed that the operations team will "figure something out" through improvisation. The truth is that these tasks are important and cannot be done well or at all without specific features. In the worst case, systems are designed in ways that work against the ability to "improvise" a solution.

Rather than the term "operational requirements," some organizations use the term "non-functional requirements." We consider this term misleading. While these features are not directly responsible for the function of the application or service, the term "non-functional" implies that these features do not have a function. A service cannot exist without the support of these features; they are essential.

The remainder of this chapter discusses these operational aspects and features that enable them. Many of these will seem obvious to someone with operational experience. Yet, each of them appears on this list because we have observed at least one system that suffered from its omission.

2.1.1 Configuration

The system must be configurable by automated means. This includes initial configuration as well as changes made later. It must be possible to perform the following tasks:

- Make a backup of a configuration and restore it
- View the difference between one archived copy and another revision
- Archive the running configuration without taking the system down

A typical way to achieve all of these goals is for the configuration to take the form of a text file with a well-defined format. Automated systems can easily generate such a file. Text files are easy to parse and therefore auditable. They can be archived easily. They can also be stored in a source code repository and analyzed with standard text comparison tools such as UNIX `diff`.

In some systems the configuration is dynamically updated as the system runs. This "state" may be reflected back into the primary configuration file or may be a separate entity. In this case there are additional requirements.

There must be a way for automation to read and update the state. This step may be carried out through an API or by reading and updating a configuration file. If a file is used, a locking protocol must exist to prevent both the service and external automation from reading the file in an incomplete state and to prevent update collisions. Tools should be available for doing sanity checks on configurations that do not involve activating the configuration on a live system.

An inferior option would be a configuration file that is an opaque binary blob. Such a file is not human readable. In these types of systems it is impossible to keep a history of the configuration and see change over time. Often strange problems are debugged by analyzing changes to a configuration file, where a change may be too small to be remembered but just big enough to cause a problem. This type of analysis is not possible if the file is not plain text.

We have been burned by systems that provide an API for extracting the entire configuration but where the result turns out not to actually represent the entire configuration. All too often, the omission is found only during a disaster recovery exercise or emergency. For that reason each new release should be tested to verify that the configuration data does not omit anything.

From an operational perspective, the ideal is for the configuration to consist of one or more plain text files that can be easily examined, archived, and compared.

Some systems read their configuration directly from a source code repository, which is convenient and highly recommended. However, it must also be possible to disable this feature and provide configurations directly. Such an approach may be used in an emergency, when the source code repository is down, and for experimentation. The use of this feature must be exposed in a way that the monitoring system can detect it. Other users can then be made aware that it is happening—for example, by showing this status in dashboards. It may also be an alertable event, in which case alerts can be generated if this feature is used on production systems. Alerting if this feature is disabled for more than a certain amount of time assures that temporary fixes are not forgotten.

Easy Configuration Does Not Require a GUI

A product manager from IBM once told Tom that the company had spent a lot of money adding a graphical user interface (GUI) to a system administration tool. This was done to make it easier to configure. To the team's dismay, the majority of their customers did not use the GUI because they had written Perl scripts to generate the configuration files.

2.1.2 Startup and Shutdown

The service should restart automatically when a machine boots up. If the machine is shut down properly, the system should include the proper operating system (OS) hooks to shut the service down properly. If the machine crashes suddenly, the next restart of the system should automatically perform data validations or repairs before providing service.

Ensuring that a service restarts after a reboot can be as simple as installing a boot-time script, or using a system that monitors processes and restarts them (such as Ubuntu Upstart). Alternatively, it can be an entire process management system like Apache Mesos (Metz 2013) or Google Omega (Schwarzkopf, Konwinski, Abd-El-Malek & Wilkes 2013), which not only restarts a process when a machine reboots, but also is able to restart the process on an entirely different machine in the event of machine death.

The amount of time required to start up or shut down a system should be documented. This is needed for preparing for disaster recovery situations. One needs to know how quickly a system can be safely shut down to plan the battery capacity of uninterruptible power supply (UPS) systems. Most UPS batteries can sustain a system for about five minutes. After a power outage, starting up thousands of servers can be very complex. Knowing expected startup times and procedures can dramatically reduce recovery time.

Testing for how a system behaves when all systems lose power concurrently is important. It's a common datacenter stressor. Thousands of hard disk motors spinning up at the same time create a huge power draw that can overload power systems. In general, one can expect 1 to 5 percent of machines to not boot on the first try. In a system with 1000 machines, a large team of people might be required to resuscitate them all.

Related to this is the concept of "crash-only" software. Candea & Fox (2003) observe that the post-crash recovery procedure in most systems is critical to system reliability, yet receives a disproportionately small amount of quality assurance (QA) testing. A service that is expected to have high availability should rarely use the orderly shutdown process. To align the importance of the recovery procedure with the amount of testing it should receive, these authors propose not implementing the orderly shutdown procedure or the orderly startup procedures. Thus, the only way to stop the software is to crash it, and the only way to start it is to exercise the crash recovery system. In this way, the crash recovery process is exercised frequently and test processes are less likely to ignore it.

2.1.3 Queue Draining

There must be an orderly shutdown process that can be triggered to take the system out of service for maintenance. A **drain** occurs when the service is told to stop accepting new requests but complete any requests that are "in flight." This is sometimes called **lame-duck mode**.

This mechanism is particularly important when using a load balancer with multiple backend replicas, as described in Section 1.3.1. Software upgrades are implemented by removing one replica at a time, upgrading it, and returning it to service. If each replica is simply "killed," any in-flight requests will be lost. It is better to have a draining mode, where the replica continues to process requests but intentionally fails the load balancer's health check requests. If it sees the health check requests fail, the load balancer stops sending new requests to the replica. Once no new requests have been received for a while and the existing requests are completed, it is safe to kill the replica and perform the upgrade.

Emptying the Queue

While developing the pioneering Palm VII wireless messaging service, the team realized the main application did not have the ability to be drained. Any attempt to shut it down would lose any messages that were in flight. Strata negotiated to add this feature. This "drain and exit" feature enabled the operations team to be able to take servers down for maintenance or swap them out for service reliability without losing messages.

Similarly, it is useful for the service to be able to start in drained mode. In this case, the load balancer will not send new traffic to the replica, but operations can send messages directly to it for testing. Once confidence is achieved, undraining the replica signals the load balancer to send traffic.

2.1.4 Software Upgrades

It must be possible for software upgrades to be implemented without taking down the service. Usually the software is located behind a load balancer and upgraded by swapping out replicas as they are upgraded.

Some systems can be upgraded while running, which is riskier and requires careful design and extensive testing.

Nonreplicated systems are difficult to upgrade without downtime. Often the only alternative is to clone the system, upgrade the clone, and swap the newly upgraded system into place faster than customers will notice. This is usually a risky—and sometimes improvised—solution. Clones of production systems tend to be imperfect copies because it is difficult to assure that the clone was made precisely when no changes are in progress.

2.1.5 Backups and Restores

It must be possible to back up and restore the service's data while the system is running.

Often legacy systems must be taken down to do backups or restores. This approach may suffice for a small office with 10 understanding users, but it is not reasonable for a web site with hundreds or millions of users. The design of a system that permits live backups and restores is very different

One way to achieve live backups without interfering with the service is to perform the backup on a read-only replica of the database. If the system can dynamically add and remove replicas, a replica is removed from service, frozen, and used to make the backup. This replica is then added back to the system later. It is common to have a particular replica dedicated to this process.

Live restores are often done by providing a special API for inserting data during a restore operation. The architecture should allow for the restoration of a single account, preferably without locking that user or group out of the service.

For example, an email system should be able to restore a single user's account without having to restore all accounts. It should be able to do this live so that the user may continue using the service while the restoring messages appear.

Both backups and restores create additional load on a system. This burden must be accounted for in capacity planning (headroom) and latency calculations.

2.1.6 Redundancy

Many reliability and scaling techniques are predicated on the ability to run multiple, redundant replicas of a service. Therefore services should be designed to support such configurations. Service replicas are discussed in Section 1.3.1. The challenge of replicating state between replicas is discussed in Section 1.5.

If a service wasn't designed to work behind a load balancer, it may work through "luck," which is not a recommended way to do system administration. Only the most rudimentary services will work in such a situation. It is more likely that the system will not work or, worse, will seem to work but develop problems later that are difficult to trace.

A common issue is that a user's login state is stored locally by a web server but not communicated to replicas. When the load balancer receives future requests from the same user, if they are sent to a different replica the user will be asked to log in again. This will repeat until the user has logged into every replica. Solutions to this problem are discussed in Section 4.2.3.

2.1.7 Replicated Databases

Systems that access databases should do so in a way that supports database scaling. The most common way to scale database access in a distributed system is to create one or more read-only replicas. The master database does all transactions that mutate (make changes to) the database. Updates are then passed to the read-only replicas via bulk transfers. Services can access the master database as normal, or if a query does not make any mutations it is sent to a read-only replica. Most database access is read-only, so the majority of work is off-loaded to the replicas. The replicas offer fast, though slightly out of date, access. The master offers full-service access to the "freshest" data, though it might be slower.

Software that uses a database must be specifically engineered to support read-only replicas. Rather than opening a connection to the database, two connections are created: a connection to the database master and a connection to one of the read-only replicas. As developers code each query, they give serious consideration to which connection it should be sent over, trading off speed for freshness and realizing that every query sent directly to the master "just in case" is consuming the master database's very precious resources.

It is good practice to segregate these kinds of queries even if the database does not have any replicas and both connections go to the same server. Someday you will want to add read-only replicas. Deciding which connection a query should use is best done when the query is originally being invented, not months or years later. That said, if you find yourself retrofitting a system after the fact, it may be a better use of your time to identify a few heavy hitters that can be moved to the read-only replica, rather than examine every single query in the source code. Alternatively, you may create a read-only replica for a specific purpose, such as backups.

Unlucky Read-Only Replicas

At Google Tom experienced a race condition between a database master and its replicas. The system carefully sent writes to the master and did all reads from the replicas. However, one component read data soon after it was updated and often became confused because it saw outdated information from the replica. As the team had no time to recode the component, it was simply reconfigured so that both the write and read connections went to the master. Even though only one read query out of many had to go to the master, all were sent to the master. Since the component was used just once or twice a day, this did not create an undue burden on the master.

As time went on, usage patterns changed and this component was used more frequently, until eventually it was used all day long. One day there was an outage because the master became overloaded due to the load from this component. At that point, the component had to be re-engineered to properly segregate queries.

One more warning against relying on luck rather than official support from the developers: luck runs out. Relying on luck today may result in disaster at the next software release. Even though it may be a long-standing policy for the operations staff, it will appear to the developers as a "surprise request" to support this configuration. The developers could rightfully refuse to fix the problem because it had not been a supported configuration in the first place. You can imagine the confusion and the resulting conflict.

2.1.8 Hot Swaps

Service components should be able to be swapped in or out of their service roles without triggering an overall service outage. Software components may be self-sufficient for completing a hot swap or may simply be compatible with a load balancer or other redirection service that controls the process.

Some physical components, such as power supplies or disk drives, can be swapped while still electrically powered on, or "hot." **Hot-swappable** devices can be changed without affecting the rest of the machine. For example, power supplies can be replaced without stopping operations. **Hot-pluggable** devices can be installed or removed while the machine is running. Administrative tasks may be required before or after this operation is performed. For example, a hard drive may not be recognized unless the operating system is told to scan for new disks. A new network interface card may be recognized, but the application server software may not see it without being restarted unless it has been specifically programmed to periodically scan for new interfaces.

It is often unclear what vendors mean by "hot-pluggable" and "hot-swappable." Directly test the system to understand the ramifications of the process and to see how application-level software responds.

2.1.9 Toggles for Individual Features

A configuration setting (a **toggle**) should be present to enable or disable each new feature. This allows roll-outs of new software releases to be independent of when the new feature is made available to users. For example, if a new feature is to appear on the site precisely at noon on Wednesday, it is very difficult to coordinate a new binary "push" exactly at that time. However, if each new feature can be individually enabled, the software can be deployed early and the feature can be enabled via changing a configuration setting at the desired time. This is often called a **flag flip**.

This approach is also useful for dealing with new features that cause problems. It is easier to disable the individual feature via a flag flip than to roll back to the previous binary.

More sophisticated toggles can be enabled for particular groups of users. A feature may be enabled for a small group of trusted testers who receive early access. Once it is validated, the toggle can enable the feature for all users, perhaps by enabling it for successively larger groups.

See Section 11.7 for more details.

2.1.10 Graceful Degradation

Graceful degradation means software acts differently when it is becoming overloaded or when systems it depends on are down. For example, a web site might have two user interfaces: one is rich and full of images, while the other is lightweight and all text. Normally users receive the rich interface. However, if the system is overloaded or at risk of hitting bandwidth limits, it switches to the lightweight mode.

Graceful degradation also requires the software to act smartly during outages. A service may become read-only if the database stops accepting writes (a common administrative defense when corruption is detected). If a database becomes completely inaccessible, the software works from its cache so that users see partial results rather than an error message.

When a service can no longer access services it depends on, related features may disappear rather than just displaying a broken web page or a "404 page not found" error.

Even small sites have learned that it is better to put up a temporary web server that displays the same "under construction" page no matter what the query, than to have the users receive no service at all. There are simple web server software packages made just for this situation.

Case Study: Graceful Degradation in Google Apps

Google Docs deploys many graceful degradation techniques. Google's word processor can switch into read-only mode when only a read-only database replica is available. The client-side JavaScript can work with the cached data in the browser if the server is inaccessible. Gmail provides a rich, JavaScript-based user interface as well as a slimmer HTML-only interface that appears automatically as needed. If the entire system is unavailable, the user is sent to a generic front page that displays the system status rather than simply receiving no response.

2.1.11 Access Controls and Rate Limits

If a service provides an API, that API should include an Access Control List (ACL) mechanism that determines which users are permitted or denied access, and also determines rate-limiting settings.

An ACL is a list of users, along with an indication of whether they are authorized to access the system. For example, access could be restricted to certain Internet Protocol (IP) addresses or blocks, to certain users or processes, or by other identification mechanisms. IP addresses are the weakest form of identification because they can be easily forged. Something better should be used, such as a public key infrastructure (PKI) that uses digital certificates to prove identity.

The most simple ACL is a list of users that are permitted access; everyone else is banned. This is called a **default closed** policy; the list is called the **whitelist**. The reverse would be a **default open** policy, where the default is to give access to all users unless they appear on a **blacklist**.

A more sophisticated ACL is an ordered list of users and/or groups annotated as either being "permitted" or "denied." If a user is not mentioned in the ACL, the default action might be to permit the user (**fail open**) or, alternatively, to deny the user (**fail closed**).

In addition to indicating permission, ACLs can indicate rate limits. Different users might be permitted different queries per second (QPS) rates, with requests that go over that rate being denied. For example, the service may give premium customers an unlimited QPS rate, regular paid customers a moderate QPS rate, and unpaid customers a low QPS rate or no access at all.

Case Study: ACLs at Google

Google's Remote Procedure Call (RPC) protocol, used by all internal APIs, has a powerful ACL system. Connections are authenticated via a PKI so that the service is assured of the client's identity and knows which groups that client is a member of. Identity and groups are globally defined and represent products and services as opposed to individual external customers. The ACLs specify the access allowed for that individual or group: permit, deny, or permit with a rate limit. Teams negotiate QPS rates for accessing a service as part of the service's capacity planning. Teams that have not negotiated rates get access but at a very low rate limit. This enables all teams to try out new services and eliminates the need for the service team to expend effort negotiating hundreds of lightweight or casual use requests.

2.1.12 Data Import Controls

If a service periodically imports data, mechanisms should be established that permit operations staff to control which data is accepted, rejected, or replaced.

The quality of incoming data varies, and the system importing the data needs a way to restrict what is actually imported so that known bad data can be disregarded. If a bad record causes a problem with the system, one must be able to block it via configuration rather than waiting for a software update.

Such a system uses the same whitelist/blacklist terminology we saw earlier. A blacklist is a way of specifying input that is to be rejected, with the assumption that all other data is accepted. A whitelist is used to specify data that is to be accepted; all other data is rejected.

In addition to control the incoming data stream, we need a way to augment an imported data source with locally provided data. This is accomplished using an augmentation file of data to import.

Establishing a change limit can also prevent problems. For example, if a weekly data import typically changes less than 20 percent of all records, one might want to require manual approval if the change will affect 30 or more percent of all records. This can prevent a disaster caused by a software bug or a bad batch of new data.

Case Study: Google Maps Local Business Listing

Google subscribes to listings of businesses from various "local business directory" services for use in its map-related products. These information providers periodically send data that must be processed and imported into the map system. The quality of the data is disheartening: listings are often incorrect, mangled, or somehow useless. Corrections are reported to the provider but could take months to appear in the data feed. Some sources provide data that has good quality for certain states and countries but categorically bad data for others. Therefore the system that imports this data has a whitelist, a blacklist, and an augmentation file.

The whitelist indicates which regions to include. It is used when the information from a particular provider might be of high quality only for certain regions. Once the quality of data for a particular region is verified, it is added to the whitelist. If the quality drops, the data for that region is removed.

The blacklist identifies known bad records. It includes records that have been identified as bad or incorrect in past batches.

The data from the business directories is augmented by data that Google produces independently of the source. This includes information sourced by Google itself, overrides for known bad data that Google has independently corrected, and "Easter eggs" (jokes to be included in the listings).

2.1.13 Monitoring

Operations requires visibility into how the system is working. Therefore each component of a system must expose metrics to the monitoring system. These metrics are used to monitor availability and performance, for capacity planning, and as part of troubleshooting.

Chapters 16 and 17 cover this topic in greater detail.

2.1.14 Auditing

Logging, permissions, and role accounts are set up to enable the service to be examined for, and pass, security and compliance audits. This area is changing rapidly, so it is always best to consult your legal department for information about the latest laws. The biggest concerns for corporations that are considering using public cloud services revolve around compliance with the relevant laws governing their business: if they choose to use a public cloud service, will they fail their next audit, and subsequently face massive fines or be prevented from conducting business until they pass another audit?

Although local labor laws usually do not directly affect compliance or governance issues, some countries strongly believe that people from other countries doing IT administration can be a compliance issue. Consider the system administrator who is sitting in Orange, New Jersey, and doing some administration on a server in Frankfurt, Germany. The system administrator has no knowledge of the local labor laws or the European Union (EU) Data Protection Directive and moves a virtual server across the company intranet as a scheduled and approved change. That system administrator may have violated at least two EU mandates, inadvertently making her employer non compliant and subject to sanctions, fines, or both.

Examples of regulations with specific IT audit requirements are SOX, j-SOX, c-SOX, PCI DSS, the EU Data Protection Directive, and Singapore MAS. More than 150 such regulatory mandates can be found across the world. In addition, some global standards apply to various governance scenarios, such as CobiT 5 and ISO/IEC 27001, 27002, and 27005. IT governance and compliance are covered more fully in Volume 1 of this series (Limoncelli, Hogan & Chalup, forthcoming 2015).

2.1.15 Debug Instrumentation

Software needs to generate logs that are useful when debugging. Such logs should be both human-readable and machine-parseable. The kind of logging that is appropriate for debugging differs from the kind of logging that is needed for auditing. A debug log usually records the parameters sent to and returned from any important function call. What constitutes "important" varies.

Large systems should permit debug logging to be enabled on individual modules. Otherwise, the volume of information can be overwhelming.

In some software methodologies, any logged information must be matched with documentation that indicates what the message means and how to use it. The message and the documentation must be translated into all (human) languages supported by the system and must be approved by marketing, product management, and legal personnel. Such a policy is a fast path to ending any and all productivity through bureaucratic paralysis. Debugging logs should be exempt from such rules because these messages are not visible to external users. Every developer should feel empowered to add a debug logging statement for any information he or she sees fit. The documentation on how to consume such information is the source code itself, which should be available to operations personnel.

2.1.16 Exception Collection

When software generates an exception, it should be collected centrally for analysis. A software exception is an error so severe that the program intentionally exits. For example, the software author may decide that handling a particular situation is unlikely to happen and will be difficult to recover from; therefore the program declares an exception and exits in this situation. Certain data corruption scenarios are better handled by a human than by the software itself. If you've ever seen an operating system "panic" or present a "blue screen of death," that is an exception.

When designing software for operability, it is common to use a software framework that detects exceptions, gathers the error message and other information, and submits it to a centralized database. Such a framework is referred to as an exception collector.

Exception collection systems offer three benefits. First, since most software systems have some kind of automatic restart capability, certain exceptions may go unnoticed. If you never see that the exceptions are occurring, of course, you can't deal with the underlying causes. An exception collector, however, makes the invisible visible.

Second, exception collection helps determine the health of a system. If there are many exceptions, maintenance such as rolling out new software releases should be cancelled. If a sharp increase in exceptions is seen during a roll-out, it may be an indication that the release is bad and the roll-out should stop.

The third benefit from using an exception collector is that the history of exceptions can be studied for trends. A simple trend to study is whether the sheer volume of exceptions is going up or down. Usually exception levels can be correlated to a particular software release. The other trend to look for is repetition. If a particular type of exception is recorded, the fact that it is happening more or less frequently is telling. If it occurs less frequently, that means the software quality is improving. If it is increasing in frequency, then there is the opportunity to detect it and fix the root cause before it becomes a bigger problem.

2.1.17 Documentation for Operations

Developers and operational staff should work together to create a playbook of operating procedures for the service. A playbook augments the developer-written documentation by adding operations steps that are informed by the larger business view. For example, the developers might write the precise steps required to fail over a system to a hot spare. The playbook would document when such a failover is to be done, who should be notified, which additional checks must be done before and after failover, and so on. It is critical that every procedure include a test suite that verifies success or failure. Following is an example database failover procedure:

1. Announce the impending failover to the db-team and manager-team mailing lists.
2. Verify the hot spare has at least 10 terabytes of free disk space.

3. Verify these dependencies are all operating within parameters: (link to server control panel) (link to data feed control panel).
4. Perform the failover using the system failover procedure (link).
5. Verify that these dependencies have successfully switched to the hot spare and are operating correctly.
6. Reply-all to the previously sent email regarding the operation's success or failure.

Documenting the basic operational procedures for a service cannot be the sole responsibility of either the development or operations team. Instead, it needs to be a collaborative effort, with the operations team ensuring that all the operational scenarios they can foresee are addressed, and the developers ensuring that the documentation covers all error situations that can arise in their code, and how and when to use the supporting tools and procedures.

Documentation is a stepping stone to automation. Processes may change frequently when they are new. As they solidify, you can identify good candidates for automation (see Chapter 12). Writing documentation also helps you understand what can be automated easily and what will be more challenging to automate, because documenting things means explaining the steps in detail.

2.2 Implementing Design for Operations

Features designed for operations need to be implemented by someone; they are not magically present in software. For any given project, you will find that the software may have none, some, or all of the features listed in this chapter. There are four main ways that you can get these features into software:

- Build them in from the beginning.
- Request features as they are identified.
- Write the features yourself.
- Work with a third-party vendor.

2.2.1 Build Features in from the Beginning

In this instance, a savvy development and operations team has built the features into the product you are using to run your service. It is extremely rare that you will encounter this scenario outside of large, experienced shops like Google, Facebook, or Yahoo.

If you are fortunate enough to be involved in early development of a system, work with developers and help them set priorities so that these features are "baked in" from the beginning. It also helps if the business team driving the requirements can recognize the needs of operations.

2.2.2 Request Features as They Are Identified

More likely a service does not contain all of the operational features desired because it is impossible to know what will be needed before the system is in operation. If you have access to the developers, these features can be requested over time. First and foremost, speak up about your operations needs—file a feature request for every missing feature. The feature request should identify the problem that needs to be solved rather than the specific implementation. List the risks and impact to the business so that your request can be prioritized. Work collaboratively with the developers as they implement the features. Make yourself available for consultation with the developers, and offer encouragement.

Developer time and resources are limited, so it is important to prioritize your requests. One strategy for prioritization is to select the item that will have the biggest impact for the smallest amount of effort. Figure 2.1 shows a graph where the x-axis is the expected impact of a change, ranging from low- to high-impact. The y-axis represents the amount of effort required to create the change, also ranging from easy (low effort) to hard (high effort). It is tempting to focus on the easiest tasks or "low-hanging fruit." However, this often ends up wasting resources on easy tasks that have very little impact. That outcome may be emotionally satisfying but does not solve operational problems. Instead, you should focus on the high-impact items exclusively, starting with the low-effort projects while selectively choosing the ones that require larger effort.

Fixing the biggest bottleneck usually has the biggest impact. This point will be discussed in greater detail in Section 12.4.3.

One of the differences we have found between high-performing teams and low-performing teams is that the high-performing teams focus on impact.

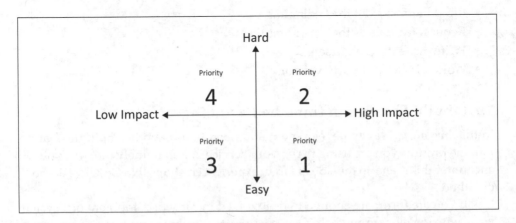

Figure 2.1: Implementation priorities for design for operations

Case Study: An 80/20 Rule for Operational Features

When Tom was at Lumeta, a disagreement arose over how much developer time should be spent on operational issues versus new features. The product manager came up with a very creative solution. The product alternated big releases and small releases. Big releases were expected to have major new features. Small releases were expected to fix bugs from the previous major release.

It was negotiated that big releases would have 20 percent of developer time spent on issues requested by the operations team. The small releases were not intended to add major new features, but it was useful to have one or two high-priority features included. Therefore, for small releases, 80 percent of developer time was spent on operational requests. Since the releases were smaller, the same number of hours was spent on operational requests for both big and small releases.

2.2.3 Write the Features Yourself

When developers are unwilling to add operational features, one option is to write the features yourself. This is a bad option for two reasons.

First, the developers might not accept your code. As an outsider, you do not know their coding standards, the internal infrastructure, and their overall vision for the future software architecture. Any bugs in your code will receive magnified blame.

Second, it sets a bad precedent. It sends a message that developers do not need to care about operational features because if they delay long enough you'll write them yourself.

Operational staff should spend time coding operational services that create the ecosystem in which services run. Write frameworks that developers can use to improve operations. For example, write a library that can be linked to that makes it easy to report status to the monitoring system. Write tools that let developers be self-sufficient rather than dependent on operations. For example, write a tool that gathers exceptions and core dumps for analysis rather than emailing requests to operations anytime that step is needed.

There are exceptions to this rule. Code submissions from outsiders are easier to accept when they are small. In a highly collaborative organization, people may simply be more accustomed to receiving code contributions from many sources. This is typical on open source projects. At Google there is a code approval process that makes it easy for outsiders to contribute to a project and assure the code meets team standards. This system permits feedback and revisions until the code change is deemed acceptable by both parties; only then is the code accepted into the system. It also helps that there is a corporate-wide high standard for code quality and style. In such a system, the code quality and style you are used to writing will probably be compatible with that of other teams.

When possible, operational staff should be embedded with developers so they can learn the code base, become familiar with the release and testing process, and build a relationship with the code. However, even that is no replacement for getting operational features added by the developers themselves. Therefore it is better to embed developers with the operations staff, possibly in six-month rotations, so that they understand the operational need for such features.

What works best may be dictated by the size of the organization and the scale of the system being operated. For example, a high degree of collaboration may be easier to achieve in small organizations.

2.2.4 Work with a Third-Party Vendor

Working with a third-party vendor is quite similar to working with your own development team. Many of the same processes need to be followed, such as filing bugs and having periodic meetings to discuss feature requests.

Always raise the visibility of your issues in a constructive way, as vendors are sensitive to criticism of their products. For example, write a postmortem report that includes the feature request so that the vendor can see the context of the request. (See Section 14.3.2 for more details on writing good postmortem reports.)

If the vendor is unresponsive to your requests, you may be able to write code that builds frameworks around the vendor's software. For example, you might create a wrapper that provides startup and shutdown services in a clean manner around vendor software that handles those tasks ungracefully. We highly recommend publishing such systems externally as open source products. If you need them, someone else will, too. Developing a community around your code will make its support less dependent on your own efforts.

2.3 Improving the Model

Good design for operations makes operations easy. Great design for operations helps eliminate some operational duties entirely. It's a force multiplier often equivalent to hiring an extra person. When possible, strive to create systems that embed knowledge or capability into the process, replacing the need for operational intervention. The job of the operations staff then changes from performing repetitive operational tasks to building, maintaining, and improving the automation that handles those tasks.

Tom once worked in an environment where resource allocations were requested via email and processed manually. Once an API was made available, the entire process became self-service; users could manage their own resources.

Some provisioning systems let you specify how much RAM, disk, and CPU each "job" will need. A better system does not require you to specify any resources at all: it monitors use and allocates what is needed, maintaining an effective balance among all the jobs on a cluster, and reallocating them and shifting resources around over time.

A common operational task is future capacity planning—that is, predicting how many resources will be needed 3 to 12 months out. It can be a lot of work. Alternatively, a thoughtfully constructed data collection and analysis system can make these predictions for you. For more information on capacity planning, see Chapter 18.

Creating alert thresholds and fine-tuning them can be an endless task. That work can be eliminated if the monitoring system sets its own thresholds. For example, one web site developed an accurate prediction model for how many QPS it should receive every hour of the year. The system administrators could then set an alert if the actual QPS was more than 10 percent above or below the prediction. Monitoring hundreds of replicas around the world can't be done manually without huge investments in staff. By eliminating this operational duty, the system scaled better and required less operational support.

2.4 Summary

Services should include features that benefit operations, not just the end users. Features requested by operations staff are aimed at building a stable, reliable, high-performing service, which scales well and can be run in a cost-effective manner. Even though these features are not directly requested by customers, the better operational effectiveness ultimately benefits the customer.

Operations staff need many features to support day-to-day operations. They also need full documentation of all the operational processes, failure scenarios, and feature controls. They need authentication, authorization, and access control mechanisms, as well as rate-limiting functionality. Operations staff need to be able to enable and disable new features with toggles, globally for roll-out and roll-back, and on a per-user basis for beta testing and premium services.

Services should degrade gracefully when there are problems, rather than become completely unusable. Services that import data from other sources must allow the operations staff to apply controls to those data sources, based on their data quality or other criteria.

Systems are easier to maintain when this functionality is designed into them from inception. Operations staff can work with developers to ensure that operational features are included in a system, particularly if the software is developed in-house.

Exercises

1. Why is design for operations so important?
2. How is automated configuration typically supported?
3. List the important factors for redundancy through replication.
4. Give an example of a partially implemented process in your current environment. What would you do to fully implement it?
5. Why might you not want to solve an issue by coding the solution yourself?
6. Which type of problems should appear first on your priority list?
7. Which factors can you bring to an outside vendor to get the vendor to take your issue seriously?

Chapter 3

Selecting a Service Platform

> When I hear someone touting the
> cloud as a magic-bullet for all
> computing problems, I silently
> replace "cloud" with "clown" and
> carry on with a zen-like smile.
>
> —Amy Rich

A service runs on a computing infrastructure called a platform. This chapter provides an overview of the various types of platforms available in cloud computing, what each of them provides, and their strengths and weaknesses. It does not offer an examination of specific products but rather a categorization that will help you understand the variety of offerings. Strategies for choosing between these different services are summarized at the end of the chapter.

The term "cloud" is ambiguous; it means different things to different people and has been made meaningless by marketing hype. Instead, we use the following terms to be specific:

- **Infrastructure as a Service (IaaS):** Computer and network hardware, real or virtual, ready for you to use.
- **Platform as a Service (PaaS):** Your software running in a vendor-provided framework or stack.
- **Software as a Service (SaaS):** An application provided as a web site.

Figure 3.1 depicts the typical consumer of each service. SaaS applications are for end users and fulfill a particular market niche. PaaS provides platforms for developers. IaaS is for operators looking to build their own platforms on which applications will be built, thus providing the most customizability.

In this chapter, we will discuss these services in terms of being provided by a third-party vendor since that is the general case.

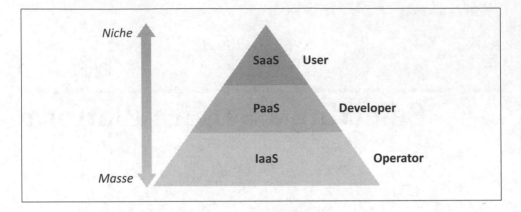

Figure 3.1: The consumers of SaaS, PaaS, and IaaS

A platform may be described along three axes:

- **Level of service abstraction:** IaaS, PaaS, SaaS
- **Type of machine:** Physical, virtual, or process container
- **Level of resource sharing:** Shared or private

3.1 Level of Service Abstraction

Abstraction is, essentially, how far users are kept from the details of the raw machine itself. That is, are you offered a raw machine (low abstraction) or are services provided as a high-level API that encapsulates what you need done rather than how to do it (high abstraction)? The closer you are to the raw machine, the more control you have. The higher the level of abstraction, the less you have to concern yourself with technical details of building infrastructure and the more you can focus on the application.

3.1.1 Infrastructure as a Service

IaaS provides bare machines, networked and ready for you to install the operating system and your own software. The service provider provides the infrastructure so that the customer can focus on the application itself.

The machines provided by the vendor are usually virtual machines but may be physical machines. The provider takes care of the infrastructure: the machines themselves, power, cooling, and networking, providing internet access, and all datacenter operations.

Terms to Know

Server: Software that provides a function or API. (Not a piece of hardware.)

Service: A user-visible system or product composed of many servers.

Machine: A virtual or physical machine.

Oversubscribed: A system that provides capacity X is used in a place where Y capacity is needed, when $X < Y$. Used to describe a potential or actual need.

Undersubscribed: The opposite of oversubscribed.

Although the service provider manages its layers of the infrastructure, IaaS does not relieve you from all work. A lot of work must be done to coordinate all the pieces, understand and tune the various parts so they work well together, and manage the operating system (since you have total control of the OS).

Providers charge for compute time, storage, and network traffic. These costs will affect how your application is architected. Keeping information locally versus retrieving it over a network may have different costs, affecting your design choices. If information is accessed frequently over the network, the network charges can be reduced by caching or storing more information locally. However, the additional local storage may have its own cost. Such engineering details are important, because otherwise you may find yourself with a startlingly large bill at the end of the month. These are important points to work out with the development and business teams. The software and operational choices have real costs and tradeoffs.

The performance characteristics of providers may vary wildly. When comparing providers, it is important to benchmark local storage, remote storage, CPU, and network performance. Some providers' remote storage is significantly faster than others. Repeat any such benchmarks at different times of the day—some service providers may experience high packet loss at daily peak times. Design decisions made for one provider may not be the right choice for other providers.

Within an IaaS offering, partitions or "reliability zones" segment the service geographically to provide regional uptime guarantees. While all attempts are made to ensure reliable service, it is inevitable that some downtime will be required for maintenance or due to unavoidable circumstances such as a natural disaster. The service provider should segment its service into multiple zones and provide guarantees that planned downtime will not occur in multiple zones at the same time. Each zone should be far enough apart from the others that natural disasters are unlikely to strike more than one zone at a time. This permits customers to keep their service in one zone and fail over to another zone if necessary.

For example, a service provider may offer four zones: U.S. East Coast, U.S. West Coast, Western Europe, and Eastern Europe. Each zone is built and managed to have limited dependencies on the others. At a minimum, customers should locate a service in one zone with plans for failover in another zone. A more sophisticated plan would be to have the service run in each zone with load balancing between all locations, automatically shifting traffic away from any zone that is down. We will cover this in more detail in Chapter 6.

Such geographic diversity also permits customers to better manage the latency of their service. Information takes time to travel, so it is generally faster to provide service to someone from a nearby datacenter. For example, a service may be architected such that a user's data is stored in one zone with a backup kept in one other zone. Users from New York would have their data stored in the U.S. East Coast zone, with backup copies stored in the Western Europe zone. During an outage, the user is served from the backup zone; the service would not be as fast in such a case, but at least the data would be accessible.

IaaS providers have expanded beyond offering just simple machines and networks. Some provide a variety of storage options, including relational (SQL) and non-relational (NoSQL or key/value) databases, high-speed storage options, and **cold storage** (bulk data storage that is inexpensive but has latency on the order of hours or days). More advanced networking options include virtual private network (VPN)–accessible private networks and load balancing services. Many provide both local load balancing and global load balancing, as will be described in Chapter 4. Some provide elastic scaling services, which automatically allocate and configure additional machines on demand as capacity is needed.

Providers that offer both IaaS and PaaS often blur the line between the two by providing high-level managed services that are available to both.

3.1.2 Platform as a Service

PaaS enables you to run your applications from a vendor-provided framework. These services offer you a high level of value, as they manage all aspects of the infrastructure, even much of the application stack. They offer very elastic scaling services, handling additional load without any input required from you. Generally you are not even aware of the specific resources dedicated to your application.

For example, in Google AppEngine, you upload application-level software and Google takes care of the rest. The framework (platform) automatically provides load balancing and scaling. The more active your users are, the more machines Google allocates to your application. Internally the system is managing bandwidth, CPU allocations, and even authentication. Your application and hundreds of others might be sharing the same machine or your application may require the resources of hundreds of dedicated machines. You do not have to manage such decisions except to limit resource use to control costs.

PaaS providers charge for their services based on how much CPU, bandwidth, and storage are used. This is similar to IaaS except the charges are higher to compensate for the more extensive framework that is provided.

The downside of PaaS is that you are restricted to using what the vendor's platform provides. The platform is generally programmable but not necessarily extensible. You do not have direct access to the operating system. For instance, you may not be able to add binaries or use popular libraries until the vendor makes them part of its service. Generally processes run in a secure "jail" (similar to UNIX's "chroot" restricted environment), which aims to prevent them from breaking out of the service's framework. For example, one PaaS offered the Python language but not the Python Imaging Library (PIL). It could not be installed by users because the framework does not permit Python libraries that include portions written in compiled languages.

PaaS provides many high-level services including storage services, database services, and many of the same services available in IaaS offerings. Some offer more esoteric services such as Google's Machine Learning service, which can be used to build a recommendation engine. Additional services are announced periodically.

3.1.3 Software as a Service

SaaS is what we used to call a web site before the marketing department decided adding "as a service" made it more appealing. SaaS is a web-accessible application. The application is the service, and you interact with it as you would any web site. The provider handles all the details of hardware, operating system, and platform.

Some common examples include Salesforce.com, which replaces locally run sales team management software; Google Apps, which eliminates the need for locally run email and calendaring software; and Basecamp, which replaces locally run project management software. Nearly any business process that is common among many companies is offered as SaaS: human resources (HR) functions such as hiring and performance management; accounting functions such as payroll, expense tracking, and general ledgers; IT incident, request, and change management systems; and many aspects of marketing and sales management.

The major selling point of SaaS is that customers do not have to concern themselves with software installation, upgrades, and operations. There is no client software to download. The service is fully managed, upgraded, and maintained by the provider. Because the service is accessed via the web, it can be used from any location.

As a SaaS provider, you need to design the service to obscure upgrades and other operational details. Developers must avoid features that require client software or browser plug-ins. In designing the service you need to recognize that since it *can* be accessed from anywhere, it *will* be accessed from anywhere, including mobile devices. This affects architecture and security decisions.

Make it easy for customers to get started using your service. Rather than having to speak with a salesperson to sign up, signing up should be possible via the web site, possibly requiring submission of a credit card or other payment information. Facebook would not have gotten to where it is today if each user had to first speak to a customer service representative and arrange for an account to be created. Importing data and enabling features should also be self-service. A product like Salesforce.com would not have been able to grow at the rate it has if importing data or other operations required working with customer support personnel.

It is also important that people can leave the service in a self-service manner. This means users should be able to export or retrieve their data and close their accounts, even if this makes it easier to leave and move to a competitor. Customers will be concerned about their ability to migrate out of the application at the end of the contract or if they are dissatisfied. We believe it is unethical to lock people into a product by making it impossible or difficult to export their data. This practice, called vendor lock-in, should be considered a "red flag" that the product is not trustworthy. The best way to demonstrate confidence in your product is to make it easy to leave. It also makes it easy for users to back up their data.

Many SaaS offerings are upgraded frequently, often without warning, providing little opportunity for training. Users should be able to access major new releases for the purpose of planning, training, and user acceptance testing. Provide a mechanism for users to select the day they will be moved to major releases, or provide two tracks: a "rapid release" track for customers that want new features without delay and a "scheduled release" track for customers that would like new features to appear on a published schedule, perhaps two to three weeks after the rapid release track.

Finally, conflicts may exist between your data privacy and application hosting policies and those of your customers. Your privacy policy will need to be a superset of all your customers' privacy policies. You may need to provide heightened security for certain customers, possibly segmenting them from other customers.

3.2 Type of Machine

There are three options for the type of machine that a service runs on: physical machine, virtual machine, and process container. The decision between physical, virtual, and container is a technical decision. Each has different performance, resource efficiency, and isolation capabilities. The desired technical attributes should guide your decision on which to use.

IaaS generally provides the widest variety of options. PaaS generally obscures what is used, as the user works in a framework that hides the distinction. That said, most PaaS providers use containers.

3.2.1 Physical Machines

A **physical machine** is a traditional computer with one or more CPUs, and subsystems for memory, disk, and network. These resources are controlled by the operating system, whose job it is to act as the traffic cop coordinating all the processes that want to share these resources. The resources allocated to a running process (a program running on the system) are actual hardware resources. As a result their performance is relatively predictable.

3.2.2 Virtual Machines

Virtual machines are created when a physical machine is partitioned to run a separate operating system for each partition. Processes running on a virtual machine have little or no awareness that they are not on a physical machine. They cannot access the resources, such as disk or memory, of other virtual machines running on the same physical machine.

Virtual machines can make computing more efficient. Physical machines today are so fast and powerful that some applications do not need the full resources of a single machine. The excess capacity is called **stranded capacity** because it is unusable in its current form. Sharing a large physical machine's power among many smaller virtual machines helps reduce stranded capacity by permitting the creation of virtual machines that are the right size for their requirements.

Stranded capacity can also be mitigated by running multiple servers on the same machine. However, virtualization provides better isolation than simple multitasking.

For example, when two applications share a machine, when one application gets overloaded or has a problem that causes it to consume large amounts of CPU, disk space, or memory, it will affect the performance of the other application. Now suppose those two programs each ran on their own virtual machines, each with a certain amount of CPU, disk space, and memory allocated. This arrangement provides better isolation for each application from problems caused by the other.

Sometimes the reason for using virtual machines is organizational. Different departments within an organization may not trust each other enough or have sufficient cross-department billing options to run software on the same machine. Nevertheless, they can share a pool of physical machines if each is able to create its own virtual machine.

Sometimes the reason for using virtual machines is logistical. Running five services on one machine requires that any OS patches or upgrades be approved by all five services. If each service runs in its own virtual machine, then upgrades and patches can be done on different schedules for different services. In all these cases, virtual machines permit isolation at the OS level.

Benefits of Virtual Machines

Virtual machines are fast to create and destroy. There is very little lead time between when one is requested and when the virtual machine is usable. Some systems can spin up a new virtual machine in less than a minute. Consequently, it is easy to create a virtual machine for a specific task and delete it when the task is completed. Such a virtual machine is called an **ephemeral machine** or short-lived machine. Some systems create hundreds of ephemeral machines across many physical machines, run a parallel compute job, and then destroy the machines when the job is complete.

Because virtual machines are controlled through software, virtualization systems are programmable. An API can be used to create, start, stop, modify, and destroy virtual machines. Software can be written to orchestrate these functions on a large scale. This is not possible with physical machines, which have to be racked, cabled, and configured via manual labor.

Virtual machine functionality is provided by a combination of virtualization support in modern CPUs and virtualization control software called the **virtual machine monitor** (VMM). Modern CPUs have special features for partitioning memory and CPU time to create virtual machines. Access to disk, network, and other I/O devices is handled by emulation at the chip or device level.

Some virtualization systems permit a virtual machine to be moved between physical machines. Like a laptop that is put to sleep and woken up later, the VMM puts the machine to sleep, copies its memory and all other state to a different physical machine, and continues its activities there. The process can be coordinated so that most of the copying happens ahead of time, so that the machine freeze lasts for less than a second. This permits a virtual machine to be moved to a different physical machine when the current one needs to be upgraded or repaired, or moved to a different failure domain in advance of a planned maintenance outage.

I/O in a Virtual Environment

A **hardware virtual machine** (HVM) performs I/O emulation at the chip level. With HVMs, the virtual machine's operating system thinks there is, for example, an actual SATA hard drive controller installed. This lets the virtual machine use an unmodified operating system. However, such emulation is rather slow. On an HVM, every time the OS tries to access the SATA controller, the CPU's virtualization feature detects this access, stops the virtual machine, and gives control to the VMM. The VMM performs the disk request, emulating a real SATA controller and placing the result where the actual chip would have. The virtual machine is then allowed to continue where it left off. It sees the result and is none the wiser.

Paravirtualization (PV) performs I/O emulation at the device level. PV requires the operating system to be modified so that the I/O calls it would normally perform are instead done by requests to the VMM. The VMM handles the I/O and returns the result. The modifications usually take the form of device drivers that look like standard hard disks, video displays, keyboards, and so on, but are actually talking to the VMM. PV is able to perform the requests more efficiently since it captures the request at a higher level of abstraction.

Virtual machines are allocated a fixed amount of disk space, memory, and CPU from the physical machine. The hard drive a VM sees actually may be a single large file on the physical machine.

Disadvantages of Virtual Machines

Some resources, such as CPU cores, are shared. Suppose a physical machine has a four-core CPU. Three virtual cores may be allocated to one virtual machine and three virtual cores may be allocated to another virtual machine. The VMM will load-share the six virtual cores on the four physical cores. There may be times when one virtual machine is relatively idle and does not need all three virtual cores it was allocated. However, if both virtual machines are running hard and require all six virtual cores, each will receive a fraction of the CPU's attention and so will run more slowly.

A virtual machine can detect CPU contention. In Linux and the Xen hypervisor, this is called "steal time": it is the amount of CPU time that your virtual machine is missing because it was allocated to other virtual machines (Haynes 2013). IaaS providers usually cannot provide guarantees of how much steal time will exist, nor can they provide mechanisms to control it. Netflix found the only way it could deal with this issue was to be reactionary. If high steal time was detected on a virtual machine in Amazon Web Services (AWS), Netflix would delete the virtual machine and have it re-created. If the company was lucky, the new virtual machine would be created on a physical machine that was less oversubscribed. This is a sorry state of affairs (Link 2013).

Some resources are shared in an unbounded manner. For example, if one virtual machine is generating a huge amount of network traffic, the other virtual machines may suffer. This is also typical of disk I/O. A hard drive can perform only so much disk I/O per second, with the amount being limited by the bandwidth from the computer to the disk. Where there is a resource shortage such as disk I/O bandwidth, the situation is called **resource contention**.

Virtual machines are very heavy-weight. They run a full operating system, which requires a lot of disk space. They hold on to all the memory allocated to them, even if it isn't being used. The underlying OS cannot reallocate this memory to other machines. Because virtual machines run a complete operating system, the operational burden is similar to a full machine that needs to be monitored, patched, upgraded, and so on. Also, because a complete operating system is running, each OS is running many background service processes such as maintenance tasks and service daemons. Those take up resources and add to the operational burden on the system administration team.

3.2.3 Containers

A **container** is a group of processes running on an operating system that are isolated from other such groups of processes. Each container has an environment with its own process name space, network configuration, and other resources. The file system to which the processes have access consists of a subdirectory on the host machine. The processes in a particular container see that subdirectory as their root directory, and cannot access files outside that subdirectory (and its subdirectories) without special accommodation from the host machine. The processes all run on the same operating system or kernel. As a consequence, you cannot, for example, have some processes running under Linux and others running under Windows as you can with virtual machines.

Unlike a virtual machine, which is allocated a large chunk of RAM and disk, containers consume resources at the same fine-grained level as processes. Thus they are less wasteful.

Processes in a container are controlled as a group. If the container is configured to have a memory limit, the sum total of memory used by all processes in that container cannot exceed that limit. If the container is allocated a certain amount of disk bandwidth, that limit is enforced on the processes in the container as a whole. Solaris containers, called Zones, can be allocated network interfaces and have their network bandwidth regulated to control bandwidth resource contention. Containers on Linux can assign a different amount of disk cache to each container so that one container's buffer thrashing will not affect the buffers of another container.

Processes in a container are isolated in other ways. A container can kill or otherwise interact with only processes in its container. In contrast, processes that are not in containers can kill or interact with all processes, even ones in individual containers. For example, the shell command ps, when running in a FreeBSD container (called a "jail"), displays only processes running in that container. This is not a parlor trick; the container has no visibility to other processes. However, when the same command is run on the host from outside any container, it shows all processes, including those inside the each container. Thus, if you are logged into the main host (no particular container), you have global visibility and can serve as administrator for all containers.

Each container has its own copy of the packages, shared libraries, and other supporting files that it requires. Two containers running on the same machine cannot have dependency or version conflicts. For example, without containers one program might require a particular version of a library while another requires a very different version and cannot operate with the other version installed. This "dependency hell" is common. When each program is put in a different container, however, each can have its own copy of the library and thus the conflict is avoided.

Containers are very lightweight because they do not require an entire OS. Only the specific system files needed by the software are copied into the container. The system allocates disk space as files are needed, as opposed to allocating a large virtual disk ahead of time. A container runs fewer processes because it needs to run only the ones related to the software. System background processes such as SSH and other daemons do not run in the container since they are available in the outside operating system. When using virtual machines, each machine has a full complement of such daemons.

Containers are different from virtual machines. Each virtual machine is a blackbox. An administrator logged into the physical machine cannot (without tricks) peer into the individual virtual machines. A virtual machine can run a different operating system than its host physical machine because it is emulating a full machine. A virtual machine is a larger, less granular allocation of resources. When the virtual machine starts, a certain amount of RAM and disk space is allocated and dedicated to that virtual machine. If it does not use all of the RAM, the RAM can't be used by anything else. Virtual disks are often difficult to resize, so you create them larger than needed to reduce the chance that the container will need to be enlarged. The extra capacity cannot be used by other virtual machines—a situation called having **stranded resources**.

Containers do share some of the downsides of virtual machines. Downtime of the host machine affects all containers. This means that planned downtime for patching the host as well as unplanned outages affect all containers. Nevertheless, the host machine doesn't have to do much, so it can run a stripped-down version of the operating system. Thus there is less to patch and maintain.

So far we have discussed the technical aspects of containers. What can be done with them, however, is much more exciting.

Containers are usually the underlying technology in PaaS. They enable customers to be isolated from each other while still sharing physical machines. Because they consume the exact amount of resources they need at the time, containers are also much more efficient means of providing such shared services.

Systems like Docker define a standardized container for software. Rather than distributing software as a package, one can distribute a container that includes the software and everything needed for it to run. This container can be created once and run on many systems.

Being self-contained, containers eliminate dependencies and conflicts. Rather than shipping a software package plus a list of other dependent packages and system requirements, all that is needed is the standardized container and a system that supports the standard. This greatly simplifies the creation, storage, and delivery and distribution of software. Since many containers can coexist on the same machine, the resulting machine works much like a large hotel that is able to provide for many customers, treating them all the same way, even though they are all unique.

> ### Standardized Shipping Containers
>
> A common way for industries to dramatically improve processes is to standardize their delivery mechanism. The introduction of standardized shipping containers revolutionized the freight industry.
>
> Previously individual items were loaded and unloaded from ships, usually by hand. Each item was a different size and shape, so each had to be handled differently.
>
> Standardized shipping containers resulted in an entirely different way to ship products. Because each shipping container was the same shape and size, loading and unloading could be done much faster. A single container might hold many individual items, but since they were transported as a group, transferring the items between modes of transport was quick work. Customs could approve all the items in a particular container and seal it, eliminating the need for customs checks at remaining hops on the container's journey as long as the seal remained unbroken.
>
> As other modes of transportation adopted the standard shipping container, the concept of intermodal shipping was born. A container would be loaded at a factory and remain as a unit whether it was on a truck, train, or ship.
>
> All of this started in April 1956, when Malcom McLean's company SeaLand organized the first shipment using standardized containers from New Jersey (where Tom lives) to Texas. (Levinson 2008).

3.3 Level of Resource Sharing

In a "public cloud," a third party owns the infrastructure and uses it to provide service for many customers. The sharing may be fine-grained, mixing processing and data of different customers on the same machine. Alternatively, the sharing may be more segmented, like tenants in an apartment building with well-defined partitions between them. In a "private cloud," a company runs its own computing infrastructure on its own premises. This infrastructure may be set up for a dedicated internal project or, more commonly, done as an internal service provider that makes the offering available to projects and departments within the company. Hybrids may also be created, such as private clouds run in rented datacenter space.

The choice between private or public use of a platform is a business decision based on four factors: compliance, privacy, cost, and control.

3.3.1 Compliance

Companies are governed by varying amounts of regulation depending on their business, size, locations, and public or private status. Their compliance with all applicable regulations can be audited, and failing an audit can have significant consequences, such as the company being unable to conduct business until it passes a subsequent audit.

Using a public cloud for certain data or services may cause a company to fail a compliance audit. For example, the EU Data Protection Directive dictates that certain data about EU citizens may not leave the EU. Unless the public cloud provider has sufficient controls in place to ensure that will not happen, even in a failover scenario, a company that moves the data into the public cloud would fail an audit.

3.3.2 Privacy

Using a public cloud means your data and code reside on someone else's equipment, in someone else's facility. They may not have direct access to your data, but they could potentially gain access without your knowledge. Curious employees, with or without malicious intent, could poke around using diagnostic tools that would enable them to view your data. Data might be accidentally leaked by a service provider that disposed of old equipment without properly erasing storage systems.

Because of these risks, service providers spell out how they will take care of your data in their contracts. Contracts aside, vendors know that they must earn their users' trust if they are to retain them as customers. They maintain that trust by being transparent about their policies, and they submit to external audits to verify that they are abiding by the rules they set out.

Another issue with the public cloud is how law enforcement requests are handled. If law enforcement officials have a warrant to access the data, they can make a third party provide access without telling you. In contrast, in a private cloud, their only avenue to access your data involves making you aware of their request (although clandestine techniques can be hidden even at your own site).

There is also the possibility of accidental exposure of your data. Due to software bugs, employee mistakes, or other issues, your data could be exposed to other customers or the entire world. In a private cloud, the other customers are all from the same company, which may be considered an acceptable risk; the incident can be contained and not become public knowledge. In a public cloud, the exposure could be to anyone, possibly your competitors, and could be front-page news.

3.3.3 Cost

The cost of using a public cloud may or may not be less than the cost of building the necessary infrastructure yourself. Building such infrastructure requires large amounts of engineering talent, from physical engineering of a datacenter's cooling system, electric service, and design, to technical expertise in running a datacenter and providing the services themselves. All of this can be very expensive. Amortizing the expense over many customers reduces cost. By comparison, doing it yourself saves money due to the benefits of **vertical integration**. Vertical integration means saving money by handling all levels of service delivery yourself, eliminating the uplift in cost due to "middle men" and service provider profit margins. There is a break-even point where vertical integration becomes more economical. Calculating the total cost of ownership (TCO) and return on investment (ROI) will help determine which is the best option.

Deciding whether the cost of private versus public clouds is appropriate is similar to making a rent versus own decision about where you live. In the long term, it is less expensive to own a house than to rent one. In the short term, however, it may be less expensive to rent. Renting a hotel room for a night makes more sense than buying a building in a city and selling it the next day.

Similarly, building a private cloud makes sense if you will use all of it and need it for as long as it takes to pay for itself. Using a third-party provider makes sense if the need is small or short term.

3.3.4 Control

A private cloud affords you more control. You can specify exactly what kind of hardware will be used, which network topology will be set up, and so on. Any feature you need is a matter of creating it yourself, acquiring it, or licensing it. Changes can happen as fast as your organization can make them. In a public cloud you have less control. You must choose from a finite set of features. While most providers are responsive to feature requests, you are merely one customer among many. Providers need to focus on those features that will be used by many customers and may not be able to provide the specialized features you need.

Letting the vendor take care of all hardware selection means losing the ability to specify low-level hardware requirements (specific CPU types or storage products).

Contract Questions for Hosting Providers

The contract you sign is the baseline of what to expect and what obligations the provider has toward you, the customer. Here are some key questions to ask your potential providers:

1. If you want to exit the contract, will you be able to take all your data with you?

2. In the case of physical machines, if you wish to leave, can you buy the machine itself?

3. What happens to your servers and data if the vendor goes bankrupt? Will they be tied up in bankruptcy proceedings?

4. Is internet bandwidth provided by the vendor or do you have to arrange for it yourself? If provided, which Internet service providers (ISPs) do you connect to and how much oversubscription is done? What's the hardware and peering transit redundancy?

5. Are backups performed? If so, with what frequency and retention policy? Can you access the backups by request or are they solely for use by the vendor in case of a vendor emergency? How often are restores tested?

6. How does the vendor guarantee its service level agreement (SLA) numbers for capacity and bandwidth? Are refunds given in the event of an SLA violation?

3.4 Colocation

While not particularly considered a "cloud environment," **colocation** is a useful way to provide services. Colocation occurs when a datacenter owner rents space to other people, called tenants. Renting datacenter space is very economical for small, medium, and even large businesses. Building your own datacenter is a huge investment and requires specialized knowledge about cooling, design, networking, location selection, real-estate management, and so on.

The term "colocation" comes from the telecommunications world. In the past, telecommunication companies were among the rare businesses that built datacenters, which they used to house their equipment and systems. Some third-party companies offered services to the customers of the telecommunication companies, and it was easier to do so if they could put their own equipment in the telecommunication company's datacenters. Thus, they colocated their equipment with the telecommunication company's equipment. In more recent years, any rental of datacenter space has been called colocation service.

This service is ideal when you need a small or medium amount of datacenter space. Such datacenters tend to be well designed and well run. While it can take years to procure space and build a datacenter, using a colocation facility can get you up and running quickly.

Colocation is also useful when you need many small spaces. For example, a company might want to have a single rack of equipment in each of a dozen countries to provide better access for its customers in those countries.

ISPs often extend their network into colocation provider spaces so that tenants can easily connect to them directly. Being directly connected to an ISP improves access time for the ISP's users. Alternatively, colocation providers may provide internet access as a service to tenants, often by blending connections from two or more ISPs. Tenants can take advantage of this capability rather than manage their own ISP connections and relationships.

3.5 Selection Strategies

There are many strategies one may use to choose between IaaS, PaaS, and SaaS. Here are a few we have used:

- **Default to Virtual:** Use containers or virtual machines wherever possible, opting for physical machines only when performance goals cannot be achieved any other way. For example, physical machines are generally better at disk I/O and network I/O. It is common to see a fully virtualized environment with the exception of a particularly demanding database with high I/O requirements. A web load balancer may also be a candidate for physical hardware because of the availability of high-bandwidth network interface cards or the benefit of predictable performance gained from dedicated network connections.

- **Make a Cost-Based Decision:** Select a public cloud solution or a private cloud solution based on cost. Create a business plan that describes the total cost of a project if it is done in-house, on a private infrastructure, versus using a public cloud provider. Choose the option with the lower cost. For a multiyear project, it may be less expensive to do it yourself. For a short-term project, a public cloud is probably the cheaper option.

- **Leverage Provider Expertise:** Use the expertise of cloud providers in creating an infrastructure so your employees can focus on the application. This strategy is especially appealing for small companies and startups. With only one or two developers, it is difficult to imagine building large amounts of infrastructure when public cloud services are available. Public clouds are generally run more professionally than private clouds because of the dynamics of competing against other providers for customers. Of course, private clouds *can* be run professionally, but it is difficult to do at a small scale, especially without a dedicated staff.

- **Get Started Quickly:** Leverage cloud providers to get up and running as fast as possible. Often the biggest cost is "opportunity cost": if you miss an opportunity because you moved too slowly, it doesn't matter how much money you were going to save. Contracting with a public cloud provider may be more expensive than doing it yourself, but doing it yourself may take months or years to build the infrastructure and by then the opportunity may have disappeared. It is also true that building infrastructure is a waste of time when the product's success is uncertain. Early in a product's life the entire idea may be experimental, involving trying new things rapidly and iterating over and over to try new features. Getting a minimal product available to early testers to see if the product is viable can be quickly done using public cloud services. If the product is viable, private infrastructure can be considered. If the product is not viable, no time was wasted building infrastructure that is no longer needed.

- **Implement Ephemeral Computing:** Use ephemeral computing for short-term projects. Ephemeral computing entails setting up a large computing infrastructure for a short amount of time. For example, imagine a company is doing an advertising campaign that will draw millions of users to its web site for a few weeks, with a sharp drop-off occurring after that. Using a public provider enables the company to expand to thousands of machines briefly and then dispose of them when they are no longer needed. This is commonly done for large data processing and analysis projects, proof-of-concept projects, biotechnology data mining, and handling unexpected bursts of web site traffic. It is unreasonable to build a large infrastructure to be used for such a short span time, but a cloud service provider may specialize in providing such computing facilities. In the aggregate the utilization will smooth out and be a constant load.

- **Use the Cloud for Overflow Capacity:** Establish baseline capacity requirements and build those in-house. Then use the cloud to burst beyond your normal capacity. This is often more cost-effective than either building in-house capacity or exclusively using a public provider.

- **Leverage Superior Infrastructure:** Gain an edge through superior infrastructure. In this strategy the ability to create customized infrastructure is leveraged to gain competitive advantage. This may include building your own datacenters to control cost and resource utilization, or selecting IaaS over PaaS to take advantage of the ability to customize at the OS and software level.

- **Develop an In-House Service Provider:** Create an in-house service provider to control costs and maintain privacy. Often computing infrastructures are only cost-effective at very large scale, which is why public cloud providers can offer services so economically. However, a large company can achieve similar economies of scale by building a large infrastructure that is shared by many in-house customers. Because it is in-house, it is private—a criterion often required by industries that are highly regulated.

- **Contract for an On-Premises, Externally Run Service:** Some companies will run an in-house cloud service for you. They differ in how much control and customization they provide. You benefit from their expertise and mitigate privacy issues by owning and controlling the equipment.

- **Maximize Hardware Output:** Pursue a strategy of squeezing every bit of productivity and efficiency out of computers by eschewing virtualization.

When an infrastructure has hundreds of thousands of computers or millions of cores, improving efficiency by 1 percent can be the equivalent of gaining thousands of new computers. The loss of efficiency from virtualization can be a huge expense. In this strategy physical machines, rather than virtual machines, are used and services are tightly packed on them to maximize utilization.

- **Implement a Bare Metal Cloud:** Manage physical machine infrastructure like a virtual machine cloud. Provide physical machines via the same API used for provisioning virtual machines. The benefits of being able to spin up virtual machines can be applied to physical machines with some planning. Rather than selecting the exact custom configuration needed for each physical machine, some companies opt to purchase hundreds or thousands of machines all configured the same way and manage them as a pool that can be reserved by departments or individuals. They do this by providing an API for allocating machines, wiping and reinstalling their OS, rebooting them, controlling access, and returning them to the pool. The allocations may not be as fast or as dynamic as virtual machines, but many of the same benefits can be achieved.

3.6 Summary

This chapter examined a number of platforms. Infrastructure as a Service (IaaS) provides a physical or virtual machine for your OS and application installs. Platform as a Service (PaaS) provides the OS and application stack or framework for you. Software as a Service (SaaS) is a web-based application.

You can create your own cloud with physical or virtual servers, hosting them yourself or using an IaaS provider for the machines. Your specific business needs will guide you in determining the best course of action for your organization.

There is a wide palette of choices from which to construct a robust and reliable architecture for any given service or application. In the next chapter we examine the various architectures themselves.

Exercises

1. Compare IaaS, PaaS, and SaaS on the basis of cost, configurability, and control.
2. What are the caveats to consider in adopting Software as a Service?
3. List the key advantages of virtual machines.
4. Why might you choose physical over virtual machines?
5. Which factors might make you choose private over public cloud services?
6. Which selection strategy does your current organization use? What are the benefits and caveats of using this strategy?

Chapter 4

Application Architectures

> Patterns are solutions to recurring
> problems in a context.
>
> —Christopher Alexander

This chapter examines the building blocks used when designing applications and
other services. The previous chapter discussed cloud platform options. Now we
move up one layer to the application architecture.

We start with an examination of common web service architectures beginning
with a single web server, to multi-machine designs, growing larger and larger until
we have a design that is appropriate for a large global service. Then we examine architectures that are common behind the scenes of web applications: message
buses and service-oriented architectures.

Most examples in this chapter will assume that the service is a web-based
application using the Hyper-Text Transfer Protocol (HTTP). The user runs a web
browser such as Firefox, Chrome, or Internet Explorer. In HTTP terminology, this is
called the client. Each request for a web page involves speaking the HTTP protocol
to a web server, usually running on a machine elsewhere on the internet. The web
server speaks the server side of the HTTP protocol, receives the HTTP connection,
parses the request, and processes it to generate the reply. The reply is an HTML
page or other file that is sent to the client. The client then displays the web page or
file to the user. Generally each HTTP request, or **query**, is a separate TCP/IP connection, although there are extensions to the protocol that let one session process
many HTTP requests.

Some applications use protocols other than HTTP. For example, they may
implement their own protocol. Some non-web applications use HTTP. For example, mobile phone apps may use HTTP to talk to APIs to make requests or gather
information. While most of our examples will assume web browsers speaking the
HTTP protocol, the principles apply to any client/server application and protocol.

4.1 Single-Machine Web Server

The first design pattern we examine is a single self-sufficient machine used to provide web service (Figure 4.1). The machine runs software that speaks the HTTP protocol, receiving requests, processing them, generating a result, and sending the reply. Many typical small web sites and web-based applications use this architecture.

The web server generates web pages from three different sources:

- **Static Content:** Files are read from local storage and sent to the user unchanged. These may be HTML pages, images, and other content like music, video, or downloadable software.
- **Dynamic Content:** Programs running on the web server generate HTML and possibly other output that is sent to the user. They may do so independently or based on input received from the user.
- **Database-Driven Dynamic Content:** This is a special case of dynamic content where the programs running on the web server consult a database for information and use that to generate the web page. In this architecture, the database software and its data are on the same machine as the web server.

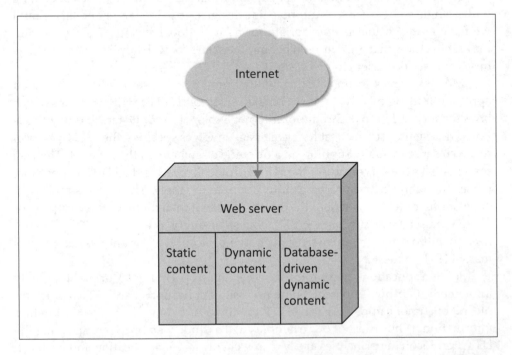

Figure 4.1: Single-machine web service architecture

Not all web servers have all three kinds of traffic. A static web server has no dynamic content. Dynamic content servers may or may not need a database.

The single-machine web server is a very common configuration for web sites and applications. It is sufficient for many small applications, but it does have limits. For example, it cannot store or access more data than can fit on a single machine. The number of simultaneous users it can service is limited by the capacity of the machine's CPU, memory, and I/O capacity.

The system is also only as reliable as one machine can be. If the machine crashes or dies, web service stops until the machine is repaired. Doing maintenance on the machine is also difficult. Software upgrades, content changes, and so on all are disruptions that may require downtime.

As the amount of traffic received by the machine grows, the single-machine web server may become overloaded. We can add more memory, more disk, and more CPUs, but eventually we will hit the limits of the machine. These might be design limits that dictate the hardware's physical connections (number of physical slots and ports) or internal limits such as the amount of bandwidth on the internal interconnections between disk and memory. We can purchase a larger, more powerful machine, but we will eventually reach limits with that, too. As traffic grows, the system will inevitably reach a limit and the only solution will be to implement a different architecture.

Another problem has to do with buffer thrashing. Modern operating systems use all otherwise unused memory as a disk cache. This improves disk I/O performance. An operating system can use many different algorithms to tune the disk cache, all having to do with deciding which blocks to discard when memory is needed for other processes or newer disk blocks. For example, if a machine is running a web server, the OS will self-tune for the memory footprint of the web server. If a machine is running a database server, the OS will tune itself differently, possibly even selecting an entirely different block replacement algorithm.

The problem is that if a machine is running a web server and a database server, the memory footprint may be complex enough that the operating system cannot self-tune for the situation. It may pick an algorithm that is optimal for only one application, or it may simply give up and pick a default scheme that is non-optimal for all. Attempts at improving this include Linux "containers" systems like LXC and Lmctfy.

4.2 Three-Tier Web Service

The three-tier web service is a pattern built from three layers: the load balancer layer, the web server layer, and the data service layer (see Figure 4.2). The web servers all rely on a common backend data server, often an SQL database. Requests enter the system by going to the load balancer. The load balancer picks one of the

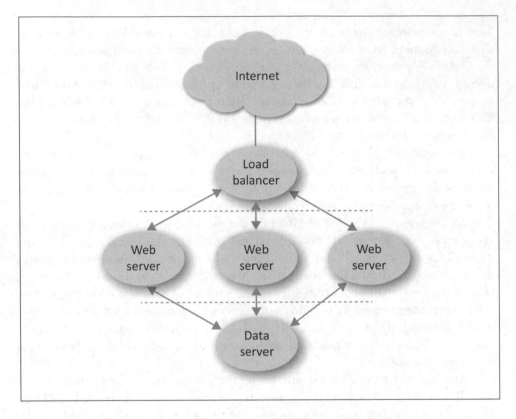

Figure 4.2: Three-tier web service architecture

machines in the middle layer and relays the request to that web server. The web server processes the request, possibly querying the database to aid it in doing so. The reply is generated and sent back via the load balancer.

A load balancer works by receiving requests and forwarding them to one of many replicas—that is, web servers that are configured such that they can all service the same URLs. Users talk to the load balancer as if it is a web server; they do not realize it is a frontend for many replicas.

4.2.1 Load Balancer Types

There are many ways to create a load balancer. In general, they fall into three categories:

- **DNS Round Robin:** This works by listing the IP addresses of all replicas in the DNS entry for the name of the web server. Web browsers will receive all the IP addresses but will randomly pick one of them to try first. Thus, when a multitude of web browsers visit the site, the load will be distributed almost evenly among the replicas. The benefit to this technique is that it is easy to implement and free. There is no actual hardware involved other than the DNS server, which already exists. However, this technique is rarely used because it doesn't work very well and is difficult to control. It is not very responsive. If one replica dies unexpectedly, clients will continue to try to access it as they cache DNS heavily. The site will appear to be down until those DNS caches expire. There is very little control over which servers receive which requests. There is no simple way to reduce the traffic sent to one particular replica if it is becoming unusually overloaded.

- **Layer 3 and 4 Load Balancers:** L3 and L4 load balancers receive each TCP session and redirect it to one of the replicas. Every packet of the session goes first through the load balancer and then to the replica. The reply packets from the replica go back through the load balancer. The names come from the ISO protocol stack definitions: Layer 3 is the network (IP) layer; Layer 4 is the session (TCP) layer. L3 load balancers track TCP sessions based on source and destination IP addresses (i.e., the network layer). All traffic from a given source address will be sent to the same server regardless of the number of TCP sessions it has generated. L4 load balancers track source and destination ports in addition to IP addresses (i.e., the session layer). This permits a finer granularity. The benefit of these load balancers is that they are simple and fast. Also, if a replica goes down, the load balancer will route traffic to the remaining replicas.

- **Layer 7 Load Balancer:** L7 load balancers work similarly to L3/L4 load balancers but make decisions based on what can be seen by peering into the application layer (Layer 7) of the protocol stack. They can examine what is inside the HTTP protocol itself (cookies, headers, URLs, and so on) and make decisions based on what was found. As a result they offer a richer mix of features than the previous load balancers. For example, the L7 load balancer can check whether a cookie has been set and send traffic to a different set of servers based on that criterion. This is how some companies handle logged-in users differently. Some companies set a special cookie when their most important customers log in and configure the load balancer to detect that cookie and send their traffic to especially fast servers.

Some load balancers are transparent: the source IP address of the request is unaltered. Most, however, are not: the source IP address of each request the backend sees is the IP address of the load balancer itself. That is, from the backend's perspective, it looks as if all requests are coming from a single source, the load balancer. The actual source IP of the requests is obscured.

When all requests appear to come from the same IP address, debugging and log analysis may be impossible at worst and confusing at best. The usual way to deal with this issue is for the load balancer to inject an additional header that indicates the IP address of the original requester. Backends can access this information as needed. This header is called X-Forwarded-For:. It contains a list of IP addresses starting with the client's and includes all the previous proxies or load balancers that the request has passed through. Note that the client and intermediate devices can add invalid or forged addresses to the list. Therefore you can only trust the address added by your own load balancer. Using the rest is insecure and risky.

4.2.2 Load Balancing Methods

For each request, an L3, L4, or L7 load balancer has to decide which backend to send it to. There are different algorithms for making this decision:

- **Round Robin (RR):** The machines are rotated in a loop. If there are three replicas, the rotation would look something like A-B-C-A-B-C. Down machines are skipped.
- **Weighted RR:** This scheme is similar to RR but gives more queries to the backends with more capacity. Usually a manually configured **weight** is assigned to each backend. For example, if there are three backends, two of equal capacity but a third that is huge and can handle twice as much traffic, the rotation would be A-C-B-C.
- **Least Loaded (LL):** The load balancer receives information from each backend indicating how loaded it is. Incoming requests always go to the least loaded backend.
- **Least Loaded with Slow Start:** This scheme is similar to LL, but when a new backend comes online it is not immediately flooded with queries. Instead, it starts receiving a low rate of traffic that slowly builds until it is receiving an appropriate amount of traffic. This fixes the problems with LL as described in Section 1.3.1.
- **Utilization Limit:** Each server estimates how many more QPS it can handle and communicates this to the load balancer. The estimates may be based on current throughput or data gathered from synthetic load tests.
- **Latency:** The load balancer stops forwarding requests to a backend based on the latency of recent requests. For example, when requests are taking more than 100 ms, the load balancer assumes this backend is overloaded. This technique manages bursts of slow requests or pathologically overloaded situations.
- **Cascade:** The first replica receives all requests until it is at capacity. Any overflow is directed to the next replica, and so on. In this case the load balancer must know precisely how much traffic each replica can handle, usually by static configuration based on synthetic load tests.

4.2.3 Load Balancing with Shared State

Another issue with load balancing among many replicas is shared state. Suppose one HTTP request generates some information that is needed by the next HTTP request. A single web server can store that information locally so that it is available when the second HTTP request arrives. But what if the load balancer sends the next HTTP request to a different backend? It doesn't have that information (state). This can cause confusion.

Consider the commonly encountered case in which one HTTP request takes a user's name and password and validates it, letting the user log in. The server stores the fact that the user is logged in and reads his or her profile from the database. This is stored locally for fast access. Future HTTP requests to the same machine know that the user is logged in and have the user profile on hand, so there's no need to access the database.

What if the load balancer sends the next HTTP request to a different backend? This backend will not know that the user is logged in and will ask the user to log in again. This is annoying to the user and creates extra work for the database.

There are a few strategies for dealing with this situation:

- **Sticky Connections:** Load balancers have a feature called **stickiness**, which means if a user's previous HTTP request went to a particular backend, the next one should go there as well. That solves the problem discussed earlier, at least initially. However, if that backend dies, the load balancer will send requests from that user to another backend; it has no choice. This new backend will not know the user is logged in. The user will be asked to log in again. Thus, this is only a partial solution.

- **Shared State:** In this case the fact that the user has logged in and the user's profile information are stored somewhere that all backends can access. For each HTTP connection, the user's state is fetched from this shared area. With this approach, it doesn't matter if each HTTP request goes to a different machine. The user is not asked to log in every time the backends are switched.

- **Hybrid:** When a user's state moves from one backend to another, it generally creates a little extra work for the web server. Sometimes this burden is small and tolerable. For some applications, however, it is extremely inconvenient and requires a lot more processing. In that case using both sticky connections and shared state is the best solution.

There are many schemes for storing and retrieving the sharing state. A simple approach is to use a database table on a database server to which all backends have access. Unfortunately, databases may respond slowly, as they are not optimized for this type of operation. Other systems are specifically designed for shared state storage, often holding all the information in RAM for fastest access. Memcached and Redis are two examples. In any event, you should avoid using a directory on an NFS server, as that does not provide failover in the event of a server outage or reliable file locking.

4.2.4 User Identity

Although the interaction with a web site appears to the user to be one seamless session, in truth it is made up of many distinct HTTP requests. The backends need to know that many HTTP requests are from the same user. They cannot use the source IP address of the HTTP request: due to the use of network address translation (NAT), many different machines are often seen as using the same IP address. Even if that weren't the case, the IP address of a particular machine changes from time to time: when a laptop moves from one WiFi network to another, when a mobile device moves from WiFi to cellular and back, or if any machine is turned off and turned on again on a different (or sometimes even the same) network. Using the IP address as an identity wouldn't even work for one user running two web browsers on the same machine.

Instead, when a user logs into a web application, the web application generates a secret and includes it with the reply. The secret is something generated randomly and given to only that user on that web browser. In the future, whenever that web browser sends an HTTP request to that same web app, it also sends the secret. Because this secret was not sent to any other user, and because the secret is difficult to guess, the web app can trust that this is the same user. This scheme is known as a **cookie** and the secret is often referred to as a **session ID**.

4.2.5 Scaling

The three-tier web service has many advantages over the single web server. It is more expandable; replicas can be added. If each replica can process 500 queries per second, they can continue to be added until the total required capacity is achieved. By splitting the database service onto its own platform, it can be grown independently.

This pattern is also very flexible. This leads to many variations:

- **Replica Groups:** The load balancer can serve many groups of replicas, not just one. Each group serves a different web site. The number of replicas in each group can be grown independently as that web site requires.
- **Dual Load Balancers:** There can be multiple load balancers, each a replica of the other. If one fails, the other can take over. This topic is discussed further in Section 6.6.3.

- **Multiple Data Stores:** There may be many different data stores. Each replica group may have its own data store, or all of the data stores may be shared. The data stores may each use the same or different technology. For example, there may be one data store dedicated to shared state and another that stores a product catalog or other information needed for the service.

4.3 Four-Tier Web Service

A four-tier web service is used when there are many individual applications with a common frontend infrastructure (Figure 4.3). In this pattern, web requests come in as usual to the load balancer, which divides the traffic among the various frontends.

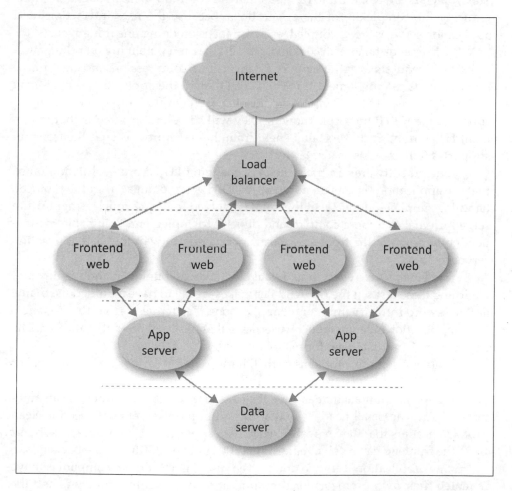

Figure 4.3: Four-tier web service architecture

The frontends handle interactions with the users, and communicate to the application servers for content. The application servers access shared data sources in the final layer.

The difference between the three-tier and four-tier designs is that the application and the web servers run on different machines. The benefits of using the latter design pattern are that we decouple the customer-facing interaction, protocols, and security issues from the applications. The downside is that it takes a certain amount of trust for application service teams to rely on a centralized frontend platform team. It also takes management discipline to not allow exceptions.

4.3.1 Frontends

The frontends are responsible for tasks that are common to all applications, thus reducing the complexity of the applications. Because the user interactions and application services are decoupled, each can focus on doing one thing well.

The frontends handle all cookie processing, session pipelining (handling multiple HTTP requests over the same TCP connection), compression, and encryption. The frontends can implement HTTP 2.0 even though the application servers may still be stuck on HTTP 1.1. In fact, application servers often implement a simpler subset of the HTTP protocol, knowing they will be behind frontends that implement HTTP fully. End users still benefit from these features because the frontend supports them and acts as a gateway.

Frontend software can track the ever-changing HTTP protocol definition so that the application servers do not have to. HTTP started out as a simple protocol, handling simple requests. Over time, it has evolved to have a much richer feature set, which makes it more complex and difficult to implement. Being able to independently upgrade the frontends means not having to wait for each application server to do so.

Frontends process everything related to the users logging in and logging out. Handling these tasks at the frontend tier makes it easy to have a unified username and password infrastructure for all applications. The requests from the frontends to the application layer include the username that has been pre-authenticated. The applications can trust this information implicitly.

Frontends often fix problems so that the application servers don't have to. For example, HTTP headers are case insensitive, but some application servers have broken implementations that assume they are case sensitive. Frontends can automatically downcase all headers so that the application servers only see the clean protocol headers that they naively expect. If an application server doesn't support IPv6, the frontend can receive requests via IPv6 but speak IPv4 to the backends.

Some application servers don't even use HTTP. Some companies have invented their own protocols for communication between the frontends and the application servers that are much faster and more efficient.

Encryption and Certificate Management

Encryption is particularly important to centralize at one layer because certificate management is quite complex. It is easy for the non-expert to make mistakes that weaken the security of the system at best and make the service stop working at worst. By centralizing the encryption function, you can assure that the people managing it are experts in their field. Typically each application server is run by a different team. Expecting each team to be highly qualified at crypto certificate management as well as their application is unreasonable.

Even if they all had a high degree of security expertise, there is still another issue: trust. Each person who manages the crypto certificates has to be trusted not to expose or steal the keys. Giving that trust to one specialized team is more secure than giving that trust to members of many individual teams. In some cases all services use the same key, which means an accidental leak of the key by any one team would weaken security for all applications. As Cheswick, Bellovin, and Rubin (2003) suggest, often the best security policy is to put all your eggs in one basket and then make sure it is a really strong basket.

Security Benefits

The frontends are the one part of the system that is directly exposed to the Internet. This reduces the number of places that have to be secured against attacks. In the security field this approach is called reducing the **attack surface area**. By decoupling these functions from the applications, bugs and security holes can be fixed more rapidly.

HTTP is a complex protocol and becomes more complex with every revision. The more complex something is, the more likely it is to contain bugs or security holes. Being able to upgrade the frontends rapidly and independently of any application server upgrade schedule is important. Application teams have their own priorities and may not be willing or able to do a software upgrade at the drop of a hat. There are often dozens or hundreds of individual applications and application teams, and tracking all of their upgrades would be impossible.

4.3.2 Application Servers

The frontends send queries to the application servers. Because all HTTP processing is handled by the frontends, this permits the frontend-to-application protocol to be something other than HTTP. HTTP is a general protocol, so it is slow and not as good at serving API requests as a purpose-built protocol can be.

Splitting application servers from the frontends also means that different applications can run on different servers. Having dedicated servers for frontends and for each application means that each component can be scaled independently. Also, it brings even greater reliability because problems in one application do not affect other applications or the frontends.

4.3.3 Configuration Options

Splitting functionality into frontend, application server, and data service layers also permits one to pick hardware specifically appropriate for each layer. The frontends generally need high network throughput and very little storage. They are also located in a special place in the network so they have direct internet access. The application servers may be on machines that are configured differently for each application based on their needs. The database service most likely has a need for large amounts of disk storage or may be a **server tree** (as described in Section 1.3.3).

4.4 Reverse Proxy Service

A reverse proxy enables one web server to provide content from another web server transparently. The user sees one cohesive web site, even though it is actually made up of a patchwork of applications.

For example, suppose there is a web site that provides users with sports news, weather reports, financial news, an email service, plus a main page:

- www.company.com/ (the main page)
- www.company.com/sports
- www.company.com/weather
- www.company.com/finance
- www.company.com/email

Each of those web features is provided by a very different web service, but all of them can be combined into a seamlessly unified user experience by a reverse proxy. Requests go to the reverse proxy, which interprets the URL and collects the required pages from the appropriate server or service. This result is then relayed to the original requester.

Like the frontend four-tier web service, this scheme permits centralizing security and other services. Having many applications behind one domain simplifies many administrative tasks, such as maintaining per-domain crypto certificates.

The difference between a reverse proxy and the frontend of the four-tier web service is that a reverse proxy is simpler and usually just connects the web browsers and the patchwork of HTTP servers that sit behind it. Sometimes reverse proxies are stand-alone software, but the functionality is so simple that it is often a feature built into general web server software.

4.5 Cloud-Scale Service

Cloud-scale services are globally distributed. The service infrastructure uses one of the previously discussed architectures, such as the four-tier web service, which is then replicated in many places around the world. A global load balancer is used to direct traffic to the nearest location (Figure 4.4).

It takes time for packets to travel across the internet. The farther the distance, the longer it takes. Anyone who has spent significant time in Australia accessing computers in the United States will tell you that even though data can travel at the speed of light, that's just not fast enough. The latency over such a great distance gives such terrible performance for interactive applications that they are unusable.

We fix this problem by bringing the data and computation closer to the users. We build multiple datacenters around the world, or we rent space in other people's datacenters, and replicate our services in each of them.

4.5.1 Global Load Balancer

A global load balancer (GLB) is a DNS server that directs traffic to the nearest datacenter. Normally a DNS server returns the same answer to a query no matter where the query originated. A GLB examines the source IP address of the query and returns a different result depending on the geolocation of the source IP address.

Geolocation is the process of determining the physical location of a machine on the internet. This is a very difficult task. Unlike a phone number, whose country code and area code give a fairly accurate indication of where the user is (although this, too, is less accurate in the age of cell phones), an IP address has no concrete geographic meaning. There is a small industry consisting of companies that use various means (and a lot of guessing) to determine where each IP subnet is physically located. They sell databases of this information for the purpose of geolocation.

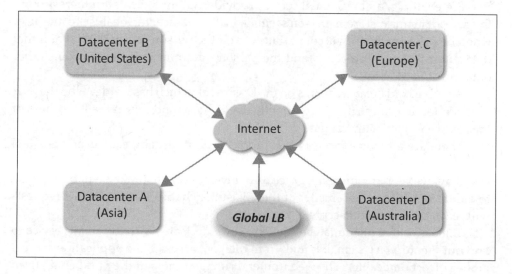

Figure 4.4: Cloud-scale web service architecture

4.5.2 Global Load Balancing Methods

A GLB maintains a list of replicas, their locations, and their IP addresses. When a GLB is asked to translate a domain name to an IP address, it takes into account the geolocation of the requester when determining which IP address to send in the reply.

GLBs use many different techniques:

- **Nearest:** Strictly selects the nearest datacenter to the requester.
- **Nearest with Limits:** The nearest datacenter is selected until that site is full. At that point, the next nearest datacenter is selected. Slow start, as described previously, is included for the same reasons as on local load balancers.
- **Nearest by Other Metric:** The best location may be determined not by distance but rather by another metric such as latency or cost. Latency and distance are usually the same but not always. For example, for a long time the only route between most South American countries was via the United States. In Section 4.5.4 we'll see that cost is not always a function of distance, either.

4.5.3 Global Load Balancing with User-Specific Data

Now that the HTTP request is directed to a particular datacenter, it will be handled by local load balancers, frontends, and whatever else makes up the service. This brings up another architectural issue. Suppose the service stores information for a user. What happens if that user's data is stored at some other datacenter?

For example, a global email service provider might have datacenters around the world. It may store a person's email in the datacenter nearest to the user when he or she creates an account. But what if the person moves? Or what if that datacenter is decommissioned and the person's account is moved to some other datacenter?

A global load balancer works on the DNS level, which has no idea who the user is. It cannot determine that Mary sent the DNS query and return the IP address of the service replica with her data.

There are a few solutions to this problem. First, usually each user's email is stored in two different datacenters. That way, if one datacenter goes down, the data is still available. Now there are twice as many chances that Mary will be directed to a datacenter with her email, but there is still a chance that her HTTP requests will reach the wrong datacenter.

To resolve this dilemma, the frontend communicates with the email service to find out where Mary's email is and, from then on, accesses the application servers in the correct datacenter. The web frontends are generic, but they pull email from the specific datacenter.

To do this the company must have connections between each datacenter so that the frontends can talk to any application server. They could communicate between datacenters over the internet, but typically a company in this situation owns private, dedicated wide area network (WAN) connections between datacenters. A dedicated WAN gives the company more control and more reliable performance.

4.5.4   Internal Backbone

The private WAN links that connect datacenters form an **internal backbone.** An internal backbone is not visible to the internet at large. It is a private network.

This internal network connects to the internet in many places. Wherever there is a datacenter, the datacenter will generally connect to many ISPs in the area. Connecting to an ISP directly has speed and cost benefits. If you do not have a direct connection to a particular ISP, then sending data to users of that ISP involves sending the data through another ISP that connects your ISP and theirs. This ISP in the middle is called a **transit ISP**. The transit ISP charges the other ISPs for the privilege of permitting packets to travel over its network. There are often multiple transit ISPs between you and your customers. The more transits, the slower, less reliable, and more expensive the connections become.

POPs

A **point of presence (POP)** is a small, remote facility used for connection to local ISPs. It is advantageous to connect to many ISPs but they cannot always connect to your datacenter. For example, your datacenter may not be in the state or country they operate in. Since they cannot go to you, you must extend your network to someplace near them. For example, you might create a POP in Berlin to connect to many different German ISPs.

A POP is usually a rack of equipment in a colocation center or a small space that resembles a closet. It contains network equipment and connections from various telecom providers, but no general-purpose computers.

A POP plus a small number of computers is called a **satellite**. The computers are used for frontend and content distribution services. The frontends terminate HTTP connections and proxy to application servers in other datacenters. **Content distribution servers** are machines that cache large amounts of content. For example, they may store the 1000 most popular videos being viewed at the time (Figure 4.5).

Thus an internal network connects datacenters, POPs, and satellites.

Global Load Balancing and POPs

This brings up an interesting question: should the GLB direct traffic to the nearest frontend or to the nearest datacenter that has application servers for that

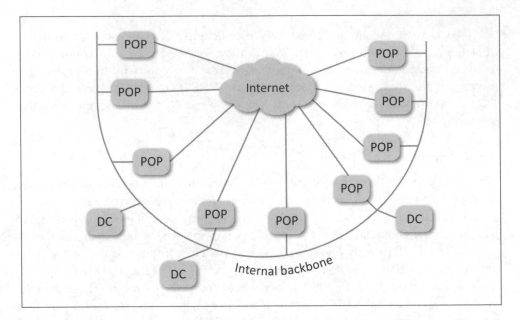

Figure 4.5: A private network backbone connecting many datacenters (DCs) and points of presence (POPs) on the Internet

particular service? For example, imagine (and these numbers are completely fictitious) Google had 20 POPs, satellites, and datacenters but Google Maps was served out of only 5 of the datacenters. There are two paths to get to a server that provides the Google Maps service.

The first path is to go to the nearest frontend. Whether that frontend is in a datacenter or satellite doesn't matter. There's a good chance it won't be in one of the five datacenters that host Google Maps, so the frontend will then talk across the private backbone to the nearest datacenter that does host Maps. This solution will be very fast because Google has total control over its private backbone, which can be engineered to provide the exact latency and bandwidth required. There are no other customers on the backbone that could hog bandwidth or overload the link. However, every packet sent on the backbone has a cost associated with it, and Google pays that expense.

The second path is to go to a frontend at the nearest datacenter that hosts Google Maps. If that datacenter is very far away, the query may traverse multiple ISPs to get there, possibly going over oceans. This solution will be rather slow. These transcontinental links tend to be overloaded and there is no incentive for the ISPs involved to provide stellar performance for someone else's traffic. Even so, the cost of the transmission is a burden on the ISP, not Google. It may be slow, but someone else is bearing the cost.

Which path does Google Maps traffic take? The fast/expensive one or the cheap/slow one? The answer is: both!

Google wants its service to be fast and responsive to the user. Therefore traffic related to the user interface (UI) is sent over the first path. This data is HTML and is generally very small.

The other part of Google Maps is delivering the map tiles—that is, the graphics that make up the maps. Even though they are compressed, they are big and bulky and use a lot of bandwidth. However, they are loaded "off screen" by very crafty JavaScript code, so responsiveness isn't required. The map tiles can load very slowly and it would not hinder the users' experience. Therefore the map tile requests take the slow but inexpensive path.

If you look at the HTML code of Google Maps, you will see that the URLs of the UI and map tiles refer to different hostnames. This way the global DNS load balancer can assign different paths to the different types of traffic. The GLB is configured so that maps.google.com, which is used for all the elements related to the UI, returns the IP address of the nearest frontend. The map tiles are loaded using URLs that contain a different hostname. The GLB is configured so that this hostname returns the IP address of a frontend in the nearest datacenter that serves Google Maps. Thus users get fast interaction and Google pays less for bandwidth.

4.6 Message Bus Architectures

A message bus is a many-to-many communication mechanism between servers. It is a convenient way to distribute information among different services. Message buses are becoming a popular architecture used behind the scenes in system administration systems, web-based services, and enterprise systems. This approach is more efficient than repeatedly polling a database to see if new information has arrived.

A message bus is a mechanism whereby servers send messages to "channels" (like a radio channel) and other servers listen to the channels they need. A server that sends messages is a **publisher** and the receivers are **subscribers**. A server can be a publisher or subscriber of a given channel, or it can simply ignore the channel. This permits one-to-many, many-to-many, and many-to-one communication. One-to-many communication enables one server to quickly send information to a large set of machines. Many-to-many communication resembles a chat room application, where many people all hear what is being said. Many-to-one communication enables a funnel-like configuration where many machines can produce information and one machine takes it in. A central authority, or master, manages which servers are connected to which channels.

The messages being sent may contain any kind of data. They may be real-time updates such as chat room messages, database updates, or notifications that update a user's display to indicate there are messages waiting in the inbox. They may be low-priority or batch updates communicating status changes, service requests, or logging information.

Message bus technology goes by many names, including message queue, queue service, or pubsub service. For example, Amazon provides the Simple Queue Service (SQS), MCollective is described as publish subscribe middleware, and RabbitMQ calls itself a message broker.

A message bus system is efficient in that clients receive a message only if they are subscribed. There may be hundreds or thousands of machines involved, but different subsets of machines will typically be subscribed to different channels. Messages are transmitted only to the subscribed machines. Thus network bandwidth and processing are conserved. This approach is more efficient than a broadcast system that sends all messages to all machines and lets the receiving machines filter out the messages they aren't interested in.

Message bus systems are operations-friendly. It's trivial to connect a command-line client to listen to messages and see what is being emitted. This capability is very handy when debugging requires peering into information flows.

4.6.1 Message Bus Designs

The message bus master learns the underlying network topology and for each channel determines the shortest path a message needs to follow. IP multicast is often used to send a message to many machines on the same subnet at the same time. IP unicast is used to transmit a message between subnets or when IP multicast isn't available. Determining and optimizing the unique topology of each channel separately requires a lot of calculations, especially when there are thousands of channels.

Some message bus systems require all messages to first go to the master for distribution. Consequently, the master may become a bottleneck. Other systems are more sophisticated and either have multiple masters, one master per channel, or have a master that controls topology but does not require all messages to go through it.

Channels may be open to anyone, or they may be tightly controlled with ACLs determining who can publish and who can subscribe. On some systems the listeners can send a reply to the message sender. Other systems do not have this feature and instead create a second channel for publishing replies.

There may be one channel, or thousands. Different message bus systems are optimized for different sizes. Google's PubSub2 system (Publish Subscribe Version 2) can handle hundreds of channels and tens of thousands of hosts. Google's Thialfi system can handle 2.3 million subscribers (Adya, Cooper, Myers & Piatek 2011).

4.6.2 Message Bus Reliability

Message bus systems usually guarantee that every message will be received. For example, some message bus systems require subscribers to acknowledge each message received. If the subscriber crashes, when it returns to service it is guaranteed to receive all the unacknowledged messages again; if the acknowledgment did not make it back to the message bus system, the subscriber may receive a second copy of the message. It is up to the subscriber to detect and skip duplicates.

However, message bus systems do vary in how they handle long subscriber outages. In some systems, subscribers miss messages when they are down. In others, messages are stored up for a certain amount of time and are lost only if the subscriber is down for more than a defined length of time. Some message bus systems might hold things in RAM for just a few minutes before giving up and queueing messages to disk. When a subscriber comes back online, it will get the backlog of messages in a flood.

Message bus systems do not guarantee that messages will be received in the same order as they were sent. Doing so would mean that if one message was being retried, all other messages would have to wait for that message to succeed. In the meantime, millions of messages might be delayed.

For this reason, the subscriber must be able to handle messages arriving out of order. The messages usually include timestamps, which help the subscriber detect when messages do arrive out of order. However, reordering them is difficult, if not impossible. You could hold messages until any late ones have arrived, but how would you know how long to wait? If you waited an hour, a slow-poke message might arrive 61 minutes late. It is best to write code that does not depend on perfectly ordered messages than to try to reorder them.

Because messages may be missed or lost, usually services have a mechanism that is not based on the message bus but that enables clients to catch up on anything they missed. For example, if the message bus is used to keep a database in sync, there may be a way to receive a list of all database keys and the date they were last updated. Receiving this list once a day enables the subscriber to notice any missing data and request it.

As systems get larger, message bus architectures become more appealing because they are fast, they are efficient, and they push control and operational responsibility to the listeners. A good resource for using message bus architectures is *Enterprise Integration Patterns: Designing, Building, and Deploying Messaging Solutions* by Hohpe and Woolf (2003).

4.6.3 Example 1: Link-Shortening Site

A link-shortening site very much like bit.ly had a message bus architecture used by its components to communicate. The application had two user-visible components: the control panel (a web UI for registering new URLs to be shortened) and the web service that took in short links and responded with the redirect code to the expanded URL.

The company wanted fast updates between the user interface and the redirect servers. It was common for users to create a short link via the control panel and then immediately try to use the link to make sure that it worked. Initially there was a multi-minute delay between when the link was created and when the redirection service was able to redirect it. The new link had to be indexed and processed, then added to the database, and the database changes had to propagate to all the redirection servers.

To fix this problem the company set up a message bus system that connected all machines. There were two channels: one called "new shortlinks" and one called "shortlinks used."

As depicted in Figure 4.6, the architecture had four elements:

- **Control Panel:** A web frontend that was the portal people used to create new shortlinks.
- **Main Database:** A database server that stored all the shortlink information.
- **Trend Server:** A server that kept track of "trending links" statistics.

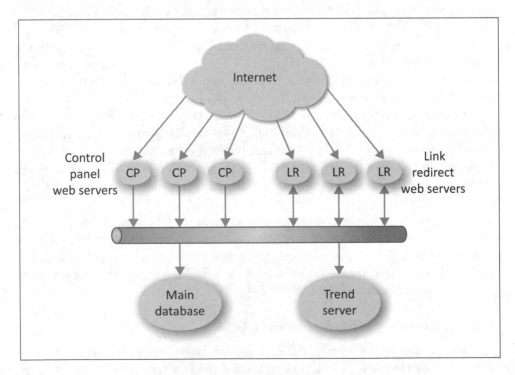

Figure 4.6: Link-shortening architecture

- **Link Redirect Servers:** Web servers that received requests with short URLs and replied with a redirect to the expanded URL.

When any control panel server received a new shortlink from a user, it would publish it on the "new shortlink" channel. Subscribers to that channel included the database (which stored the new shortlink information) as well as all the redirect servers (which stored the new information in their lookup cache). When performing a redirect, each redirect server relied on information from its local cache and consulted the database only in case of a cache miss. Since it could take minutes or hours for the main database to ingest a new shortlink (due to indexing and other issues), the message bus architecture enabled the redirect servers to always be up to date.

When a redirect server used a shortlink, it would publish this fact on the "shortlinks used" channel. There were only two subscribers to this channel: the main database and the trend server. The main database updated the usage statistics for that database entry. The trend server kept an in-memory database of which URLs had been used recently so that the company could always display an accurate list of trending URLs.

Imagine how difficult creating this functionality would have been without a message bus. The control panel machines would need an "always up-to-date" list of all the redirect servers. It would have to handle down machines, new machines, and so on. The communication would not be optimized for the network topology. It would be very difficult to achieve the same quality of service as that provided by message bus.

Without a message bus system, adding a new service would mean changing all the data providers to also send a copy to it. Suppose an entirely new mechanism for calculating trending links was devised. Without a message bus, the redirect servers would have to be updated to send information to them. With the message bus system, the new trend server could be added and run in parallel without requiring changes to the other servers. If it proved successful, the old trend server could be disconnected just as easily.

4.6.4 Example 2: Employee Human Resources Data Updates

An enterprise had a large employee base. Each day many new employees were hired, left the company, changed names, or changed other database attributes. Meanwhile, there were numerous consumers of this information: the login/authentication system, the payroll system, the door-lock systems, and many others.

In the first incarnation of the system, a single database was maintained. All systems queried the database for changes. As the company grew, however, the database got more and more overloaded.

In the second incarnation, any department that needed to be informed of user change requests had to write a plug-in that would be called for each change. The plug-in had to handle subcommands including add, update, remove, name-change, and others. The plug-ins all ran under the same role account, which meant this one account had privileged access to every critical system in the company. It was a nightmare. If one department's plug-in had a bug, it would take down the entire system. This system remained in operation for years even though it was very brittle and required a lot of work to keep it running.

The newest version of the system implemented a message bus. All changes went through one system that was the publisher on a channel called "user updates." Any department that needed to be informed of changes would subscribe to that channel. The department could run its system on its own role account, which isolated each department into its own security domain. Each department also had its own failure domain, as the failure of one listener did not affect any of the others. A synchronization mechanism talked to each department once a day so that any missed updates could be processed.

New departments could join the system at will without affecting any others. Best of all, this system was very easy to maintain. Responsibility was distributed to each department. The main group simply had to make sure the publisher was working.

4.7 Service-Oriented Architecture

Service-oriented architecture (SOA) enables large services to be managed more easily. With this architecture, each subsystem is a self-contained service providing its functionality as a consumable service via an API. The various services communicate with one another by making API calls.

A goal of SOAs is to have the services be loosely coupled. That is, each API presents its service at a high level of abstraction. This makes it easier to improve and even replace a service. The replacement must simply provide the same abstraction. Loosely coupled systems do not know the internal workings of the other systems that are part of the architecture. If they did, they would be tightly bound to each other.

As an example, imagine a job scheduler service. It accepts requests to perform various actions, schedules them, coordinates them, and reports back progress as it executes. In a tightly coupled system, the API would be tightly linked to the inner workings of the job scheduler. Users of the API could specify details related to how the jobs work rather than what is needed. For example, the API might provide direct access to the status of the lock mechanism used to prevent the same job from being executed twice.

Suppose a new internal design was proposed that prevented duplicate job execution but did locking some other way. This change could not be made without changing the code of all the services that used the API. In a loosely coupled system, the API would provide job status at a higher level of abstraction: is the job waiting, is it running, where is it running, can it be stopped, and so on. No matter what the internal implementation was, these requests could be processed.

4.7.1 Flexibility

An SOA makes it easier for services to cooperate. Services can be combined in many, often unexpected, ways to create new applications. New applications can be designed without consultation of all the other services as long as the API meets the new application's needs. Each subsystem can be managed as a discrete system. It is easier to manage a few, small, easy-to-understand services than one large system with ill-defined internal interconnections. When the touch-points between services are well-defined APIs that implement high-level abstractions, it makes it easier to evolve and/or replace the service.

4.7.2 Support

SOAs have benefits at the people management level, too. As a system grows, the team that develops and operates it tends to grow as well. Large teams are more difficult to manage than smaller, focused teams. With an SOA it is easy to split up a team every time it grows beyond a manageable limit. Each team can focus on a related set of subsystems. They can even trade subsystems between teams as skills and demands require. Contrast this to a large, tightly coupled system that cannot be easily divided and managed by separate teams.

> **Splitting Teams by Functionality**
>
> At Google, Gmail was originally maintained by one group of Google site reliability engineers (SREs). As the system grew, subteams split off to focus on subsystems such as the storage layer, the anti-spam layer, the message receiving system, the message delivery system, and so on. This was possible because of the SOA design of the system.

4.7.3 Best Practices

Following are some best practices for running an SOA:

- Use the same underlying RPC protocol to implement the APIs on all services. This way any tool related to the RPC mechanism is leveraged for all services.

- Have a consistent monitoring mechanism. All services should expose measurements to the monitoring system the same way.
- Use the same techniques with each service as much as possible. Use the same load balancing system, management techniques, coding standards, and so on. As services move between teams, it will be easier for people to get up to speed if these things are consistent.
- Adopt some form of API governance. When so many APIs are being designed, it becomes important to maintain standards for how they work. These standards often impart knowledge learned through painful failures in the past that the organization does not want to see repeated.

When a tightly coupled system becomes difficult to maintain, one option is to evolve it into a loosely coupled system. Often when systems are new, they start out tightly coupled with the justification, real or not, of being more resource efficient or faster to develop. Decoupling the components can be a long and difficult journey. Start by identifying pieces that can be spilt out as services one at a time. Do not pick the easiest pieces but rather the pieces most in need of the benefits of SOA: flexibility, ease of upgrade and replacement, and so on.

4.8 Summary

Web-based applications need to grow and scale. A small service can run on a single machine, serving content that is static, dynamic, or database driven. When the limits of one machine are reached, a three-tier architecture is used. It moves each function to a different machine: a load balancer to direct traffic among web servers, and one or more data servers providing static or database content.

Local load balancers distribute traffic between replicas within a datacenter. They work by intercepting traffic and redirecting it to web replicas. There are many load balancing technologies, and many algorithms for deciding how to distribute traffic. When an application is divided among replicas, synchronizing user identity and other state information becomes complex. This goal is usually achieved by having some kind of server that stores state common to all replicas.

A four-tier architecture creates a frontend to many three-tier systems. The new tier handles common services, often related to user sessions, security, and logging. A reverse proxy ensures that many application servers appear to be a single large application.

Cloud-scale services take this architecture and replicate it to many datacenters around the world. They use global load balancers to direct traffic to particular datacenters. A private network between datacenters may be used if one would benefit from being able to control inter-datacenter network quality. This private network may connect to the internet at many points of presence to improve connectivity at many ISPs. POPs may have servers that terminate HTTP sessions and relay data to datacenters using more efficient protocols.

Other architecture patterns are appropriate for non-web applications. Message bus architectures create a message-passing system that decouples communication from the services that need the information. Service-oriented architectures involve many small services that cooperate to create larger services. Each service in an SOA can be independently scaled, upgraded, and even replaced.

Chapter 1 discussed composition, server trees, and other patterns. These rudimentary elements make up many of the patterns discussed in this chapter. Chapter 5 will discuss patterns for data storage; in particular, Section 5.5 will describe the distributed hash table.

All of these architecture patterns have tradeoffs on cost, scalability, and resiliency to failure. Understanding these tradeoffs is key to knowing when to use each pattern.

Exercises

1. Describe the single-machine, three-tier, and four-tier web application architectures.
2. Describe how a single-machine web server, which uses a database to generate content, might evolve to a three-tier web server. How would this be done with minimal downtime?
3. Describe the common web service architectures, in order from smallest to largest.
4. Describe how different local load balancer types work and what their pros and cons are. You may choose to make a comparison chart.
5. What is "shared state" and how is it maintained between replicas?
6. What are the services that a four-tier architecture provides in the first tier?
7. What does a reverse proxy do? When is it needed?
8. Suppose you wanted to build a simple image-sharing web site. How would you design it if the site was intended to serve people in one region of the world? How would you then expand it to work globally?
9. What is a message bus architecture and how might one be used?
10. What is an SOA?
11. Why are SOAs loosely coupled?
12. How would you design an email system as an SOA?
13. Who was Christopher Alexander and what was his contribution to architecture?

Chapter 5

Design Patterns for Scaling

> The only real problem is scaling.
> Everything else is a sub-problem.
>
> —O'Dell's Axiom

A system's ability to scale is its ability to process a growing workload, usually measured in transactions per second, amount of data, or number of users. There is a limit to how far a system can scale before reengineering is required to permit additional growth.

Distributed systems must be built to be scalable from the start because growth is expected. Whether you are building a web-based service or a batch-processing data analytics platform, the goal is always to be successful, which usually means attracting more users, uses, or data.

Making sure a service is fast and stays fast is critical. If your service does not scale, or if it gets too slow as it becomes more popular, users will go elsewhere. Google found that an artificial 400-ms delay inserted into its search results would make users conduct 0.2 to 0.6 percent fewer searches. This could translate into millions or billions of dollars of lost revenue.

Ironically, a slow web service is more frustrating than one that is down. If a site is down, users understand that fact immediately and can go to a competing site or find something else to do until it comes back up. If it is slow, the experience is just painful and frustrating.

Building a scalable system does not happen by accident. A distributed system is not automatically scalable. The initial design must be engineered to scale to meet the requirements of the service, but it also must include features that create options for future growth. Once the system is in operation, we will always be optimizing the system to help it scale better.

In previous chapters we've discussed many techniques that enable distributed systems to grow to extreme sizes. In this chapter we will revisit these techniques in greater detail. We will review terminology related to scaling, examine the theory behind scaling techniques, and describe specific techniques used to scale. Mathematical terms used to describe how systems perform and scale can be found in Appendix C.

5.1 General Strategy

The basic strategy for building a scalable system is to design it with scalability in mind from the start and to avoid design elements that will prevent additional scaling in the future.

The initial requirements should include approximations of the desired scale: the size of data being stored, the throughput of the systems that process it, the amount of traffic the service currently receives, and expected growth rates. All of these factors then guide the design. This process was described previously in Section 1.7.

Once the system is running, performance limits will be discovered. This is where the design features that enable further scaling come into play.

While every effort is made to foresee potential scaling issues, not all of them can receive engineering attention. The additional design and coding effort that will help deal with future potential scaling issues is lower priority than writing code to fix the immediate issues of the day. Spending too much time preventing scaling problems that may or may not happen is called **premature optimization** and should be avoided.

5.1.1 Identify Bottlenecks

A bottleneck is a point in the system where congestion occurs. It is a point that is resource starved in a way that limits performance. Every system has a bottleneck. If a system is underperforming, the bottleneck can be fixed to permit the system to perform better. If the system is performing well, knowing the location of the bottleneck can be useful because it enables us to predict and prevent future problems. In this case the bottleneck can be found by generating additional load, possibly in a test environment, to see at which point performance suffers.

Deciding what to scale is a matter of finding the bottleneck in the system and eliminating it. The bottleneck is where a backlog of work accumulates. Optimizations done to the process upstream of the bottleneck simply make the backlog grow faster. Optimizations made downstream of the bottleneck may improve the efficiency of that part but do not improve the total throughput of the system. Therefore any effort not spent focused on the bottleneck is wasteful.

5.1.2 Reengineer Components

Some scaling issues can be resolved through adjustments to the current system. For example, enlarging a cache might be as simple as adjusting a configuration file. Other scaling issues require engineering effort.

Rewriting parts of a system is called **reengineering** and is usually done to improve speed, functionality, or resource consumption. Sometimes reengineering is difficult because of earlier design decisions that led to particular code or design structures. It is often best to first replace such code with code that is functionally equivalent but has an internal organization that makes other reengineering efforts easier to accomplish. Restructuring an existing body of code—namely, altering its internal structure without changing its external behavior—is called **refactoring**.

5.1.3 Measure Results

Scaling solutions must be evaluated using evidence, meaning data collected from a real system. Take measurements, try a solution, and repeat the same measurements to see the effect. If the effect is minimal or negative, the solution is not deployed.

For example, if performance is slow and measurements indicate that a cache hit rate is very low, the cache is probably too small. In such a case, we would measure performance, resize the cache, and then measure performance again. While the cache may be performing better with such an adjustment, the overall effect on the system may not be a significant improvement or may not be big enough to justify the cost of the additional RAM required.

If we do not measure before and after a change is made, we cannot be sure whether our changes were actually effective. Making changes without measurement would be system administration by luck at best, and by ego at worst. It is often tempting to rush ahead with a solution and measure only after the change is made. This is as bad as not measuring at all, because there is no baseline for comparison.

While past experience should inform and guide us, we must resist the temptation to skip the scientific process of using measurement and analysis to guide our decisions. Distributed systems are always too large for any one person to "just know" the right thing to do. A hunch or guess by an experienced system administrator should be trumped by the recommendation of a more junior person who has taken the time to perform scientific analysis: set up data collection mechanisms, take measurements, verify a hypothesis about what is wrong, test a theory of what might fix it, and analyze the results.

5.1.4 Be Proactive

The best time to fix a bottleneck is before it becomes a problem. Ideally, the fix will arrive just in time, immediately before this point is reached. If we fix a problem too soon, we may be wasting effort on a problem that never arises—effort that could have been better spent elsewhere. If we begin to design and implement a solution too late, the problem will arise before the solution is deployed. If we wait much too long, the problem will surprise us, catching us off guard, and we will be "firefighting" to find a solution. Engineering takes time and doing it in a rushed fashion leads to mistakes and more problems. We want the Goldilocks solution: not too early, not too late, just right.

Every system has a bottleneck or constraint. This is not a bad thing. Constraints are inherent in all systems. A constraint dictates the rate at which processing can happen, or how much work can flow through the process. If the current rate is sufficient, the bottleneck is not a problem. In other words, the constraint becomes a problem only if it actually hampers the system's ability to achieve its goal.

The best strategy for scaling a running system, then, is to predict problems far enough in advance that there is enough time to engineer a proper solution. This means one should always be collecting enough measurements to be aware of where the bottlenecks are. These measurements should be analyzed so that the point at which the bottleneck will become a problem can be predicted. For example, simply measuring how much internet bandwidth is being consumed and graphing it can make it easy to predict when the capacity of your internet link will be exhausted. If it takes 6 weeks to order more bandwidth, then you need to be able to order that bandwidth at least 6 weeks ahead of time, and preferably 12 weeks ahead of time to permit one failed attempt and do-over.

Some solutions can be implemented quickly, by adjusting a configuration setting. Others require weeks or months of engineering effort to solve, often involving rewriting or replacing major systems.

5.2 Scaling Up

The simplest methodology for scaling a system is to use bigger, faster equipment. A system that runs too slowly can be moved to a machine with a faster CPU, more CPUs, more RAM, faster disks, faster network interfaces, and so on. Often an existing computer can have one of those attributes improved without replacing the entire machine. This is called **scaling up** because the system is increasing in size.

When this solution works well, it is often the easiest solution because it does not require a redesign of the software. However, there are many problems with scaling this way.

First, there are limits to system size. The fastest, largest, most powerful computer available may not be sufficient for the task at hand. No one computer can store the entire corpus of a web search engine or has the CPU power to process petabyte-scale datasets or respond to millions of HTTP queries per second. There are limits as to what is available on the market today.

Second, this approach is not economical. A machine that is twice as fast costs more than twice as much. Such machines are not sold very often and, therefore, are not mass produced. You pay a premium when buying the latest CPU, disk drives, and other components.

Finally, and most importantly, scaling up simply won't work in all situations. Buying a faster, more powerful machine without changing the design of the software being used usually won't result in proportionally faster throughput. Software that is single-threaded will not run faster on a machine with multiple processors. Software that is written to spread across all processors may not see much performance improvement beyond a certain number of CPUs due to bottlenecks such as lock contention.

Likewise, improving the performance of any one component is not guaranteed to improve overall system performance. A faster network connection will not improve throughput, for example, if the protocol performs badly when latency is high.

Appendix B goes into more detail about these issues and the history of how such problems led to the invention of distributed computing.

5.3   The AKF Scaling Cube

Methodologies for scaling to massive proportions boil down to three basic options: replicate the entire system (horizontal duplication); split the system into individual functions, services, or resources (functional or service splits); and split the system into individual chunks (lookup or formulaic splits).

Figure 5.1, the AKF Scaling Cube, was developed by Abbott, Keeven, and Fisher and conceptualizes these categories as x-, y-, and z-axes (Abbott & Fisher 2009).

5.3.1 x: Horizontal Duplication

Horizontal duplication increases throughput by replicating the service. It is also known as **horizontal scaling** or **scaling out**.

This kind of replication has been discussed in past chapters. For example, the technique of using many replicas of a web server behind a load balancer is an example of horizontal scaling.

A group of shared resources is called a resource pool. When adding resources to a pool, it is necessary for each replica to be able to handle the same transactions, resulting in the same or equivalent results.

The x-axis does not scale well with increases in data or with complex transactions that require special handling. If each transaction can be completed independently on all replicas, then the performance improvement can be proportional to the number of replicas. There is no loss of efficiency at scale.

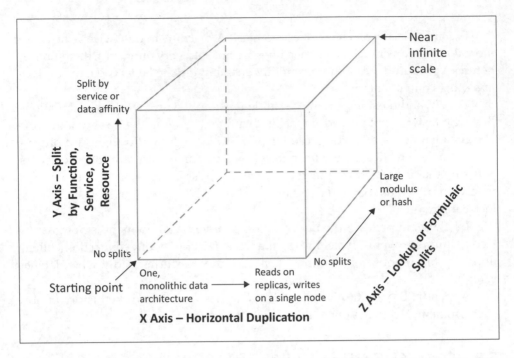

Figure 5.1: The AKF Scaling Cube. Trademark AKF Partners. Reprinted with permission from *Scalability Rules: 50 Principles for Scaling Web Sites*.

Recommended Books on Scalability

The Art of Scalability: Scalable Web Architecture, Processes, and Organizations for the Modern Enterprise by Abbott and Fisher (2009) is an extensive catalog of techniques and discussion of scalability of people, processes, and technologies.

Scalability Rules: 50 Principles for Scaling Web Sites, also by Abbott and Fisher (2011), is a slimmer volume, focused on technical strategy and techniques.

When the transactions require replicas to communicate, the scaling is less efficient. For example, transactions that write new data that must be communicated to all replicas may require all replicas to hold off on any future transactions related to the update until all replicas have received the change. This is related to the CAP Principle (discussed in Section 1.5).

Techniques that involve x-axis scaling include the following:

- Adding more machines or replicas
- Adding more disk spindles
- Adding more network connections

5.3.2 y: Functional or Service Splits

A **functional or service split** means scaling a system by splitting out each individual function so that it can be allocated additional resources.

An example of this was discussed in Section 4.1, where we had a single machine that was used for a web server, a database, and an application server (dynamic content generation). The three functions all compete for resources such as disk buffer cache, CPU, and the bandwidth to the disk, memory, and memory subsystems. By moving the three major functions to separate machines, each is able to perform better because it has dedicated resources.

Separating the functions requires making them less tightly coupled to each other. When they are loosely coupled, it becomes easier to scale each one independently. For example, we could apply x-axis scaling techniques to a single subsystem. Scaling individual parts has advantages. It is less complicated to replicate a small part rather than an entire system. It is also often less expensive to replicate one part that needs more capacity than the entire system, much of which may be performing adequately at the current scale.

In addition to splitting along subsystem boundaries, y axis scaling may involve splitting workflows or transaction types.

Perhaps some category of transactions might be better handled as a special case rather than being treated the same way as all the other requests. This type of transaction might be split off to be processed by a dedicated pool of machines.

For example, it is expensive to engineer a system that has very low latency for all requests. If all traffic is placed in the same bucket, you need far more hardware to keep latencies low for the few requests that care. A better alternative might be to separate requests that come from batch processing systems versus interactive services. The latter can be processed by machines that are less oversubscribed or are on networks with different quality of service (QoS) settings.

One can also mark special customers for special treatment. One financial services web site sets a cookie if a user invests multiple millions of dollars with the firm. The web load balancer detects the cookie and sends its traffic to a pool of servers that are dedicated to very important customers.

Alternatively, there may be an infrequent type of transaction that is particularly burdensome, such that moving it to its own pool would prevent it from overloading the general transactions. For example, a particular query might negatively affect the cache infrastructure. Such queries might be directed to a separate set of machines that uses a different cache algorithm.

Techniques that involve y-axis scaling include the following:

- Splitting by function, with each function on its own machine
- Splitting by function, with each function on its own pool of machines
- Splitting by transaction type
- Splitting by type of user

Case Study: Separating Traffic Types at ServerFault.com

ServerFault.com is a question-and-answer web site for system administrators. When displaying a question (and its answers) to a logged-in user, the page is augmented and customized for the particular person. Anonymous users (users who are not logged in) all see the same generic page.

To scale the system on the y-axis, the two ways to generate the same page were split out. The anonymous pages are now handled by a different system that generates the HTML once and caches it for future requests. Since the vast majority of queries are from anonymous users, this division greatly improved performance.

Anonymous page views are subdivided one additional way. Search engines such as Google and Bing crawl every page at Serverfault.com looking for new content. Since this crawling hits every page, it might potentially overload the service, due to both the volume of requests and the fact that hitting every page in order exhausts the cache. Both factors make performance suffer for other users. Therefore requests from web crawlers are sent to a dedicated pool of replicas. These replicas are configured not to cache the HTML pages that are generated. Because the pool is separate, if the crawlers overload it, regular users will not be affected.

5.3.3 z: Lookup-Oriented Split

A **lookup-oriented split** scales a system by splitting the data into identifiable segments, each of which is given dedicated resources. z-axis scaling is similar to y-axis scaling except that it divides the data instead of the processing.

A simple example of this is to divide, or **segment**, a database by date. If the database is an accumulation of data, such as log data, one can start a new database server every time the current one fills up. There may be a database for 2013 data, 2014 data, and so on. Queries that involve a single year go to the appropriate database server. Queries that span years are sent to all the appropriate database servers and the responses are combined. If a particular year's database is accessed so often that it becomes overloaded, it can be scaled using the x-axis technique of replication. Since no new data is written to past years' servers, most servers can be simple read-only replicas.

Case Study: Twitter's Early Database Architecture

When Twitter was very new, the history of all Tweets fit on a single database server running MySQL. When that server filled up, Twitter started a new database server and modified its software to handle the fact that its data was now segmented by date.

As Twitter became more popular, the amount of time between a new segment being started and that new database filling up decreased rapidly. It became a race for the operations team to keep up with demand. This solution was not sustainable. Load was unbalanced, as older machines didn't get much traffic. This solution was also expensive, as each machine required many replicas. It was logistically complex as well.

Eventually, Twitter moved to a home-grown database system called T-bird, based on Gizzard, which smoothly scales automatically.

Another way to segment data is by geography. In a global service it is common practice to set up many individual data stores around the world. Each user's data is kept on the nearest store. This approach also gives users faster access to their data because it is stored closer to them.

Going from an unsegmented database to a segmented one may require considerable refactoring of application code. Thus scaling on the z-axis is often undertaken only when scaling using the x- and y-axes is exhausted.

Additional ways to segment data include the following:

- **By Hash Prefix:** This is known as sharding and is discussed later.
- **By Customer Functionality:** For example, eBay segments by product—cars, electronics, and so on.
- **By Utilization:** Putting high-use users in dedicated segments.
- **By Organizational Division:** For example, sales, engineering, business development.

- **Hierarchically:** The segments are kept in a hierarchy. DNS uses this pattern, looking up an address like www.everythingsysadmin.com first in the root servers, then in the servers for com, and finally in the servers for the domain everythingsysadmin.
- **By Arbitrary Group:** If a cluster of machines can reliably scale to 50,000 users, then start a new cluster for each 50,000 users. Email services often use this strategy.

5.3.4 Combinations

Many scaling techniques combine multiple axes of the AKF Scaling Cube. Some examples include the following:

- **Segment plus Replicas:** Segments that are being accessed more frequently can be replicated at a greater depth. This enables scaling to larger datasets (more segments) and better performance (more replicas of a segment).
- **Dynamic Replicas:** Replicas are added and removed dynamically to achieve required performance. If latency is too high, add replicas. If utilization is too low, remove replicas.
- **Architectural Change:** Replicas are moved to faster or slower technology based on need. Infrequently accessed shards are moved to slower, less expensive technology such as disk. Shards in higher demand are moved to faster technology such as solid-state drives (SSD). Extremely old segments might be archived to tape or optical disk.

5.4 Caching

A cache is a small data store using fast/expensive media, intended to improve a slow/cheap bigger data store. For example, recent database queries may be stored in RAM so that if the same query is repeated, the disk access can be avoided. Caching is a distinct pattern all its own, considered an optimization of the z-axis of the AKF Scaling Cube.

Consider lookups in a very large data table. If the table was stored in RAM, lookups could be very fast. Assume the data table is larger than will fit in RAM, so it is stored on disk. Lookups on the disk are slow. To improve performance, we allocate a certain amount of RAM and use it as a cache. Now when we do a lookup, first we check whether the result can be found in the cache. If it is, the result is used. This is called a **cache hit**. If it is not found, the normal lookup is done from the disk. This is called a **cache miss**. The result is returned as normal and in addition is stored in the cache so that future duplicate requests will be faster.

Figure 1.10 lists performance comparisons useful for estimating the speed of a cache hit and miss. For example, if your database is in Netherlands and you are in California, a disk-based cache is faster if it requires fewer than 10 seeks and two or three 1MB disk reads. In contrast, if your database queries are within the same datacenter, your cache needs to be significantly faster, such as RAM or a cache server on the same subnet.

5.4.1 Cache Effectiveness

The effectiveness of a cache is measured by the **cache hit ratio**, sometimes called a **cache hit rate**. It is the ratio of the number of cache hits over the total number of lookups. For example, if 500 lookups are performed and 100 were serviced from the cache, the cache hit ratio would be 1/5 or 20 percent.

Performance

A cache is a net benefit in performance if the time saved during cache hits exceeds the time lost from the additional overhead. We can estimate this using weighted averages. If the typical time for a regular lookup is L, a cache hit is H, a cache miss is M, and the cache hit ratio is R, then using the cache is more effective if $H \times R + M \times (1 - R) < L$.

When doing engineering estimates we can simplify the formula if cache lookups and updates are extremely fast or nearly zero. In that case we can assume the performance benefit will be a function of the cache hit ratio. For example, suppose a typical lookup took 6 seconds and we predict a cache hit rate of 33 percent. We know that in a perfect world with an instant, zero-overhead cache, the average lookup would fall by 33 percent to 4 seconds. This gives us a best-case scenario, which is useful for planning purposes. Realistically, performance will improve slightly less than this ideal.

Cost-Effectiveness

A cache is cost-effective only if the benefit from the cache is greater than the cost of implementing the cache. Recall that accessing RAM is faster than accessing disk, but much more expensive. The performance and costs of the items in Figure 1.10 will inevitably change over time. We recommend building your own chart based on the performance and costs in your specific environment.

Suppose a system without caching required 20 replicas, but with caching required only 15. If each replica is a machine, this means the cache is more cost-effective if it costs less than purchasing 5 machines.

Purchase price is not always the only consideration. If being able to provide a faster service will improve sales by 20 percent, then cost should be weighed against that improvement.

5.4.2 Cache Placement

Caching can be local, in which case the software is performing its own caching, saving itself the trouble of requesting a lookup for each cache hit (Figure 5.2a). Caching can be external to the application, with a cache placed between the server and the external resources. For example, a web cache sits between a web browser and the web server, intercepting requests and caching them when possible (Figure 5.2b). Caches can also be at the server side. For example, a server that provides an API for looking up certain information might maintain its own cache that services requests when possible (Figure 5.2c). If there are multiple caches, some might potentially be outdated. The CAP Principle, described in Section 1.5, then applies.

Not all caches are found in RAM. The cache medium simply must be faster than the main medium. A disk can cache for data that has to be gathered from a remote server because disks are generally faster than remote retrieval. For example, YouTube videos are cached in many servers around the world to conserve internet bandwidth. Very fast RAM can cache for normal RAM. For example, the L1 cache of a CPU caches the computer's main memory. Caches are not just used to improve data lookups. For example, calculations can be cached. A function that does a difficult mathematical calculation might cache recent calculation results if they are likely to be requested again.

5.4.3 Cache Persistence

When a system starts, the cache is usually empty, or **cold**. The cache hit ratio will be very low and performance will remain slow until enough queries have **warmed**

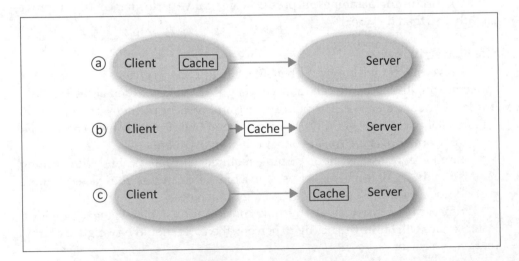

Figure 5.2: Cache placement

the cache. Some caches are persistent, meaning they survive restarts. For example, a cache stored on disk is persistent across restarts. RAM is not persistent and is lost between restarts. If a system has a cache that is slow to warm up and is stored in RAM, it may be beneficial to save the cache to disk before a shutdown and read it back in on startup.

> **Case Study: Saving a RAM Cache to Disk**
>
> Stack Exchange's web sites depend on a database that is heavily cached in RAM by Redis. If Redis is restarted, its performance will be unacceptably slow for 10 to 15 minutes while the cache warms. Redis has many features that prevent this problem, including the ability to snapshot the data held in RAM to disk, or to use a second Redis server to store a copy of the cache.

5.4.4 Cache Replacement Algorithms

When a cache miss is processed, the data gathered by the regular lookup is added to the cache. If the cache is full some data must be thrown away to make room. There are many different replacement algorithms available to handle the cache manipulation.

In general, better algorithms keep track of more usage information to improve the cache hit ratio. Different algorithms work best for different data access patterns.

The Least Recently Used (LRU) algorithm tracks when each cache entry was used and discards the least recently accessed entry. It works well for access patterns where queries are repeated often within a small time period. For example, a DNS server might use this algorithm: if a domain has not been accessed in a long time, chances are it won't be accessed again. Typos, for example, rarely repeat and will eventually expire from the cache.

The Least Frequently Used (LFU) algorithm counts the number of times a cache entry is accessed and discards the least active entries. It may track total accesses, or keep an hourly or daily count. This algorithm is a good choice when more popular data tends to be accessed the most. For example, a video service might cache certain popular videos that are viewed often while other videos are viewed once and rarely ever rewatched.

New algorithms are being invented all the time. Tom's favorite algorithm, Adaptive Replacement Cache (ARC), was invented in 2003 (Megiddo & Modha 2003). Most algorithms do not perform well with a sudden influx of otherwise little-used data. For example, backing up a database involves reading every record one at a time and leaves the cache filled with otherwise little-used data. At that point, the cache is cold, so performance suffers. ARC solves this problem by putting newly cached data in a probationary state. If it is accessed a second time, it gets out of probation and is put into the main cache. A single pass through the database flushes the probationary cache, not the main cache.

Many other algorithms exist, but most are variations on the LRU, LFU, and ARC options.

5.4.5 Cache Entry Invalidation

When data in the primary storage location changes, any related cache entries become obsolete. There are many ways to deal with this situation.

One method is to ignore it. If the primary storage does not change, the cache entries do not become obsolete. In other cases, the cache is very small and obsolete entries will be eventually be replaced via the cache replacement algorithm. If the system can tolerate occasional outdated information, this may be sufficient. Such situations are rather rare.

Another method is to invalidate the entire cache anytime the database changes. The benefit of this method is that it is very simple to implement. It leaves the cache cold, however, and performance suffers until it warms again. This is acceptable in applications where the cache warms quickly.

The main storage may communicate to the cache the need to invalidate an entry whenever the data in the cache has changed. This may create a lot of work if there are many caches and updates occur frequently. This is also an example of how the CAP Principle, described in Section 1.5, comes into play: for perfect consistency, processing of queries involving the updated entry must pause until all caches have been notified.

Some methods eliminate the need for the main storage to communicate directly to the caches. The cache can, for example, assume a cache entry is valid only for a certain number of seconds. The cache can record a timestamp on each entry when it is created and expire entries after a certain amount of time.

Alternatively, the server can help by including how long an entry may be cached when it answers a query. For example, suppose a DNS server responds to all queries with not just the answer, but also how many seconds each entry in the answer may be cached. This is called the time to live (TTL) value. Likewise, an HTTP server can annotate a response with an expiration date, an indication of how long the item can be cached. If you do not control the client software, you cannot be assured that clients will abide by such instructions. Many ISPs cache DNS entries for 24 hours at a minimum, much to the frustration of those using DNS as part of a global load balancer. Many web browsers are guilty of ignoring expiration dates sent by HTTP servers.

Lastly, the cache can poll the server to see if a local cache should be invalidated. For example, an HTTP client can query the server about whether an item has changed to find out if an item in its cache is fresh. This method works when the query for freshness can be processed significantly faster than the full answer is sent.

5.4.6 Cache Size

Picking the right cache size is difficult but important. If it is too small, performance will suffer, which may potentially be worse than having no cache at all. If it is too large, we have wasted money when a smaller cache would do. If we have thousands of machines, a few dollars wasted on each machine adds up quickly.

Caches are usually a fixed size. This size usually consists of a fixed number of cache entries or a fixed amount of total storage, in which case the number of potential entries is adjusted accordingly.

There are several approaches to selecting a cache size. The most accurate way to determine the correct cache size for a given situation is to take measurements on a running system. Caches are complex, especially due to interactions between replacement algorithms and cache size. Measuring a running system involves all these factors, but may not always be possible.

One approach is to run the system with a variety of cache sizes, measuring performance achieved by each one. Benchmarks like this can be done with real or simulated data on a separate system set up for benchmark tests. Such operations can be done on live systems for the most accurate measurements, though this may be risky. One way to limit such risks is to adjust cache sizes on just one replica of many. Negative effects are then less likely to be noticed.

Another approach is to configure a system with a larger cache size than the application could possibly need. If the cache entries expire fast enough, the cache will grow to a certain size and then stop growing. This gives an upper bound of how big the cache needs to be. If the cache size does not stabilize, eventually the replacement algorithm will kick in. Take a snapshot of the age of all the entries. Review the snapshot to see which entires are hot (frequently being used) and cold (less frequently used). Often you will see a pattern surface. For example, you may see that 80 percent of the cache entries have been used recently and the rest are significantly older. The 80 percent size represents approximately the amount of cache that is contributing to improving performance.

Another approach is to estimate the cache hit ratio. If we are considering adding a cache to a running system, we can collect logs of data and estimate what the cache hit ratio will be. For example, we could collect 24 hours' worth of query logs and count duplicate requests. The ratio of duplicates to total queries is a good predictor of what the cache hit ratio will be be if caching is added. This assumes an infinite cache with no expiration. If even under these theoretically perfect conditions the cache hit ratio is low, we know that a cache will not help. However, if there are duplicate queries, the cumulative size of the responses to those queries will give a good estimate for sizing the cache.

The problem with measurements from live or benchmark systems is that they require the system to exist. When designing a system it is important to be able to make a reasonable prediction of what cache size will be required.

We can improve our estimate by using a cache simulator. These tools can be used to provide "what if" analysis to determine the minimum cache size.

Once the cache is in place, the cache hit ratio should be monitored. The cache size can be reevaluated periodically, increasing it to improve performance as needed.

5.5 Data Sharding

Sharding is a way to segment a database (z-axis) that is flexible, scalable, and resilient. It divides the database based on the hash value of the database keys.

A hash function is an algorithm that maps data of varying lengths to a fixed-length value. The result is considered probabilistically unique. For example, the MD5 algorithm returns a 128-bit number for any input. Because there are 340,282,366,920,938,463,463,374,607,431,768,211,456 possible combinations, the chance of two inputs producing the same hash is very small. Even a small change in the data creates a big change in the hash. The MD5 hash of "Jennifer" is e1f6a14cd07069692017b53a8ae881f6 but the MD5 hash of "Gennifer" is 1e49bbe95b90646dca5c46a8d8368dab.

To divide a database into two shards, generate the hash of the key and store keys with even hashes in one database and keys with odd hashes in the other database. To divide a database into four shards, split the database based on the remainder of the key's hash divided by 4 (i.e., the hash $mod 4$). Since the remainder will be 0, 1, 2, or 3, this will indicate which of the four shards will store that key. Because the hash values are randomly distributed between the shards, each shard will store approximately the same number of keys automatically. This pattern is called a **distributed hash table (DHT)** since it distributes the data over many machines, and uses hashes to determine where the data is stored.

The Power of 2

We use a power of 2 to optimize the hash-to-shard mapping process. When you want the remainder of the hash when divided by 2^n, you just need to look at the last n bits of the hash. This is a very fast operation, much faster than getting the modulus using a number that is not a power of 2.

Shards can be replicated on multiple machines to improve performance. With such an approach, each replica processes a share of the queries destined for that shard. Replication can also provide better availability. If multiple machines store any shard, then any machine can crash or be taken down for maintenance and the other replicas will continue to service the requests.

As more data are stored, the shards may outgrow the machine. The database can then be split over twice as many shards. The number of shards doubles, and the old data is divided among the new shards. Each key's hash is evaluated to determine if the key should stay in the current shard or if it belongs to the new shard. Systems that perform this step while live have complex algorithms to manage queries received during the expansion.

It is rather inflexible to require that the number of segments be a power of 2. For example, going from one shard to two requires adding just one machine, which is easy to purchase. However, as the system grows, you may find yourself needing to go from 32 machines to 64 machines, which is quite a large purchase. The next jump is twice as big. If the new machines are more powerful, this extra capacity will be wasted until all the smaller machines are eliminated. Also, while the number of keys is evenly divided between shards, each key may not store exactly the same amount of data. Thus a machine may have one fourth of the keys, but more data than can fit on the machine. One must increase the number of shards based on the largest shard, which could be considerably bigger than the smallest.

The solution to these problems is to create more, smaller shards and store multiple shards on each machine. Now you can vary the number of shards on a machine to compensate for uneven shard sizes and different machine sizes. For example, you could divide the hash value by a larger power of 2 and produce, for example, 8192 buckets. Divide those buckets across as many machines as needed. For example, if there are three machines, one twice as large as the other two, the larger machine might store keys that fall into bucket 0...4095 (4096 total) in the larger server and store buckets 4096...6143 and 6144...8191 (2048 keys each) in the second and third machines, respectively.

As new, more powerful hardware becomes available, one can pack more shards on a machine. More shards mean more queries will be directed to that machine. Thus, more CPU and network bandwidth is required. It is possible that when the machine stores the maximum number of shards, the CPU or network bandwidth will be exhausted and performance suffer. New hardware models should be benchmarked to determine the usable capacity before being put into service. Ideally CPU, shard storage, and network bandwidth will all top out at the same time.

If shards are used for a read/write database, each write updates the appropriate shards. Replicas must be kept up-to-date, abiding by the CAP Principle discussed in Chapter 1.

In reality, shards are often used to distribute a read-only corpus of information. For example, a search engine collects data and indexes it, producing shards of a read-only database. These then need to be distributed to each search cluster replica. Distribution can be rather complex. Transmitting an updated shard can take a long time. If it is copied over the old data, the server cannot respond to requests on that shard until the update is complete. If the transfer fails for some reason, the shard will be unusable. Alternatively, one could set aside storage space for temporary use by shards as they are transmitted. Of course, this means there is unused space when updates are not being done. To eliminate this waste, one can stop advertising that the shard is on this machine so that the replicas will process any requests instead. Now it can be upgraded. The process of unadvertising until no new requests are received is called **draining**. One must be aware that while a shard is being drained, there is one fewer replica—so performance may suffer. It is important to globally coordinate shard upgrades so that enough replicas exist at any given moment to maintain reliability and meet performance goals.

5.6 Threading

Data can be processed in different ways to achieve better scale. Simply processing one request at a time has its limits. Threading is a technique that can be used to improve system throughput by processing many requests at the same time.

Threading is a technique used by modern operating systems to allow sequences of instructions to execute independently. Threads are subsets of processes; it's typically faster to switch operations among threads than among processes. We use threading to get a fine granularity of control over processing for use in complex algorithms.

In a single-thread process, we receive a query, process it, send the result, and get the next query. This is simple and direct. A disadvantage is that a single long request will stall the requests behind it. It is like wanting to buy a pack of gum but being in line behind a person with a full shopping cart. In this so-called **head of line blocking**, the head of the line is blocked by a big request. The result is high latency for requests that otherwise could be serviced quickly.

A second disadvantage to single-threading is that in a flood of requests, some requests will be dropped. The kernel will queue up incoming connections while waiting for the program to take the next one and process it. The kernel limits how many waiting connections are permitted, so if there is a flood of new connections, some will be dropped.

Finally, in a multi-core machine, the single thread will be bound to a single CPU, leaving the other cores idle. Multithreaded code can take advantage of all cores, thereby making maximum use of a machine.

In multithreading, a **main thread** receives new requests. For each request, it creates a new thread, called a **worker thread**, to do the actual work and send the reply. Since thread creation is fast, the main thread can keep up with a flood of new requests and none will be dropped. Throughput is improved because requests are processed in parallel, multiple CPUs are utilized, and head of line blocking is reduced or eliminated.

That said, multithreading is more difficult to implement. If multiple threads have to access the same resources in memory, locks or signaling flags (semaphores) are needed to prevent resource collision. Locking is complex and error prone.

There are limits to the number of threads a machine can handle, based on RAM and CPU core limits. If any one core becomes overloaded, performance will quickly drop for that core. Connection floods can still cause dropped requests, but the number of connections being handled is increased.

5.7 Queueing

Another way that data can be processed differently to achieve better scale is called **queuing**. A **queue** is a data structure that holds requests until the software is ready to process them. Most queues release elements in the order that they were received, called first in, first out (FIFO) processing.

Queueing is similar to multithreading in that there is a master thread and worker threads. The master thread collects requests and places them in the queue. There is usually a fixed number of worker threads. Each one takes a request from the queue, processes it, sends a reply, and then takes another item from the queue. This workflow is called **feeding from a queue**.

5.7.1 Benefits

Queueing shares many of the advantages and disadvantages of multithreading. At the same time, it has several advantages over basic multithreading.

With queueing, you are less likely to overload the machine since the number of worker threads is fixed and remains constant. There is also an advantage in retaining the same threads to service multiple requests. This avoids the overhead associated with new thread creation. Thread creation is lightweight, but on a massive scale the overhead can add up.

Another benefit of the queuing model is that it is easier to implement a priority scheme. High-priority requests can go to the head of the queue. A plethora of queueing algorithms may be available depending on the type of priority scheme you want to implement. In **fair queueing**, the algorithm prevents a low-priority item from being "starved" by a flood of high-priority items. Other algorithms dynamically shift priorities so that bursty or intermittent traffic does not overload the system or starve other priorities from being processed.

5.7.2 Variations

Variations of the queueing model can optimize performance. It is common to have the ability to shrink or grow the number of threads. This may be automatic based on demand, or it may be manually controlled. Another variation is for threads to kill and re-create themselves periodically so that they remain "fresh." This mitigates memory leaks and other problems, but in doing so hides them and makes them more difficult to find.

Finally, it is common practice to use processes instead of threads. Process creation can be expensive, but the fixed population of worker processes means that you pay that overhead once and then get the benefit of using processes. Processes can do things that threads cannot, because they have their own address space, memory, and open file tables. Processes are self-isolating, in that a process that is corrupted cannot hurt other processes, whereas one ill-behaved thread can adversely affect other threads.

An example of queueing implemented with processes is the Prefork processing module for the Apache web server. On startup, Apache forks off a certain number of subprocesses. Requests are distributed to subprocesses by a master process. Requests are processed faster because the subprocess already exists, which hides the long process creation time. Processes are configured to die and be refreshed to every *n* requests so that memory leaks are averted. The number of subprocesses used can be adjusted dynamically.

5.8 Content Delivery Networks

A **content delivery network** (CDN) is a web-acceleration service that delivers content (web pages, images, video) more efficiently on behalf of your service. CDNs cache content on servers all over the world. Requests for content are serviced from the cache nearest the user. Geolocation techniques are used to identify the network location of the requesting web browser.

CDNs do not copy all content to all caches. Instead, they notice usage trends and determine where to cache certain content. For example, seeing a surge of use from Germany for a particular image, the CDN might copy all images for that customer to its servers in Germany. These images may displace cached images that have not been accessed as recently.

CDNs have extremely large, fast connections to the internet. They have more bandwidth to the internet than most web sites.

CDNs often place their cache servers in the datacenters of ISPs, in arrangements called **colocation**. As a result, the ISP-to-ISP traffic is reduced. Considering that ISPs charge each other for this traffic, such a reduction can pay for itself quickly.

Typically, an image in the middle of a web page might come from a URL on the same server. However, this image rarely, if ever, changes. A web site that uses a CDN would upload a copy of this image to the CDN, which then serves it from a URL that points to the CDN's servers. The web site then uses the CDN's URL to refer to the image. When users load the web page, the image comes from the CDN's servers. The CDN uses various techniques to deliver the image faster than the web site could.

Uploading content to a CDN is automatic. Your web site serves the content as it normally does. A link to this content is called a native URL. To activate the CDN, you replace the native URLs in the HTML being generated with URLs that point to the CDN's servers. The URL encodes the native URL. If the CDN has the content cached already, it serves the content as one expects. If this is the first time that particular content is accessed, the CDN loads the content from the native URL, caches it, and serves the content to the requester. The idea to encode the native URL in the CDN URL is quite smart; it means that there is no special step for uploading to the CDN that must be performed.

Best practice is to use a flag or software switch to determine whether native URLs or CDN URLs are output as your system generates web pages. Sometimes CDNs have problems and you will want to be able to switch back to native URLs easily. Sometimes the problem is not the CDN but rather a configuration error that you have caused. No amount of marketing material expounding the reliability of a CDN product will save you from this situation. Also, while a new web site is in the testing phase, you may not want to use a CDN, especially if you are testing new, secret features that should not be exposed to the world yet. Lastly, having such a switch enables you to switch between CDN vendors easily.

CDNs are great choices for small sites. Once the site becomes extremely large, however, it may be more cost-effective to run your own private CDN. Google initially used a third-party CDN to improve performance and achieved an order of magnitude better uptime than it could achieve when it was a young company. As Google grew, it established its own datacenter space all over the world. At that point Google built its own private CDN, which permitted it to achieve another order of magnitude better uptime.

CDNs didn't appear until the late 1990s. At that time they focused on static content delivery for images and HTML files. The next generation of CDN products added video hosting. In the past, file sizes were limited, but video hosting requires the CDN to be able to handle larger content plus deal with protocols related to skipping around within a video. The current generation of CDN products, therefore, can act as a proxy. All requests go through the CDN, which acts as a middle man, performing caching services, rewriting HTML to be more efficient, and supporting other features.

CDNs now compete on price, geographic coverage, and an ever-growing list of new features. Some CDNs specialize in a particular part of the world, either offering lower prices for web sites that have users only in their part of the world, or offering special services such as being licensed to serve content in China from inside the Great Firewall of China (that is, assisting clients with the difficult and complex censorship requirements placed on such traffic).

New features include the ability to serve dynamic content, serve different content to mobile devices, and provide security services. HTTPS (encrypted HTTP) service can be complex and difficult to administer. Some CDNs can process the HTTPS connections on your behalf, relieving you of managing such complexity. The connection between your web servers and the CDN can then use an easier-to-manage transport mechanism, or no encryption at all.

5.9 Summary

Most approaches to scaling fall under one of the axes of the AKF Scaling Cube. The x-axis (horizontal scaling) is a power multiplier, cloning systems or increasing their capacities to achieve greater performance. The y-axis (vertical scaling) scales by isolating transactions by their type or scope, such as using read-only database replicas for read queries and sequestering writes to the master database only. Finally, the z-axis (lookup-based scaling) is about splitting data across servers so that the workload is distributed according to data usage or physical geography.

Sharding scales large databases by putting horizontal partitions of your database (rows) on multiple servers, gaining the advantage of smaller indices and distributed queries. Replicating the shards onto additional servers produces speed and reliability benefits, at the cost of data freshness.

Another optimization for data retrieval is a cache, a comparatively small data store on fast and/or expensive media. A cache aggregates recently requested data, performing updates on itself when data that isn't in the cache is requested. Subsequent queries will then go directly to the cache and an overall improvement in performance will be realized.

Threading and queueing give us the tools to deal with floods of requests, aggregating them into a structure that allows us to service them individually. Content delivery networks provide web-acceleration services, usually by caching content closer to the user.

Exercises

1. What is scaling?
2. What are the options for scaling a service that is CPU bound?
3. What are the options for scaling a service whose storage requirements are growing?
4. The data in Figure 1.10 is outdated because hardware tends to get less expensive every year. Update the chart for the current year. Which items changed the least? Which changed the most?

5. Rewrite the data in Figure 1.10 in terms of proportion. If reading from main memory took 1 second, how long would the other operations take? For extra credit, draw your answer to resemble a calendar or the solar system.

6. Take the data table in Figure 1.10 and add a column that identifies the cost of each item. Scale the costs to the same unit—for example, the cost of 1 terabyte of RAM, 1 terabyte of disk, and 1 terabyte of L1 cache. Add another column that shows the ratio of performance to cost.

7. What is the theoretical model that describes the different kinds of scaling techniques?

8. How do you know when scaling is needed?

9. What are the most common scaling techniques and how do they work? When are they most appropriate to use?

10. Which scaling techniques also improve resiliency?

11. Describe how your environment uses a CDN or research how it could be used.

12. Research Amdahl's Law and explain how it relates to the AKF Scaling Cube.

Chapter 6

Design Patterns for Resiliency

> Success is not final, failure is not
> fatal: it is the courage to continue
> that counts.

—Winston Churchill

Resiliency is a system's ability to constructively deal with failures. A resilient system detects failure and routes around it. Nonresilient systems fall down when faced with a malfunction. This chapter is about software-based resiliency and documents the most common techniques used.

Resiliency is important because no one goes to a web site that is down. Hardware fails—that is a fact of life. You can buy the most reliable, expensive hardware in the world and there will be some amount of failures. In a sufficiently large system, a one in a million failure is a daily occurrence.

During the first year of a typical Google datacenter, there will be five rack-wide outages, three router failures large enough to require diverting processing away from connected machines, and eight network scheduled maintenance windows, half of which cause 30-minute random connectivity losses. At the same time 1 to 5 percent of all disks will die and each machine will crash at least twice (2 to 4 percent failure rate) (Dean 2009).

Graceful degradation, discussed previously, means software is designed to survive failures or periods of high load by providing reduced functionality. For example, a movie streaming service might automatically reduce video resolution to conserve bandwidth when some of its internet connections are down or otherwise overloaded. The other strategy is **defense in depth**, which means that all layers of design detect and respond the failures. This includes failures as small as a single process and as large as an entire datacenter.

An older, more traditional strategy for achieving reliability is to reduce the chance of failure at every place it can happen. Use the best servers and the best network equipment, and put it in the most reliable datacenter: There will still

> ### *Terms to Know*
> **Outage:** A user-visible lack of service.
> **Failure:** A system, subsystem, or component that has stopped working.
> **Malfunction:** Used interchangeably with "failure."
> **Server:** Software that provides a function or API. (Not a piece of hardware.)
> **Service:** A user-visible system or product composed of one or more servers.
> **Machine:** A virtual or physical machine.
> **QPS:** Queries per second. Usually how many web hits or API calls are received per second.

be outages when this strategy is pursued, but they will be rare. This is the most expensive strategy. Another strategy is to perform a dependency analysis and verify that each system depends on high-quality parts. Manufacturers calculate their components' reliability and publish their mean time between failure (MTBF) ratings. By analyzing the dependencies within the system, one can predict MTBF for the entire system. The MTBF of the system is only as high as that of its lowest-MTBF part.

Such a strategy is predictive, meaning that it predicts the likelihood of failure or the reliability of the system.

Resilient systems continue where predictive strategies leave off. Assuming that failure will happen, we build systems that react and respond intelligently so that the system as a whole survives and continues to provide service. In other words, resilient systems are responsive to failure. Rather than avoiding failure through better hardware or responding to it with human effort (and apologies), they take a proactive stance and put in place mechanisms that expect and survive failure.

Resilient systems decouple component failure from user-visible outages. In traditional computing, where there is a failed component, there is a user-visible outage. When we build **survivable systems**, the two concepts are decoupled.

This chapter is about the various ways we can design systems that detect failure and work around it. This is how we build survivable systems. The techniques are grouped into four categories: physical failures, attacks, human errors, and unexpected load.

6.1 Software Resiliency Beats Hardware Reliability

You can build a reliable system by selecting better hardware or better software. Better hardware means special-purpose CPUs, components, and storage systems.

Better software means adding intelligence to a system so that it detects failures and works around them.

Software solutions are favored for many reasons. First and foremost, they are more economical. Once software is written, it can be applied to many services and many machines with no additional cost (assuming it is home-grown, is open source, or does not require a per-machine license.) Software is also more malleable than hardware. It is easier to fix, upgrade, and replace. Unlike hardware upgrades, software upgrades can be automated. As a result, software is replaced often. New features can be introduced faster and more frequently. It is easy to experiment. As software gets older, it gets stronger: Bugs are fixed; rare edge cases are handled better. Spolsky's (2004) essay, "Things You Should Never Do," gives many examples.

Using better hardware, by comparison, is more expensive. The initial purchase price is higher. More reliable CPUs, components, and storage systems are much more expensive than commodity parts. This strategy is also more expensive because you pay the extra expense with each machine as you grow. Upgrading hardware has a per-machine cost for the hardware itself, installation labor, capital depreciation, and the disposal of old parts. Designing hardware takes longer, so upgrades become available less frequently and it is more difficult to experiment and try new things. As hardware gets older, it becomes more brittle and fails more often.

6.2 Everything Malfunctions Eventually

Malfunctions are a part of every environment. They can happen at every level. For example, they happen at the component level (chips and other electronic parts), the device level (hard drives, motherboards, network interfaces), and the system level (computers, network equipment, power systems). Malfunctions also occur regionally: racks lose power, entire datacenters go offline, cities and entire regions of the world are struck with disaster. Humans are also responsible for malfunctions ranging from typos to software bugs, from accidentally kicking a power cable out of its socket to intentionally malicious attacks.

6.2.1 MTBF in Distributed Systems

Large systems magnify small problems. In large systems a "one in a million" problem happens a lot. A hard drive with an MTBF of 1 million hours has a 1 in 114 chance of failing this year. If you have 100,000 such hard disks, you can expect two to fail every day.

A bug in a CPU that is triggered with a probability of one in 10 million might be why your parents' home PC crashed once in 2010. They cursed, rebooted, and didn't think of it again. Such a bug would be hardly within the chip maker's ability to detect. That same bug in a distributed computing system, however, would be observed frequently enough to show up as a pattern in a crash detection and analysis system. It would be reported to the vendor, which would be dismayed that it existed, shocked that anyone found it, and embarrassed that it had been in the core CPU design for multiple chip generations. The vendor would also be unlikely to give permission to have the specifics documented in a book on system administration.

Failures cluster so that it appears as if the machines are ganging up on us. Racks of machines trying to boot at the same time after a power outage expose marginal power supplies unable to provide enough juice to spin up dozens of disks at once. Old solder joints shrink and crack, leading to mysterious failures. Components from the same manufacturing batch have similar mortality curves, resulting in a sudden rush of failures.

With our discussion of the many potential malfunctions and failures, we hope we haven't scared you away from the field of system administration!

6.2.2 The Traditional Approach

Traditional software assumes a perfect, malfunction-free world. This leaves the hardware systems engineer with the impossible task of delivering hardware that never fails. We fake it by using redundant array of inexpensive [independent] disks (RAID) systems that let the software go on pretending that disks never fail. Sheltered from the reality of a world full of malfunctions, we enable software developers to continue writing software that assumes a perfect, malfunction-free world (which, of course, does not exist).

For example, UNIX applications are written with the assumption that reading and writing files will happen without error. As a result, applications do not check for errors when writing files. If they did, it would be a waste of time because the blocks may not be written to disk until later, possibly after the application has been exited. Microsoft Word is written with the assumption that the computer it runs on will continue to run.

Hyperbole Warning

The previous paragraph included two slight exaggerations. The application layer of UNIX assumes a perfect file system but the underlying layers do not assume perfect disks. Microsoft Word checkpoints documents so that the user does not lose data in the event of a crash. However, during that crash the user is unable to edit the document.

Attempts to achieve this impossible malfunction-free world cause companies to spend a lot of money. CPUs, components, and storage systems known for high reliability are demonstrably more expensive than commodity parts. Appendix B details the history of this strategy and explains the economic benefits of distributed computing techniques discussed in this chapter.

6.2.3 The Distributed Computing Approach

Distributed computing, in contrast to the traditional approach, embraces components' failures and malfunctions. It takes a reality-based approach that accepts malfunctions as a fact of life. Google Docs continues to let a user edit a document even if a machine fails at Google: another machine takes over and the user does not even notice the handoff.

Traditional computing goes to great lengths to achieve reliability through hardware and then either accepts a small number of failures as "normal" or adds intelligence to detect and route around failures. If your software can route around failure, it is wasteful to also spend money on expensive hardware.

A popular bumper-sticker says "Eat right. Exercise. Die anyway." If your hardware is going to fail no matter how expensive it is, why buy the best? Why pay for reliability twice?

Buying Failed Memory

Early in its history, Google tried to see how far it could push the limits of using intelligent software to manage unreliable hardware. To do so, the company purchased failed RAM chips and found ways to make them useful.

Google was purchasing terabytes of RAM for machines that ran software that was highly resilient to failure. If a chip failed, the OS would mark that area of RAM as unusable and kill any process using it. The killed processes would be restarted automatically. The fact that the chip was bad was recorded so that it was ignored by the OS even after reboot.

As a result, a machine didn't need to be repaired just because one chip had failed. The machine could run until the machine's capacity was reduced below usable limits.

To understand what happened next, you must understand that the difference between high-quality RAM chips and normal-quality chips is how much testing they pass. RAM chips are manufactured and then tested. The ones that pass the most QA testing are sold as "high quality" at a high price. The ones that pass the standard QA tests are sold as normal for the regular price. All others are thrown away.

Google's purchasing people are formidable negotiators. Google had already been saving money by purchasing the normal-quality chips, relying on the custom software Google wrote to work around failures. One day the purchasing department thought to ask if it was possible to purchase the chips that were being thrown away. The manufacturers had never received such a request before and were willing to sell the defective chips for pennies on the dollar.

The "failed" RAM chips worked perfectly for Google's need. Some didn't work from the start and others failed soon after. However, services were able to keep running.

Google eventually ended this practice but for many years the company was able to build servers with enormous amounts of RAM for less money than any of its competitors. When your business is charging pennies for advertisements, saving dollars is a big advantage!

6.3 Resiliency through Spare Capacity

The general strategy used to gain resiliency is to have redundant units of capacity that can fail independently of each other. Failures are detected and those units are removed from service. The total capacity of the system is reduced but the system is still able to run. This means that systems must be built with **spare capacity** to begin with.

Let's use the example of a web server that serves the static images displayed on a web site. Such a server is easy to replicate because the content does not change frequently. We can, for example, build multiple such servers and load balance between them. (How load balancers work was discussed in Section 4.2.1.) We call these servers **replicas** because the same service is replicated by each server. They are duplicates in that they all respond to the same queries and give equivalent results. In this case the same images are accessed at the same URLs.

Suppose each replica can handle 100 QPS and the service receives 300 QPS at peak times. Three servers would be required to provide the 300 QPS capacity. An additional replica is needed to provide the spare capacity required to survive one failed replica. Failure of any one replica is detected and that replica is taken out of service automatically. The load is now balanced over the surviving three replicas. The total capacity of the system is reduced to 300 QPS, which is sufficient.

We call this $N + M$ **redundancy**. Such systems require N units to provide capacity and have M units of extra capacity. Units are the smallest discrete system that provides the service. The term $N + 1$ **redundancy** is used when we wish to indicate that there is enough spare capacity for one failure, such as in our example.

If we added a fifth server, the system would be able to survive two simultaneous failures and would be described as N + 2 **redundancy**.

What if we had 3 + 1 redundancy and a series of failures? After the first failure, the system is described as 3 + 0. It is still running but there is no redundancy. The second failure (a double failure) would result in the system being **oversubscribed**. That is, there is less capacity available than needed.

Continuing our previous example, when there are two failed replicas, there is 200 QPS of capacity. The system is now 3:2 oversubscribed: two replicas exist where three are needed. If we are lucky, this has happened at a time of day that does not draw many users and 200 QPS is sufficient. However, if we are unlucky, this has happened at peak usage time and our two remaining servers are faced with 300 QPS, more than they are designed to handle. Dealing with such an overload is covered later in Section 6.7.1.

6.3.1 How Much Spare Capacity

Spare capacity is like an insurance policy: it is an expense you pay now to prepare for future trouble that you hope does not happen. It is better to have insurance and not need it than to need insurance and not have it. That said, paying for too much insurance is wasteful and not good business. Selecting the granularity of our unit of capacity enables us to manage the efficiency. For example, in a 1 + 1 redundant system, 50 percent of the capacity is spare. In a 20 + 1 redundant system, less than 5 percent of the capacity is spare. The latter is more cost-efficient.

The other factors in selecting the amount of redundancy are how quickly we can bring up additional capacity and how likely it is that a second failure will happen during that time. The time it takes to repair or replace the down capacity is called the mean time to repair (MTTR). The probability an outage will happen during that time is the reciprocal of the mean time between failures. The percent probability that a second failure will happen during the repair window is MTTR/MTBF × 100.

If a second failure means data loss, the probability of a second failure becomes an important factor in how many spares you should have.

Suppose it takes a week (168 hours) to repair the capacity and the MTBF is 100,000 hours. There is a $168/1,000,000 \times 100 = 1.7$ percent, or 1 in 60, chance of a second failure.

Now suppose the MTBF is two weeks (336 hours). In this case, there is a $168/336 \times 100 = 50$ percent, or 1 in 2, chance of a second failure—the same as a coin flip. Adding an additional replica becomes prudent.

MTTR is a function of a number of factors. A process that dies and needs to be restarted has a very fast MTTR. A broken hardware component may take only a few minutes to replace, but if that server is in a datacenter 9000 miles away, it may take a month before someone is able to reach it. Spare parts need to be ordered, shipped, and delivered. Even if a disk can be replaced within minutes of failure, if it is in a RAID configuration there may be a long, slow rebuild time where the system is still $N + 0$ until the rebuild is complete.

If all this math makes your head spin, here is a simple rule of thumb: $N + 1$ is a minimum for a service; $N + 2$ is needed if a second outage is likely while you are fixing the first one.

Digital computers are either on or off, and we think in terms of a service as either running or not: it is either up or down. When we use resiliency through replication, the service is more like an analog device: it can be on, off, or anywhere in between. We are no longer monitoring the service to determine if it is up or down. Instead, we are monitoring the amount of capacity in the system and determining whether we should be adding more. This changes the way we think about our systems and how we do operations. Rather than being awakened in the middle of the night because a machine is down, we are alerted only if the needle of a gauge gets near the danger zone.

6.3.2 Load Sharing versus Hot Spares

In the previous examples, the replicas are load sharing: all are active, are sharing the workload equally (approximately), and have equal amounts of spare capacity (approximately). Another strategy is to have primary and secondary replicas. In this approach, the primary replica receives the entire workload but the secondary replica is ready to take over at any time. This is sometimes called the **hot spare** or "hot standby" strategy since the spare is connected to the system, running (hot), and can be switched into operation instantly. It is also known as an active–passive or master–slave pair. Often there are multiple secondaries. Because there is only one master, these configurations are $1 + M$ configurations.

Sometimes the term "active–active" or "master–master" pair will be used to refer to two replicas that are load sharing. "Active–active" is more commonly used with network links. "Master–master" is more commonly used in the database world and in situations where the two are tightly coupled.

6.4 Failure Domains

A **failure domain** is the bounded area beyond which failure has no impact. For example, when a car fails on a highway, its failure does not make the entire highway unusable. The impact of the failure is bounded to its failure domain.

The failure domain of a fuse in a home circuit breaker box is the room or two that is covered by that circuit. If a power line is cut, the failure domain affects a number of houses or perhaps a city block. The failure domain of a power grid might be the town, region, or county that it feeds (which is why some datacenters are located strategically so they have access to two power grids).

A failure domain may be prescriptive—that is, a design goal or requirement. You might plan that two groups of servers are each their own failure domain and then engineer the system to meet that goal, assuring that the failure domains that they themselves rely on are independent. Each group may be in different racks, different power circuits, and so on. Whether they should be in different datacenters depends on the scope of the failure domain goal.

Alternatively, a failure domain may be descriptive. Often we find ourselves exploring a system trying to determine, or reverse-engineer, what the resulting failure domain has become. Due to a failed machine, a server may have been moved temporarily to a spare machine in another rack. We can determine the new failure domain by exploring the implications of this move.

Determining a failure domain is done within a particular scope or assumptions about how large an outage we are willing to consider. For example, we may keep off-site backups 1000 miles away, assuming that an outage that affects two buildings that far apart is an acceptable risk, or that a disaster that large would mean we'd have other problems to worry about.

Unaligned Failure Domains Increase Outage Impact

A company with many large datacenters used an architecture in which a power bus was shared by every group of six racks. A network subsystem provided network connectivity for every eight racks. The network subsystem received power from the first rack of each of its groups.

If a power bus needed to be turned off for maintenance, the outage this would create would involve the six racks directly attached to it for power, plus other racks would lose network connectivity if they were unlucky enough to be on a network subsystem that got power from an affected rack. This extended the failure domain to as many as 13 racks. Many users felt it was unfair that they were suffering even though the repair didn't directly affect them.

There were additional unaligned failure domains related to cooling and which machines were managed by which cluster manager. As a result, these misalignments were not just an inconvenience to some but a major factor contributing to system availability.

Eventually a new datacenter design was created that aligned all physical failure domains to a common multiple. In some cases, this meant working with vendors to create custom designs. Old datacenters were eventually retrofitted to the new design at great expense.

We commonly hear of datacenters that have perfect alignment of power, networking, and other factors but in which an unexpected misalignment results in a major outage. For example, consider a datacenter with 10 domains, each independently powered, cooled, and networked. Suppose the building has two connections to the outside world and the related equipment is located based on where the connections come into the building. If cooling fails in the two domains that include those connections, suddenly all 10 domains have no connectivity to the outside world.

6.5 Software Failures

As long as there has been software, there have been software bugs. Long-running software can die unexpectedly. Software can hang and not respond. For all these reasons, software needs resilience features, too.

6.5.1 Software Crashes

A common failure in a system is that software crashes, or prematurely exits. There are many reasons software may crash and many ways to respond. Server software is generally intended to be long lived. For example, a server that provides a particular API is expected to run forever unless the configuration changes in a way that requires a restart or the service is decommissioned.

There are two categories of crashes:

- **A regular crash** occurs when the software does something prohibited by the operating system. For example, due to a software bug, the program may try to write to memory that is marked read-only by the operating system. The OS detects this and kills the process.
- **A panic** occurs when the software itself detects something is wrong and decides the best course is to exit. For example, the software may detect a situation that shouldn't exist and cannot be corrected. The software's author may have decided the safest thing to do in such a scenario is to exit. For example, if internal data structures are corrupted and there is no safe way to rectify them, it is best to stop work immediately rather than continue with bad data. A panic is, essentially, an intentional crash.

Automated Restarts and Escalation

The easiest way to deal with a software crash is to restart the software. Sometimes the problem is transient and a restart is all that is needed to fix it. Such restarts should be automated. With thousands of servers, it is inefficient for a human to constantly be checking processes to see if they are down and restarting them as needed. A program that handles this task called a **process watcher**.

However, restarting a down process is not as easy as it sounds. If it immediately crashes again and again, we need to do something else; otherwise, we will be wasting CPU time without improving the situation. Usually the process watcher will detect that the process has been restarted x times in y minutes and consider that behavior cause to escalate the issue. Escalation involves not restarting the process and instead reporting the problem to a human. An example threshold might be that something has restarted more than five times in a minute.

Less frequent restarts are often a sign of other problems. One restart every hour is not cause for alarm but it should be investigated. Often these slower restart issues are detected by the monitoring system rather than the process watcher.

Automated Crash Data Collection and Analysis

Every crash should be logged. Crashes usually leave behind a lot of information in a crash report. The crash report includes statistics such as amount of RAM and CPU usage at the time of the process's death, as well as detailed information such as a **traceback** of which function call and line of code was executing when the problem occurred. A **coredump**—a file containing the contents of the process's memory—is often written out during a crash. Developers use this file to aid debugging.

Automated collection and storage of crash reports is useful because this information may be lost if it is not collected quickly; the information may be deleted or the machine may go away. Collecting the information is inconvenient for humans but easy for automation. This is especially true in a system with hundreds of machines and hundreds of thousands of processes. Storing the reports centrally permits data mining and analysis. A simple analytical result, such as which systems crash the most, can be a useful engineering metric. More intricate analysis can find bugs in common software libraries, the operating system, hardware, or even particular chips.

6.5.2 Software Hangs

Sometimes when software has a problem it does not crash, but instead hangs or gets caught in an infinite loop.

A strategy for detecting hangs is to monitor the server and detect if it has stopped processing requests. We can passively observe request counts or actively test the system by sending requests and verifying that a reply is generated within a certain amount of time. These active requests, which are called pings, are designed to be light-weight, simply verifying basic functionality.

If pings are sent at a specific, periodic rate and are used to detect hangs as well as crashes, they are called **heartbeat requests**. When hangs are detected, an error can be generated, an alert sent, or an attempt to restart the service can be made. If the server is one of many replicas behind a load balancer, rather than simply restarting it, you can remove it from the load balancing rotation and investigate the problem. Sometimes adding a new replica is significantly more work than returning a replica that has been repaired to service. For example, in the Google File System, a new replica added to the system requires replicating possibly tera-bytes of files. This can flood the network. Fixing a hung replica and returning it to service simply results in the existing data being revalidated, which is a much more light-weight task.

Another technique for dealing with software hangs is called a **watchdog timer**. A hardware clock keeps incrementing a counter. If the counter exceeds a certain value, a hardware subsystem will detect this and reboot the system. Software run-ning on the system resets the counter to zero after any successful operation. If the software hangs, the resets will stop and soon the system will be rebooted. As long as the software keeps running, the counter will be reset frequently enough to prevent a reboot.

A watchdog timer is most commonly used with operating system kernels and embedded systems. Enabling the Linux kernel watchdog timer on a system with appropriate hardware can be used to reduce the need to physically visit a machine when the kernel hangs or to avoid the need to purchase expensive remote power control systems.

Like crashes, hangs should be logged and analyzed. Frequent hangs are an indication of hardware issues, locking problems, and other bugs that should be fixed before they become big problems.

6.5.3 Query of Death

Sometimes a particular API call or query exercises an untested code path that causes a crash, a long delay, or an infinite loop. We call such a query a **query of death** because it kills the service.

When users discover a query of death for a popular web site, they let all of their friends know. Soon much of the internet will also be trying it to see what a crashing web site looks like. The better known your company is, the faster word will spread.

The best fix is to eliminate the bug that causes the problem. Unfortunately, it can take a long time to fix the code and push a new release. A quick fix is needed in the meantime.

A widely used strategy is to have a **banned query list** that is easy to update and communicate to all the frontends. The frontends automatically reject any query that is found on the banned query list.

However, that solution still requires human intervention. A more automated mechanism is required, especially when a query has a large fan-out. For example, suppose the query is received and then sent to 1000 other servers, each one holding

1/1000th of the database. A query of death would kill 1000 servers along with all the other queries that are in flight.

Dean and Barroso (2013) describe a preventive measure pioneered at Google called **canary requests**. In situations where one would normally send the same request to thousands of leaf servers, systems using this approach send the query to one or two leaf servers. These are the canary requests. Queries are sent to the remaining servers only if replies to the canary requests are received in a reasonable period of time. If the leaf servers crash or hang while the canary requests are being processed, the system flags the request as potentially dangerous and prevents further crashes by not sending it to the remaining leaf servers. Using this technique Google is able to achieve a measure of robustness in the face of difficult-to-predict programming errors as well as malicious denial-of-service attacks.

6.6 Physical Failures

Distributed systems also need to be resilient when faced with physical failures. The physical devices used in a distributed system can fail on many levels. Physical failures can range from the smallest electronic component all the way up to a country's power grid. Providing resiliency through the use of redundancy at every level is expensive and difficult to scale. You need a strategy for providing resiliency against hardware failures without adding excessive cost.

6.6.1 Parts and Components

Many components of a computer can fail. The parts whose utilization you monitor can fail, such as the CPU, the RAM, the disks, and the network interfaces. Supporting components can also fail, such as fans, power supplies, batteries, and motherboards.

Historically, when the CPU died, the entire machine was unusable. Multiprocessor computers are now quite common, however, so it is more likely that a machine can survive so long as one processor is still functioning. If the machine is already resilient in that way, we must monitor for $N + 0$ situations.

RAM

RAM often fails for strange reasons. Sometimes a slight power surge can affect RAM. Other times a single bit flips its value because a cosmic ray from another star system just happened to fly through it. Really!

Many memory systems store with each byte an additional bit (a **parity bit**) that enables them to detect errors, or two additional bits (**error-correcting code** or ECC memory) that enable them to perform error correction. This adds cost. It also drags down reliability because now there are 25 percent more bits and, therefore, the MTTF becomes 25 percent worse. (Although most of these failures are now corrected invisibly, the failures are still happening and can be detected via monitoring systems. If the failures persist, the component needs to be replaced.)

When writing to parity bit memory, the system counts how many 1 bits are in the byte and stores a 0 in the parity bit if the total is even, or a 1 if the total is odd. Anytime memory is read, the parity is checked and mismatches are reported to the operating system. This is sufficient to detect all single-bit errors, or any multiple-bit errors that do not preserve parity. ECC memory uses two additional bits and Hamming code algorithms that can correct single-bit errors and detect multiple-bit errors.

The likelihood of two or more bit errors increases the longer that values sit in memory unread and the more RAM there is in a system.

One can save money by having no parity or ECC bits—an approach commonly used with low-end chipsets—but then all software has to do its own checksumming and error correction. This is slow and costly, and you or your developers probably won't do it. So spend the money on ECC, instead.

Disks

Disks fail often because they have moving parts. Solid-state drives (SSDs), which have no moving parts, wear out since each block is rated to be written only a certain number of times.

The usual solution is to use RAID level 1 or higher to achieve $N + 1$ redundancy or better. However, RAID systems are costly and their internal firmware is often a source of frustration, as it is difficult to configure without interrupting service. (A full explanation of RAID levels is not included here but can be found in our other book, *The Practice of System and Network Administration*.)

File systems such as ZFS, Btrfs and Hadoop HDFS store data reliably by providing their own RAID or RAID-like functionality. In those cases hardware RAID controllers are not needed.

We recommend the strategic use of RAID controllers, deploying them only where required. For example, a widely used distributed computing environment is the Apache Hadoop system. The first three machines in a Hadoop cluster are special master service machines that store critical configuration information. This information is not replicated and is difficult to rebuild if lost. The other machines in a Hadoop cluster are data nodes that store replicas of data. In this environment RAID is normally used on the master machines. Implementing RAID there has a fixed cost, as no more than three machines with RAID controllers are needed. Data nodes are added when more capacity is needed. They are built without RAID since Hadoop replicates data as needed, detecting failures and creating new replicas as needed. This strategy has a cost benefit in that the expensive hardware is a fixed quantity while the nodes used to expand the system are the inexpensive ones.

Power Supplies

Each machine has a **power supply** that converts standard electric voltages into levels needed by the computer. Power supplies frequently die. Servers, network equipment, and many other systems can be purchased with redundant power supplies. $N + 1$ and $N + 2$ configurations are commonly available.

As with RAID, a strategic use of redundant power supplies is best. They are not needed when the system itself is a replica or some other resilience technique is used at a higher level. Do use such power supplies for the remaining systems that are not redundant.

Network Interfaces

Network interfaces or network connections themselves often fail. Multiple links can be used in $N + 1$ configurations. There are many standards, too many to detail here.

Some are load sharing, others are active–passive. Some require that all the near-end (machine) connections be plugged into the same network interface controller (NIC) daughterboard. If two physical ports share the same daughterboard, the failure of one may cause the other to fail. Some require that all the far-end (switch) connections be plugged into the same switch, while others do not have such a limit. The latter approach provides resiliency against switch failure, not just NIC failure.

Many different algorithms are available for determining which packets go over which physical link. With some, it is possible for packets to arrive out of order. While all protocols should handle this situation, many do not do it well.

Longitudinal Studies on Hardware Failures

Google has published to two longitudinal studies of hardware failures. Most studies of such failures are done in laboratory environments. Google meticulously collects component failure information on its entire fleet of machines, providing probably the best insight into actual failure patterns. Both studies are worth reading.

"Failure Trends in a Large Disk Drive Population" (Pinheiro, Weber & Barroso 2007) analyzed a large population of hard disks over many years. The authors did not find temperature or activity levels to correlate with drive failures. They found that after a single scan error was detected, drives are 39 times more likely to fail within the next 60 days. They discovered the "bathtub failure curve" where failures tend to happen either in the first month or only many years later.

"DRAM Errors in the Wild: A Large-Scale Field Study" (Schroeder, Pinheiro & Weber 2009) analyzed memory errors in a large fleet of machines in datacenters over a period of 2.5 years. These authors found that error rates were orders of magnitude higher than previously reported and were dominated by hard errors—the kind that ECC can detect but not correct. Temperature had comparatively small effect compared to other factors.

6.6.2 Machines

Machine failures are generally the result of components that have died. If the system has subsystems that are $N + 1$, a double failure results in machine death.

A machine that crashes will often come back to life if it is power cycled off and back on, often with a delay to let the components drain. This process can be automated, although it is important that the automation be able to distinguish between not being able to reach the machine and the machine being down.

If a power cycle does not revive the machine, the machine must be diagnosed, repaired, and brought back into service. Much of this can be automated, especially the reinstallation of the operating system. This topic is covered in more detail in Section 10.4.1.

Earlier we described situations where machines fail to boot up after a power outage. These problems can be discovered preemptively by periodically rebooting them. For example, Google drains machines one by one for kernel upgrades. As a result of this practice, each machine is rebooted in a controlled way approximately every three months. This reduces the number of surprises found during power outages.

6.6.3 Load Balancers

Whether a server fails because of a dead machine, a network issue, or a bug, a resilient way to deal with this failure is by use of replicas and some kind of load balancer.

The same load balancer described previously to gain scale is also used to gain resiliency. However, when using this approach to gain scale, each replica added was intended to add capacity that would be used. Now we are adding spare capacity that is an insurance policy we hope not to use.

When using a load balancer it is important to consider whether it is being used for scaling, resiliency, or both. We have observed situations where it was assumed that the presence of a load balancer means the system scales and is resilient automatically. This is not true. The load balancer is not magic. It is a technology that can be used for many different things.

Scale versus Resiliency

If we are load balancing over two machines, each at 40 percent utilization, then either machine can die and the remaining machines will be 80 percent utilized. In such a case, the load balancer is used for resiliency.

If we are load balancing over two machines, each at 80 percent utilization, then there is no spare capacity available if one goes down. If one machine died, the remaining replica would receive all the traffic, which is 160 percent of what the machine can handle. The machine will be overloaded and may cease to function. Two machines each at 80 percent utilization represents an $N + 0$ configuration. In this situation, the load balancer is used for scale, not resiliency.

In both of the previous examples, the same configuration was used: two machines and a load balancer. Yet in one case resiliency was achieved and in the other case scale was achieved. The difference between the two was the utilization, or traffic, being processed. In other words, 50 percent is 100 full when you have only two servers.

If we take the second example and add a third replica but the amount of traffic does not change, then 160 percent of the total 300 percent capacity is in use. This is an $N + 1$ configuration since one replica can die and the remaining replicas can still handle the load. In this case, the load balancer is used for both scale and resiliency.

A load balancer provides scale when we use it to keep up with capacity, and resiliency when we use it to exceed capacity. If utilization increases and we have not added additional replicas, we run the risk of no longer being able to claim resiliency. If traffic is high during the day and low at night, we can end up with a system that is resilient during some hours of the day and not others.

Load Balancer Resiliency

Load balancers themselves can become a single point of failure (SPOF). Redundant pairs of load balancers are often used to remedy this shortcoming.

One strategy is a simple failover. One load balancer (the primary) receives all traffic, and the other load balancer (the secondary) monitors the health of the primary by sending heartbeat messages to it. If a loss of heartbeat is detected, the secondary takes over and becomes the active load balancer. Any TCP connections that were "in flight" are disconnected since the primary is unaware of them.

Another strategy is stateful failover. It resembles simple failover except that the two load balancers exchange enough information, or state, so that both know all existing TCP connections. As a consequence, those connections are not lost in case of failover.

A single pair of load balancers are often used for many different services—for example, many different web sites. All the web sites are homed at one load balancer and the other is used for failover. When using non-stateful load balancers, a common trick is to home half the web sites on one load balancer and half the web sites on the other load balancer. In this case, in the event of a failover half as many connections are lost.

Hardware or Software Load Balancers

Load balancers may be hardware appliances that are purpose-built for the task. They may also be software-based programs that run on standard computers. The hardware appliances are usually highly tuned and feature-rich. The software-based ones are more flexible.

For smaller services, the load balancer software might run on the machines providing the services. Pushing the load balancing function to the machines themselves reduces the amount of hardware to be managed. However, now the processing of the load balancing software competes for CPU and other resources with the services running on the box. This approach is not recommended for high-volume load balancing but is fine for many situations.

Software load balancing can also be pushed even further down the stack to the clients themselves. Client-side load balancing requires that the client software know which servers are available and do its own health checking, server selection, and so on. This is frequently done for internal services since they are usually more tightly controlled. The client library can load the configuration from a central place, load balance requests, and detect and route around failures. The downside is that to change algorithms or fix bugs, the client library must be changed, which requires updating the software anywhere it is used.

6.6.4 Racks

Racks themselves do not usually fail. They are steel and have no active components. However, many failures are rack-wide. For example, a rack may have a single power feed or network uplink that is shared by all the equipment in the rack. Intrusive maintenance is often done one rack at a time.

As a result, a rack is usually a failure domain. In fact, intentionally designing each rack to be its own failure domain turns out to be a good, manageable size for most distributed systems.

Rack Diversity

You can choose to break a service into many replicas and put one replica in each rack. With this arrangement, the service has **rack diversity**. A simple example would be a DNS service where each DNS server is in a different rack so that a rack-wide failure does not cause a service outage.

In a Hadoop cluster, data files are stored on multiple machines for safety. The system tries to achieve rack diversity by making sure that at least one replica of any data block is in a different rack than the other data blocks.

Rack Locality

Making a service component self-contained within a single rack also offers certain benefits. Bandwidth is plentiful within a rack but sparse between racks. All the machines in the rack connect to the same switch at the top of the rack. This switch has enough internal bandwidth that any machine can talk to any machine within the rack at full bandwidth, and all machines can do this at the same time—a scheme called **non-blocking bandwidth**. Between racks there is less bandwidth. Rack uplinks are often 10 times the links between the machines, but they are a shared resource used by all the machines in the rack (typically 20 or 40). There is contention for bandwidth between racks. The article "A Guided Tour through Data-center Networking" (Abts & Felderman 2012) drills down into this topic using Google's networks as examples.

Because bandwidth is plentiful inside the rack and the rack is a failure domain, often a service component is designed to fit within a rack. Small queries come in, they use a lot of bandwidth to generate the answer, and a small or medium-size reply leaves. This model fits well given the bandwidth restrictions.

The service component is then replicated on many racks. Each replica has **rack locality**, in that it is self-contained within the rack. It is designed to take advantage of the high bandwidth and the rack-sized failure domain.

Rack-sized replicas are sometimes called **pods**. A pod is self-contained and often forms its own security domain. For example, a billing system may be made up of pods, each one self-contained and designed to handle bill processing for a specific group of customers.

Clos Networking

It is reasonable to expect that eventually there will be network products on the open market that provide non-blocking, full-speed connectivity between any two machines in an entire datacenter. We've known how to do this since 1953 (Clos 1953). When this product introduction happens, it will change how we design services.

6.6.5 Datacenters

Datacenters can also be failure domains. An entire datacenter can go down due to natural disasters, cooling failures, power failures, or an unfortunate backhoe dig that takes out all network connections in one swipe.

Similar to rack diversity and rack locality, datacenter diversity and datacenter locality also exist. Bandwidth within a datacenter is generally fast, though not as fast as within a rack. Bandwidth between datacenters is generally slower and, unlike with data transmitted within a datacenter, is often billed for by the gigabyte.

Each replica of a service should be self-contained within a datacenter but the entire service should have datacenter diversity. Google requires $N + 2$ diversity as a minimum requirement for user-facing services. That way, when one datacenter is intentionally brought down for maintenance, another can go down due to unforeseen circumstances without impacting the service.

6.7 Overload Failures

Distributed systems need to be resilient when faced with high levels of load that can happen as the result of a temporary surge in traffic, an intentional attack, or automated systems querying the system at a high rate, possibly for malicious reasons.

6.7.1 Traffic Surges

Systems should be resilient against temporary periods of high load. For example, a small service may become overloaded after being mentioned in a popular web site or news broadcast. Even a large service can become overloaded due to load being shifted to the remaining replicas when one fails.

The primary strategy for dealing with this problem in user-facing services is graceful degradation. This topic was covered in Section 2.1.10.

Dynamic Resource Allocation

Another strategy is to add capacity dynamically. With this approach, a system would detect that a service is becoming overloaded and allocate an unused machine from a pool of idle machines that are running but otherwise unconfigured. An automated system would configure the machine and use it to add capacity to the overloaded service, thereby resolving the issue.

It can be costly to have idle capacity but this cost can be mitigated by using a **shared pool**. That is, one pool of idle machines serves a group of services. The first service to become overloaded allocates the machines. If the pool is large enough, more than one service can become overloaded at the same time. There should also be a mechanism for services to give back machines when the need disappears.

Additional capacity can be found at other service providers as well. A public cloud computing provider can be used as the shared pool. Usually you will not have to pay for unused capacity.

Shared resource pools are not just appropriate for machines, but may also be used for storage and other resources.

Load Shedding

Another strategy is **load shedding**. With this strategy the service turns away some users so that other users can have a good experience.

To make an analogy, an overloaded phone system doesn't suddenly disconnect all existing calls. Instead, it responds to any new attempts to make a call with a "fast busy" tone so that the person will try to make the call later. An overloaded web site should likewise give some users an immediate response, such as a simple "come back later" web page, rather than requiring them to time out after minutes of waiting.

A variation of load shedding is stopping certain tasks that can be put off until later. For example, low-priority database updates could be queued up for processing later; a social network that stores reputation points for users might store the fact that points have been awarded rather than processing them; nightly bulk file transfers might be delayed if the network is overloaded.

That said, tasks that can be put off for a couple of hours might cause problems if they are put off forever. There is, after all, a reason they exist. For any activity that is delayed due to load shedding, there must be a plan on how such a delay is handled. Establish a service level agreement (SLA) to determine how long something can be delayed and to identify a timeline of actions that should be undertaken to mitigate problems or extend the deadlines. Low-priority updates might become a high priority after a certain amount of time. If many systems are turned off due to load shedding, it might be possible to enable them, one at a time, to let each catch up.

To be able to manage such situations one must have visibility into the system so that prioritization decisions can be made. For example, knowing the age of a task (how long it has been delayed), predicting how long it will take to process, and indicating how close it is to a deadline will permit operations personnel to gauge when delayed items should be continued.

Delayed Work Reduces Quality

An old version of Google Web Search had two parts: the user-facing web front-end and the system that received and processed updates to the search index (corpus). These updates arrived in large chunks that had to be distributed to each frontend.

The quality of the search system was measured in terms of how fresh the corpus was across all the web frontends.

The monitoring dashboard displayed the freshness of shards in each frontend. It listed how many shards were in each freshness bucket: up-to-date, 1 hour old, 2 hours old, 4 hours old, and so on. With this visibility, operations staff could see when something was wrong and gain an insight into which frontends were the most out of date.

If the system was overloaded, the updater system was paused to free up resources for handling the additional load. The dashboard enabled operations staff to understand the effects of the pause. They could unpause high-priority updates to maintain at least minimal freshness.

6.7.2 DoS and DDoS Attacks

A **denial-of-service (DoS)** attack is an attempt to bring down a service by sending a large volume of queries. A **distributed denial-of-service (DDoS)** attack occurs when many computers around the Internet are used in a coordinated fashion to create an extremely large DoS attack. DDoS attacks are commonly initiated from **botnets**, which are large collections of computers around the world that have been successfully infiltrated and are now controlled centrally, without the knowledge of their owners.

Blocking the requests is usually not a successful defense against a DDoS attack. Attackers can forge packets in a way that obscures where the attack is coming from, thereby making it impossible for you to construct filters that would block the attack without blocking legitimate traffic. If they do come from a fixed set of sources, simply not responding to the requests still hogs bandwidth used to receive the attack—and that alone can overload a network. The attack must be blocked from outside your network, usually by the ISP you connect to. Most ISPs do not provide this kind of filtering.

The best defense is to simply have more bandwidth than the attacker. This is very difficult considering that most DDoS attacks involve thousands of machines. Very large companies are able to use this line of defense. Smaller companies can use DDoS attack mitigation services. Many CDN vendors (see Section 5.8) provide this service since they have bandwidth available.

Sometimes a DDoS attack does not aim to exhaust bandwidth but rather to consume large amounts of processing time or load. For example, one might find a small query that demands a large amount of resources to reply to. In this case the banned query list described previously can be used to block this query until a software release fixes the problem.

6.7.3 Scraping Attacks

A scraping attack is an automated process that acts like a web browser to query for information and then extracts (scrapes) the useful information from the HTML pages it receives. For example, if you wanted a list of every book ever published but didn't want to pay for such a database from a library supply company, you could write a program that sends millions of search requests to Amazon.com, parse the HTML pages, and extract the book titles to build your database. This use of Amazon is considered an attack because it violates the company's terms of service.

Such an attack must be defended against to prevent theft of information, to prevent someone from violating the terms of service, and because a very fast scraper is equivalent to a DoS attack. Detecting such an attack is usually done by having all frontends report information about the queries they are receiving to a central scraping detector service.

The scraping detector warns the frontends of any suspected attacks. If there is high confidence that a particular source is involved in an attack, the frontends can block or refuse to answer the queries. If confidence in the source of the attack is low, the frontends can respond in other ways. For example, they can ask the user to prove that he or she is a human by using a Captcha or other system that can distinguish human from machine input.

Some scraping is permitted, even desired. A scraping detector should have a whitelist that permits search engine crawlers and other permitted agents to do their job.

6.8 Human Error

As we design systems to be more resilient to hardware and software failures, the remaining failures are likely to be due to human error. While this sounds obvious, this trend was not recognized until the groundbreaking paper "Why Do Internet Services Fail, and What Can Be Done about It?" was published in 2003 (Oppenheimer, Ganapathi & Patterson 2003).

The strategies for dealing with human error can be categorized as getting better humans, removing humans from the loop, and detecting human errors and working around them.

We get better humans by having better operational practices, especially those that exercise the skills and behaviors that most need improvement. (See Chapter 15.)

We remove humans from the loop through automation. Humans may get sloppy and not do as much checking for errors during a procedure, but automation, once written, will always check its work (See Chapter 12.)

Detecting human errors and working around them is also a function of automation. A **pre-check** is automation that checks inputs and prevents a process from running if the tests fail. For example, a pre-check can verify that a recently edited configuration file has no syntax errors and meets certain other quality criteria. Failing the pre-check would prevent the configuration file from being put into use.

While pre-checks are intended to prevent problems, the reality is that they tend to lag behind experience. That is, after each outage we add new pre-checks to prevent that same human error from creating future outages.

Another common pre-check is for large changes. If a typical change usually consists of only a few lines, a pre-check might require additional approval if the change is larger than a particular number of lines. The change might be in the size of the input, the number of changed lines between the current input and new input, or the number of changed lines between the current and new output. For example, a configuration file may be used to control a system that generates other files. The growth of the output by more than a certain percentage may trigger additional approval.

Another way to be resilient to human error is to have two humans check all changes. Many source code control systems can be configured to not accept changes from a user until a second user approves them. All system administration that is done via changes to files in a source code repository are then checked by a second pair of eyes. This is a very common operational method at Google.

6.9 Summary

Resiliency is a system's ability to constructively deal with failures. A resilient system detects failure and routes around it.

Failure is a normal part of operations and can occur at any level. Large systems magnify the risk of small failures. A one in a million failure is a daily occurrence if you have enough machines.

Failures come from many sources. Software can fail unintentionally due to bugs or intentionally to prevent a bad situation from getting worse. Hardware can also fail, with the scope of the failure ranging from the smallest component to the largest network. Failure domains can be any size: a device, a computer, a rack, a datacenter, or even an entire company.

The amount of capacity in a system is $N + M$, where N is the amount of capacity used to provide a service and M is the amount of spare capacity available, which can be used in the event of a failure. A system that is $N + 1$ fault tolerant can survive one unit of failure and remain operational.

The most common way to route around failure is through replication of services. A service may be replicated one or more times per failure domain to provide resilience greater than the domain.

Failures can also come from external sources that overload a system, and from human mistakes. There are countermeasures to nearly every failure imaginable. We can't anticipate all failures, but we can plan for them, design solutions, prioritize their implementation, and repeat the process.

Exercises

1. What are the major sources of failure in distributed computing systems?
2. What are the most common failures: software, hardware, or human? Justify your answer.
3. Select one resiliency technique and give an example of a failure and the way in which the resiliency technique would prevent a user-visible outage. Do this for one technique in each of these sections: 6.5, 6.6, 6.7, and 6.8.
4. If a load balancer is being used, the system is automatically scalable and resilient. Do you agree or disagree with this statement? Justify your answer.
5. Which resiliency techniques or technologies are in use in your environment?
6. Where would you like to add resiliency in your current environment? Describe what you would change and which techniques you would apply.
7. In your environment, give an example of graceful degradation under load, or explain how you would implement it if it doesn't currently exist.
8. How big can a RAID5 array be? For example, how large can it be before the parity checking scheme is likely to miss an error? How long can the rebuild time be before MTBF puts the system at risk of a second failure?
9. The phrase "Eat right. Exercise. Die anyway." is mentioned on page 123. Explain how this relates to distributed computing.

Part II

Operations: Running It

Chapter 7

Operations in a Distributed World

> The rate at which organizations learn may soon become the only sustainable source of competitive advantage.
>
> —Peter Senge

Part I of this book discussed how to build distributed systems. Now we discuss how to run such systems.

The work done to keep a system running is called **operations**. More specifically, operations is the work done to keep a system running in a way that meets or exceeds operating parameters specified by a service level agreement (SLA). Operations includes all aspects of a service's life cycle: from initial launch to the final decommissioning and everything in between.

Operational work tends to focus on availability, speed and performance, security, capacity planning, and software/hardware upgrades. The failure to do any of these well results in a system that is unreliable. If a service is slow, users will assume it is broken. If a system is insecure, outsiders can take it down. Without proper capacity planning, it will become overloaded and fail. Upgrades, done badly, result in downtime. If upgrades aren't done at all, bugs will go unfixed. Because all of these activities ultimately affect the reliability of the system, Google calls its operations team Site Reliability Engineering (SRE). Many companies have followed suit.

Operations is a team sport. Operations is not done by a single person but rather by a team of people working together. For that reason much of what we describe will be processes and policies that help you work as a team, not as a group of individuals. In some companies, processes seem to be bureaucratic mazes that slow things down. As we describe here—and more important, in our professional experience—good processes are exactly what makes it possible to run very large

> *Terms to Know*
>
> **Innovate:** Doing (good) things we haven't done before.
>
> **Machine:** A virtual or physical machine.
>
> **Oncall:** Being available as first responder to an outage or alert.
>
> **Server:** Software that provides a function or API. (Not a piece of hardware.)
>
> **Service:** A user-visible system or product composed of one or more servers.
>
> **Soft launch:** Launching a new service without publicly announcing it. This way traffic grows slowly as word of mouth spreads, which gives operations some cushion to fix problems or scale the system before too many people have seen it.
>
> **SRE:** Site Reliability Engineer, the Google term for systems administrators who maintain live services.
>
> **Stakeholders:** People and organizations that are seen as having an interest in a project's success.

computing systems. In other words, process is what makes it possible for teams to do the right thing, again and again.

This chapter starts with some operations management background, then discusses the operations service life cycle, and ends with a discussion of typical operations work strategies. All of these topics will be expanded upon in the chapters that follow.

7.1 Distributed Systems Operations

To understand distributed systems operations, one must first understand how it is different from typical enterprise IT. One must also understand the source of tension between operations and developers, and basic techniques for scaling operations.

7.1.1 SRE versus Traditional Enterprise IT

System administration is a continuum. On one end is a typical IT department, responsible for traditional desktop and client–server computing infrastructure, often called enterprise IT. On the other end is an SRE or similar team responsible for a distributed computing environment, often associated with web sites and other services. While this may be a broad generalization, it serves to illustrate some important differences.

SRE is different from an enterprise IT department because SREs tend to be focused on providing a single service or a well-defined set of services. A traditional enterprise IT department tends to have broad responsibility for desktop services, back-office services, and everything in between ("everything with a power plug"). SRE's customers tend to be the product management of the service while IT customers are the end users themselves. This means SRE efforts are focused on a few select business metrics rather than being pulled in many directions by users, each of whom has his or her own priorities.

Another difference is in the attitude toward uptime. SREs maintain services that have demanding, 24×7 uptime requirements. This creates a focus on preventing problems rather than reacting to outages, and on performing complex but non-intrusive maintenance procedures. IT tends to be granted flexibility with respect to scheduling downtime and has SLAs that focus on how quickly service can be restored in the event of an outage. In the SRE view, downtime is something to be avoided and service should not stop while services are undergoing maintenance.

SREs tend to manage services that are constantly changing due to new software releases and additions to capacity. IT tends to run services that are upgraded rarely. Often IT services are built by external contractors who go away once the system is stable.

SREs maintain systems that are constantly being scaled to handle more traffic and larger workloads. Latency, or how fast a particular request takes to process, is managed as well as overall throughput. Efficiency becomes a concern because a little waste per machine becomes a big waste when there are hundreds or thousands of machines. In IT, systems are often built for environments that expect a modest increase in workload per year. In this case a workable strategy is to build the system large enough to handle the projected workload for the next few years, when the system is expected to be replaced.

As a result of these requirements, systems in SRE tend to be bespoke systems, built on platforms that are home-grown or integrated from open source or other third-party components. They are not "off the shelf" or turn key systems. They are actively managed, while IT systems may be unchanged from their initial delivery state. Because of these differences, distributed computing services are best managed by a separate team, with separate management, with bespoke operational and management practices.

While there are many such differences, recently IT departments have begun to see a demand for uptime and scalability similar to that seen in SRE environments. Therefore the management techniques from distributed computing are rapidly being adopted in the enterprise.

7.1.2   Change versus Stability

There is a tension between the desire for stability and the desire for change. Operations teams tend to favor stability; developers desire change. Consider how each group is evaluated during end-of-the-year performance reviews. A developer is praised for writing code that makes it into production. Changes that result in a tangible difference to the service are rewarded above any other accomplishment. Therefore, developers want new releases pushed into production often. Operations, in contrast, is rewarded for achieving compliance with SLAs, most of which relate to uptime. Therefore stability is the priority.

A system starts at a baseline of stability. A change is then made. All changes have some kind of a destabilizing effect. Eventually the system becomes stable again, usually through some kind of intervention. This is called the **change-instability cycle**.

All software roll-outs affect stability. A change may introduce bugs, which are fixed through workarounds and new software releases. A release that introduces no new bugs still creates a destabilizing effect due to the process of shifting workloads away from machines about to be upgraded. Non-software changes also have a destabilizing effect. A network change may make the local network less stable while the change propagates throughout the network.

Because of the tension between the operational desire for stability and the developer desire for change, there must be mechanisms to reach a balance.

One strategy is to prioritize work that improves stability over work that adds new features. For example, bug fixes would have a higher priority than feature requests. With this approach, a major release introduces many new features, the next few releases focus on fixing bugs, and then a new major release starts the cycle over again. If engineering management is pressured to focus on new features and neglect bug fixes, the result is a system that slowly destabilizes until it spins out of control.

Another strategy is to align the goals of developers and operational staff. Both parties become responsible for SLA compliance as well as the velocity (rate of change) of the system. Both have a component of their annual review that is tied to SLA compliance and both have a portion tied to the on-time delivery of new features.

Organizations that have been the most successful at aligning goals like this have restructured themselves so that developers and operations work as one team. This is the premise of the DevOps movement, which will be described in Chapter 8.

Another strategy is to budget time for stability improvements and time for new features. Software engineering organizations usually have a way to estimate the size of a software request or the amount of time it is expected to take to complete. Each new release has a certain size or time budget; within that budget a certain amount of stability-improvement work is allocated. The case study at the end of Section 2.2.2 is an example of this approach. Similarly, this allocation can be achieved by assigning dedicated people to stability-related code changes.

The budget can also be based on an SLA. A certain amount of instability is expected each month, which is considered a budget. Each roll-out uses some of the budget, as do instability-related bugs. Developers can maximize the number of roll-outs that can be done each month by dedicating effort to improve the code that causes this instability. This creates a positive feedback loop. An example of this is Google's Error Budgets, which are more fully explained in Section 19.4.

7.1.3 Defining SRE

The core practices of SRE were refined for more than 10 years at Google before being enumerated in public. In his keynote address at the first USENIX SREcon, Benjamin Treynor Sloss (2014), Vice President of Site Reliability Engineering at Google, listed them as follows:

Site Reliability Practices

1. Hire only coders.
2. Have an SLA for your service.
3. Measure and report performance against the SLA.
4. Use Error Budgets and gate launches on them.
5. Have a common staffing pool for SRE and Developers.
6. Have excess Ops work overflow to the Dev team.
7. Cap SRE operational load at 50 percent.
8. Share 5 percent of Ops work with the Dev team.
9. Oncall teams should have at least eight people at one location, or six people at each of multiple locations.
10. Aim for a maximum of two events per oncall shift.
11. Do a postmortem for every event.
12. Postmortems are blameless and focus on process and technology, not people.

The first principle for site reliability engineering is that SREs must be able to code. An SRE might not be a full-time software developer, but he or she should be able to solve nontrivial problems by writing code. When asked to do 30 iterations of a task, an SRE should do the first two, get bored, and automate the rest. An SRE must have enough software development experience to be able to communicate with developers on their level and have an appreciation for what developers do, and for what computers can and can't do.

When SREs and developers come from a common staffing pool, that means that projects are allocated a certain number of engineers; these engineers may be developers or SREs. The end result is that each SRE needed means one fewer developer in the team. Contrast this to the case at most companies where system administrators and developers are allocated from teams with separate budgets. Rationally a project wants to maximize the number of developers, since they write new features. The common staffing pool encourages the developers to create systems that can be operated efficiently so as to minimize the number of SREs needed.

Another way to encourage developers to write code that minimizes operational load is to require that excess operational work overflows to the developers. This practice discourages developers from taking shortcuts that create undue operational load. The developers would share any such burden. Likewise, by requiring developers to perform 5 percent of operational work, developers stay in tune with operational realities.

Within the SRE team, capping the operational load at 50 percent limits the amount of manual labor done. Manual labor has a lower return on investment than, for example, writing code to replace the need for such labor. This is discussed in Section 12.4.2, "Reducing Toil."

Many SRE practices relate to finding balance between the desire for change and the need for stability. The most important of these is the Google SRE practice called Error Budgets, explained in detail in Section 19.4.

Central to the Error Budget is the SLA. All services must have an SLA, which specifies how reliable the system is going to be. The SLA becomes the standard by which all work is ultimately measured. SLAs are discussed in Chapter 16.

Any outage or other major SLA-related event should be followed by the creation of a written postmortem that includes details of what happened, along with analysis and suggestions for how to prevent such a situation in the future. This report is shared within the company so that the entire organization can learn from the experience. Postmortems focus on the process and the technology, not finding who to blame. Postmortems are the topic of Section 14.3.2. The person who is oncall is responsible for responding to any SLA-related events and producing the postmortem report.

Oncall is not just a way to react to problems, but rather a way to reduce future problems. It must be done in a way that is not unsustainably stressful for those oncall, and it drives behaviors that encourage long-term fixes and problem prevention. Oncall teams are made up of at least eight members at one location, or six members at two locations. Teams of this size will be oncall often enough that their skills do not get stale, and their shifts can be short enough that each catches no more than two outage events. As a result, each member has enough time to follow through on each event, performing the required long-term solution. Managing oncall this way is the topic of Chapter 14.

Other companies have adopted the SRE job title for their system administrators who maintain live production services. Each company applies a different set of practices to the role. These are the practices that define SRE at Google and are core to its success.

7.1.4 Operations at Scale

Operations in distributed computing is operations at a large scale. Distributed computing involves hundreds and often thousands of computers working together. As a result, operations is different than traditional computing administration.

Manual processes do not scale. When tasks are manual, if there are twice as many tasks, there is twice as much human effort required. A system that is scaling to thousands of machines, servers, or processes, therefore, becomes untenable if a process involves manually manipulating things. In contrast, automation does scale. Code written once can be used thousands of times. Processes that involve many machines, processes, servers, or services should be automated. This idea applies to allocating machines, configuring operating systems, installing software, and watching for trouble. Automation is not a "nice to have" but a "must have." (Automation is the subject of Chapter 12.)

When operations is automated, system administration is more like an assembly line than a craft. The job of the system administrator changes from being the person who does the work to the person who maintains the robotics of an assembly line. Mass production techniques become viable and we can borrow operational practices from manufacturing. For example, by collecting measurements from every stage of production, we can apply statistical analysis that helps us improve system throughput. Manufacturing techniques such as **continuous improvement** are the basis for the Three Ways of DevOps. (See Section 8.2.)

Three categories of things are not automated: things that should be automated but have not been yet, things that are not worth automating, and human processes that can't be automated.

Tasks That Are Not Yet Automated

It takes time to create, test, and deploy automation, so there will always be things that are waiting to be automated. There is never enough time to automate everything, so we must prioritize and choose our methods wisely. (See Section 2.2.2 and Section 12.1.1.)

For processes that are not, or have not yet been, automated, creating procedural documentation, called a **playbook**, helps make the process repeatable and consistent. A good playbook makes it easier to automate the process in the future. Often the most difficult part of automating something is simply describing the process accurately. If a playbook does that, the actual coding is relatively easy.

Tasks That Are Not Worth Automating

Some things are not worth automating because they happen infrequently, they are too difficult to automate, or the process changes so often that automation is not possible. Automation is an investment in time and effort and the return on investment (ROI) does not always make automation viable.

Nevertheless, there are some common cases that are worth automating. Often when those are automated, the more rare cases (**edge cases**) can be consolidated or eliminated. In many situations, the newly automated common case provides such superior service that the edge-case customers will suddenly lose their need to be so unique.

Benefits of Automating the Common Case

At one company there were three ways that virtual machines were being provisioned. All three were manual processes, and customers often waited days until a system administrator was available to do the task. A project to automate provisioning was stalled because of the complexity of handling all three variations. Users of the two less common cases demanded that their provisioning process be different because they were (in their own eyes) unique and beautiful snowflakes. They had very serious justifications based on very serious (anecdotal) evidence and waved their hands vigorously to prove their point. To get the project moving, it was decided to automate just the most common case and promise the two edge cases would be added later.

This was much easier to implement than the original all-singing, all-dancing, provisioning system. With the initial automation, provisioning time was reduced to a few minutes and could happen without system administrator involvement. Provisioning could even happen at night and on weekends. At that point an amazing thing happened. The other two cases suddenly discovered that their uniqueness had vanished! They adopted the automated method. The system administrators never automated the two edge cases and the provisioning system remained uncomplicated and easy to maintain.

Tasks That Cannot Be Automated

Some tasks cannot be automated because they are human processes: maintaining your relationship with a stakeholder, managing the bidding process to make a large purchase, evaluating new technology, or negotiating within a team to assemble an oncall schedule. While they cannot be eliminated through automation, they can be streamlined:

- Many interactions with stakeholders can be eliminated through better documentation. Stakeholders can be more self-sufficient if provided with introductory documentation, user documentation, best practices recommendations, a style guide, and so on. If your service will be used by many other services or service teams, it becomes more important to have good documentation. Video instruction is also useful and does not require much effort if you simply make a video recording of presentations you already give.
- Some interactions with stakeholders can be eliminated by making common requests self-service. Rather than meeting individually with customers to understand future capacity requirements, their forecasts can be collected via a web user interface or an API. For example, if you provide a service to hundreds

of other teams, forecasting can be become a full-time job for a project manager; alternatively, it can be very little work with proper automation that integrates with the company's supply-chain management system.

- Evaluating new technology can be labor intensive, but if a common case is identified, the end-to-end process can be turned into an assembly-line process and optimized. For example, if hard drives are purchased by the thousand, it is wise to add a new model to the mix only periodically and only after a thorough evaluation. The evaluation process should be standardized and automated, and results stored automatically for analysis.

- Automation can replace or accelerate team processes. Creating the oncall schedule can evolve into a chaotic mess of negotiations between team members battling to take time off during an important holiday. Automation turns this into a self-service system that permits people to list their availability and that churns out an optimal schedule for the next few months. Thus, it solves the problem better and reduces stress.

- Meta-processes such as communication, status, and process tracking can be facilitated through online systems. As teams grow, just tracking the interaction and communication among all parties can become a burden. Automating that can eliminate hours of manual work for each person. For example, a web-based system that lets people see the status of their order as it works its way through approval processes eliminates the need for status reports, leaving people to deal with just exceptions and problems. If a process has many complex handoffs between teams, a system that provides a status dashboard and automatically notifies teams when hand-offs happen can reduce the need for legions of project managers.

- The best process optimization is elimination. A task that is eliminated does not need to be performed or maintained, nor will it have bugs or security flaws. For example, if production machines run three different operating systems, narrowing that number down to two eliminates a lot of work. If you provide a service to other service teams and require a lengthy approval process for each new team, it may be better to streamline the approval process by automatically approving certain kinds of users.

7.2 Service Life Cycle

Operations is responsible for the entire **service life cycle**: launch, maintenance (both regular and emergency), upgrades, and decommissioning. Each phase has unique requirements, so you'll need a strategy for managing each phase differently.

The stages of the life cycle are:

- **Service Launch:** Launching a service the first time. The service is brought to life, initial customers use it, and problems that were not discovered prior to the launch are discovered and remedied. (Section 7.2.1)
- **Emergency Tasks:** Handling exceptional or unexpected events. This includes handling outages and, more importantly, detecting and fixing conditions that precipitate outages. (Chapter 14)
- **Nonemergency Tasks:** Performing all manual work required as part of the normally functioning system. This may include periodic (weekly or monthly) maintenance tasks (for example, preparation for monthly billing events) as well as processing requests from users (for example, requests to enable the service for use by another internal service or team). (Section 7.3)
- **Upgrades:** Deploying new software releases and hardware platforms. The better we can do this, the more aggressively the company can try new things and innovate. Each new software release is built and tested before deployment. Tests include system tests, done by developers, as well as user acceptance tests (UAT), done by operations. UAT might include tests to verify there are no **performance regressions** (unexpected declines in performance). Vulnerability assessments are done to detect security issues. New hardware must go through a **hardware qualification** to test for compatibility, performance regressions, and any changes in operational processes. (Section 10.2)
- **Decommissioning:** Turning off a service. It is the opposite of a service launch: removing the remaining users, turning off the service, removing references to the service from any related service configurations, giving back any resources, archiving old data, and erasing or scrubbing data from any hardware before it is repurposed, sold, or disposed. (Section 7.2.2)
- **Project Work:** Performing tasks large enough to require the allocation of dedicated resources and planning. While not directly part of the service life cycle, along the way tasks will arise that are larger than others. Examples include fixing a repeating but intermittent failure, working with stakeholders on roadmaps and plans for the product's future, moving the service to a new datacenter, and scaling the service in new ways. (Section 7.3)

Most of the life-cycle stages listed here are covered in detail elsewhere in this book. Service launches and decommissioning are covered in detail next.

7.2.1 Service Launches

Nothing is more embarrassing than the failed public launch of a new service. Often we see a new service launch that is so successful that it receives too much traffic, becomes overloaded, and goes down. This is ironic but not funny.

Each time we launch a new service, we learn something new. If we launch new services rarely, then remembering those lessons until the next launch is difficult. Therefore, if launches are rare, we should maintain a checklist of things to do and record the things you should remember to do next time. As the checklist grows with each launch, we become better at launching services.

If we launch new services frequently, then there are probably many people doing the launches. Some will be less experienced than others. In this case we should maintain a checklist to share our experience. Every addition increases our **organizational memory**, the collection of knowledge within our organization, thereby making the organization smarter.

A common problem is that other teams may not realize that planning a launch requires effort. They may not allocate time for this effort and surprise operations teams at or near the launch date. These teams are unaware of all the potential pitfalls and problems that the checklist is intended to prevent. For this reason the launch checklist should be something mentioned frequently in documentation, socialized among product managers, and made easy to access. The best-case scenario occurs when a service team comes to operations wishing to launch something and has been using the checklist as a guide throughout development. Such a team has "done their homework"; they have been working on the items in the checklist in parallel as the product was being developed. This does not happen by accident; the checklist must be available, be advertised, and become part of the company culture.

A simple strategy is to create a checklist of actions that need to be completed prior to launch. A more sophisticated strategy is for the checklist to be a series of questions that are audited by a Launch Readiness Engineer (LRE) or a Launch Committee.

Here is a sample launch readiness review checklist:

Sample Launch Readiness Review Survey
The purpose of this document is to gather information to be evaluated by a Launch Readiness Engineer (LRE) when approving the launch of a new service. Please complete the survey prior to meeting with your LRE.

- General Launch Information:
  - What is the service name?
  - When is the launch date/time?
  - Is this a soft or hard launch?
- Architecture:
  - Describe the system architecture. Link to architecture documents if possible.
  - How does the failover work in the event of single-machine, rack, and datacenter failure?
  - How is the system designed to scale under normal conditions?

- Capacity:
  - What is the expected initial volume of users and QPS?
  - How was this number arrived at? (Link to load tests and reports.)
  - What is expected to happen if the initial volume is 2× expected? 5×? (Link to emergency capacity documents.)
  - What is the expected external (internet) bandwidth usage?
  - What are the requirements for network and storage after 1, 3, and 12 months? (Link to confirmation documents from the network and storage teams capacity planner.)
- Dependencies:
  - Which systems does this depend on? (Link to dependency/data flow diagram.)
  - Which RPC limits are in place with these dependencies? (Link to limits and confirmation from external groups they can handle the traffic.)
  - What will happen if these RPC limits are exceeded ?
  - For each dependency, list the ticket number where this new service's use of the dependency (and QPS rate) was requested and positively acknowledged.
- Monitoring:
  - Are all subsystems monitored? Describe the monitoring strategy and document what is monitored.
  - Does a dashboard exist for all major subsystems?
  - Do metrics dashboards exist? Are they in business, not technical, terms?
  - Was the number of "false alarm" alerts in the last month less than x?
  - Is the number of alerts received in a typical week less than x?
- Documentation:
  - Does a playbook exist and include entries for all operational tasks and alerts?
  - Have an LRE review each entry for accuracy and completeness.
  - Is the number of open documentation-related bugs less than x?
- Oncall:
  - Is the oncall schedule complete for the next n months?
  - Is the oncall schedule arranged such that each shift is likely to get fewer than x alerts?
- Disaster Preparedness:
  - What is the plan in case first-day usage is 10 times greater than expected?
  - Do backups work and have restores been tested?
- Operational Hygiene:
  - Are "spammy alerts" adjusted or corrected in a timely manner?

  - Are bugs filed to raise visibility of issues—even minor annoyances or issues with commonly known workarounds?
  - Do stability-related bugs take priority over new features?
  - Is a system in place to assure that the number of open bugs is kept low?
- Approvals:
  - Has marketing approved all logos, verbiage, and URL formats?
  - Has the security team audited and approved the service?
  - Has a privacy audit been completed and all issues remediated?

Because a launch is complex, with many moving parts, we recommend that a single person (the **launch lead**) take a leadership or coordinator role. If the developer and operations teams are very separate, one person from each might be selected to represent each team.

The launch lead then works through the checklist, delegating work, filing bugs for any omissions, and tracking all issues until launch is approved and executed. The launch lead may also be responsible for coordinating post-launch problem resolution.

Case Study: Self-Service Launches at Google

Google launches so many services that it needed a way to make the launch process streamlined and able to be initiated independently by a team. In addition to providing APIs and portals for the technical parts, the Launch Readiness Review (LRR) made the launch process itself self-service.

The LRR included a checklist and instructions on how to achieve each item. An SRE engineer was assigned to shepherd the team through the process and hold them to some very high standards.

Some checklist items were technical—for example, making sure that the Google load balancing system was used properly. Other items were cautionary, to prevent a launch team from repeating other teams' past mistakes. For example, one team had a failed launch because it received 10 times more users than expected. There was no plan for how to handle this situation. The LRR checklist required teams to create a plan to handle this situation and demonstrate that it had been tested ahead of time.

Other checklist items were business related. Marketing, legal, and other departments were required to sign off on the launch. Each department had its own checklist. The SRE team made the service visible externally only after verifying that all of those sign-offs were complete.

7.2.2 Service Decommissioning

Decommissioning (or just "decomm"), or turning off a service, involves three major phases: removal of users, deallocation of resources, and disposal of resources.

Removing users is often a product management task. Usually it involves making the users aware that they must move. Sometimes it is a technical issue of moving them to another service. User data may need to be moved or archived.

Resource deallocation can cover many aspects. There may be DNS entries to be removed, machines to power off, database connections to be disabled, and so on. Usually there are complex dependencies involved. Often nothing can begin until the last user is off the service; certain resources cannot be deallocated before others, and so on. For example, typically a DNS entry is not removed until the machine is no longer in use. Network connections must remain in place if deallocating other services depends on network connectivity.

Resource disposal includes securely erasing disks and other media and disposing of all hardware. The hardware may be repurposed, sold, or scrapped.

If decommissioning is done incorrectly or items are missed, resources will remain allocated. A checklist, that is added to over time, will help assure decommissioning is done completely and the tasks are done in the right order.

7.3 Organizing Strategy for Operational Teams

An operational team needs to get work done. Therefore teams need a strategy that assures that all incoming work is received, scheduled, and completed. Broadly speaking, there are three sources of operational work and these work items fall into three categories. To understand how to best organize a team, first you must understand these sources and categories.

The three sources of work are life-cycle management, interacting with stakeholders, and process improvement and automation. Life-cycle management is the operational work involved in running the service. Interacting with stakeholders refers to both maintaining the relationship with people who use and depend on the service, and prioritizing and fulfilling their requests. Process improvement and automation is work inspired by the business desire for continuous improvement.

No matter the source, this work tends to fall into one of these three broad categories:

- **Emergency Issues:** Outages, and issues that indicate a pending outage that can be prevented, and emergency requests from other teams. Usually initiated by an alert sent by the monitoring system via SMS or pager. (Chapter 14)

- **Normal Requests:** Process work (repeatable processes that have not yet been automated), non-urgent trouble reports, informational questions, and initial consulting that results in larger projects. Usually initiated by a request ticket system. (Section 14.1.3)
- **Project Work:** Small and large projects that evolve the system. Managed with whatever project management style the team selects. (Section 12.4.2)

To assure that all sources and categories of work receive attention, we recommend this simple organizing principle: people should always be working on projects, with exceptions made to assure that emergency issues receive immediate attention and non-project customer requests are triaged and worked in a timely manner.

More specifically, at any given moment, the highest priority for one person on the team should be responding to emergencies, the highest priority for one other person on the team should be responding to normal requests, and the rest of the team should be focused on project work.

This is counter to the way operations teams often work: everyone running from emergency to emergency with no time for project work. If there is no effort dedicated to improving the situation, the team will simply run from emergency to emergency until they are burned out.

Major improvements come from project work. Project work requires concentration and focus. If you are constantly being interrupted with emergency issues and requests, you will not be able to get projects done. If an entire team is focused on emergencies and requests, nobody is working on projects.

It can be tempting to organize an operations team into three subteams, each focusing on one source of work or one category of work. Either of these approaches will create silos of responsibility. Process improvement is best done by the people involved in the process, not by observers.

To implement our recommended strategy, all members of the team focus on project work as their main priority. However, team members take turns being responsible for emergency issues as they arise. This responsibility is called **oncall**. Likewise, team members take turns being responsible for normal requests from other teams. This responsibility is called **ticket duty**.

It is common that oncall duty and ticket duty are scheduled in a rotation. For example, a team of eight people may use an eight-week cycle. Each person is assigned a week where he or she is on call: expected to respond to alerts, spending any remaining time on projects. Each person is also assigned a different week where he or she is on ticket duty: expected to focus on triaging and responding to request tickets first, working on other projects only if there is remaining time. This gives team members six weeks out of the cycle that can be focused on project work.

Limiting each rotation to a specific person makes for smoother handoffs to the next shift. In such a case, there are two people doing the handoff rather than a large operations team meeting. If more than 25 percent of a team needs to be dedicated to ticket duty and oncall, there is a serious problem with firefighting and a lack of automation.

The team manager should be part of the operational rotation. This practice ensures the manager is aware of the operational load and firefighting that goes on. It also ensures that nontechnical managers don't accidentally get hired into the operations organization.

Teams may combine oncall and ticket duty into one position if the amount of work in those categories is sufficiently small. Some teams may need to designate multiple people to fill each role.

Project work is best done in small teams. Solo projects can damage a team by making members feel disconnected or by permitting individuals to work without constructive feedback. Designs are better with at least some peer review. Without feedback, members may end up working on projects they feel are important but have marginal benefit. Conversely, large teams often get stalled by lack of consensus. In their case, focusing on shipping quickly overcomes many of these problems. It helps by making progress visible to the project members, the wider team, and management. Course corrections are easier to make when feedback is frequent.

The Agile methodology, discussed in Section 8.6, is an effective way to organize project work.

Meta-work

There is also meta-work: meetings, status reports, company functions. These generally eat into project time and should be minimized. For advice, see Chapter 11, "Eliminating Time Wasters," in the book *Time Management for System Administrators* by Limoncelli (2005).

7.3.1 Team Member Day Types

Now that we have established an organizing principle for the team's work, each team member can organize his or her work based on what kind of day it is: a project-focused day, an oncall day, or a ticket duty day.

Project-Focused Days

Most days should be project days for operational staff. Specifically, most days should be spent developing software that automates or optimizes aspects of the team's responsibilities. Non-software projects include shepherding a new launch or working with stakeholders on requirements for future releases.

Organizing the work of a team through a single bug tracking system has the benefit of reducing time spent checking different systems for status. Bug tracking systems provide an easy way for people to prioritize and track their work. On a typical project day the staff member starts by checking the bug tracking system to review the bugs assigned to him or her, or possibly to review unassigned issues of higher priority the team member might need to take on.

Software development in operations tends to mirror the Agile methodology: rather than making large, sudden changes, many small projects evolve the system over time. Chapter 12 will discuss automation and software engineering topics in more detail.

Projects that do not involve software development may involve technical work. Moving a service to a new datacenter is highly technical work that cannot be automated because it happens infrequently.

Operations staff tend not to physically touch hardware not just because of the heavy use of virtual machines, but also because even physical machines are located in datacenters that are located far away. Datacenter technicians act as **remote hands**, applying physical changes when needed.

Oncall Days

Oncall days are spent working on projects until an alert is received, usually by SMS, text message, or pager.

Once an alert is received, the issue is worked until it is resolved. Often there are multiple solutions to a problem, usually including one that will fix the problem quickly but temporarily and others that are long-term fixes. Generally the quick fix is employed because returning the service to normal operating parameters is paramount.

Once the alert is resolved, a number of other tasks should always be done. The alert should be categorized and annotated in some form of electronic alert journal so that trends may be discovered. If a quick fix was employed, a bug should be filed requesting a longer-term fix. The oncall person may take some time to update the playbook entry for this alert, thereby building organizational memory. If there was a user-visible outage or an SLA violation, a postmortem report should be written. An investigation should be conducted to ascertain the root cause of the problem. Writing a postmortem report, filing bugs, and root causes identification are all ways that we raise the visibility of issues so that they get attention. Otherwise, we will continually muddle through ad hoc workarounds and nothing will ever get better. Postmortem reports (possibly redacted for technical content) can be shared with the user community to build confidence in the service.

The benefit of having a specific person assigned to oncall duty at any given time is that it enables the rest of the team to remain focused on project work. Studies have found that the key to software developer productivity is to have long periods of uninterrupted time. That said, if a major crisis appears, the oncall person will pull people away from their projects to assist.

If oncall shifts are too long, the oncall person will be overloaded with follow-up work. If the shifts are too close together, there will not be time to complete the follow-up work. Many great ideas for new projects and improvements are first imagined while servicing alerts. Between oncall shifts people should have enough time to pursue such projects.

Chapter 14 will discuss oncall in greater detail.

Ticket Duty Days

Ticket duty days are spent working on requests from customers. Here the customers are the internal users of the service, such as other service teams that use your service's API. These are not tickets from external users. Those items should be handled by customer support representatives.

While oncall is expected to have very fast reaction time, tickets generally have an expected response time measured in days.

Typical tickets may consist of questions about the service, which can lead to some consulting on how to use the service. They may also be requests for activation of a service, reports of problems or difficulties people are experiencing, and so forth. Sometimes tickets are created by automated systems. For example, a monitoring system may detect a situation that is not so urgent that it needs immediate response and may open a ticket instead.

Some long-running tickets left from the previous shift may need follow-up. Often there is a policy that if we are waiting for a reply from the customer, every three days the customer will be politely "poked" to make sure the issue is not forgotten. If the customer is waiting for follow-up from us, there may be a policy that urgent tickets will have a status update posted daily, with longer stretches of time for other priorities.

If a ticket will not be completed by the end of a shift, its status should be included in the shift report so that the next person can pick up where the previous person left off.

By dedicating a person to ticket duty, that individual can be more focused while responding to tickets. All tickets can be triaged and prioritized. There is more time to categorize tickets so that trends can be spotted. Efficiencies can be realized by batching up similar tickets to be done in a row. More importantly, by dedicating a person to tickets, that individual should have time to go deeper into each ticket: to update documentation and playbooks along the way, to deep-dive into bugs rather than find superficial workarounds, to fix complex broken processes. Ticket duty should not be a chore, but rather should be part of the strategy to reduce the overall work faced by the team.

Every operations team should have a goal of eliminating the need for people to open tickets with them, similar to how there should always be a goal to automate manual processes. A ticket requesting information is an indication that documentation should be improved. It is best to respond to the question by adding the requested information to the service's FAQ or other user documentation and then directing the user to that document. Requests for service activation, allocations, or configuration changes indicate an opportunity to create a web-based portal or API to make such requests obsolete. Any ticket created by an automated system should have a corresponding playbook entry that explains how to process it, with a link to the bug ID requesting that the automation be improved to eliminate the need to open such tickets.

At the end of oncall and ticket duty shifts, it is common for the person to email out a shift report to the entire team. This report should mention any trends noticed and any advice or status information to be passed on to the next person. The oncall end-of-shift report should also include a log of which alerts were received and what was done in response.

When you are oncall or doing ticket duty, that is your main project. Other project work that is accomplished, if any, is a bonus. Management should not expect other projects to get done, nor should people be penalized for having the proper focus. When people end their oncall or ticket duty time, they should not complain that they weren't able to get any project work done; their project, so to speak, was ticket duty.

7.3.2 Other Strategies

There are many other ways to organize the work of a team. The team can rotate though projects focused on a particular goal or subsystem, it can focus on reducing toil, or special days can be set aside for reducing technical debt.

Focus or Theme

One can pick a category of issues to focus on for a month or two, changing themes periodically or when the current theme is complete. For example, at the start of a theme, a number of security-related issues can be selected and everyone commit to focusing on them until they are complete. Once these items are complete, the next theme begins. Some common themes include monitoring, a particular service or subservice, or automating a particular task.

If the team cohesion was low, this can help everyone feel as if they are working as a team again. It can also enhance productivity: if everyone has familiarized themselves with the same part of the code base, everyone can do a better job of helping each other.

Introducing a theme can also provide a certain amount of motivation. If the team is looking forward to the next theme (because it is more interesting, novel, or fun), they will be motivated to meet the goals of the current theme so they can start the next one.

Toil Reduction

Toil is manual work that is particularly exhausting. If a team calculates the number of hours spent on toil versus normal project work, that ratio should be as low as possible. Management may set a threshold such that if it goes above 50 percent, the team pauses all new features and works to solve the big problems that are the source of so much toil. (See Section 12.4.2.)

Fix-It Days

A day (or series of days) can be set aside to reduce technical debt. **Technical debt** is the accumulation of small unfinished amounts of work. By themselves, these bits and pieces are not urgent, but the accumulation of them starts to become a problem. For example, a Documentation Fix-It Day would involve everyone stopping all other work to focus on bugs related to documentation that needs to be improved. Alternatively, a Fix-It Week might be declared to focus on bringing all monitoring configurations up to a particular standard.

Often teams turn fix-its into a game. For example, at the start a list of tasks (or bugs) is published. Prizes are given out to the people who resolve the most bugs. If done company-wide, teams may receive T-shirts for participating and/or prizes for completing the most tasks.

7.4 Virtual Office

Many operations teams work from home rather than an office. Since work is virtual, with remote hands touching hardware when needed, we can work from anywhere. Therefore, it is common to work from anywhere. When necessary, the team meets in chat rooms or other virtual meeting spaces rather than physical meeting rooms. When teams work this way, communication must be more intentional because you don't just happen to see each other in the office.

It is good to have a policy that anyone who is not working from the office takes responsibility for staying in touch with the team. They should clearly and periodically communicate their status. In turn, the entire team should take responsibility for making sure remote workers do not feel isolated. Everyone should know what their team members are working on and take the time to include everyone in discussions. There are many tools that can help achieve this.

7.4.1 Communication Mechanisms

Chat rooms are commonly used for staying in touch throughout the day. Chat room transcripts should be stored and accessible so people can read what they may have missed. There are many chat room "bots" (software robots that join the chat room and provide services) that can provide transcription services, pass messages to offline members, announce when oncall shifts change, and broadcast any alerts generated by the monitoring system. Some bots provide entertainment: At Google, a bot keeps track of who has received the most virtual high-fives. At Stack Exchange, a bot notices if anyone types the phrase "not my fault" and responds by selecting a random person from the room and announcing this person has been randomly designated to be blamed.

Higher-bandwidth communication systems include voice and video systems as well as screen sharing applications. The higher the bandwidth, the better the fidelity of communication that can be achieved. Text-chat is not good at conveying emotions, while voice and video can. Always switch to higher-fidelity communication systems when conveying emotions is more important, especially when an intense or heated debate starts.

The communication medium with the highest fidelity is the in-person meeting. Virtual teams greatly benefit from periodic in-person meetings. Everyone travels to the same place for a few days of meetings that focus on long-term planning, team building, and other issues that cannot be solved online.

7.4.2 Communication Policies

Many teams establish a communication agreement that clarifies which methods will be used in which situations. For example, a common agreement is that chat rooms will be the primary communication channel but only for ephemeral discussions. If a decision is made in the chat room or an announcement needs to be made, it will be broadcast via email. Email is for information that needs to carry across oncall shifts or day boundaries. Announcements with lasting effects, such as major policies or design decisions, need to be recorded in the team wiki or other document system (and the creation of said document needs to be announced via email). Establishing this chat–email–document paradigm can go a long way in reducing communication problems.

7.5 Summary

Operations is different from typical enterprise IT because it is focused on a particular service or group of services and because it has more demanding uptime requirements.

There is a tension between the operations team's desire for stability and the developers' desire to get new code into production. There are many ways to reach a balance. Most ways involve aligning goals by sharing responsibility for both uptime and velocity of new features.

Operations in distributed computing is done at a large scale. Processes that have to be done manually do not scale. Constant process improvement and automation are essential.

Operations is responsible for the life cycle of a service: launch, maintenance, upgrades, and decommissioning. Maintenance tasks include emergency and non-emergency response. In addition, related projects maintain and evolve the service.

Launches, decommissioning of services, and other tasks that are done infrequently require an attention to detail that is best assured by use of checklists. Checklists ensure that lessons learned in the past are carried forward.

The most productive use of time for operational staff is time spent automating and optimizing processes. This should be their primary responsibility. In addition, two other kinds of work require attention. Emergency tasks need fast response. Nonemergency requests need to be managed such that they are prioritized and worked in a timely manner. To make sure all these things happen, at any given time one person on the operations team should be focused on responding to emergencies; another should be assigned to prioritizing and working on nonemergency requests. When team members take turns addressing these responsibilities, they receive the dedicated resources required to assure they happen correctly by sharing the responsibility across the team. People also avoid burning out.

Operations teams generally work far from the actual machines that run their services. Since they operate the service remotely, they can work from anywhere there is a network connection. Therefore teams often work from different places, collaborating and communicating in a chat room or other virtual office. Many tools are available to enable this type of organizational structure. In such an environment, it becomes important to change the communication medium based on the type of communication required. Chat rooms are sufficient for general communication but voice and video are more appropriate for more intense discussions. Email is more appropriate when a record of the communication is required, or if it is important to reach people who are not currently online.

Exercises

1. What is operations? What are its major areas of responsibilities?
2. How does operations in distributed computing differ from traditional desktop support or enterprise client–server support?
3. Describe the service life cycle as it relates to a service you have experience with.
4. Section 7.1.2 discusses the change-instability cycle. Draw a series of graphs where the x-axis is time and the y-axis is the measure of stability. Each graph should represent two months of project time.

Each Monday, a major software release that introduces instability (9 bugs) is rolled out. On Tuesday through Friday, the team has an opportunity to roll out a "bug-fix" release, each of which fixes three bugs. Graph these scenarios:

(a) No bug-fix releases
(b) Two bug-fix releases after every major release
(c) Three bug-fix releases after every major release
(d) Four bug-fix releases after every major release
(e) No bug-fix release after odd releases, five bug-fix releases after even releases

5. What do you observe about the graphs from Exercise 4?
6. For a service you provide or have experience with, who are the stakeholders? Which interactions did you or your team have with them?
7. What are some of the ways operations work can be organized? How does this compare to how your current team is organized?
8. For a service you are involved with, give examples of work whose source is life-cycle management, interacting with stakeholders, and process improvement and automation.
9. For a service you are involved with, give examples of emergency issues, normal requests, and project work.

In other words, technology has become so reliable that the remaining problems are in the processes used to manage it. We need better practices.

The canonical way to improve large-scale operations is through "quality management" techniques such as W. Edwards Deming's "Shewhart cycle" (Deming 2000) or "Lean Manufacturing" (Spear & Bowen 1999). DevOps's key principles are an application of these principles to web system administration. The book *The Phoenix Project* (Kim, Behr & Spafford 2013) explains these principles in the form of a fictional story about a team that learns these principles as they reform a failing IT organization.

8.1 What Is DevOps?

DevOps is a combination of culture and practices—system administrators, software developers, and web operations staff all contribute to the DevOps environment. With DevOps, sysadmins and developers share responsibility for a service and its availability. DevOps aligns the priorities of developers (dev) and system administrators or operations staff (ops) by making them both responsible for uptime. DevOps also brings all of the various environments, from development through test and production, under software version management and control.

> At its most fundamental level, DevOps is about breaking down silos and removing bottlenecks and risks that screw up an organization's Development to Operations delivery lifecycle. The goal is to enable change to flow quickly and reliably from specification through to running features in a customer-facing environment. (Edwards 2012)

DevOps is an emerging field in operations. The practice of DevOps typically appears in web application and cloud environments, but its influence is spreading to all parts of all industries.

DevOps is about improving operations. Theo Schlossnagle (2011) says DevOps is "the operationalism of the world." Increasingly companies are putting a greater importance on the operational part of their business. This is because of an increasing trend to be concerned with the total cost of ownership (TCO) of a project, not just the initial purchase price, as well as increasing pressure to achieve higher reliability and velocity of change. The ability to make changes is required to improve efficiency and to introduce new features and innovations. While traditionally change has been seen as a potential destabilizer, DevOps shows that infrastructure change can be done rapidly and frequently in a way that increases overall stability.

DevOps is not a job title; you cannot hire a "DevOp." It is not a product; you cannot purchase "DevOps software." There are teams and organizations that exhibit DevOps culture and practices. Many of the practices are aided by one software package or another. But there is no box you can purchase, press the DevOps button, and magically "have" DevOps. Adam Jacob's seminal "Choose Your Own Adventure" talk at Velocity 2010 (Jacob 2010) makes the case that DevOps is not a job description, but rather an inclusive movement that codifies a culture. In this culture everyone involved knows how the entire system works, and everyone is clear about the underlying business value they bring to the table. As a result availability becomes the problem for the entire organization, not just for the system administrators.

DevOps is not just about developers and system administrators. In his blog post "DevOps is not a technology problem. DevOps is a business problem," Damon Edwards (2010) emphasizes that DevOps is about collaboration and optimization across the whole organization. DevOps expands to help the process from idea to customer. It isn't just about leveraging cool new tools. In fact, it's not just about software.

The organizational changes involved in creating a DevOps environment are best understood in contrast to the traditional software development approach. The DevOps approach evolved because of the drawbacks of such methods when developing custom web applications or cloud service offerings, and the need to meet the higher availability requirements of these environments.

8.1.1 The Traditional Approach

For software packages sold in shrink-wrapped packages at computer stores or downloaded over the Internet, the developer is finished when the software is complete and ships. Operational concerns directly affect only the customer; the developer is far removed from the operations. At best, operational problems may be fed back to the developer in the form of bug reports or requests for enhancement. But developers are not directly affected by operational issues caused by their code.

Traditional software development uses the **waterfall methodology**, where each step—gather requirements, design, implement, test, verify, and deploy—is done by a different team, each in isolation from the other steps. Each step (team) produces a deliverable to be handed off to the next step (team).

This is called "waterfall development" because the steps look like a cascading waterfall (see Figure 8.1). Information flows down, like the water.

It is impossible to understand the operational requirements of a system until at least the design is complete, or in many cases until it is deployed and in active use. Therefore the operational requirements cannot be taken into account in the requirements gathering stage, after which the features are "locked." Thus the result of this approach is that operational requirements are not considered until it is too late to do anything about them.

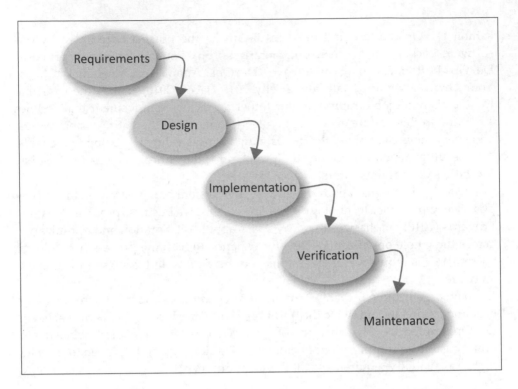

Figure 8.1: The waterfall methodology: information flows down. Unidirectional information flows are the antithesis of DevOps.

In the waterfall method, system administrators are involved only in deploying the software, and thereafter are solely responsible for operations and meeting uptime requirements. System administrators have very little chance of influencing the development of the software to better meet their needs. In many cases they have no direct contact with the software developers.

Companies that have a business model based on the web, or a significant web presence, develop their own custom software. Traditionally there was very little interaction between software developers and system administrators even if they worked for the same company. They worked in "silos," with each group unaware of the concerns of the other, and neither side seeing the "big picture." In an organizational chart, their hierarchies might meet only at the CEO level. The software developers continued to develop software in isolation, without a motivating sense of its future use, and the sysadmins continued to struggle to meet high availability requirements with buggy software.

In such a situation, operations is generally improved through ad hoc solutions, by working around problems and creating optimizations that are limited in scope. Excellence in operational efficiency, performance, and uptime is hindered by this approach. Alas, the waterfall approach is from a time when we didn't know any better.[1]

8.1.2 The DevOps Approach

Companies with a business model based on the web found that traditional software development practices did not work well for meeting very high availability requirements. Operational concerns are key for high availability, so these companies needed a new approach with tightly coupled development and operations. A new set of practices evolved as a result, and the term "DevOps" was coined to describe them. (See Appendix B for a historical perspective.)

Web-based companies typically introduce new features much more frequently than those that sell packaged software. Since it is so easy for end users to switch from one web search engine to another, for example, these companies need to keep improving their products to maintain their customer base. Also, web companies release more often because they can—they don't have to manufacture physical media and distribute it to a customer. With the traditional packaged software approach, each new release is viewed as having a destabilizing influence—it is a source of new, unknown bugs.

In a DevOps environment, developers and sysadmins share the responsibility for meeting uptime requirements, so much so that both share oncall duties. Developers have a vested interest in making sure that their software can meet the high availability requirements of the site. Developers collaborate in creating operational strategies, and operations staff work closely with developers to provide implementation and development input. Development and operations are both handled by a single team, with developers and sysadmins participating in all stages and being jointly responsible for the final result. The development cycle should be a seamless set of procedures and processes that result in a finished product—the service. There is no concept of "them," as in "hand off to them"; there is only "us"—the team working on the product. Team members are largely generalists with deep specialties.

Most DevOps organizations are focused on clear business objectives such as scale, efficiency, and high uptime. By emphasizing people and process over ad hoc tool use, DevOps allows tight alignment of operations with business needs and thus with customer needs.

---

1. Or did we? Royce's 1970 paper, which is credited with "inventing" the model, actually identifies it so Royce can criticize it and suggest improvements. He wrote it is "risky and invites failure" because "design iterations are never confined to the successive step." What Royce suggests as an alternative is similar to what we now call Agile. Sadly, multiple generations of software developers have had to suffer through waterfall projects thanks to people who, we can only assume, didn't read the entire paper (Pfeiffer 2012).

By mandating that operations, development, and business departments work together, the operations process in a DevOps environment becomes a shared responsibility that can respond more quickly and efficiently to needs of the service being operated. The result of the DevOps approach is higher uptime and lower operational costs.

8.2 The Three Ways of DevOps

"The Three Ways of DevOps" is a strategy for improving operations. It describes the values and philosophies that frame the processes, procedures, and practices of DevOps. The Three Ways strategy was popularized by Kim et al.'s (2013) book *The Phoenix Project*. It borrows from "Lean Manufacturing" (Spear & Bowen 1999) and the Toyota Production System's Kaizen improvement model.

8.2.1 The First Way: Workflow

Workflow looks at getting the process correct from beginning to end and improving the speed at which the process can be done. The process is a *value stream*—it provides value to the business. The speed is referred to as *flow rate* or just simply *flow*.

If the steps in the process are listed on a timeline, one can think of this as improving the process as it moves from left to right. On the left is the business (development) and on the right is the customer (operations).

For example, a software release process has multiple stages: code is committed to a code repository, unit-tested, packaged, integration-tested, and deployed into production. To put an emphasis on getting the process correct from start to end:

- **Ensure each step is done in a repeatable way.** Haphazard and ad hoc steps are replaced with repeatable processes.
- **Never pass defects to the next step.** Testing is done as early as possible rather than only on the final product. Each step has validation or quality assurance checks.
- **Ensure no local optimizations degrade global performance.** For example, it might be faster to not package the software but instead have each step pull the software from the source repository. This saves time for the developers because it eliminates a step for them. At the same time, it introduces uncertainty that the remaining steps will all be working with the same exact bits, causing confusion and increasing errors. Therefore it is a global regression and we would not do it.
- **Increase the flow of work.** Now that the steps are done in a repeatable way, the process can be analyzed and improved. For example, steps could

be automated to improve speed. Alternatively there may be steps where work is redone multiple times; the duplicate work can be eliminated.

8.2.2 The Second Way: Improve Feedback

A feedback loop is established when information (a complaint or request) is communicated upstream or downstream. Amplifying feedback loops means making sure that what is learned while going from left (dev) to right (ops) is communicated back to the left and through the system again. Feedback (information about problems, concerns, or potential improvements) is made visible rather than hidden. As we move from left to right, we learn things; if the lessons learned are thrown away at the end, we have missed an opportunity to improve the system. Conversely, if what we learn is amplified and made visible, it can be used to improve the system.

Continuing our software release example, to put an emphasis on amplifying feedback loops:

- **Understand and respond to all customers, internal and external.** Each step is a customer of the previous steps in addition to the obvious "customer" at the end of the process. Understanding the customer means understanding what the subsequent steps need. Responding means there is a way for the customer to communicate and a way to assure that the request is responded to.
- **Shorten feedback loops.** Shortening a feedback loop means making the communication as direct as possible. The more stages a message must pass through to communicate, the less effective it will be. If the feedback is given to a manager, who types it up and presents it to a vice president, who communicates it down to a manager, who tells an engineer, you know you have too many steps. The loop is as short as possible if the person who experienced the problem is able to directly communicate it to the person who can fix the problem.
- **Amplify all feedback.** The opposite would be someone noticing a problem and muddling through it with their own workaround. The person may think he or she is being a hero for working around the problem, but actually the individual is hiding the problem and preventing it from being fixed. Amplifying feedback makes the issue more visible. It can be as simple as filing a bug report or as dramatic as stopping the process until a management decision is made with regard to how to proceed. When all feedback is brought to the surface, then we have the most information available to improve a process.
- **Embed knowledge where it is needed.** Specialized knowledge such as configuration information or business requirements is "embedded" in the process through the use of appropriate documentation and managed via source code control. As you move from left to right in the process, the details of what is

needed are available at every stage and do not require going outside of the loop to acquire them.

8.2.3 The Third Way: Continual Experimentation and Learning

The third way involves creating a culture where everyone is encouraged to try new things. This is a requirement for innovation to happen. In the third way, everyone understands two things: (1) that we learn from the failures that happen when we experiment and take risks and (2) that to master a skill requires repetition and practice.

In our software release example this means:

- **Rituals are created that reward risk taking.** Trying new things, even when the new thing fails, is rewarded at review time if valuable lessons were learned.
- **Management allocates time for projects that improve the system.** The backlog of "technical debt" is considered important. Resources are allocated to fix the bugs filed when feedback is amplified. Mistakes are not repeated.
- **Faults are introduced into the system to increase resilience.** Fire drills (discussed in Chapter 15) intentionally take down machines or networks to make sure redundant systems kick in.
- **You try "crazy" or audacious things.** For example, you might try to get the flow time from one week down to one day.

When a team can identify its "value streams" (the processes that the business depends on) and apply the Three Ways of DevOps to them, the processes don't just get better—the company also values the IT team more.

8.2.4 Small Batches Are Better

Another principle of DevOps is that small batches are better.

Small batches means doing a lot of small releases with a few features rather than a small number of large releases with lots of features. It's very risky to do large, infrequent releases. The abundance of new features makes it difficult to home in on bugs in the code. Features may interfere with each other, creating new bugs. To lower overall risk, it's better to do many small releases containing only a few features each.

The first benefit of this pattern is that each new release is smaller, enabling you to isolate bugs more easily. The second benefit is that code latency is reduced. Code latency is how fast code gets from the first check-in to production, where it can be making money for you. From a financial standpoint, the code going into production sooner means the code can be generating return on investment (ROI) sooner. Lastly, small batches mean the process is done over many iterations. This means getting more practice at it, so you have more opportunities to get better at the process. This reduces risk.

Velocity is how many times you ship in a month. High velocity and low latency are realized through releasing small batches.

The small batches principle is counter-intuitive because there is a human tendency to avoid risky behavior. Deploying software in production involves risk; therefore businesses traditionally minimize the frequency of deployments. While this makes them feel better, they actually are shooting themselves in the foot because the deployments that are done are bigger and riskier, and the team doing them is out of practice by the time the next one rolls around.

This principle applies to deployments and any other process that involves making frequent changes.

8.2.5 Adopting the Strategies

The first step in adopting the Three Ways is to identify the team's value streams—processes done for the business, or requested by the business.

Go through each process several times until it can be done from beginning to end without failure. It doesn't have to be optimal, but each step needs to be clearly defined so that it can be done in a repeatable fashion. That is, a reasonably well-trained person should be able to do the step and the result will be the same as the result from another reasonably trained person. Now the process is defined.

Once the process is defined, amplify the feedback loops. That is, make sure each step has a way to raise the visibility of problems so that they are worked on, not ignored. Collect measurements on the length, frequency, and failure rate of the steps. Make this data available to all involved.

This feedback is used to optimize the process. Find the steps that are the most error prone, unreliable, or slow. Replace them, improve them, or eliminate them. The two biggest inefficiencies are rework (fixing mistakes) and redundant work (duplicate effort that can be consolidated).

Every process has a bottleneck—a place where work is delayed while it waits on other dependencies. The most beneficial place to put energy into improvement is at the bottleneck. In fact, optimizations anywhere else are wasted energy. Above the bottleneck, incomplete work accumulates. Below the bottleneck, workers are starved for things to do. Optimizing steps above the bottleneck simply makes more work accumulate. Optimizing steps below the bottleneck simply improves steps that are underutilized. Therefore fixing the bottleneck is the only logical thing to do.

Making all of this happen requires a culture of innovation and a willingness to take risks. Risk must be rewarded and failure embraced. In fact, once the Three Ways of DevOps have been used to make the process smooth and optimized, you should introduce defects into the system to verify that they are detected and handled. By embracing failure this way, we go from optimized to resilient.

8.3 History of DevOps

The term "DevOps" was coined by Patrick Debois in 2008. Debois noticed that some sites had evolved the practice of system administration into something fundamentally different. That is, they had independently reached the conclusion that web sites could be better run when development and operations were done in collaboration. Debois thought there would be value in getting these people together to share what they had learned. He started a series of mini-conferences called "DevOps Days" starting in 2009 in Belgium. The name came from the concept of bringing developers (dev) and operations people (ops) together.

DevOps Days was a big success and helped popularize the term "DevOps." The conversations continued on mailing lists and blogs. In May 2010, John Willis and Damon Edwards started the DevOps Cafe Podcast, which soon became a clearinghouse for DevOps ideas and discussion. The hashtag "#devops" arose as a way for DevOps followers to identify themselves on Twitter, which was a relatively new service at the time. The 2011 USENIX LISA Conference (Large Installation System Administration) selected DevOps as its theme and since then has evolved to incorporate a DevOps focus.

8.3.1 Evolution

Some practitioners say that DevOps is a logical evolution of having sysadmins and developers participating in an Agile development cycle together and using Agile techniques for system work. While the use of Agile tools is common in DevOps, Agile is merely one of many ways to apply DevOps principles. Techniques such as pair programming or scrum teams are not required to create a DevOps environment. However, adherence to some of the basic Agile principles is definitely required.

Other practitioners say that DevOps is the logical evolution of developers doing system administration themselves due to the popularity of Amazon AWS and (later) similar services. In other words, it is developers reinventing system administration. In the past, setting up a new machine required the skill and training of a sysadmin. Now developers were allocating virtual machines using API calls. Without the need for full-time sysadmins, developers were learning more and more system skills and bringing with them their penchant to automate tasks. By making deployment and test coding part of the development cycle, they created a new emphasis on repeatability that led to many of the techniques discussed in this chapter.

Other practitioners counter by saying that some sysadmins have always had an emphasis on automation, though outside of web environments management did not value such skills. From their perspective, DevOps was driven by sysadmins who concentrated on their coding skills and began collaborating with the developers on deployment and code testing. Taking these steps into the development cycle led to closer ties with developers and working as a tight-knit group to accomplish the shared goal of increased uptime and bug-free deploys. More cynically, DevOps can be viewed as system administration reinvented by sysadmins who finally had management support to do it the right way.

8.3.2 Site Reliability Engineering

Around the same time, companies such as Google started being more open about their internet sysadmin practices. Google had evolved system administration into the concept of a **Site Reliability Engineer** (SRE) by recognizing that all functions of system administration, from capacity planning to security, were crucial to the reliability of a site. Since 2005, Google's SRE model has organized the company's developers and operational engineers to share responsibility for reliability and performance. The SRE model can be thought of as DevOps at large scale: how do you empower 10,000 developers and 1000 SREs to work together? First, each product or infrastructure component has a small team responsible for it. For critical and highly visible systems, developers and SREs work together in an arrangement that mirrors the DevOps model. Unfortunately, there are not enough SREs to go around. Therefore the vast majority of these teams consist of developers using tools developed by the SREs. The tools are engineered to make operations self-service for developers. This empowers developers to do their own operations. The SREs build tools that are specifically engineered to make it easy to achieve high-quality results without advanced knowledge.

DevOps is rapidly expanding from a niche technique for running web sites to something that can also be applied to enterprise and industrial system administration. There is nothing uniquely web-centric about DevOps. Marc Andreessen famously said, "Software eats the world" (Anderson 2012). As this happens, all facets of society will require well-run operations. Thus, DevOps will be applied to all facets of computing.

8.4 DevOps Values and Principles

DevOps can be divided into roughly four main areas of practice (Kartar 2010):

* Relationships
* Integration

- Automation
- Continuous improvement

8.4.1 Relationships

In a traditional environment, the tools and scripts are seen as the primary focus of operational maintenance. DevOps gives more weight to the relationships among the teams and the various roles in the organization. Developers, release managers, sysadmins, and managers—all need to be in close coordination to achieve the shared goal of highly reliable and continuously improving services.

Relationships are so important in a DevOps environment that a common motto is "People over process over tools." Once the right people are performing the right process consistently, only then does one create a tool to automate the function. One of the key defining principles of DevOps is the focus on people and process over writing a script and then figuring out who should run it and when.

8.4.2 Integration

Part of breaking down silos is ensuring that processes are integrated across teams. Rather than seeing operational duties as merely following a script, in a DevOps environment one views them as end-to-end processes that combine tools and data with people processes such as peer reviews or coordination meetings. Processes must be linked across domains of responsibility to deliver end-to-end functionality.

Integration of the communities responsible for different parts of the service operation is also a given for DevOps. A quick way to assess the DevOps culture in your environment might be to ask sysadmins who they have lunch with regularly. If the answer is "Mostly sysadmins," and hardly ever folks from software development, web operations, networking, or security, this is a sign that integration of teams has not been achieved.

8.4.3 Automation

Under the auspices of automation, DevOps strives for simplicity and repeatability. Configurations and scripts are handled as source code and kept under version control. Building and management of the source code are scripted to the fullest extent possible once the entire process is understood.

Simplicity increases the efficiency and speed of communication and avoids confusion. It also saves time in training, documentation, and support. The goal is to design simple, repeatable, reusable solutions.

8.4.4 Continuous Improvement

Each time a process is carried out, the goal is to make it dependably repeatable and more functional. For example, every time there is a failure, tests are added to the release process to detect that failure mode and prevent another release with the same failure from being passed to the next step. Another example might be improving a process that needs occasional manual intervention by handling more edge cases in the tool, until eventually manual intervention is no longer required.

By taking an end-to-end view, we often find opportunities to eliminate processes and tools, thus simplifying the system. Problems are fixed by looking for root causes rather than making local optimizations that degrade global performance.

The mindset required is eloquently summed up by Kartar (2010):

> Treat your processes like applications and build error handling into them. You can't predict every ... pitfall ... but you can ensure that if you hit one your process isn't derailed.

8.4.5 Common Nontechnical DevOps Practices

DevOps includes many nontechnical practices that fall under the DevOps umbrella. Not all DevOps organizations use all of these techniques. In fact, it is important to pick and choose among them, using the techniques that are needed rather than blindly following all the practices for completeness. These are the "people processes"; the more technical practices will be covered in the next section.

- **Early Collaboration and Involvement:** Ops staff are included in development planning meetings, and developers have full access to ops monitoring. Key issues such as architecting for scalability are jointly developed in the planning stage. (See Chapter 5.)
- **New Features Review:** Ops staff participate in and guide development toward best practices for operability during design time, not as an after-thought. Key monitoring indicators for services are defined through collaboration. Deployment details are sketched out so development of deployment code and tests are part of the main development effort. (See Chapter 2.)
- **Shared Oncall Responsibilities:** These responsibilities include not only pager duties shared between developers and Ops staff, but also shared review of oncall trends—for example, a weekly meeting to review SLA compliance and any outages. Developers have full access to all monitoring output, and Ops staff have full access to all build/deploy output. That way everyone is fully empowered to research any issues that come up while oncall or during a failure analysis.

- **Postmortem Process:** In addition to a regular stand-up meeting to review outages and trends, there should be a thorough postmortem or failure analysis done for every outage. Recurring patterns of minor failures can point to a larger gap in process. Findings of a postmortem—specifically, tasks needed to correct issues—should be added to the current development backlog and prioritized accordingly.

- **Game Day Exercises:** Sometimes known as "fire drills," these are deliberate attempts to test failover and redundancy by triggering service disruption in a planned fashion. Teams of people are standing by to ensure that the "right thing" happens, and to fix things manually if it does not. Only by inducing failure can you actually test what will happen when service components fail. A simple example of a game-day exercise is rebooting randomly selected machines periodically to make sure all failover systems function properly.

- **Error Budgets:** Striving for perfection discourages innovation, but too much innovation means taking on too much risk. A system like Google's Error Budgets brings the two into equilibrium. A certain amount of downtime is permitted each month (the budget). Until the budget is exhausted, developers may do as many releases as they wish. Once the budget is exhausted, they may do only emergency security fixes for the rest of the month. To conserve the Error Budgets, they can dedicate more time for testing and building frameworks that assure successful releases. This aligns the priorities of operations and developers and helps them work together better. See Section 19.4 for a full description.

8.4.6 Common Technical DevOps Practices

DevOps is, fundamentally, a structural and organizational paradigm. However, to meet the goals of DevOps, a number of technical practices have been adopted or developed. Again, not all of them are used by every DevOps organization. These practices are tools in your toolbox, and you should choose those that will best serve your situation.

- **Same Development and Operations Toolchain:** Development and operations can best speak the same language by using the same tools wherever possible. This can be as simple as using the same bug-tracking system for both development and operations/deployment issues. Another example is having a unified source code management system that stores not just the product's source code, but also the source code of operational tools and system configurations.

- **Consistent Software Development Life Cycle (SDLC):** Bringing both the application itself and the deployment/operations code together into the same

SDLC is key to keeping the two in sync. The "throw it over the wall to deployment" model is anathema in DevOps, where development and operations are tightly coupled. The deployment tools are developed and tested in lockstep with the applications themselves, following a shared release cycle.

- **Managed Configuration and Automation:** The configuration files of all applications that are required for the service are kept in source code control and are subject to the same change management as the rest of the code. The same is true for all automation scripts.

- **Infrastructure as Code:** With a software-defined datacenter (i.e., virtual machines), you can keep a description of the entire infrastructure as code that can be maintained under revision control. Infrastructure as code is further described in Section 10.6.

- **Automated Provisioning and Deployment:** Every step of the deployment process is automated and/or scripted so that one can trigger a build that will go all the way through self-test to a deployment, or can trigger a deployment via a separate build command.

- **Artifact-Scripted Database Changes:** Rather than manual manipulation of database schema, changes to databases are also treated as code. They are scripted, tested, versioned, and released into staging environments.

- **Automated Build and Release:** The output of a build cycle is a valid set of application and deployment objects that can be deployed to a staged environment. Builds have makefiles or other configuration files that treat the build as a series of dependencies and contracts to fulfill, and can be triggered by check-ins or by specific command. Assembling stages of a build by hand is counter to repeatability and ease of operation.

- **Release Vehicle Packaging:** As noted earlier, the build cycle creates packaging for the application to facilitate its deployment. The end product of a build does not require by-hand packaging to prepare it for deployment, nor is software deployed to live systems via checkout from a repository or compiled on each host before use.

- **Abstracted Administration:** Abstracted administration describes system administration tasks at a high level and lets automation decide the right steps to perform for a given operating system. Thus we might have a configuration file to provision a new user that says "create user" rather than the steps required for Linux ("append this line to /etc/passwd, this line to /etc/shadow, and this line to /etc/group") or Windows ("create the user in ActiveDirectory"). By doing the initial setup work with the tools, we simplify the interface between goals and configurations. Some commonly used tools in this area include CFEngine, Puppet, and Chef.

8.4.7 Release Engineering DevOps Practices

Certain release engineering practices have become closely related to DevOps practices. Release engineering is the process of taking software in source form, building it, packaging it, testing it, and deploying it into the field.

While not DevOps practices in themselves, these development practices have a great deal to offer in achieving operational efficiency (DevOps-Toolchain 2010). Each of these practices is discussed in more detail in Chapters 9, 10 and 11.

- **Continuous Build:** With each change, attempt to compile the code base and generate the packaged software. This detects build-related problems as soon as possible.
- **Continuous Test:** The software is tested in an automated fashion with each change to the code base. This prevents problems from becoming embedded in the system.
- **Automated Deployment:** The process of deploying the software for use in test and live environments is automated.
- **Continuous Deployment:** With fully automated build, test, and deployment, the decision whether to deploy a particular release is also automated. Multiple releases are deployed in the field each day.
- **Automated Provisioning:** Additional resources, such as CPU, storage, memory, and bandwidth, are allocated based on a predictive model. As the system detects that more resources are needed, they are allocated for use by the system.

8.5 Converting to DevOps

Before implementing any of these recommendations, developers and operations need to open a dialogue. Building bridges between the groups needs to start by forming collegial connections. This is often best done away from the office, preferably over a beer or other beverage. That is when operations and developers really start talking to each other, sharing their perspectives, and finding common ground that make adopting DevOps practices happen. In an interview on the DevOps Cafe podcast, Jesse Robbins noted that spending $50 on fries and drinks may be the best investment some companies ever make (Willis & Edwards 2011).

When adopting DevOps principles in a traditional, non-DevOps organization, it is important to start slowly. Adopt a few new practices at first and add more practices as they get buy-in from the team. There are three basic phases involved in this type of conversion.

First, make operations feedback available to the overall project team. This can take several forms. Most commonly, organizations make monitoring available to developers and ask them to do joint root causes analysis of issues or failures, identify recurring problems, and collaborate on solutions.

Second, begin to embed product knowledge into operations. Invite developers to key operations meetings on deployment and maintenance, and set escalation paths that involve developers being reachable after hours.

Third, enable operations knowledge to be available during all project phases. This involves operations being included in daily or weekly status meetings, being involved in prioritization of the product backlog tasks, and being a full partner in planning meetings.

8.5.1 Getting Started

To start a DevOps relationship, you must first get off the computer and begin face-to-face discussions. Where do you start? Begin with development, product managers, or other members of the product team for the product(s) you support.

It is best to choose someone approachable, with whom you may already have some rapport. You can arrange a meeting or simply go get coffee some afternoon.

Your initial conversation should be about mutual problems that can be solved. As part of the conversation, explain the improvements that could come from closer collaboration, such as improved release efficiency or better operations response to developers' needs.

As you discuss problems to solve, you will find one that will be a good starting point for a joint DevOps project. Choose something that has obvious benefits to the development team rather than something that is primarily operations focused. It is best to describe the project in terms of mutual benefits.

As part of the collaboration on this project, get·in the habit of holding regular meetings with the development and product teams. Attend their planning meetings, and invite them to yours.

As you successfully complete your starter project, identify another project for collaboration. Good candidates are processes that affect both development and operations, such as roll-outs or build toolchains. Involving multiple stakeholders from development, operations, and the product team is a good way to build relationships.

Once again, one easy way to measure your DevOps success is to ask, "Who do you go to lunch with?" If you're routinely going to lunch with folks from development, networking, release, or similar groups, chances are very good that you are doing DevOps.

8.5.2 DevOps at the Business Level

The next stage of conversion to a DevOps environment is getting your management to buy into the DevOps philosophy. A true DevOps environment often involves changes to the organizational chart that break down the barriers between development and operations. The organizational structure needs to foster a close relationship between development and operations. Ideally, get development and operations under one management team, the same vice president, or something similar. Also try to colocate the groups so that they are near each other, or at least in the same building or time zone. This kind of change can open up a whole new level of functionality. Getting buy-in is fairly difficult. Management needs to have the value explained in business terms.

DevOps doesn't stop with collaboration between developers and operations staff. It can be useful up and down the entire organizational chain. Recently one of the authors witnessed an internal project where developers, operations staff, product management, and the legal department worked side by side to create a solution that would properly handle a tight set of constraints. The staff from the legal department were amazed at the level of collaboration and commitment that could be focused on the problem. Buying an expensive third-party system that would have needed configuration and outside management was avoided.

DevOps: Not Just for the Web

A Practical Approach to Large-Scale Agile Development: How HP Transformed HP LaserJet FutureSmart Firmware by Gruver, Young, and Fulghum (2012) describes applying DevOps to the creation of HP LaserJet software. The result was that developers spent less time doing manual testing, which gave them more time to develop new features. Their success story is summarized in Episode 33 of the DevOps Cafe Podcast (Willis, Edwards & Humble 2012).

8.6 Agile and Continuous Delivery

DevOps is a natural outgrowth of the software development methodology known as "Agile" and the practices called "continuous delivery." While this book is not about either of those topics, a brief look at both Agile and continuous delivery is helpful to show the origins of many DevOps practices. The principles involved are directly transferable to DevOps practices and serve as a strong foundation for a DevOps mindset.

8.6.1 What Is Agile?

Agile is a collection of software development principles that originated in an unusual summit of representatives from various nontraditional software practices such as Extreme Programming, Scrum, and Pragmatic Programming, to name a few. They called themselves "The Agile Alliance" and created the highly influential "Agile Manifesto" (Beck et al. 2001).

The Agile Manifesto

- Individuals and interactions over processes and tools
- Working code over comprehensive documentation
- Customer collaboration over contract negotiation
- Responding to change over following a plan

As a coda to the Agile Manifesto, the authors added, "While there is value in the items on the right, we value the items on the left more." Agile practices stress direct connections between the business objectives and the development team. Developers work closely with product owners to build software that meets specific business objectives. The waterfall method of development is bypassed in favor of collaborative methods such as pair programming, where two developers work on code together, or scrum, where a whole team commits to "sprints" of one to four weeks working on a prioritized backlog of features. Plain statements called "user stories" provide requirements for software development—for example, "As a bank customer, I want to receive an electronic bill for my credit card statement" or "As a photo site user, I want to crop and edit pictures in my web browser."

In Agile development, waterfall methods are also bypassed with respect to testing and integration. Unit and integration tests are created with new feature code, and testing is applied automatically during the build process. Often the only documentation for code releases is the user stories that provided the initial requirements, in strong contrast to waterfall's functional specifications and requirements documents. The user stories come out of a prioritized backlog of feature stories maintained by the product owner. By keeping a prioritized list that can change with business needs, the agility of the development process is maintained and development can respond to changing business needs easily without wasted effort and rework.

DevOps is the application of Agile methodology to system administration.

8.6.2 What Is Continuous Delivery?

Continuous delivery (CD) is a set of principles and practices for delivery of software and updates on an ongoing basis. Software delivery means the process by which software goes from source code to ready-to-use installation packages. Included in this process are the building (compiling) of the software packages as well as any quality testing. The process stops if the build or testing fails. CD began as a design pattern in Extreme Programming but has since become a discipline of its own.

For example, an organization that practices CD builds the software frequently, often immediately after any new source code changes are detected. The change triggers the build process, which, on successful completion, triggers an automated testing process. On successful completion of the tests, the software packages are made available for use.

CD is different from traditional software methodologies where new software releases are infrequent, perhaps yearly. In the latter approach, when the software release date is near, the packages are built, possibly involving a very manual process involving human intervention and perhaps ad hoc processes. The testing is a mixture of automation and manual testing that may last for days. If any problems are found, the entire process starts all over.

Continuous delivery stresses automation, packaging, and repeatability, with a culture of shared responsibility for good outcomes. In continuous delivery we recognize that every step of the process is part of the ultimate delivery of the software and updates, and that the process is always occurring at every stage.

System operations and maintenance can be thought of as a form of continuous delivery. Operations tasks are part of how software gets from a packaged build on the repository onto the system. While these principles and practices came from software development, it is easy to map them onto operations tasks and gain efficiency and reliability.

The eight principles of continuous delivery are codified by Humble and Farley (2010).

The Eight Principles of Continuous Delivery

1. The process for releasing/deploying *must* be repeatable and reliable.
2. Automate everything.
3. If something is difficult or painful, do it more often to improve and automate it.
4. Keep everything in source control.
5. "Done" means "released, working properly, in the hands of the end user."
6. Build quality in.
7. Everybody has responsibility for the release process.
8. Improve continuously.

While most of these principles are self-explanatory, it is worthwhile expanding on the third principle. Often our response to error-prone, painful, and difficult tasks is to find ways to do them less often. Continuous delivery says to do them more often to improve our skill ("Practice makes perfect"), fix the problems in the processes, and automate them.

There are also four practices of continuous delivery.

The Four Practices of Continuous Delivery

1. Build binaries only once.
2. Use the same repeatable process for deployment to every environment.
3. Do basic functionality tests ("smoke tests") on your deployment (e.g., include diagnostics).
4. If anything fails, stop the line and start again.

For any given release cycle, binary packages are built only once. Contrast this with environments where QA builds a package and tests it, and then deployment checks out the same code and builds the package to be used in deployment. Not only is this duplication of effort, but errors can also creep in. Multiple build requests may be confused or miscommunicated, resulting in packages being built from slightly different source code revisions each time. One team may be tempted to "slip in a few small fixes," which might seem helpful but is dangerous because it means some new code did not receive the full, end-to-end testing. It is difficult to verify that the second time the package is built, the same exact OS release, compiler release, and build environment are used.

> ### Version-Controlled Builds
>
> At one of Tom's former employers, the build system checked the MD5 hash of the OS kernel, compiler, and a number of other files. The build tools team would determine that version x.y was to be built with a specific tool-chain and the build system wouldn't let you build that version with any other toolchain. If a customer five years later required a patch to version X, the company knew it could build the software exactly as needed with only the patch being the different item, not the compiler, OS, or other tool. This was particularly important because the company made software for designing chips, and chip designers didn't change toolchains once a design was started. If you started a design with version X, the vendor promised it could fix bugs in that specific version until your chip design was finished.

By automating as much as possible and creating documented processes for steps that cannot be automated, we create a repeatable process for deployment.

In a traditional software development methodology, release engineers hand-build binaries for the QA environment and deploy them in an ad hoc fashion. In continuous deployment, the build is automated and each stage uses the same process for deployment.

A "smoke test" is a basic functionality test, like plugging in a device and seeing if it starts to smoke (it shouldn't!). Including built-in diagnostic tests as part of your build and deployment automation gives you high confidence that what you just deployed meets the basic functionality requirements. The build or deploy will error out if the built-in tests fail, letting you know something is wrong.

Instead of patching a failure and proceeding with patches, continuous delivery wants us to find a root cause and fix the problem. We then work the process again to verify that the problem has disappeared.

CD produces an installation package that is tested sufficiently so that it can be deployed into production. However, actually pushing that release into production is a business decision. Deployments are usually less frequent, perhaps daily or weekly. There may be additional tests that the deployment team performs and the actual deployment itself may be complex and manual. Automating those practices and doing them frequently (perhaps as frequently as new packages are available) constitutes continuous deployment. This approach is discussed further in Section 11.10.

8.7 Summary

In this chapter, we examined the culture and principles of DevOps and looked at its historical antecedents—namely, Agile and continuous delivery. The principles and practices in this chapter serve as a strong foundation for a shift in culture and attitude in the workplace about operations and maintenance tasks. This shift brings measurable efficiency and increased uptime when it is strongly applied, and you should explore it for yourself.

Theo Schlossnagle (2011) describes DevOps as the natural response to "the operationalism of the world." As velocity increases in companies of every type, the most successful competitors will be those organizations that are "operationally focused" in every business unit.

DevOps is not about a technology. DevOps is about solving business problems (Edwards 2010). It starts with understanding the business needs and optimizing processes to best solve them.

DevOps makes businesses run more smoothly and enables the people involved to work together more effectively. It gives us hope that operations can be done well at any scale.

Exercises

1. What are the fundamental principles behind DevOps?
2. How does a waterfall environment differ from a DevOps environment?
3. Why is DevOps not intended to be a job title?
4. Describe the relationship between Agile and DevOps practices.
5. Whose participation is vital to DevOps collaboration, at a minimum?
6. Name three release engineering best practices.
7. What are the basic steps involved in converting a process to DevOps?
8. Describe your release process (code submission to running in production). Identify the manual steps, team-to-team handoffs, and steps that are ill defined or broken. Based on the Three Ways of DevOps, which improvements could be made?

Chapter 9

Service Delivery: The Build Phase

And they're certainly not showing
any signs that they are slowing.

—Willy Wonka

Service delivery is the technical process of how a service is created. It starts with source code created by developers and ends with a service running in production. The system that does all of this is called the **service delivery platform**. It includes two major phases: build and deploy. The **build phase** starts with the software source code and results in installable packages. That phase is covered in this chapter. The **deployment phase** takes those packages, readies the service infrastructure (machines, networks, storage, and so on), and produces the running system. The deployment phase is covered in Chapter 10.

The service delivery flow is like an assembly line. Certain work is done at each step. Tests are performed along the way to verify that the product is working correctly before being passed along to the next step. Defects are detected and monitored.

The faster the entire process can run, the sooner the test results are known. However, comprehensive tests take a long time. Therefore the earlier tests should be the fastest, broadest tests. As confidence builds, the slower, more detailed tests are done. This way the most likely failures happen early on, removing the need for the other tests. For example, the early stages compile the software, which is sensitive to easy-to-detect syntax errors but provides little guarantee that the software works. Testing performance, security, and usability can be the most time consuming. Manual tests are saved for the end, after all other failures have been detected, conserving manual labor.

Terms to Know

Innovate: Doing (good) things we haven't done before.

Stakeholders: People and organizations that are seen as having an interest in a project's success.

Artifacts: Any kind of tangible by-product produced during the development of software—source files, executables, documentation, use cases, diagrams, packages, and so on.

Service Delivery Flow: The trip through the system from beginning to end; often shortened to **flow**.

Cycle Time: How frequently a flow completes.

Deployment: The process of pushing a release into production; often shortened to **deploy**.

Gate: An intentional limit that prevents flow. For example, the deploy step is gated by whether quality assurance tests succeeded.

Release Candidate: The end result of the build phase. Not all release candidates are deployed.

Release: The successful completion of an entire flow, including deploy. May result in users seeing a visible change.

A good service delivery platform takes into account the fact that a service is not just software, but also the infrastructure on which the service runs. This includes machines with an operating system loaded and properly configured, the software packages installed and configured, plus network, storage, and other resources available. While infrastructure can be set up manually, it is best to automate that process. Virtualization enables this kind of automation because virtual machines can be manipulated via software, as can software-defined networks. The more we treat infrastructure as code, the more we can benefit from software development techniques such as revision control and testing. This automation should be treated like any other software product and put through the same service delivery flow as any application.

When service delivery is done right, it provides confidence, speed, and continuous improvement. Building, testing, and deployment of both an application and virtual infrastructure can be done in a completely automated fashion, which is streamlined, consistent, and efficient. Alternatively, it can be done via manual, ad hoc processes, inconsistently and inefficiently. It is your mission to achieve the former.

9.1 Service Delivery Strategies

There are many possible service delivery strategies. Most methodologies fall along the continuum between the older waterfall methodology and the more modern methodology associated with the DevOps world. We recommend the latter because it gets better results and encourages faster rates of innovation. It focuses on automation, instrumentation, and improvement based on data.

9.1.1 Pattern: Modern DevOps Methodology

The DevOps methodology divides the platform into two phases: the build phase and the deployment phase. The build phase is concerned with taking the source code and producing installation packages. The deployment phase takes those packages and installs them in the environment where they are to be run. At each step along the way tests are performed. If any test fails, the process is stopped. Source code is revised and the process starts again from the beginning.

Figure 9.1 represents this service delivery platform. There are two primary flows. The upper flow delivers the application. The lower flow delivers the infrastructure. The four quadrants represent the build and deployment phases of each flow.

Each phase has a repository: The build phase uses the source repository. The deployment phase uses the package repository. Each phase has a console that provides visibility into what is going on. The application flow and the infrastructure flow have the same steps and should use the same tools when possible.

Deployments are done in one of at least two environments: the test environment and the live production environment. The service is created initially in the test environment, which is not exposed to customers. In this environment, a series of tests are run against the release. When a release passes these tests, it becomes a release candidate. A release candidate is a version with the potential to be a final product—that is, one that is deployed in production for customer use.

The software may be deployed in other environments, such as a **private sandbox** environment where the engineering team conducts experiments too disruptive to attempt in the test environment. Individual developers should each have at least one private environment for their own development needs. These environments are generally scaled-down versions of the larger system and may even run on the developers' own laptops. There may be other separate environments for other reasons. For example, there may be a demo environment used to give previews of new releases to stakeholders. Alternatively, new releases may be deployed in an intermediate production environment used by "early access customers" before they are deployed into the main production environment.

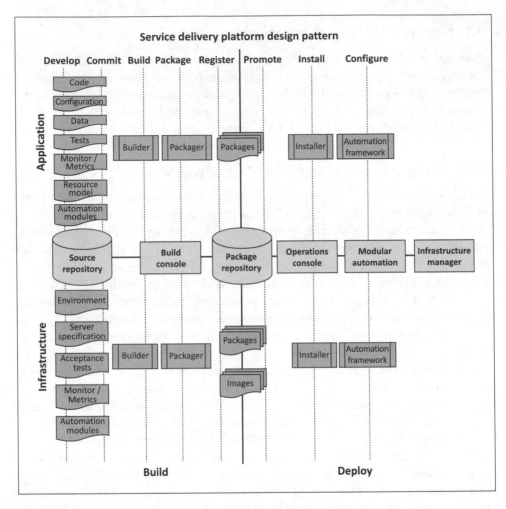

Figure 9.1: The parts of the modern service delivery platform pattern. (Reprinted with permission from Damon Edwards of DTO Solutions.)

At a minimum, every site must have separate testing and production environments, where the testing environment is built exactly like production. Developers' own environments are typically less well controlled, and testing in such an environment may miss some issues. It is negligent to move a release straight from developer testing into production, or to not have an environment for testing the configuration management systems. There is no good reason to not invest in the additional infrastructure for a proper test environment—it always pays for itself in increased service availability.

While one may think of the build phase as the domain of developers and the deployment phase as the domain of operations, this is not true in a DevOps environment. Both groups share responsibility for the construction and use of the entire system. The handoff between steps marks the flow of work, not organizational boundaries.

9.1.2 Anti-pattern: Waterfall Methodology

The waterfall methodology works differently from the modern DevOps methodology. It is predicated on multiple phases, each controlled by a different organization. Handoffs not only mark the flow of work, but also indicate the end of each organization's responsibility. The waterfall methodology was previously discussed in Section 8.1.1.

The waterfall methodology has many phases. The first phase is controlled by the development organization, which has two teams: software engineers (SWEs) and quality assurance (QA) engineers. The SWEs create the source code, which they compile and package. The QA team tests the packages in its own environment. When the team approves the software, it is designated as a release candidate and passed to the next phase. The next phase is controlled by the system administration team. This team uses the release candidate to build a beta environment; the beta environment is used to verify that the software works. Product management then gets involved and verifies that the software is functioning as expected. Once the release is approved, the system administrators use it to upgrade the live production environment.

There are many problems with the waterfall approach. First, both QA and operations build their own environments, each using different methods. This means there is a duplication of effort, with each team developing overlapping tools. Second, because the QA environment is built using different methods, it is not a valid test of how the system will work in production. The production environment might not have the same OS release, host configuration, or supporting packages. As a consequence, the testing is incomplete. It also makes it difficult for developers to reproduce bugs found in QA.

Another problem with the waterfall methodology is that because the handoff between phases is also a handoff between organizations, the discovery of bugs or other problems can become a game of finger pointing. Is the software not working in production because developers didn't do their job, or did the problem arise because operations didn't build the test environment correctly? Why find out the truth when it is easier to create a political battle and see who can shift blame the fastest?

The DevOps methodology has many benefits. Rather than the two phases creating a dividing wall between two organizations, the developers and operations staff work collaboratively on each phase. The testing and production environments are built using the same tools, so testing is more accurate. The reuse of tools is more efficient and means that the improvements made to the tools benefit all. Because both teams have a shared responsibility for the entire process, cooperation trumps finger pointing.

The DevOps methodology is also more simple. There are just two distinct phases, each with well-defined concerns, inputs, and outputs.

9.2 The Virtuous Cycle of Quality

Good flow creates a virtuous cycle of quality. Rigorous testing creates a solid foundation that results in better releases. This improves confidence, which in turn encourages faster and better releases. Because they are smaller releases, testing is improved. The cycle then repeats.

When discussing service delivery, people often focus on how fast their release cycle has become. When someone brags about improving cycle time from six weeks to an hour, they are missing the point.

What's really important is confidence in the quality of the final product. Improved code management, speed, packaging, and cycle time are all means, not ends. Confidence is a result of the platform's ability to provide better testing and other processes that are automated to assure consistency. An excellent discussion of this can be heard in Episode 33 of the DevOps Cafe Podcast (Willis, Edwards & Humble 2012).

More specifically, a good service delivery platform should result in the following outcomes:

- **Confidence:** We want a process that assures a high likelihood that each deployment into production will be successful. Success means application bugs are found and resolved early, ensuring a trouble-free deployment without outages. The more confident we are in our service delivery process, the more aggressively we can try new things. Innovation requires the ability to aggressively and fearlessly experiment. Consider the opposite case: a company full of people who resist change does not innovate. As fear of change increases, innovation declines. If we can confidently try new things, then we can experiment and innovate, knowing that we can count on our service delivery system to support our innovations.

- **Reduced Risk:** Faster iterations are less risky. As discussed in Section 8.2.4, more frequent releases mean that each release will contain a smaller number of changes and, therefore, is less risky.

- **Shorter Interval from Keyboard to Production:** We want the end-to-end process to happen quickly. We want to have our capital—the code developers create—in the hands of the customers as quickly as possible. Compare yearly releases to weekly releases. With the former, new features sit idle for months before they see the light of day. That would be like an automotive factory making cars all year but selling them only in December. Faster iterations mean features get into production faster. This is important because the investment required to create a new feature is huge.

- **Less Wait Time:** Faster iterations also mean code gets to the testing process sooner. This improves productivity because it is easier to debug code that was written recently. Developers lose context over time; regaining lost context takes time and is error prone. Less work has to be redone because testing helps get things right the first time.

- **Less Rework:** We want to reduce the amount of effort spent redoing work that was done previously. It is more efficient to get things right the first time.

- **Improved Execution:** Doing faster iterations improves our ability to execute all the phases. When there is a lot of time between each iteration, any manual steps become less practiced and we don't do them as well. If releases are extremely infrequent, the processes will have changed enough that it gives us an excuse not to automate. We throw up our hands and revert to old, manual methods. Frequent releases keep automation fresh and encourage us to update it to reflect small changes before they turn into major ones.

- **A Culture of Continuous Improvement:** The ideal process is always evolving and improving. Initially it might have manual steps. That's to be expected, as processes are malleable when initially being invented. Once the end-to-end process is automated, it can be instrumented and metrics can be collected automatically. With metrics we can make data-driven improvements. For a process to be continuously improved, we not only need the right technology but also need a culture that embraces change.

- **Improved Job Satisfaction:** It is exciting and highly motivating to see our changes rapidly put into production. When the interval between doing work and receiving the reward is small enough, we associate the two. Our job satisfaction improves because we get instant gratification from the work we do.

Rather than focusing purely on cycle time, a team should have metrics that balance the velocity of individual aspects of the software delivery platform. We recommend that every DevOps team collect the following metrics:

1. **Bug lead time:** Time from initial bug report to production deployment of fixed code.
2. **Code lead time:** Time from code commit to production deployment.
3. **Patch lead time:** Time from vendor patch release to production deployment.
4. **Frequency of deployment:** How many deployments to production are done each month.
5. **Mean time to restore service:** Duration of outages; from initial discovery to return to service.
6. **Change success rate:** Ratio of successful production deployments to total production deployments.

9.3 Build-Phase Steps

The goal of the build phase is to create installation packages for use by the deployment phase. It has five steps:

1. Code is developed.
2. Code is committed to the source repository.
3. Code is built.
4. Build results are packaged.
5. Packages are registered.

Each step includes some kind of testing. For example, building the software verifies that it compiles and packaging it verifies that all the required files are available.

As Figure 9.1 shows, the source repository is used as the primary storage facility for this phase. The final output is handed off to the next phase by stashing it in the package repository.

9.3.1 Develop

During the **develop** step, engineers write code or produce other files. For example, they may write C++, Python, or JavaScript code. Graphic designers create images and other artifacts.

Engineers check out the existing files from the source repository, downloading the source onto the engineer's machine or workspace. From there, the files are edited, revised, and altered. New files are created. For example, a software engineer working on a new feature may make many revisions to all related files, compiling and running the code, and repeating this process until the source code compiles and functions as desired.

9.3.2 Commit

During the **commit** step, the files being developed are uploaded to the source repository. Generally this is done infrequently, as it indicates the files have reached a certain level of completeness. All committed code should be working code. If not, other developers' work will come to a halt. They will pull recent changes into their workspaces and the result will be code that doesn't work. They will not be able to tell if the problem is due to their own error or if the source is just in bad shape. Checking in code that does not work is known as "breaking the build." It may be broken in that the code no longer compiles, or because the code compiles but automated tests (discussed later) fail. If the build is broken, returning it to working state should be considered a high priority.

The gate for this step is the **pre-submit check**. To prevent obviously bad or broken code from entering, source repository systems can be configured to call programs that will check the new files for basic validity and reject attempts to commit code that fails. The checks are not able to determine that the code is perfect and bug free, but obvious mistakes can be detected such as syntax errors. Often unit tests, described later, are run to verify the change does not break basic functionality. Pre-submit checks often check for style guide conformance (discussed later in Section 12.7.4).

Because pre-submit checks can call any program, people have found many creative uses for them beyond simple sanity checks. Pre-submit checks can be used to enforce policies, update status displays, and check for common bugs. For example, we once experienced an outage caused by a file with incorrect permissions. Now a pre-submit check prevents that same problem from reoccurring.

9.3.3 Build

During the **build** step, source files are processed to generate new artifacts. This usually means source code is compiled to produce executable files. Other tasks such as converting images from one format to another, extracting documentation from source code, running unit tests, and so on might also be performed during this step.

This step is gated based on whether all the build processes complete successfully. The most important of these checks are the **unit tests**. Unit tests are quality assurance tests that can run on compilation units such as function libraries and object class definitions. In contrast, **system tests**, discussed in the next chapter, involve running the service and testing its complete functionality.

Unit tests often take the form of an additional executable that does nothing except call functions in the code in many different ways, checking whether the results are as expected. For example, suppose the source code includes a library of functions for manipulating usernames. Suppose one function in the library tests whether a string can be used as a valid username. The unit test may call that function many times, each time testing a string that is known to be invalid a different way (too short, too long, contains spaces, contains invalid characters) to verify that all of those cases are rejected. Another unit test may do the inverse for strings that are known to be valid.

Unit tests can be rather sophisticated. For example, to test functions that need access to a database, the unit test code may set up a mini-database with sample data. Setting up a database is complex, so testing frameworks have been developed that permit one to replace functions for testing purposes. For example, suppose you are testing a function that opens a connection to a database, sends a query, and manipulates the results. You might replace the "connect to database" function with one that does nothing and replace the "query database" function with one that always returns a particular set of results. Now you can test the function without needing to have an actual database.

This step provides us with an opportunity to perform aggressive testing early in the process to avoid wasted effort later.

9.3.4 Package

During the **package** step, the files left behind from the previous step are used to create the installation packages. A package is a single file that encodes all the files to be installed plus the machine-readable instructions for how to perform the installation. Because it is a single file, it is more convenient to transport.

This step is gated based on whether package creation happened successfully.

A simple package format would be a Zip or tar file that contains all the files that will be installed plus an installation script. When the installer runs, it reads the package, extracts all the files, and then runs the installation script. A more detailed description appears in the "Software Repositories" chapter of the third edition of *The Practice of System and Network Administration* (Limoncelli, Hogan & Chalup 2015).

Software packages should be designed to run in any environment. Do not create separate packages for the testing environment and the production environment. Or worse, do not build the package for testing, then after testing rebuild it for the production environment. Production should run packages that were tested, not packages that are similar to ones that were tested.

What Is a Software Package?

A software package is a container. This single file contains everything needed to install an application, patch, or library. Packages typically include the binary executables to be installed, any related data files, configuration data, and machine-interpretable instructions describing how to install and remove the software. You may be familiar with file formats such as Zip, UNIX tar, and cpio. Such files contain the contents of many smaller files plus metadata. The metadata as a whole is like a table of contents or index. It encodes information needed to unpack the individual files plus file ownership, permissions, and timestamps.

9.3.5 Register

During the **register** step, the package is uploaded to the package repository. At this point the package is ready to be handed off to the deploy phase. This step is gated based on whether upload is a success.

9.4 Build Console

The **build console** is software that manages all of the build steps, making it easy to view results and past history, and to keep statistics on success rates, the amount of time the process takes, and more. Build consoles are invariably web-based tools that provide a dashboard to view status as well as control panels to manage the processes. There are many such tools, including Hudson, Jenkins CI, TeamCity, Go Continuous Delivery, and Atlassian Bamboo.

Once you find a tool that you like, you will find yourself wanting to use it with everything. Therefore, when selecting such a tool, make sure it operates with the tools you currently use—source code repository software, compilers and other build tools—and offers support for all your operating systems and platforms. Such tools generally can be extended through a plug-in mechanism. This way you are not at the whim of the vendor to extend it. If there is a community of open source developers who maintain freely available plug-ins, that is a good sign. It usually means that the tool is extensible and well maintained.

A build console also should have an API for controlling it. You will want to be able to write tools that interact with it, kick off jobs, query it, and so on. One of the most simple and useful APIs is an RSS feed of recently completed builds. Many other systems can read RSS feeds.

> **Case Study: RSS Feeds of Build Status**
>
> StackExchange has an internal chat room system. It has the ability to monitor an RSS feed and announce any new entries in a given room. The SRE chat room monitors an RSS feed of build completions. Every time a build completes, there is an announcement of what was built and whether it was successful, plus a link to the status page. This way the entire team has visibility to their builds.

9.5 Continuous Integration

Continuous integration (CI) is the practice of doing the build phase many times a day in an automated fashion. Each run of the build phase is triggered by some event, usually a code commit. All the build-phase steps then run in a fully automated fashion.

All builds are done from the main trunk of the source code repository. All developers contribute code directly to the trunk. There are no long-lived branches or independent work areas, created for feature development.

that the same bits are used in testing as well as deployment. Deployment may happen hours or weeks after testing and it is important that the same files be used for other deployments. Otherwise, untested changes can slip in.

It is easier to manage a package than the individual files. Packages are usually cryptographically hashed or digitally signed so that the receiving end can verify that the file was not altered along the way. It is safer to upload a single file than a hierarchy of files. Because the metadata is encoded inside the package, there is no worry that it will be accidentally changed along the way.

Other mechanisms for passing files between phases should be avoided. We've seen individual files emailed between teams, losing any permissions and ownership metadata. We've seen organizations that do their handoff by placing all the individual files in a particular subdirectory on a file server. There was no easy way to tell if the files had changed between test and deploy. The person maintaining the directory could not prepare the next release until we were done with the current files. In this system there was no way to access older releases. Even worse, we've seen this process involve a subdirectory in a particular person's home directory, which meant if that individual left the company, the entire process would break.

Also avoid using the source code repository as the handoff mechanism. Source repositories usually have a feature that lets you label, or **tag**, all files at a particular moment in time. The tag name is then given to the deployment phase as the handoff. This approach may create many problems. For example, it is difficult to verify the integrity of all the files and the metadata. Permissions may be accidentally changed. File ownership, by design, is changed. If this technique is used and binaries are checked into the repository, the repository will grow quite large and unwieldy. If binaries are not checked in, it means deployment will have to build them. This is a duplication of effort and risks introducing subtle changes that will have bypassed testing.

9.7 Summary

This chapter was an overview of service delivery and a detailed examination of the build phase. The next chapter will examine the deployment phase in detail.

Service delivery comprises the technical processes involved in turning source code into a running service. The service delivery platform is the software and automation that drives the process.

Service delivery has two phases: build and deploy. Build turns source code into packages. Deploy takes the packages and deploys them in an environment. There are different environments for different purposes. The test environment is used to test the service. The live environment is where the service runs to provide service for customers. The two environments should be engineered and built the same way to make testing as meaningful as possible. The test environment typically differs only in its size and the fact that it stores fictional data instead of real user data. There are many other environments, including some used for exploratory testing, performance testing, beta testing, and so on.

A flow is one trip through the service delivery platform. Each step includes testing with the aim of finding bugs as early as possible. Bugs found in the live environment are the result of insufficient testing in earlier phases and environments.

When a service delivery platform is functioning at its best, the result is high confidence in the service being delivered. As a result, the organization can be more aggressive with making changes, and features can be released faster. In other words, innovation is accelerated. Compare this to an organization that is unsure of its delivery system. In such a case, releases take months to produce. Bugs are found long after code is written, making it more difficult to correct problems. Innovation is hindered because change becomes stifled as fear and despair rule.

The handoff from build to deploy is a package, a file that contains many files. A package is easier to transport, more secure, and less error prone than transporting many individual files.

Exercises

1. Describe the steps of the service delivery platform's build phase.
2. Why are the build and deployment phases separate?
3. Why are the application and infrastructure flows separate?
4. What are the pros and cons of the waterfall methodology compared with the modern DevOps methodology?
5. How does "good flow" enable a business to reach its goals?
6. Describe continuous integration and its benefits.
7. Why do testing and production need separate environments?
8. Describe the service delivery platform used in your organization. Based on the benefits described in this chapter, which changes would you recommend?
9. What are the benefits of using packages as the handoff mechanism?
10. Does your your organization use CI? Which parts of your current platform would need to change to achieve CI?

Chapter 10

Service Delivery: The Deployment Phase

Let 'er roll!

—Elvia Allman
to Lucy and Ethel

In the previous chapter we examined the build phase, which ends with the creation of a software package. In this chapter we'll examine the deployment phase, which uses the package to create a running service.

The deployment phase creates the service in one or more testing and production environments. Deciding if a release used in the testing environment is ready to be used in the production environment requires approval.

The goal of the deployment phase is to create a running environment. This environment is then used for testing or for live production services.

As Figure 9.1 (page 198) showed, packages are retrieved from the package repository and then installed and configured to create an environment. The environment created may be the testing environment, which is set up to verify that all the pieces of the system work together. It may also be the live environment, which provides service to users. Alternatively, it may be one of the other environments described previously in Section 9.1.1.

10.1 Deployment-Phase Steps

There are three steps in the deployment phase: packages are promoted, installed, and configured.

10.1.1 Promotion

The **promotion** step is where a release is selected and promoted for use in the desired environment. The desired version is selected and marked as the right version for the environment being built.

For example, suppose building an environment requires three packages called A, B, and C. Each trip through the build phase results in a new package. Package A has versions 1.1, 1.2, and 1.3. B has versions 1.1, 1.2, 1.3, and 1.4. There are more versions because there have been more check-ins. C has versions 1.1 and 1.3 (1.2 is missing because there was a build failure).

Let's say that the combination of A-1.2, B-1.4, and C-1.3 has been tested together and approved for production. The promotion step would tell the package repository to mark them as the designated production versions.

Selecting specific versions like this is generally done for production, beta, and early access environments, as mentioned in Section 9.1.1. However, development and testing environments may simply use the latest release: A-1.3, B-1.4, and C-1.3.

How packages are marked for particular environments depends on the package repository system. Some have a tagging mechanism, such that only one version of a particular package can have the "production" tag at a time. There may be many packages, each with one version designated as the production version. There is usually a virtual tag called "latest" that automatically refers to the newest version.

Some repository systems use a technique called **pinning**. A package is pinned at a particular version, and that version is always used even if newer versions are available. While tags are usually global, pinning is done at the environment level. For example, testing and live environments would each have packages pinned at different versions.

Other package repository systems work very differently. They can store only one version of a package at a given time. In this case, there will be multiple repositories and packages will be copied between them. For example, all new packages will be put in a repository called "development." When the package is ready to be used in the testing environment, it is copied to a repository called "testing." All machines in the testing environment point at this repository. If the package is approved for use in production, it is copied to a third repository called "production"; all the machines in the production environment read packages from this repository. The benefit of this kind of system is that the production environment cannot accidentally install unapproved packages because it does not know they exist. Nevertheless, keeping a history of past package versions is more difficult, sometimes done by some kind of separate archive subsystem.

10.1.2 Installation

In the **installation** step, the packages are copied to machines and installed. This is done by an installer that understands the package format. Most operating systems have their own installer software, each generally tied to its native package repository system.

A package can include scripts to run before and after installation. The actual installation process involves running the pre-install script, copying files from the package to their final destination, and then running the post-install script. Pre-install scripts do tasks like creating directories, setting permissions, verifying preconditions are met, and creating accounts and groups that will own the files about to be installed. Post-install scripts do tasks like copying a default configuration if one doesn't already exist, enabling services, and registering the installation with an asset manager. Post-install scripts can also perform smoke tests, such as verifying the ability to access remote services, middleware, or other infrastructure services such as databases.

10.1.3 Configuration

In the **configuration** step, local settings and data are put in place to turn the installed package into the running service.

While packages often include installation scripts that do some generic configuration, this step does machine-specific work required to create a working service. For example, installing a web server package creates a generic web server configured to host static files from a particular directory. However, determining which domains are served from this machine, making the load balancer aware of its presence, and other tasks are specific to the machine and would be done here.

This step is gated by health checks—that is, a few simple tests that verify the system is running. For example, one common health check is done by requesting a particular URL that responds only after carrying out a few quick internal tests.

There are many software frameworks for configuration management. Some popular ones include CFEngine, Puppet, and Chef. They all permit the creation of modules for configuring specific services and applying those modules to different machines as needed. Configuration management is discussed further in Section 12.6.4.

The two major strategies for configuration are called **convergent orchestration** and **direct orchestration**. Convergent orchestration takes a description of how the environment should be configured, and the configuration management system then makes individual changes that lead to the entire system converging on that desired state. If for some reason an undesired change is made (accidentally by a user, on purpose by a user, or by an external event such as a machine failure), the orchestration system will detect this and make changes until the desired configuration has converged again. When the next configuration is defined, the system starts to converge toward this new definition, making the fewest changes required to get there. Convergent orchestration can be described as getting the environment to a particular state and keeping it there.

Direct orchestration can be described as a method to execute a multistep process during which certain invariants hold true. For example, moving a database from one machine to another requires many steps that must happen in a certain order, all while the the invariant of "clients always have access to the database" remains true.

The steps might be as follows:

1. Machine B is configured to be a database replica.
2. Wait for the replica to become synchronized with the primary database.
3. The database clients are put in temporary read-only mode.
4. The roles of machines A and B are swapped, making A the read-only replica.
5. The database clients are taken out of read-only mode and configured to send writes to machine B.

Achieving this goal with convergent orchestration would require an unwieldy process. It would require creating a desired state for each step, and waiting for one state to be achieved before switching to the next.

A challenge in direct orchestration is how to handle multiple processes happening at the same time. For example, imagine this process happening at the same time as a load balancer is being added to the system and the web servers are being reconfigured to add a new service. These processes all involve overlapping sets of machines and resources. The steps have to be ordered and coordinated in ways that prevent conflicts and assure that the system does not paint itself into a corner. Currently this is done manually, which is an error-prone process. Automating such things at a large scale is the kind of thing that researchers are only just beginning to consider.

One of the barriers to moving to convergent orchestration is that systems have to be architected to support it. This is a major problem for enterprises automating their deployment and infrastructure management processes, especially with commercial products that cannot be modified. Home-grown systems can be designed with support from the start or, alternatively, modified after the fact.

10.2 Testing and Approval

Before a release is used in production, it must be tested and approved. First, automated testing is done. Next, manual testing, if there is any, is performed. Lastly, management approves or signs off on the release. The list of people or departments that must sign off on a release is called the **approval chain**. After all this activity is complete, the release can be promoted and pushed into production.

10.2.1 Testing

Testing involves many different categories of tests. In the build phase, unit testing is performed on each component. There are four kinds of testing in the deployment phase:

- **System Testing:** This testing brings together all the various pieces of the service and tests the final product or system. It is performed on the service running in the testing environment. Passing these tests is a precondition for the release being used in production and any other environment that includes external customers. Every individual feature should be tested. Multistep workflows such as making a purchase should also be tested. There are testing frameworks that can perform tests as if they are being done by a user. For example, Selenium WebDriver is an open source project that automates web site testing by sending HTTP requests as if they came from various web browsers. No matter how a user interacts with software, there is a testing tool that can automate the tests. This includes PC-based GUIs, APIs, consoles/keyboards, mobile phones, and, as documented in Gruver, Young & Fulghum (2012), even the front panels of laser printers.

- **Performance Testing:** These tests determine the speed of the service under various conditions. This testing is performed on the service while in the testing environment or in a specially built performance testing environment. It should determine if the performance meets written specifications or requirements. All too often, however, such specifications are nonexistent or vague. Therefore often the results of this testing are just compared to previous results. If the entire system, or a specific feature, works significantly more slowly than the previous release—a **performance regression**—the test fails.

- **Load Testing:** This special kind of performance testing determines how much load the system can sustain. It is usually done in the testing environment or in a special performance testing environment. Such testing involves subjecting the service to increasingly larger amounts of traffic, or load, to determine the maximum the system is able to process. As an example, Google does not use a new Linux kernel without first doing load testing to verify the kernel changes have not negatively affected how much load a search cluster can sustain. An entire cluster is built with machines running this kernel release. Search queries are artificially generated at larger and larger QPS. Eventually the cluster maxes out, unable to do more QPS, or the system gets so slow that it cannot answer queries in the required number of milliseconds. If this maximum QPS is significantly less than the previous release, Google does not upgrade to that kernel.

- **User Acceptance Testing (UAT):** This testing is done by customers to verify that the system meets their needs and to verify claims by the producer. Customers run their own tests to verify the new release meets their requirements. For example, they might run through each business process that involves the service. System testing involves developers making sure that they don't ship products with defects. UAT involves customers making sure they don't receive products with defects. Ideally, any test developed for UAT will be made known to the developers so that it can be added to their own battery of tests. This would verify such concerns earlier in the process. Sadly this is not always possible. UAT may include tests that use live data that cannot be shared, such as personally identifiable information (PII). UAT also may be used to determine if an internal process needs to be revised.

Every Step Has a Gate

The build process at StackExchange has a few different handoffs. Each is gated by a test so that defects aren't passed forward, to use the assembly-line analogy. There are many kinds of tests, each a separate module. The service delivery flow has the following handoffs and gates:

1. Code is built and then packaging is gated by unit tests.
2. Digital signature verification gates whether the packager can pass code to the test environment.
3. Promoting a release from the test environment to production is gated by system tests.
4. Production environment upgrade success is gated by health checks.

10.2.2 Approval

If all the tests pass, the release is called a **production candidate**. Candidates are put through an approval process. If they are approved they are installed in production.

At this point, the members of the approval chain are asked to sign off on the production candidate. The approval chain is a list of specific people, or their delegates, who must sign off on production releases. For example, the list might include the product manager, the director of marketing, and the director of engineering. Often departmental approval is required from the security, legal, and privacy compliance departments.

Each environment may have a different set of tests and approval chain to gate which releases may enter it. Deploying releases in the development and testing environments is automatically approved. UAT and performance testing generally select the latest release that has passed system testing. Environments that will have live users, such as beta and demo environments, may be automatically upgraded periodically. For example, it is common for demo environments to be wiped and reloaded on a specific day of the week or a certain duration before the official release date.

Environments that will be exposed to live, or revenue-generating, customers should be gated with the most scrutiny. Thus the production environment generally requires all of the preceding tests plus positive confirmation by the entire approval chain.

10.3 Operations Console

The **operations console** is software that manages the operational processes, especially the deployment steps. Like the build console, it is a web-based system that makes it easy to view results and past history, and keeps statistics about success rates, process duration, and more.

Nearly everything said about the build console can be repeated in regard to the operations console, so refer to Section 9.4. Security and authorization might be more important here because processes can affect live services. For example, there may tighter controls over who may initiate a launch for a new release into production.

10.4 Infrastructure Automation Strategies

A few strategic tips will help you fully automate the deploy phase so that it can run unattended in the console. As discussed earlier, there is a flow for deploying infrastructure and another flow for deploying the service itself. Deploying the entire stack can be broken down even further: preparing and testing the physical or virtual machine, installing the operating system, installing and configuring the service. Each of these is a discrete step that can be automated separately. In fact, in large environments you'll find different teams responsible for each step.

10.4.1 Preparing Physical Machines

Preparing a physical machine involves unboxing it, mounting it in a rack, cabling it, configuring BIOS settings, and testing. The earlier steps require physical work and are very difficult to automate. Very few companies can afford robotics to do these steps. However, we can reduce the labor by installing them one rack at a time instead of one machine at a time, thereby taking advantage of economies of mass production. Another way to improve the process is to use **blade servers**. Blade servers are a technology made up of one chassis for many individual computers, each on a "blade," which makes installation and maintenance easier. At very large scale, machines are designed with specific features to enable fast and efficient mass installation. Google and other companies design their own hardware to ensure design features meet their needs.

We have seen some impressive systems that automate the new hardware intake process. The Tumblr Invisible Touch system automates upgrading firmware, setting up the Baseboard Management Controller (BMC), adding the machine to Tumblr's inventory system, performing a multi-hour stress test, and configuring the network.

A quick-and-dirty solution is to manually install hardware and configure BIOS settings but automate the process of verifying that the settings are correct. Since BIOS settings change rarely, if at all, this may be good enough for some sites, or at least a good half-measure on the way to full automation.

Another strategy is to reduce complexity through standardization. Standardizing on a few hardware configurations makes machines interchangeable. Usually you create one model for heavy computation with lots of RAM and CPU, and one model for mass storage with lots of disk. Now all machines in a category can be treated as a pool of machines, allocating one when needed and returning it to the pool when it is not. You can create an API that permits such allocations to happen almost as easily as creating virtual machines.

10.4.2 Preparing Virtual Machines

Preparing virtual machines should be a matter of making an API call. That said, having a few standard sizes can make management easier.

For example, one might allocate VMs in sizes such that either four small, two medium, or one large VM perfectly fills the physical machine. Then there is less chance that a physical machine may have some space unused, but not enough to create a new VM.

One can also use multiples of Fibonacci numbers. If a 5-unit machine is deallocated, for example, that leaves room for five 1-unit machines, a 2-unit plus a 3-unit machine, and so on.

This not only helps fully utilize the physical machines but also makes reorganizing them easier. Imagine a situation where a medium VM is needed but the only free space is the size of a small VM on one physical machine and a small VM on another physical machine. If the VM sizes are standardized, it is easy to determine how VMs could be moved to create a medium-sized space on one physical machine. If each VM is a custom size, moving VMs around might still be possible but the movements could be like the Towers of Hanoi problem, requiring many intermediate steps and inefficiencies.

10.4.3 Installing OS and Services

Installing the operating system and service configuration can be done in many ways. The two main approaches are an image method and a configuration management method.

The **image** method involves creating a disk image for each kind of service. This image is then copied onto the disk and, after a reboot, the machine comes up preconfigured. Images can be deployed to physical machines, virtual machines, or containers, as described in Section 3.2. The image contains the operating system, all required packages, and the service in a ready-to-run form. It is known as a **baked image** because the service is "baked in."

The **configuration management** strategy involves using an installer or other mechanism to get a minimal operating system running. Configuration management tools can then install any additional packages and bring up the service. This technique is known as **frying** the image, because the image is cooked up while you wait.

Automated Baking

Baked images can be installed more rapidly because all the configuration is done ahead of time. When turning up hundreds of machines, this can be a significant win. Unfortunately, maintaining many images can be a burden. Installing a patch on many images, for example, is labor intensive. When installation is done this way, there is no version control, which is bad.

The solution is to automate the creation of baked images. Software frameworks for creating baked images include Vagrant, Docker, and Netflix Aminator. All of these options provide languages for describing how to build the image from scratch, by specifying the base OS release, packages, file settings, and so on. The image is then created from this description. The description can be kept under version control, such that the service delivery platform can be used to build, test, and deploy images.

Baked images can be used for building a new service as well as upgrading an existing one. For example, if there are 10 web servers behind a load balancer, upgrading them involves taking each one out of the load balancer's rotation, deleting it, and re-creating it from the image. All 10 web servers running the new release will then have a well-understood configuration.

Persistent Data

Not all machines can simply be wiped and reinstalled in this way. For example, a database server or file server has irreplaceable data that is not part of the build or configuration process. The solution in such a case is to put such data on virtual disks, mounted from a storage area network (SAN) or other remote storage system. The boot disk is replaced, but on boot-up it mounts its virtual disk, thereby reattaching the system to the data it needs. By decoupling where storage is provided from where it is used, machines become more disposable.

Baked versus Fried

Configuration management is often faster than upgrading a machine by installing an image. Configuration management is also less disruptive, because it makes just the minimum number of changes needed to achieve the desired configuration. Those same 10 web servers needing to be upgraded can simply be individually rotated out of the load balancer and only the desired package upgraded. With this technique, the machines are not wiped, so no data is lost.

On the downside, the machines are now in a less well-understood configuration. Imagine that an 11th web server is added. It starts out with the new software release. Does this 11th machine have the same configuration as the 10 that got to their current state through upgrades? In theory, yes, but small differences may creep in. Future upgrades require testing that covers both situations, which adds complexity. Proponents of baked images would argue that it is better to refresh a machine from scratch than to let entropy accumulate.

Different Files for Different Environments

Often there is a group of files that must be different in the testing and production environments. For example, logos and other images might have special versions used solely in the actual live service. There may also be special credentials, certificates, or other data.

One way to handle this situation is to include both sets of files in the package and use configuration management to point the server at the proper set. However, this approach does not work for certificates and other files that one might not want to expose to all environments.

Another solution is to move the environment-specific files into separate packages. Each environment then has its own **configuration package**. The installation process would install the main application package plus the one configuration package appropriate for that environment.

The problem with using environment-specific packages is that these files have, essentially, bypassed the testing process. For that reason it is best to keep the use of this mechanism to an absolute minimum, preferably restricting it to files that are low risk or files that can be tested other ways, such as via pre-submit checks.

10.5 Continuous Delivery

Continuous delivery (CD) is the technique in which testing is fully automated and triggered to run for each build. With each build, the testing environment is created, the automated testing runs, and the release is "delivered," ready to be considered for use in other environments. This doesn't mean every change is deployed to production, but rather that every change is proven to be deployable at any time.

CD has similar benefits as continuous integration. In fact, it can be considered an extension to CI. CD makes it economical and low risk to work in small batches, so that problems are found sooner and, therefore, are easier to fix. (See Section 8.2.4.)

CD incorporates all of continuous integration, plus system tests, performance tests, user acceptance tests, and all other automated tests. There's really no excuse not to adopt CD once testing is automated. If some tests are not automated, CD can deliver the release to a beta environment used for manual testing.

10.6 Infrastructure as Code

Recall in Figure 9.1 that the service delivery platform (SDP) pattern flow has quadrants that represent infrastructure as well as applications. The infrastructure for all environments should be built through automation that is treated just like any other service delivered by the SDP.

This approach is called **infrastructure as code**. Like application code, the code that describes the infrastructure is stored in the source repository, revision controlled, and tested in a test environment before being approved for deployment in the live production environment.

Configuration code includes the automation to do configuration management as well as any configuration files and data. Configuration management code and data are built, packaged, and so on just like application software. Even images for VMs and containers can be built and packaged.

When the infrastructure as code technique is done correctly, the same code can build development, testing, and production environments. Each environment differs only in terms of which machines to use, the number of replicas, and other settings. This minimizes the difference between the testing and production environments and makes testing more accurate.

Anyone should be able to build an environment for development or testing. This lets teams and individuals operate and experiment without needing to bother operations. Developers and QA personnel can build multiple test environments. SWEs can build their own sandbox environments, using virtual machines on their laptops.

Infrastructure as code becomes easier to implement as hardware becomes more and more virtual. Over time, storage, machines, and networks have all gone virtual. Storage volumes, virtual machines, and network topologies can be created, manipulated, and deallocated through software and controlled by APIs.

10.7 Other Platform Services

A few other services are involved in an SDP and are worth a brief mention in this chapter:

- **Authentication:** There needs to be some form of authentication so that the system can restrict who can access what. In turn, security facilities are needed that provide authentication, authorization, and accounting (AAA). Often this service consists of LDAP plus Kerberos, Open Directory, or Active Directory.
- **DNS:** DNS translates names of machines to IP addresses. In an SDP, machines are brought up and turned down rapidly. It is important to have the ability to update DNS zones via an API or dynamic DNS (DynDNS/DDNS).
- **Configuration Management Database (CMDB):** The deployment phase should be database driven. Configurations and machine relationships are stored in a database, and the tools that build the environment use this information to guide their work. This means modifying the environment is as simple as updating a database. For example, the database might store the list of web server frontends associated with a particular service. By adding to this list, the configuration management tools will bring up web servers on those machines.

10.8 Summary

The deployment phase of the software delivery platform is where software packages are turned into a running service. First the service is run in a testing environment. After an approval process is passed, the packages are used to build the live production environment.

The deployment phase involves selecting a group of packages that represent all the parts of the service. Together they are considered a release candidate. They are installed on the machines that make up the environment. The service is then configured and becomes ready for testing or use.

An environment requires infrastructure: hardware, network, and other components. Virtual infrastructure can be configured through automation. Physical machines can also be manipulated through software, although doing so requires more planning and is slower and less flexible. When infrastructure configuration is encoded in software, the entire infrastructure can be treated as software, with all the benefits of source code: revision control, testing, and so on.

Before a release is used in the live environment, it must pass many tests. System tests check the system as a whole. Performance and load testing verify the software's performance. User acceptance testing is an opportunity for stakeholders to approve a release. There may be other approvals such as those issued by legal, marketing, and product management.

Continuous delivery is achieved when the deployment phase and all testing is automated. New release candidates are produced automatically and confidence is improved as the testing becomes more and more extensive.

Service delivery engineering is a large and changing field. We have only scratched the surface in this chapter. We recommend the book *Continuous Delivery* (Humble & Farley 2010) for a deeper look at the subject.

Exercises

1. Describe the steps of the service delivery platform's deployment phase.
2. Describe continuous delivery and its benefits.
3. Which kinds of testing are common in service delivery?
4. In your organization's service delivery platform, which of the kinds of testing listed in Section 10.2 are and aren't done? Which benefits would you hope to gain by adding the missing tests?
5. What is the approval chain for software in your organization's service delivery process? How are the approvals requested and responses communicated?
6. How could the approval chain in your organization be automated?
7. Apply the deployment-phase techniques from this chapter to an organization that does not do software development, but instead chooses to use off-the-shelf commercial software.
8. In your environment, what are the steps to prepare a new machine? Which are automated? How could the non-automated steps be automated?
9. Does your your organization use continuous delivery? Which parts of your current platform would need to change to achieve CD?

Chapter 11

Upgrading Live Services

> The things that make you strong,
> and make you feel as though you've
> accomplished something, are not
> the easy ones.
>
> —Dr. Jerri Nielsen

This chapter is about deploying new releases to the production environment. It is different from deploying into any other environment.

The process of upgrading an environment with a new software release is called a **code push**. Pushing code into production can be tricky because we are modifying a system while it is running. This is like changing the tires of a car while it is speeding down the highway at 90 km/h: you can do it, but it requires a lot of care and planning.

Luckily there are many techniques available, each appropriate for different situations. This chapter catalogs the most common techniques. We then discuss best practices such as continuous deployment and other practical matters.

11.1 Taking the Service Down for Upgrading

One way to upgrade a service is to take it down, push the new code out to all systems, and bring the service back up. This has the benefit of being very simple to implement, and it permits testing of the service before real users are given access to the newly upgraded service.

Sadly, this technique requires downtime, which makes it unacceptable for most services. However, it may be appropriate for development and demo environments where prescheduled downtime may be permitted.

This technique also works when the service is replicated in its entirety. Each service replica can be taken down, upgraded, and brought back up if there is enough spare capacity. In this case, usually a global load balancer (GLB) divides traffic among the working replicas. One replica at a time is drained by removing it from the GLB and waiting until all in-flight requests are completed. The replica can then be taken down without affecting the service.

Upgrading Blog Search

When Tom was an SRE for Google's Blog Search service, the customer-facing stack was replicated in four datacenters. Each replica was independent of the others. There was enough capacity that any one stack could be down and the others could handle the entire traffic load. One at a time, each stack would be drained by removing it from the GLB, upgrading it, checking it, and then adding it back to the GLB.

Meanwhile, another part of the system was the "pipeline": a service that scanned for new blog posts, ingested them, produced the new corpus, and distributed it to the four customer-facing stacks. The pipeline was very important to the entire service, but if it was down customers would not notice. However, the freshness of the search results would deteriorate the longer the pipeline was down. Therefore uptime was important but not essential and upgrades were done by bringing down the entire pipeline.

Many services at Google were architected in a similar way and upgrades were done in a similar pattern.

11.2 Rolling Upgrades

In a rolling upgrade, individual machines or servers are removed from service, upgraded, and put back in service. This is repeated for each element being upgraded; the process rolls through all of them until it is complete.

The customer sees continuous service because the individual outages are hidden by a local load balancer. During the upgrade, some customers will see the new software and some will see the old software. There is a chance that a particular customer will see new features appear and disappear as sequential requests go to new and old machines. This is rare due to load balancer stickiness, discussed in Section 4.2.3, and other factors, such as deploying new features toggled off, as described in Section 2.1.9.

During the upgrade, there is a temporary reduction in capacity. If there are 10 servers, as each is upgraded the service is at 90 percent capacity. Therefore this technique requires planning to assure there is sufficient capacity.

The process works as follows. First the server or machine is drained. This can be done by reconfiguring the load balancer to stop sending requests to it or by having the replica enter "lame duck mode," as described in Section 2.1.3, where it "lies," telling the load balancer it is unhealthy so that the load balancer stops sending requests to it. Eventually no new traffic will have been received for a while and all in-flight requests will be finished. Next the server is upgraded, the upgrade is verified, and the draining process is undone. Then the upgrade process begins again with the next server.

Avoiding Code Pushes When Sleepy

The best time to do a code push is during the day. You are wide awake and more co-workers are available if something goes wrong.

Many organizations do code pushes very late at night. The typical excuse for a 3 AM upgrade is that the upgrade is risky and doing it late at night decreases exposure.

Doing critical upgrades while half-asleep is a much bigger risk. Ideally, by now we've convinced you that a much better strategy for reducing risk is automated testing and small batches.

Alternatively, you can have a team eight time zones east of your primary location that does code pushes. Those deployments will occur in the middle of the night for your customers but not for your team.

11.3 Canary

The canary process is a special form of the rolling upgrade that is more appropriate when large numbers of elements need to be upgraded. If there are hundreds or thousands of servers or machines, the rolling upgrade process can take a long time. If each server takes 10 minutes, upgrading 1000 servers will take about a week. That would be unacceptable—yet upgrading all the servers at once is too risky.

The canary process involves upgrading a very small number of replicas, waiting to see if obvious problems develop, and then moving on to progressively larger groups of machines. In the old days of coal mining, miners would bring caged canaries into the mines. These birds are far more sensitive than humans to harmful gases. If your canary started acting sick or fell from its perch, it was time to get out of the mine before you became incapacitated by the gases.

Likewise, the canary technique upgrades a single machine and then tests it for a while. Problems tend to appear in the first 5 or 10 minutes. If the canary lives, a group of machines are upgraded. There is another wait and more testing, and then a larger group is upgraded.

A common canary process is to upgrade one server, then one server per minute until 1 percent of all servers are upgraded, and then one server per second until all are upgraded. Between each group there may be an extended pause. While this is happening, verification tests are run against all the upgraded servers. These tests are usually very simplistic, generally just verifying that the code is not crashing and live queries are succeeding.

If trouble is found (i.e., if the canary dies), the process is stopped. At this point the servers that were upgraded can be rolled back. Alternatively, if there is enough capacity, they can be shut down until a new release becomes available.

Canarying is not a testing process. The canary process is a method for deploying a release into production that detects bad pushes and prevents them from being visible to users. The main difference between a testing process and a canary process is that it is acceptable for the test process to fail. If a testing process fails, you've prevented a bad release from reaching live users. More pedantically, the testing process has succeeded in detecting a defective release. That is a good thing.

Conversely, you don't want a canary process to fail. A failed canary means something was missed by the testing process. A failed canary should be so rare that it is cause to stop development and dedicate resources to determining what went wrong and which additional testing needs to be added to prevent this failure in the future. Only then can new roll-outs begin. Canarying is an insurance policy against accidental bad releases, not a way to detect bad releases.

Testing and canarying are often conflated, but should not be. What some people call canarying is really testing new releases on live users. Testing should be done in a testing environment, not on live users.

Canarying Is Not a Substitute for System Testing

We've observed situations where canarying was used to test new releases on live users. In one case it was done unintentionally—a fact that was not realized until a major outage occurred. The SREs received a thoroughly tested package and would canary it into their production environment. This worked fine for many years because the test and live environments were very similar.

Over time, however, many tools were developed by the SREs for use in the production environment. These tools were not tested by the developers' testing system. The developers were not responsible for the tools, plus many of the tools were considered ad hoc or temporary.

There's an old adage in engineering, "Nothing is more permanent than a temporary solution." Soon these tools grew and begat complex automated systems. Yet, they were not tested by the developers' testing system. Each major release broke the tools and the operations staff had to scurry to update them. These problems were trivial, however, compared to what happened next.

One day a release was pushed into production and problems were not discovered until the push was complete. Service for particular users came to a halt.

By now the hardware used in the two environments had diverged enough that kernel drivers and virtualization technology versions had diverged. The result was that virtual machines running certain operating systems stopped working.

At this point the SREs realized the environments had diverged too much. They needed to completely revamp their system testing environment to make sure it tested the specific combination of main service release, kernel version, virtualization framework version, and hardware that was used in production. In addition, they needed to incorporate their tools into the repository and the development and testing process so that each time they wouldn't have to scramble to fix incompatibilities with the tools they had developed.

Creating a proper system testing environment, and a mechanism to keep test and production in sync, required many months of effort.

11.4 Phased Roll-outs

Another strategy is to partition users into groups that are upgraded one at a time. Each group, or phase, is identified by its tolerance for risk.

For example, Facebook has clusters dedicated to providing service to its own employees. These clusters receive upgrades first because their employees are willing testers of new releases—it's part of their job. Next, a small set of outside-user clusters are upgraded. Lastly, the remaining clusters are upgraded.

Stack Exchange's upgrade process involves many phases. Stack Exchange has more than 110 web communities, plus each community has a meta-community associated with it for discussing the community itself. The same software is used for all of these communities, though the colors and designs are different. The deployment phases are the test environment, then the meta-communities, then the less populated communities, and lastly the largest and most active community. Each phase starts automatically if the previous phase saw no problems for a certain amount of time. By the time the upgrade reaches the last phase, Stack Exchange has high confidence in the release. The earliest phases can tolerate more outages for many reasons, including the fact that they are not revenue-generating units.

11.5 Proportional Shedding

Proportional shedding is a deployment technique whereby the new service is built on new machines in parallel to the old service. Then the load balancer sends, or sheds, a small percentage of traffic to the new service. If this succeeds, a larger percentage is sent. This process continues until all traffic is going to the new service.

Proportional shedding can be used to move traffic between two systems. The old cluster is not turned down until the entire process is complete. If problems are discovered, the load can be transferred back to the old cluster.

The problem with this technique is that twice as much capacity is required during the transition. If the service fits on a single machine, having two machines running for the duration of the upgrade is reasonable.

If there are 1000 machines, proportional shedding can be very expensive. Keeping 1000 spare machines around may be beyond your budget. In this case, once a certain percentage of traffic is diverted to the new cluster, some older machines can be recycled and redeployed as part of the new cluster.

11.6 Blue-Green Deployment

Blue-green deployment is similar to proportional shedding but does not require twice as many resources. There are two environments on the same machine, one called "blue" and the other called "green." Green is the live environment and blue is the environment that is dormant. Both exist on the same machine by a mechanism as simple as two different subdirectories, each of which is used as a different virtual host of the same web server. The blue environment consumes very little resources.

When the new release is to go live, traffic is directed to the blue environment. When the process is finished, the names of the environments are swapped. This system permits rolling back to the previous environment to take place easily.

This is a very simple way of providing zero-downtime deployments on applications that weren't designed for it, as long as the applications support being installed in two different places on the same machine.

11.7 Toggling Features

As discussed in Section 2.1.9, it is a common practice to tie each new feature to a software flag or configuration setting so that such features can be individually turned on or off. Toggling the switch is known as **flag flipping**. New features that are incomplete and not ready for use by live users have their flags off. When they are ready for use, the flag is turned on. The feature can be disabled if problems are found. Having a flag off is also called hiding a feature behind a flag.

Feature toggling is one way to implement the general principle of decoupling deployment and release. Deployment is putting a package into an environment. Release is making a feature available to users. We often achieve release through deployment and, therefore, assume one implies the other. In fact, feature toggles decouples these two concepts so that deployment can happen all the time while release happens on demand. Deployment becomes a purely technical activity that users are unaware of.

There are many ways to implement the flag mechanism. The flags can be command-line flags, used when starting the service. For example, starting a spell checker service with version 2 of the spell check algorithm enabled, and the morphological algorithm disabled, might involve running a command such as the following:

```
$ spellcheck-server --sp-algorithm-v2 --morphological=off
```

The flag might be set via shell environment variable. The variables are set prior to running the command:

```
$ export SP_ALGORITHM_V2=yes
$ export SP_MORPHOLOGICAL=off
$ spellcheck-server
```

This becomes cumbersome as the number of flags increases. A service may have dozens or hundreds of flags at any given time. Therefore flag systems can read flags from files instead:

```
$ cat spell.txt
sp-algorithm-v2=on
morphological=off
$ spellcheck-server --flagfile=spell.txt
```

All of these approaches suffer from the fact that to change any flag, the process must be restarted. This interrupts service. Other techniques permit flags to be updated at will. Systems like Google's Chubby and the Apache Zookeeper project can be used to store flags and efficiently notify thousands of servers when they change. With this approach, only one flag is needed—the one specifying the zookeeper namespace—to find the configuration:

```
$ spellcheck-server --zkflags=/zookeeper/config/spell
```

Flag flips are used for many reasons:

- **Rapid Development:** To enable rapid development, features are built up by a series of small changes to a main source branch. Large features take a long time to develop. The longer one waits to merge code changes into the main line source, the more difficult and risky the merge becomes. Sometimes the source code may have been changed by other developers, which creates a merge conflict. Merging small amounts of code is less error prone. (See Section 8.2.4 for more details.) Given this fact, incomplete features are hidden by flags that are disabled until the feature is ready. The flags may be enabled earlier in some environments than in others. For example, previewing a feature to product management might be done by enabling that flag in the demo environment.

- **Gradual Introduction of New Features:** Often some features are introduced to some users but not others. Beta users, for example, may receive earlier access to new features. When users are logged in, whether they have access to the beta features is dynamically controlled by adjusting the flags. Prior to the invention of this technique, beta users would go to an entirely different set of servers. It is very costly to set up a complete replica of the server environment just to support beta users. Moreover, granularity was an all-or-nothing proposition. With flags, each individual feature can be taken in and out of beta testing.

- **Finely Timed Release Dates:** Timing a flag flip is easier than timing a software deployment. If a new feature is to be announced at noon on Tuesday, it is difficult to roll out new software exactly at that time, especially if there are many servers. Instead, flags can be controlled dynamically to flip at a specific time.

- **Dynamic Roll Backs:** It is easier to disable an ill-behaved new feature by disabling a flag than by rolling back to an older release of the software. If a new release has many new features, it would be a shame to have to roll back the entire release because of one bad feature. With flag flips, just the one feature can be disabled.

- **Bug Isolation:** Having each change associated with a flag helps isolate a bug. Imagine a memory leak that may be in one of 30 recently added features. If they are all attached to toggles, a binary search can identify which feature is creating the problem. If the binary search fails to isolate the problem in a test environment, doing this bug detection in production via flags is considerably more sane than via many individual releases.

- **A-B Testing:** Often the best way to tell if users prefer one design or another is to implement both, show certain users the new feature, and observe their behavior. For example, suppose sign-ups for a product are very low. Would sign-ups be improved if a check box defaulted to checked, or if instead of a check box an entirely different mechanism was used? A group of users could be selected, half with their check box default checked (group A) and the other half with the new mechanism (group B). Whichever design has the better results would be used for all users after the test. Flag flips can be used both to control the test and to enable the winning design when the test is finished.

- **One Percent Testing:** This testing exposes a feature to a statistical sample of users. Sometimes, similar to the canary process, it is done to test a new feature before deploying it globally. Sometimes, similar to A-B testing, it is done to identify the reaction to an experimental feature before deciding whether it should be deployed at all. Sometimes it is done to collect information via statistical sampling. For example, a site might like to gather performance statistics about page load times. JavaScript code can be inserted into HTML pages that transmits back to the service data about how long the page took to load. Collecting this information would, essentially, double the number of queries that reach the service and would overload the system. Therefore, the JavaScript is inserted only 1 out of every 100 times. The flag would be set to 0 to disable collection, or a value specifying the sampling percentage.

- **Differentiated Services:** Sometimes there is a need to enable different services for different users. A good flag system can enable paid customers to see different features than unpaid users see. Many membership levels can be implemented by associating a set of flags with each one.

Sometimes a flag is used to disable everything to do with a new feature; at other times it just obscures its visibility. Suppose a web site is going to add auto-completion to an input field. This feature will require changes in the HTML that is generated for the input prompt, the addition of a new API call to the database for partial queries, and possibly other code. The flag could disable everything to do with the feature or it may simply control whether the feature appears in the UI.

Case Study: Facebook Chat's Dark Launch

In 2011 Facebook's Chuck Rossi gave a presentation titled "Pushing Millions of Lines of Code Five Days a Week" (Rossi 2011) that described an in-house tool called "Gatekeeper" that manages **dark launches**: code launched into production with no user-visible component. Rossi's talk revealed that at any given moment on Facebook.com, there is already the code for every major thing Facebook is going to launch in the next six months and beyond. Gatekeeper permits fine-grained control over which features are revealed to which users. Some filters are obvious, such as country, age, and datacenter. Others are unexpected, including one to exclude known employees of certain media outlets such as TechCrunch (Siegler 2011). (Also see the related case study in Section 18.4.)

11.8 Live Schema Changes

Sometimes a new software release expects a different database schema from the previous release. If the service could withstand downtime, one would bring down the service, upgrade the software and change the database schema, and then restart the service. However, downtime is almost always unacceptable in a web environment.

In a typical web environment there are many web server frontends, or replicas, that all talk to the same database server. The older software release is unable to understand the new database schema and will malfunction or crash. The newer software release is unable to understand the old database schema and will also malfunction. Therefore you cannot change the database schema and then do the software upgrade: the older replicas will fail as soon as the database is modified. There will be no service until replicas are upgraded. You cannot upgrade the replicas and then change the database schema because any upgraded replica will fail. The schema cannot be upgraded during the rolling upgrade: new replicas will fail, and then at the moment the database schema changes, all the failing replicas will start to work and the working replicas will start to fail. What chaos! Plus, none of these methods has a decent way to roll back changes if there is a problem.

One way to deal with this scenario is to use **database views**. Each view provides a different abstraction to the same database. A new view is coded for each new software version. This decouples software upgrades from schema changes. Now when the schema changes, each view's code must change to provide the same abstraction to the new schema. The change in schema and the upgrade of view code happen atomically, enabling smooth upgrades. For example, if a field is stored in a new format, one view would store it in the new format and the other view would convert between the old and new formats. When the schema changes, the views would reverse roles.

Sadly, this technique is not used very frequently. Views are a rare feature on relational databases. As of this writing, no key–value store (NoSQL) systems support views. Even when the feature is available, it isn't always used. In these cases another strategy is required.

An alternative is to change the database schema by making the change over a period of two software releases: one after adding any new fields to the database and another before removing any obsolete fields. We learned this technique from Stephen McHenry and refer to it as the McHenry Technique. Similar techniques have been called "expand/contract."

Here are the phases of this technique:

1. The running code reads and writes the old schema, selecting just the fields that it needs from the table or view. This is the original state.

2. Expand: The schema is modified by adding any new fields, but not removing any old ones. No code changes are made. If a roll back is needed, it's painless because the new fields are not being used.
3. Code is modified to use the new schema fields and pushed into production. If a roll back is needed, it just reverts to to Phase 2. At this time any data conversion can be done while the system is live.
4. Contract: Code that references the old, now unused fields is removed and pushed into production. If a roll back is needed, it just reverts to Phase 3.
5. Old, now unused, fields are removed from the schema. In the unlikely event that a roll back is needed at this point, the database would simply revert to Phase 4.

A simple example of this technique involves a database that stores user profiles. Suppose the ability to store the user's photograph is being added. The new field that stores photographic information is added to the schema (Phase 2). A software release is pushed that handles the new field, including the situation where the field is empty. The next software release removes the legacy code and the need for the flag. There is no need for Phase 5 because the schema change only adds fields.

As the next example, suppose a field is replaced by new fields. The user's entire name was stored in one field. The new schema uses three fields to store the first name, middle name, and last name separately. In Phase 2, the three new fields are added to the schema. In Phase 3, we introduce a software release that reads the old and new fields. The code does the right thing depending on whether the old or new fields are populated. Updates from the users write to the new individual fields and mark the old field as unused. At this time a batch job may be run that finds any profiles still using the old field and converts them to the new fields.

Once all legacy data are converted, any code that uses the old field is removed. This new release is pushed into production (Phase 4). Once this release is deployed, Phase 5 removes the old field from the database schema.

One way to streamline the process is to combine or overlap Phases 4 and 5. Another optimization is to lazily remove old fields, perhaps the next time the schema is changed. In other words, Phase 5 from schema version n is combined with Phase 2 from schema version $n+1$.

During Phase 2, software will see the new fields. This may cause problems. Software must be written to ignore them and otherwise not break when unexpected fields exist. Generally this is not a problem, as most SQL queries request the exact fields they need, and software accessing NoSQL databases tends to do this by convention. In SQL terms, this means that any use of SELECT * should not make assumptions about the number or position of fields in the data that is received. This is generally a good practice anyway, because it makes your code more robust.

- **Schedule Permission:** Automated pushes are forbidden if there is a scheduled "change freeze" for holidays, quarterly financial reporting, or days when too many key people are on vacation. A simple list of dates to pause deployments covers these situations.
- **Oncall Schedule:** To avoid dragging the current oncall engineer out of bed, pushes may be paused during typical sleeping hours. If there are multiple oncall teams, each covering different times of the day, each may have a different idea of waking hours. Even a three-shift, follow-the-sun arrangement may have hours when no one is entirely awake.
- **Manual Stop:** There should be a list of people who can, with the click of a button, halt automated pushes. This is akin to assembly lines where anyone can halt production if a defect is found. The reason for a manual pause does not have to be an emergency.
- **Push Conflicts:** A service may be made up of many subservices, each on its own release schedule. It can be prudent to permit only one subservice deployment at a time. Similarly, the next push should not start if the current one hasn't finished.
- **Intentional Delays:** It can be useful to have a pause between pushes to let the current one "soak"—that is, to run long enough to verify that it is stable. Doing pushes too rapidly may make it difficult to isolate when a problem began.
- **Resource Contention:** Pushes should be paused if resources are low—for example, if disk space is low or there is unusually high CPU utilization. Load must be below a particular threshold: don't push when when the system is flooded. Sufficient redundancy must exist: don't push if replicas are not $N + 2$.

It might seem risky to turn these hunches into automated processes. The truth is that it is safer to have them automated and always done than letting a person decide to veto a push because he or she has a gut feeling. Operations should be based on data and science. Automating these checks means they are executed every time, consistently, no matter who is on vacation. They can be fine-tuned and improved. Many times we've heard people comment that an outage happened because they lazily decided not to do a certain check. The truth is that automated checks can improve safety.

In practice, humans aren't any better at catching regressions than automated tests. In fact, to think otherwise is absurd. For example, one regression that people usually watch for is a service that requires significantly more RAM or CPU than the previous release. This is often an indication of a memory leak or other coding error. People often miss such issues even when automated systems detect them and provide warnings. Continuous deployment, when properly implemented, will not ignore such warnings.

Implementing continuous deployment is nontrivial, and easier if done at the start of new projects when the project is small. Alternatively, one can adopt a policy of using continuous deployment for any new subsystems. Older systems eventually are retired or can have continuous deployment added if they stick around.

11.11 Dealing with Failed Code Pushes

Despite all our testing and rigor, sometimes code pushed into production fails. Sometimes it is a hard failure where the software refuses to start or fails soon after starting. In theory, our canarying should detect hard failures and simply take the lone replica out of production. Unfortunately, not all services are replicated or are not replicated in a way that canarying is possible. At other times the failure is more subtle. Features may, for example, fail catastrophically in a way that is not noticed right away and cannot be mitigated through flags or other techniques. As a result, we must change the software itself.

One method is to **roll back** to the last known good release. When problems are found, the software is uninstalled and the most recent good release is reinstalled.

Another method is to **roll forward** to the next release, which presumably fixes the problem discovered in the failed release. The problem with this technique is that the next release might be hours or days away. The failed release must be resilient enough to be usable for the duration, or workarounds must be available. The resilience techniques discussed in Chapter 6 can reduce the time pressure involved. Teams wishing to adopt this technique need to focus on reducing SDP code lead time until it is short enough to make roll forward viable.

Roll forward works best when servers are highly replicated and canarying is used for deployments. A catastrophic failure, such as the server not starting, should be found in the test environment. If for some reason it was not, the first canary would fail, thus preventing the other replicas from being upgraded. There would be a slight reduction in capacity until a working release is deployed.

Critics of roll back point out that true roll back is impossible. Uninstalling software and reinstalling a known good release is still a change. In fact, it is a change that has likely not been tested in production. Doing untested processes in production should be avoided at all costs. Doing it only as an emergency measure means doing a risky thing when risk is least wanted.

Roll forward has overwhelming benefits and a continuous deployment environment creates the confidence that makes roll forward possible and less risky. Pragmatically speaking, sometimes roll forward is not possible. Therefore most sites use a hybrid solution: roll forward when you can, roll back when you have to. Also, in this situation, sometimes it is more expedient to push though a small change, one that fixes a specific, otherwise unsurmountable problem. This **emergency hotfix** is risky, as it usually has not received full testing. The emergency hotfixes and roll backs should be tracked carefully and projects should be spawned to eliminate them.

11.12 Release Atomicity

Does a release involve a specific component or the entire system?

Loosely coupled systems include many subsystems, each with its own sequence of versions. This increases the complexity of testing. It is difficult, and often impossible, to test all combinations of all versions. It is also often a waste of resources, as not all combinations will be used.

One technique is to test a particular combination of component versions: for example, Service A running release 101, Service B running release 456, and Service D running release 246. The "(101 + 456 + 246) tuple" is tested as a set, approved as a set, and deployed as a set. If a test fails, one or more components is improved and a new tuple is tested from scratch. Other combinations might work, but we develop a list of combinations that have been approved and use only those combinations. If roll back is required, we roll back to the previous approved tuple.

This technique is generally required when components are tightly coupled. For example, load balancer software, its plug-ins, and the OS kernel being used are often tested as a tuple in highly demanding environments where a performance regression would be devastating. Another example might be the tightly coupled components of a virtualization management system, such as Ganeti or OpenStack; virtualization technology, such as KVM or Xen; storage system (DRBD); and OS kernel.

The problem with this technique is that it reduces the potential rate of change. With all components moving in lock-step, one delayed release will mean the components that are ready to move forward have to wait.

If the components are loosely coupled, then each component can be tested independently and pushed at its own velocity. Problems are more isolated. The changed component may fail, in which case we know it is a problem with that component. The other components may fail, in which case we know that the changed component has introduced an incompatibility.

Such a system works only when components are loosely coupled. For example, at Google the entire infrastructure is an ecosystem of small, loosely coupled services. Services are constantly being upgraded. It is not possible to ask the entire company to stop so that your system can be tested. Google's infrastructure is more like a biological system than a mechanical clock. Because of this, each service has to take upward compatibility seriously. Incompatible changes are announced long in advance. Tools are created specifically to help manage and track such changes.

For example, when an API will change in an incompatible way, there is a way to detect uses that will soon be deprecated and warn the service owners who are affected.

11.13 Summary

Upgrading the software running in an environment is called a code push. Pushing code requires planning and techniques engineered specifically for upgrading services while they are running.

Sometimes a service can be taken down for upgrade because it runs "behind the scenes." More frequently a service is upgraded by taking down parts, upgrading them, and bringing them back up (i.e., a rolling upgrade). If there are many replicas, one can be designated as the canary, which is upgraded before the others as a test. Proportional shedding involves slowly migrating traffic from an old system to a new system, until the old system is receiving no new traffic.

Flag flips are a technique whereby new features are included in a release but are disabled. A flag or software toggle enables the feature at a designated time. This makes it easy to revert a change if problems are found: simply turn the toggle off.

Database schema changes on live systems can be difficult to coordinate. It is not possible to change the software of all clients at the exact same time as the database schema. Instead, the McHenry Technique is used to decouple the changes. New fields are added, software is upgraded to use the old and new fields, software is upgraded to use only the new fields, and any old fields are then removed from the schema.

When a push fails, it is sometimes possible to roll forward to the next release rather than reverting code back to the last known good release. Reverting code is risky, and a failed roll back can be a bigger problem than the original failed push.

Continuous deployment is the process of automating code pushes, automatically pausing or delaying them when certain criteria indicate the risk would be too high or if business conditions require a pause. As with continuous integration and continuous delivery, by doing something in an automated manner, frequently, we reduce risk and improve our processes.

Exercises

1. Summarize the different techniques for upgrading software in live services.
2. Why is a failed canary process so tragic that development should stop until the cause is found?
3. Which push techniques in this chapter are in use in your current environment?

4. Which push techniques should your current environment adopt? What would be their benefits?

5. How would, or could, a dark launch be used in your environment?

6. What is continuous deployment and what are the benefits?

7. Why are roll backs discouraged? How could they be made safer?

8. How would you begin to implement continuous deployment in your environment? If you wouldn't do so, why not?

9. Who is Dr. Jerri Nielsen?

Chapter 12

Automation

> Progressive improvement beats
> delayed perfection.
>
> —Mark Twain

Automation is when computers do work for us. The desire for automation historically has been motivated by three main goals: more precision, more stability, and more speed. Other factors, such as increased safety, increased capacity, and lower costs are desired side effects of these three basic goals. As a system administrator, automating the work that needs to be done should account for the majority of your job. We should not make changes to the system; rather, we should instruct the automation to make those changes.

Manual work has a linear payoff. That is, it is performed once and has benefits once. By comparison, time spent automating has a benefit every time the code is used. The payoff multiplies the more you use the code.

Making changes to the running system should involve making changes to code and data files stored in a revision-controlled central repository. Those changes are then picked up by the software delivery platform, tested, and deployed to production. To work in this way modern system administrators must be software developers. Ever since installing a new computer became an API call, we have all become programmers. This sort of scripting isn't heavy computer science and does not require formal training. It leads to learning more and more software development skills over time (Rockwood 2013). Automation does not put system administrators out of work. Indeed, there is always more work to be done. System administrators who can write code are more valuable to an employer. In fact, because system administration can scale only through automation, not knowing how to code puts your career at risk.

However, automation should not be approached as simply developing faster, more predictable functional replacements for the tasks that people perform. The human–computer system needs to be viewed as a whole. It is a rare system that can

> **Terms to Know**
>
> **Domain-Specific Language (DSL):** A language that was purpose-built for a particular use, such as system administration, mathematics, or text manipulation.
>
> **Toil:** Exhausting physical labor.

be fully automated. Most systems experience exceptions that cannot be handled by the automation, but rather need to be handled by people. However, if the people running the automation have no insight into how it works, it is much harder for them to figure out how and why it failed, and therefore handle the exception appropriately, than it would be if they were more involved in the process. This situation is common where the person handling the exception is not the person who wrote the automation. And at some point, that is the situation for all automation.

12.1 Approaches to Automation

There are three primary approaches to automation design. The first, and most common, approach is to automate using the "left-over" principle, where the automation handles as much as possible, with people being expected to handle whatever is left over. The second approach is the "compensatory" principle, where the work is divided between people and the automation based on which one is better at which task. The third approach is based on the complementarity principle, which aims to improve the long-term health of the combined system of people and computers.

Automation impacts things beyond the immediate intended goal. Understanding what the unintended consequences of automation are likely to be should aid you in building a healthier overall system. For example, antilock brakes (ABS) make it easier for a driver to stop a car more quickly in an emergency. In isolation, this automation should reduce accidents. However, the presence of this automation affects how people drive. They drive more quickly in slippery conditions than they would without ABS, and they leave shorter gaps to the car in front because of their confidence in the ABS automation. These are unintended consequences of the automation. When human factors are not taken into account, automation can have unexpected, and perhaps negative, consequences.

Bear in mind that not all tasks should be automated. Some difficult tasks are so rare that they happen exactly once and cannot happen again—for example, installing a large, complex, software system. This is where you outsource. Hire a consultant who has done it before, since the situation is so rare that the learning curve has no payoff. The result of the consultant's work should include a set of common tasks that are performed more frequently and are handed off to the regular operations staff or to the automation.

Also bear in mind that eliminating a task, whether it is easy, difficult, frequent, or rare, is beneficial because it becomes one less thing to know, do, or maintain. If you can eliminate the task, rather than automating it, that will be the most efficient approach. The co-creator of UNIX and the C programming language, Ken Thompson, famously wrote, "One of my most productive days was throwing away 1,000 lines of code."

12.1.1 The Left-Over Principle

Using the left-over principle, we automate everything that can be automated within reason. What's left is handled by people: situations that are too rare or too complicated to automate. This view makes the unrealistic assumption that people are are infinitely versatile and adaptable, and have no capability limitations.

The left-over principle starts by looking at the tasks that people do, and uses a number of factors to determine what to automate. In the area of system administration, there are many things that operations staff do. All of them can be classified along the axes shown in Figure 12.1.

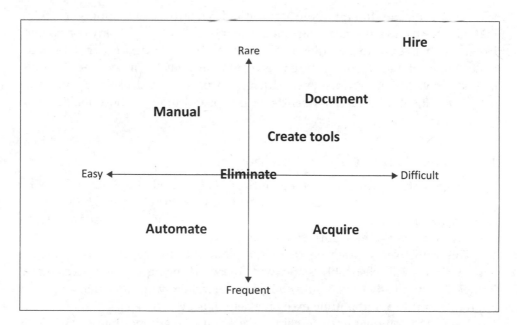

Figure 12.1: Tasks can be classified by effort and frequency, which determines the next step in how to optimize them.

The x-axis is labeled from "rare" to "frequent," representing how often a task is done. The y-axis is labeled from "easy" to "difficult," representing how much effort the task requires each time it is performed.

- Tasks classified as rare/easy can remain manual. If they are easy, anyone should be able to do them successfully. A team's culture will influence if the person does the right thing.
- Tasks classified as rare/difficult should be documented and tools should be created to assist the process. Documentation and better tools will make it easier to do the tasks correctly and consistently. This quadrant includes troubleshooting and recovery tasks that cannot be automated. However, good documentation can assist the process and good tools can remove the burden of repetition or human error.
- Tasks classified as frequent/easy should be automated. The return on investment is obvious. Interestingly enough, once something is documented, it becomes easier to do, thus sliding it toward this quadrant.
- Tasks classified as frequent/difficult should be automated, but it may be best to acquire that automation rather than write it yourself. Purchasing commercial software or using free or open source projects leverages the skills and knowledge of hundreds or thousands of other people.

With this principle, the aim is to achieve efficiency by automating everything that it is feasible to automate. The human component is not explicitly considered. However, it is easy to describe and reasonably easy to decide what to automate. Some of the lessons learned using this approach can be applied even if this is not the only principle considered. In particular, considering tasks on the easy–difficult and rare–frequent axes is a useful tool for those looking into automation.

12.1.2 The Compensatory Principle

The compensatory principle is based on Fitts's list, named after Fitts (1951), who proposed a set of attributes to use when deciding what to automate. The attributes are shown in Table 12.1. Despite the more than 60 years that have passed since Fitts performed his work, these attributes still apply reasonably well.

This principle is based on the assumption that the capabilities of people and machines are reasonably static, with the work being divided accordingly. Rather than implicitly considering humans to be infinitely versatile machines, this approach aims to avoid putting excessive demands on people.

Using the compensatory principle, we would determine that a machine is better suited than a person to collecting monitoring data at 5-minute intervals from thousands of machines. Therefore we would automate monitoring. We

Table 12.1: The Principles of the Fitts List

Attribute	Machine	Operator/Human
Speed	Much superior.	Comparatively slow, measured in seconds.
Power output	Much superior in level and consistency.	Comparatively weak, about 1500 W peak, less than 150 W during a working day.
Consistency	Ideal for consistent, repetitive actions.	Unreliable, subject to learning (habituation) and fatigue.
Information capacity	Multichannel. Information transmission in megabits/second.	Mainly single channel, low rate < 10 bits/second
Memory	Ideal for literal reproduction, access restricted and formal.	Better for principles and strategies, access versatile and innovative.
Reasoning, computation	Deductive, tedious to program. Fast, accurate. Poor error correction.	Inductive. Easy to program. Slow inaccurate. Good error correction.
Sensing	Specialized, narrow range. Good at quantitative assessment. Poor at pattern recognition.	Wide energy ranges, some multifunction capability. Good at pattern recognition.
Perceiving	Copes poorly with variations in written/spoken material. Susceptible to noise.	Copes well with variation in written/spoken material. Susceptible to noise.

also might determine that a person cannot survive walking into a highly toxic nuclear accident site, but that properly designed robots can.

According to this principle, people are considered information processing systems, and the work is described in terms of the interaction between people and computers, with each having separate, identifiable tasks. It looks at optimizing the human–computer interactions to make the processes more efficient.

12.1.3 The Complementarity Principle

The complementarity principle looks at automation from the human perspective. It aims to help people to perform efficiently in the long term, rather than just looking at short-term effects. It looks at how people's behavior will change as a result of the automation, as well as without the automation.

In this approach, one would consider what people learn over time by doing the task manually, and how that would change with the automation. For example, someone who starts doing a new task starts by understanding the primary goal of the task and the basic functions required to meet that goal. Over time the person understands more about the ecosystem surrounding that task, exceptional cases, and some bigger picture goals, and adapts his or her practices based on this knowledge. With automation, we build in the knowledge that we have accumulated so far. Does that inhibit further learning? How does that change the learning ability of a person who is new to the environment? How do a person's habits change over the longer term due to the automation?

The complementarity principle takes more of a cognitive systems engineering (CSE) approach of looking at the automation and the people together as a joint cognitive system (JCS). It takes into account the fact that people are driven by goals (proactive) as well as by events (reactive). A joint cognitive system is characterized by its ability to stay in control of a situation, despite disrupting influences from the process itself or from the environment. It takes into account the dynamics of the situation, including the fact that capabilities and needs may vary over time and with different situations.

One way of coping with changing capabilities and needs is to allow for functional overlap between the people and the automation, rather than a rigid segregation of tasks. This allows functions to be redistributed as needed. People are viewed as taking an active part in the system and are adaptive, resourceful learning partners who are essential to the functioning of the system as a whole.

Unfortunately, there is no silver bullet or easy-to-follow formula for automation using the complementarity principle. But if you remember to consider the human factor and the long-term effects of the automation on the people running the system, you have a better chance of designing good automation.

12.1.4 Automation for System Administration

In "A Model for Types and Levels of Human Interaction with Automation," Parasuraman, Sheridan, and Wickens (2000) propose an approach to automation. Much like the discussion in Section 14.2.4, they observe that there are four stages of information processing: information is gathered, that information is analyzed, a decision is made, and action is taken. These authors also observe that there are gradations between fully manual and fully automated. The various degrees include automation levels where the system makes a suggestion for a person to approve, the system makes a suggestion and executes it if a person does not veto it within a certain amount of time, the system executes its decision and informs people after the fact, and the computer decides everything and acts autonomously, not requiring or asking for any human input.

Parasuraman et al.'s conclusion is that the information gathering and analysis stages are appropriate for a high level of automation. The decision stage should be automated at a level appropriate for the function's risk. Low-risk functions should be highly automated and high-risk functions should be less automated. When it comes to taking action, however, the appropriate level of automation is somewhere in the middle for high-risk functions.

Allspaw's (2012c) two-part blog post "A Mature Role for Automation" gives a detailed explanation of Parasuraman et al.'s work and relates it to system administration. He concludes that an even better model for automation is that of a partnership—applying the complementarity principle. When automation and operations staff work together, they enhance each other's value the same way that members of a team do.

A key element of teamwork is trust and safety. Allspaw cites Lee and See's (2004) methods for making automation trustworthy:

- Design for appropriate trust, not greater trust.
- Show the past performance of the automation.
- Show the process and algorithms of the automation by revealing intermediate results in a way that is comprehensible to the operators.
- Simplify the algorithms and operation of the automation to make it more understandable.
- Show the purpose of the automation, design basis, and range of applications in a way that relates to the users' goals.
- Train operators regarding its expected reliability, the mechanisms governing its behavior, and its intended use.
- Carefully evaluate any anthropomorphizing of the automation, such as using speech to create a synthetic conversational partner, to ensure appropriate trust.

12.1.5 Lessons Learned

Efforts to automate can backfire. Automation is generally viewed as a pure engineering task, so the human component may all too often be neglected. Systems that aim to eliminate boring and tedious tasks so that people can tackle more difficult tasks leave the hardest parts to humans because they are too complex to be automated. Thus mental fatigue due to many tedious tasks is eliminated, but it is replaced by an even more burdensome mental fatigue due to the need to tackle difficult problems on a continual basis.

Automation can bring stability to a system, yet this stability results in operators becoming less skilled in maintaining the system. Emergency response becomes particularly brittle, a subject that we will address in Chapter 15.

When designing automation, ask yourself which view of the human component is being assumed by this automation. Are people a bottleneck, a source of unwanted variability, or a resource? If people are a bottleneck, can you remove the bottleneck without removing their visibility into what the system is doing, and without making it impossible for them to adjust how the system works, when necessary? If people are a source of unwanted variability, then you are constraining the environment and inputs of the automation to make it more reliable. What effect does that have on the people running the automation? How does it constrain their work? How can exceptions be handled? If people are to be a resource, then you need closer coupling between the people and the automation. But in that case, there are two thorny issues: who does which tasks (allocation) and who is in charge (responsibility)?

The long-term operation of a system can be broken down into four stages: tracking, regulating, monitoring, and targeting. Tracking covers event detection and short-term control in response to inputs or detected events. Automation typically starts at this level. Regulation covers long-term control, such as managing transition between states. The case study in Section 12.3 is an example of automation at the regulation level. Monitoring covers longer-term controls, interpreting system state and selecting plans to remain within the desired parameters. For example, capacity planning, hardware evaluation and selection, and similar tasks would fall into this category. Targeting covers setting the overall goals for the system based on the overall corporate goals—for example, using key performance indicators (KPIs; see Chapter 19) to drive the desired behavior. As you move up the chain, the higher-level tasks are generally more suited to people than to machines. As you automate further up the chain, people become more disconnected from what the system is doing and why, and the long-term health of the system as a whole may be jeopardized.

Hidden Cost of Automation

Super automated systems often require super training, which can be super expensive. Hiring becomes super difficult, which begins to limit the company's ability to grow at its desired rate. The missed opportunities that result become a burdensome cost. This opportunity cost may be more expensive than what the system saves. Such dilemmas are why companies like Google implement super aggressive recruiting campaigns to hire SREs.

12.2 Tool Building versus Automation

There is a distinction between tool building and automation. **Tool building** improves a manual task so that it can be done better. **Automation** seeks to eliminate the need for the person to do the task. A process is automated when a person does not have to do it anymore, yet this does not eliminate the need for people. Once a process is automated, a system administrator's role changes from doing the task to maintaining the automation.

12.2.1 Example: Auto Manufacturing

This is analogous to what happened in auto manufacturing. Originally the process of painting the metal panels that make up the outer body of the car was a task done by people. It was a slow, delicate, and difficult process requiring great skill. Then a high-power paint sprayer was invented to improve this process. The same person could do a better job, with less wasted paint, in less time. This technology also reduced the amount of skill required, thereby lowering the barrier to entry for this job. However, there was still a car panel painter job. The process had not been automated, but there was a better tool for the job.

In the 1970s, auto manufacturing plants automated the car painting process. They deployed robotic painting systems and the job of car panel painter was eliminated. Employees now maintain the robotic painting system, or automation, which is a very different job from painting metal panels.

12.2.2 Example: Machine Configuration

In IT we are making a similar transformation. In a typical cloud computing environment, every new machine must be configured for its role in the service. The manual process might involve loading the operating system, installing certain packages, editing configuration files, running commands, and starting services. A system administrator (SA) could write a script that does these things. For each new machine, the SA runs the script and the machine is configured. This is an improvement over the manual process. It is faster and less error prone, and the resulting machines will be more consistently configured. However, an SA still needs to run the script, so the process of setting up a new machine is not fully automated.

Automated processes do not require system administrator action, or else they reduce it to handling special cases. To continue our example, an automated solution means that when a machine boots, it discovers its identity, configures itself, and becomes available to provide service. The role for an SA who configures machines is eliminated in most cases. The SA's role is transformed into maintaining the automation that configures machines and handling unusual hardware or operating systems.

12.2.3 Example: Account Creation

Cloud administrators often maintain the systems that make up a service delivery platform. To give each new developer access, an SA might have to create accounts on several systems. The SA can create the accounts manually, but it would save a lot of time if the SA wrote a script that creates the accounts on all the relevant machines, and there would be less chance of skipping a step. Each time a new developer joins the company, the SA would use this account creation tool.

Better yet would be if the SA wrote a job that runs periodically to check if new developers are listed in the human resources database and then automatically create the new accounts. In this case, the SA no longer creates accounts; the human resources department does. The SA's job is maintaining and enhancing the account creation automation.

12.2.4 Tools Are Good, But Automation Is Better

Much of operational work consists of repeated tasks, such as configuring machines, creating accounts, building software packages, testing new releases, deploying new releases, increasing capacity, failing over services, moving services, and moving or reducing capacity. All of these tasks can be improved with better tools, and these tools are often stepping stones to automation.

Another advantage of automation is that it enables the collection of statistics about defects or, in IT terms, failures. If certain situations tend to make the automation fail, those situations can be tracked and investigated. Often automation is incomplete and certain edge cases require manual intervention. Those cases can also be tracked and categorized, and the more pervasive ones can be prioritized for automation.

Tool building is good, but automation is required for scalable cloud computing.

12.3 Goals of Automation

In cloud services, automation is a must, not a "nice to have"—it is required for growth. Cloud-based systems grow in many ways: more machines, more subsystems and services, and new operational responsibilities. If a new person had to be hired for each new service or every n new machines, a cloud-based service would not be able to function. No company could find enough new qualified SAs, nor could it afford to pay so many people. Considering that larger organizations are more difficult to manage, the people management challenge alone would be insurmountable.

There is a popular misconception that the goal of automation is to do tasks faster than they could be done manually. That is just one of the goals. Other goals include the following:

- **Help scaling.** Automation is a workforce multiplier. It permits one person to do the work of many.
- **Improve accuracy.** Automation is less error prone than people are. Automation does not get distracted or lose interest, nor does it get sloppy over time. Over time software is improved to handle more edge cases and error situations. Unlike hardware, software gets stronger over time (Spolsky 2004, p. 183).

- **Increase repeatability.** Software is more consistent than humans when doing tasks. Consistency is part of a well-controlled environment.
- **Improve reliability.** Once a process is automated, it is easier to collect statistics and metrics about the process. These data can then be used to identify problems and improve reliability.
- **Save time.** There is never enough time to do all the work that needs to be done. An automated task should require less SA time than a manual one.
- **Make processes faster.** Manual processes are slower because they involve thinking and typing. Both are error prone and correcting mistakes often has a large time penalty itself.
- **Enable more safeguards.** Adding additional pre- and post-checks to an automated process is easy. Doing so incurs a one-time cost, but improves the automation for all future iterations of the process. Adding more checks to a manual process adds a burden and creates temptation for the person to skip them.
- **Empower users.** Automation often makes it possible for a non-SA to do a task. Automation turns a task that only an expert can do into one that an end user can do using a self-service tool. In the example in Section 12.2.3, someone from the human resources department is now able to provision new accounts without the involvement of system administrators. Delegation saves time and resources.
- **Reduce user wait time.** Manual processes can be done only when an SA is available. Automation can be running all day and all night, and will usually have completed a task before an SA would have been available to start it. Even if automation were slower than a person doing the same task, the net user wait time would likely be shorter.
- **Reduce system administrator wait time.** Many manual processes involve doing one step, then waiting some time before the next step can proceed—for example, waiting for new data to propagate through a system or waiting for a machine to reboot. A process like this is said be full of "hurry up and wait" steps. If the wait is long, an SA may be able to fill the time with other work. However, this is often inefficient. All too often, we start working on something else, get distracted, and forget to return to the first task or lose context. Computers are better at waiting than people are.

For example, building software packages can be very complex. A good tool will, when the user enters one command, compile the software, run unit tests, build the package, and possibly more. Automation, however, should eliminate the need for someone to run the tool. Buildbot is a system that continuously monitors a source code repository for changes. After any change, the software is checked out, built, packaged, and tested. If all tests pass, the new package is placed in a repository so it is available to be deployed. The latest working package is always available. Many packages may be created and never used, but since no SA effort is involved, there is no additional cost, assuming that the CPU cycles are available. In addition, the automated build process should give the developers immediate feedback about any automated tests that fail, resulting in faster bug fixes and better software (see Chapter 9).

Another example involves configuring new machines. A good tool for machine configuration is run by a system administrator, perhaps with a few parameters like hostname and IP address, and the result is a fully configured machine. Automation, however, would be applied where each freshly installed machine looks up its hostname in a directory or external database to find its function. It then configures the machine's OS, installs various packages, configures them, and starts the services the machine is intended to run. The manual steps are eliminated, such that machines come to life on their own.

Sometimes automation eliminates the need for a process entirely. Typically load balancers require manual configuration to add replicas. Many tools are available that make such configuration easier or less error prone. However, a fully automated solution eliminates the need for constant reconfiguration. We've seen systems where the load balancer is configured once, and then replicas communicate their availability to the load balancer, which includes them in its rotation. Rather than automating an existing process, this project eliminates the constant reconfiguration by inventing a new way to operate.

Case Study: Automated Repair Life Cycle

Google uses the Ganeti open source virtual cluster management system to run many large clusters of physical machines, which in turn provide virtual machines to thousands of users. A physical machine rarely fails, but because of the sheer number of machines, hardware failures became quite frequent. As a result, SAs spent a lot of time dealing with hardware issues. Tom became involved in a project to automate the entire repair life cycle.

First, tools were developed to assist in common operations, all of which were complex, error prone, and required a high level of expertise:

- **Drain Tool:** When monitoring detected signs of pending hardware problems (such as correctable disk or RAM errors), all virtual machines would be migrated to other physical machines.
- **Recovery Tool:** When a physical machine unexpectedly died, this tool made several attempts to power it off and on. If these efforts failed to recover the machine, the virtual machines would be restarted from their last snapshot on another physical machine.

- **Send to Repairs Tool:** When a machine needed physical repairs, there was a procedure for notifying the datacenter technicians about which machine had a problem and what needed to be done. This tool gathered problem reports and used the machine repair API to request the work. It included the serial number of any failing disks, the memory slot of any failing RAM, and so on. In most cases the repair technician was directed to the exact problem, reducing repair time.
- **Re-assimilate Tool:** When a machine came back from repairs, it needed to be evaluated, configured, and readded to the cluster.

Each of these tools was improved over time. Soon the tools did their tasks better than people could, with more error checking than a person would be likely to do. Oncall duties involved simply running combinations of these tools.

Now the entire system could be fully automated by combining these tools. A system was built that tracked the state of a machine (alive, having problems, in repairs, being re-assimilated). It used the APIs of the monitoring system and the repair status console to create triggers that activated the right tool at the right time. As a result the oncall responsibilities were reduced from multiple alerts each day to one or two alerts each week.

The logs from the automation were used to drive business decisions. Downtime was improved dramatically by accelerating the move away from a model of hardware that proved to be the least reliable.

12.4 Creating Automation

Automation has many benefits, but it requires dedicated time and effort to create. Automation, like any programming, is best created during a block of time where there are no outside interruptions. Sometimes there is so much other work to be done that it is difficult to find a sufficient block of time to focus on creating the automation. You need to deliberately *make* the time to create the automation, not hope that eventually things will quiet down sufficiently so that you *have* the time.

In a well-run team, the majority of the team's time should be spent creating and maintaining automation, rather than on manual tasks. When manual tasks start to become the greater part of the workload, it is time to take a step back and see how new automation might restore the balance. It is important to be able to identify which automation will have the biggest impact, and to tackle that first. It is also important to understand the places where automation is not appropriate.

12.4.1 Making Time to Automate

Sometimes there isn't enough time to automate because we're so busy with urgent work that blocks long-term work such as creating automation. To use an analogy, we don't have time to shut off the leaking faucet because we're spending all of our time mopping the floor. When this happens, it can be difficult to get ourselves out of the rut and fix the root causes that prevent us from having a healthy amount of time to create automation.

Here are some suggestions for making the time to work on automation:

* Get management involved. Managers should reprioritize the work to emphasize automation.
* Find the top thing that is wrecking your ability to get the big things done and fix, mitigate, or eliminate it. This may mean ignoring other work for a time—even letting some things fail for a bit—while you fix the leaking faucet.
* Eliminate rather than automate. Find work that can be eliminated. For example, spot tasks that you do on behalf of other people and push the responsibilities back onto those people. Eliminate duplicate effort. For example, if you are maintaining 10 different Linux versions, maybe you would be best served by narrowing that number down to only a few, or one.
* Hire a temporary consultant to put into place the high-level automation framework and train people on how to use it.
* Hire a junior person (maybe even temporarily) to do the "grunge work" and free up senior people for bigger projects that would fix the root problem.
* Start small. Automating one small task can be contagious. For example, use configuration management tools such as CFEngine or Puppet to automate one aspect of configuring new machines. Once one thing is automated, doing more is much easier. Don't try to fix every problem with the first bit of automation you create.
* Don't work harder; manage your time better. Books like *Time Management for System Administrators* (Limoncelli 2005) have a lot of useful advice.

Less Is More

Etsy wrote a blog post explaining why the company decided not to adopt a new database technology. The issue wasn't that the technology wasn't good; it was that then Etsy would be maintaining two different database software systems, two ways to do backups, two testing processes, two upgrade processes, and so on. It would be too much work (McKinley 2012).

12.4.2 Reducing Toil

Toil is exhausting physical labor. It is the extreme opposite of the goal of automation. However, toil tends to build up in an operations team. It starts small and grows. For example, there may be a small project that can't be automated because it is highly specific and unlikely to repeat. Over time, it does repeat, and soon that one action becomes a huge burden. Soon the team is overloaded by toil.

A little toil isn't so bad. In fact, it is normal. Not everything is worth automating. If everything is automated perfectly and there is no work to be done, this generally means that the rate of change and innovation has been stifled.

If more than half of a team's collective time is spent on operational "toil," that fact should raise a proverbial red flag. The team should review how the members are spending their time. Usually there are a few deeper "root cause" problems that could be fixed to eliminate large chunks of manual work. Establish projects that will strike at the root of those problems. Put all other projects on hold until the 50/50 balance is achieved again.

In companies like Google, there is an established policy to deal with this type of situation. Specifically, there is an official process for a team to declare a toil emergency. The team pauses to consider its options and make a plan to fix the biggest sources of toil. Management reviews the reprioritization plans and approves putting other projects on hold until balance is achieved.

System administrator time is too valuable to be spent on something with a linear pay-off like manual work. Toil leads to burn-out and lack of morale. By reducing toil, we not only help the company but we also help ourselves.

12.4.3 Determining What to Automate First

Apply any and all effort to fix the biggest bottleneck first. There may be multiple areas where automation is needed. Choose the one with the biggest impact first.

Analyze the work and processes that the team is involved with to find the biggest bottleneck. A bottleneck is where a backlog of work accumulates. By eliminating the bottleneck, you improve throughput.

Think about the work being done as an assembly line. A project has many steps and moves down the assembly line one step at a time. One of those steps is going to be the bottleneck.

Any improvements made upstream of the bottleneck just increase the backlog. It is tempting to make improvements above the bottleneck. Often they are easy or the first thing you noticed. Sometimes fixing these items improves the efficiency of your team, but the bottleneck is buried deep in some other team's process. Therefore you have made an improvement but the total throughput of the system has not changed. It may even make the problem worse by creating a bigger traffic jam of work waiting at the bottleneck.

Improvements made downstream of the bottleneck don't help overall throughput. Again, they may be the easiest improvements that can be made, but if work is not getting to this part of the system then improving this part will not help the entire system.

The bottleneck might not involve a technical problem. It may be a particular person who is overloaded or an entire team that is unable to get important tasks done because they are drowning in small, urgent tasks.

12.5 How to Automate

You can't automate what you can't do manually. The first step in creating automation is knowing what work needs to be done. Begin by doing the process manually and documenting what is done in a step-by-step manner. Repeat the procedure, following and correcting the documentation as you go. Have someone else follow the same documentation to make sure it is clear. This is the best way to discover which steps are ill defined or missing.

The next step toward automation is prototyping. Create tools to do the individual steps in isolation, making certain that each one is self-contained and works correctly.

Now combine the individual tools into a single program. Mature automation needs logging and sanity checking of input parameters and the return values of all calls. These features should be incorporated into each stage as well as the final version. The automation should check the return value of the previous step and, if it failed, should be able to undo the prior steps.

The next stage is to make a fully automated system. Identify what would cause an SA to run the tool, and have those conditions trigger automation instead. Complete logging and robust error handling must be in place before this final step is implemented.

In some cases it is appropriate to create a self-service tool so that non-SAs can do this task. In this situation, security becomes a larger issue. There needs to be a permission model to control who may use the tool. There need to be checks to verify that people can't accidentally do bad things or circumvent the system to gain privileged access.

12.6 Language Tools

Many products, languages, and systems are available for creating automation, and each has its own pros and cons. The capabilities of these tools range from basic to quite high level.

12.6.1 Shell Scripting Languages

Shell languages provide the commands one can type at the operating system command-line prompt. It is easy to turn a sequence of commands typed inter-actively at the Bash or PowerShell prompt into a script that can be run as a single command—either manually or by another process, such as `cron`.

Shell scripts have many advantages. For example, they allow for very fast prototyping. They let the programmer work at a very high level. You can com-bine commands or programs to make larger, more powerful programs. There are also disadvantages to using shell scripts for your automation. Most importantly, shell-scripted solutions do not scale as well as other languages, are difficult to test, and cannot easily do low-level tasks.

The most common UNIX shell is the Bourne Again Shell (`bash`), a superset of the Bourne Shell (the UNIX `/bin/sh` command). In the Microsoft Windows world, PowerShell is a very powerful system that makes it easy to automate and coordinate all the Windows systems and products.

12.6.2 Scripting Languages

Scripting languages are interpreted languages designed for rapid development, often focusing on systems programming.

Some common examples include Perl, Python, and Ruby. Perl is older and very popular with system administrators because it is similar to C and awk, languages that UNIX system administrators traditionally know. Python has a cleaner design and the code is much more readable than Perl code. Ruby has a strong following in the system administrator community. It is similar to Perl and Python in syntax, but adds features that make it easy to create mini-languages, purpose-built for a specific task. More programs can then be written in that mini-language.

Scripting languages are more flexible and versatile than shell scripts. They are more expressive, permit better code organization, scale better, and encourage more modern coding practices such as object-oriented coding and functional program-ming. Better testing tools are available, and there are more prewritten libraries. Scripting languages have the ability to access networks, storage, and databases more easily than shell scripts. Better error checking is also available.

Perl, Python, and Ruby all have large libraries of modules that perform common system administration tasks such as file manipulation, date and time handling, transactions using protocols such as HTTP, and database access. You will often find the program you write is leveraging many modules, gluing them together to create the functionality you need.

A disadvantage of scripting languages is that they execute more slowly than compiled languages. This drawback has been mitigated in recent years by new, faster interpreter technology. Nevertheless, for the reasons described earlier, speed is not always essential in automation. Thus language speed is often not a factor in system administration tools whose speed is bounded by other factors. For example, if the program is always waiting on disk I/O, it might not matter if the program itself is written in a fast or slow language.

The primary disadvantage of scripting languages is that they are inappropriate for very large software projects. While nothing prevents you from writing a very large software project in Perl, Python, or Ruby (and many projects have been done this way), it becomes logistically difficult. For example, these languages are not strongly typed. That is, the type of a variable (integer, string, or object) is not checked until the variable is used. At that point the language will try to do the right thing. For example, suppose you are concatenating a string and a number: the language will automatically convert the number to a string so that it can be concatenated. Nevertheless, there are some situations the language can't fix, in which case the program will crash. These problems are discovered only at run-time, and often only in code that is rarely used or tested. Contrast this to a compiled language that checks types at compilation time, long before the code gets into the field.

For this reason scripting languages are not recommended for projects that will include tens of thousands of lines of code.

12.6.3 Compiled Languages

Compiled languages can be a good choice for large-scale automation. Automation written in a compiled language typically scales better than the same automation written in a scripting language.

Compiled languages often used by system administrators include C, C++, and Go. As described earlier, compiled languages are usually statically typed and catch more errors at compile time.

12.6.4 Configuration Management Languages

Configuration management (CM) languages are domain-specific languages (DSLs) created specifically for system administration tasks. CM systems are created for maintaining the configuration of machines, from low-level settings such as the network configuration to high-level settings such as which services should run and their configuration files.

Configuration languages are declarative. That is, the programmer writes code that describes how the world should be and the language figures out which changes are needed to achieve that goal. As discussed in Section 10.1.3 (page 213), some CM systems are designed around convergent orchestration (bringing the system to a desired state) while others favor directed orchestration (the ability to follow a multistep plan of action).

Two popular CM systems are CFEngine and Puppet. Listing 12.1 and Listing 12.2 illustrate how to specify a symbolic link in CFEngine and Puppet, respectively. Listing 12.3 and Listing 12.4 show the equivalent tasks in Python and Perl, languages that are imperative (not declarative). Notice that first two simply specify the desired state: the link name and its destination. The Python and Perl versions, in contrast, need to check if the link already exists, correct it if it is wrong, create it if it doesn't exist, and handle error conditions. A high level of expertise is needed to know that such edge cases exist, to handle them properly, and to test the code under various conditions. This is very tricky and difficult to get exactly right. The CM languages simply specify the desired state and leverage the fact that the creator of the CM system has the knowledge and experience to do things correctly.

Listing 12.1: Specifying a symbolic link in CFEngine

```
files:
    "/tmp/link-to-motd"
        link_from => ln_s("/etc/motd");
```

Listing 12.2: Specifying a symbolic link in Puppet

```
file { '/tmp/link-to-motd':
  ensure => 'link',
  target => '/etc/motd',
}
```

Listing 12.3: Creating a symbolic link in Python

```
import os

def make_symlink(filename, target):
  if os.path.lexists(filename):
    if os.path.islink(filename):
      if os.readlink(filename) == target:
        return
    os.unlink(filename)
  os.symlink(target, filename)

make_symlink('/tmp/link-to-motd', '/etc/motd')
```

Listing 12.4: Creating a symbolic link in Perl

```perl
sub make_symlink {
  my ($filename, $target) = ($_[0], $_[1]);
  if (-l $filename) {
    return if readlink($filename) eq $target;
    unlink $filename;
  } elsif (-e $filename) {
    unlink $filename;
  }
  symlink($target, $filename);
}

make_symlink('/tmp/link-to-motd', '/etc/motd');
```

Configuration management systems usually have features that let you build up definitions from other definitions. For example, there may be a definition of a "generic server," which includes the settings that all servers must have. Another definition might be for a "web server," which inherits all the attributes of a "generic server" but adds web serving software and other attributes. A "blog server" may inherit the "web server" definition and add blogging software. In contrast, an "image server" may inherit the "web server" attributes but create a machine that accesses an image database and serves the images, perhaps tuning the web server with settings that are more appropriate for serving static images.

By building up these definitions or "classes," you can build up a library that is very flexible and efficient. For example, a change to the "server" definition automatically affects all the definitions that inherit it.

The key advantages of a CM system are that SAs can define things concisely at a high level, and that it is easy to enshrine best practices in shared definitions and processes. The primary disadvantage is the steep learning curve for the domain-specific language and the need to initially create all the necessary definitions.

12.7 Software Engineering Tools and Techniques

Automation is just like any other software development project, so it needs the facilities that benefit all modern software development projects. You are probably familiar with the tools that are used for automation. Even so, we constantly find operations teams not using them or not using them to their fullest potential.

The automation tools and their support tools such as bug trackers and source code repositories should be a centralized, shared service used by all involved in software development. Such an approach makes it easier to collaborate. For example, moving bugs and other issues between projects is easier if all teams use the same bug tracking system.

The service delivery platform and related issues such as the need for continuous test, build, and deploy capabilities were discussed in Chapters 9 and 10. In this section, we discuss issue tracking systems, version control systems, packaging, and techniques such as test-driven development.

12.7.1 Issue Tracking Systems

Issue tracking systems are for recording and managing bug reports and feature requests. Every bug report and feature request should go through the system. This raises the issue's visibility, ensures the related work is recognized in statistics generated by management, and potentially allows someone else to get around to working on the issue before you do. Managing all work through one system also makes it easier to prevent overlapping work. It allows members of the team to understand what the others are working on, and it makes it easier to hand off tasks to others (this last point is especially valuable when you won't be available to work on these tasks).

Often it is tempting to not report an issue because it takes time and we are busy people, or we figure "everyone knows this issue exists" and therefore it doesn't need to be reported. These are exactly the kind of issues that need to be reported. Everyone doesn't know the issue exists, especially management. Raising the visibility of the issue is the first step toward getting it fixed.

Bugs versus Feature Requests

We colloquially refer to issue tracking systems as "bug trackers," but this is actually a misnomer. Feature requests are not bugs and need to be tracked differently. Resources are often allocated separately for bug fixing and new feature development. These workflows are often different as well. If you choose not to implement a feature request, the matter is settled and therefore it is appropriate to mark the issue as being resolved. If you choose not to fix a bug, the bug still exists. The issue should remain open, just marked at a low priority designated for issues that will not be fixed.

Issue tracking systems usually can be configured to serve different teams or projects, with each one having its bugs stored in its own **queue**. You may choose to establish a different queue for bugs and one for features ("Operations—Feature Requests" and "Operations—Bugs") or the system may have a way to tag issues as being one or the other.

Link Tickets to Subsystems

Establish a way to relate tickets to a specific subsystem. For example, you could establish a separate queue for each subsystem or use other kinds of categorization or tagging mechanisms. A small amount of planning now can prevent headaches in the future. For example, imagine there are three SRE teams, responsible for five subsystems each. Suppose a reorganization is going to change which teams are responsible for which subsystems. If each subsystem has its own queue or category, moving tickets to the new team is as simple as changing who owns a particular queue or mass-moving all tickets with a particular category marker. If there is no classification, the reorganization will be painstakingly complex. Each issue will need to be individually evaluated and moved to the proper team. This will have to be done for all current issues and, if you want to maintain history, for all past issues.

Establish Issue Naming Standards

Issues should be named in a uniform way. It simply makes it easier to read and process many issues if they are all phrased clearly. Bugs should be phrased in terms of what is wrong. If some are phrased in terms of what is wrong and others are phrased in terms of how the feature should work, it can be quite confusing when a title is ambiguous. If someone reports that "The help button links to a page about the project," for example, it is unclear if this statement describes a bug that needs to be fixed (it should link to the help page) or explains how the system should work (in which case the bug could be closed and marked "seems to already work as requested").

Feature requests should be described from the perspective of the person who desires the new capability. In Agile methodology, the recommended template is "As a [type of user], I want [some goal] so that [some reason]." For example, a request might be stated as follows: "As an SRE, I want a new machine type 'ARM64' to be supported by the configuration management system so that we can manage our new tablet-based Hadoop cluster" or "As a user, I want to be able to clone a virtual machine via an API call so that I can create clones programatically."

Choose Appropriate Issue Tracking Software

Software issue tracking systems are similar to IT helpdesk ticket systems. At the same time, they are different enough that you will need different software for the two functions. Issue tracking systems focus on the bug or feature request, whereas IT helpdesk ticket systems focus on the user. For example, in an issue tracking system, if two different people report the same bug, they are merged or the second one is closed as a duplicate. Every issue exists only once. In contrast, an IT helpdesk ticket system is a mechanism for communicating with users and helping them with problems or fulfilling requests. If two people submit similar requests, they would not be merged as each is as unique as the person who made the request.

Software issue tracking systems and IT helpdesk ticket systems also have different workflows. An issue tracking system should have a workflow that reflects the software development process: bugs are received, verified, and fixed; a different person verifies they are fixed; and then the issue is closed. This involves many handoffs. The statistics one needs to be able to generate include how much time is spent in each step of the process. The workflow for an IT helpdesk is more about the back-and-forth communication with a person.

12.7.2 Version Control Systems

A version control system (VCS) is a central repository for storing, accessing, and updating source code. Having all source code in one place makes it easier to collaborate and easier to centralize functions such as backups, build processes, and so on. A VCS stores the history of each file, including all the changes ever made. As a consequence, it is possible to see what the software looked like at a particular date, revert changes, and so on. Although version control systems were originally used for source code control, a VCS can store any file, not just source code.

VCS frameworks all have a similar workflow. Suppose you want to make a change to a system. You "check out" the source code, thus copying the entire source to your local directory. You can then edit it as needed. When your work is complete, you "commit" or "check out" your changes.

Older VCS frameworks permit only one person to check out a particular project at a given time so that people can't create conflicting changes. Newer systems permit multiple people to check out the same project. The first person to check in his or her changes has it easy; all of the others go through a process of merging their changes with past changes. VCS software helps with merges, doing non-overlapping merges automatically and bringing up an editor for you to manually merge the rest.

A distributed version control system (DVCS) is a new breed of VCS. In a DVCS, everyone has his or her own complete repository. Sets of changes are transmitted between repositories. Check-outs don't just give you a copy of the source code at a particular version, but create a local copy of the entire repository including the entire revision history. You can check in changes to the local repository independently of what is going on in the central system. You then merge a group of such changes to the master repository when you are done. This democratizes source code control. Before DVCS, you could make only one change at a time and that change had to be approved by whoever controlled the repository. It was difficult to proceed with the next change until the first change was accepted by the repository owner. In a DVCS, you are the master of your own repository. You do development in parallel with the main repository. Changes made to the main repository can be pulled into your repository in a controlled manner and only when you want to import the changes. Changes you make in your repository can be merged upstream to the main repository when desired, or not at all.

A VCS should not be used only for source code; that is, configuration files must also be revision controlled. When automation or use of tools involves configuration file changes, you should automate the steps of checking the config file out of version control, modifying it, and then checking it back in. Tools should not be allowed to modify config files outside of the VCS.

12.7.3 Software Packaging

Software, once developed, should be distributed in packages. Although this topic was discussed in Section 9.6, we raise the issue again here because the same operations people who maintain a service delivery platform often distribute their own software tools by ad hoc means.

Distributing your own software via packages enables you to take advantage of all the systems used to keep software up-to-date. Without this capability, operational tools end up being copied manually. The result is many systems, all out of date, and all the problems that can bring.

Ideally the packages should go through the same development, beta, and production phases as other software. (See Chapter 9.)

12.7.4 Style Guides

A style guide is a standard indicating how source code should be formatted and which language features are encouraged, discouraged, or banned. Having all code conform to the same style makes it easier to maintain the code and raises code quality. It sets a high bar for quality and consistency, raising standards for the entire team. A style guide also has a mentoring effect on less experienced people.

Typically programmers spend the vast majority of their time modifying code and adding features to existing code. Rarely do we have the opportunity to write a new program from scratch and be the sole maintainer for its entire life. When we work together as a team, it becomes critical to be able to look at a file for the first time and assimilate its contents quickly. This enhances productivity. When we write code that conforms to the style guide, we pay this productivity forward.

Style Guide Basics

Style guides make both formatting and feature recommendations. Formatting recommendations include specifying how indenting and whitespace are used. For example, most companies standardize on indenting with four (or less commonly two) spaces instead of tabs, eliminating extra blank lines at the end of files or whitespace at the end of lines, and placing a single blank line between functions, and possibly two blank lines before major sections or classes.

Style guides prescribe more than just aesthetics. They also recommend particular language features over others, and often outright ban certain language features that have proved to be difficult to support. Languages often have two ways of doing something, and the style guide will select which is to be used. Languages may also have features that are error prone or troublesome for other reasons; the style guide may ban or discourage those features.

Many languages have style guides of their own (Python and Puppet). Every major open source project has a style guide for its community. Most companies have a style guide for internal use. Google runs many open source projects and has published its internal style guides (minus redactions) for more than a dozen languages (`https://code.google.com/p/google-styleguide/`). This enables community members to participate and adhere to the current style. The Google style guides are very mature and are a good basis for creating your own.

Additional Recommendations

Often special notations are recommended in style guides. For example, the Google style guide recommends special notation for comments. Use TODO comments for code that is temporary, a short-term solution, or good enough but not perfect. Use NB comments to explain a non-obvious decision. Use FIXME comments to point out something that needs to be fixed and list the bug ID of the issue. The annotation is followed by the username of the person who wrote the comment. Figure 12.2 shows examples.

As mentioned in Section 9.3.2, source repositories can call programs to validate files before they are committed. Leverage these "pre-submit tests" to call style-checking programs and stop files with style violations from being committed. For example, run `PyLint` on any Python file, `puppet-lint` on any Puppet files, and even home-grown systems that pedantically reject `CHANGELOG` entries if their entries are not perfectly formatted. The result is consistency enforced consistently no matter how large the team grows.

12.7.5 Test-Driven Development

Test-driven development (TDD) is a software engineering practice that leads to code with minimal bugs and maximizes confidence.

```
TODO(george): The following works but should be refactored to use
templates.
NB(matt): This algorithm is not popular but gets the right result.
FIXME(kyle): This will break in v3, fix by 2013-03-22. See bug
12345.
```

Figure 12.2: Special-purpose comments from the Google style guide

Traditional software testing methodology involves first writing code and then writing code that tests the code. TDD reverses these steps. First one writes the code to test the code. Running these tests fails because the code hasn't been written yet. The developer then makes fast iterations of writing code and rerunning the tests; this continues until all the tests pass. At that point, the developer is done.

For example, imagine writing a function that takes a URL and breaks it down into its component parts. The function needs to handle many different kinds of URLs, with and without embedded usernames and passwords, different protocols, and so on. You would come up with a list of URLs that are examples of all the different kinds that the code should be able to handle. Next, you would write code that calls the function with each example URL and compares the result against what you think the result should be. As we saw in Section 9.3.3 and Section 10.2, these are called unit tests.

Now that the tests are written, the code itself is written. Step by step, the code is improved. The tests are run periodically. At first only the tests involving the most simple URLs work. Then more and more fancy URL formats work. When all the tests work, the function is complete.

The tests are retained, not deleted. Later you can make big changes to code with confidence that if the unit tests do not break, the changes should not have unintended side effects. Conversely, if you need to modify the code's behavior, you can start by updating the tests to expect different results and then modify the code until these tests pass again.

All modern languages have systems that make it easy to list tests and run them in sequence. They enable you to focus on writing tests and code, not managing the tests themselves.

12.7.6 Code Reviews

Code reviews are a process by which at least one other person reviews any changes to files before they are committed to the VCS. The code review system (CRS) provides a user interface that lets the reviewer(s) add commentary and feedback to particular lines of the file. The original author uses the feedback to update the files. The process repeats until all the reviewers approve the change and it is integrated into the VCS.

Software engineers conduct code reviews on source code to have a "second pair of eyes" find errors and make suggestions before code is incorporated into the main source. It is also useful to do this on configuration files. In fact, in an environment where configuration files are kept in a source repository, code reviews are a great way to ask others what they think about a change you're making.

CRS can also be used to delegate tasks to others while still being able to provide quality control. This enables scaling of authority via delegation. For example, most companies would not let just anyone edit their load balancer configurations. However, if they are kept in VCS and require approval by someone in the load balancer team, the process of load balancer updates becomes self-service. Given a good "how to" document, anyone can edit the config file and submit the proposed change to the load balancer team, who check it over and then submit the change to activate it.

There are other reasons to use a code review system:

- **Better written code.** Code review is not just a style check; it is a time to deeply consider the code and suggest better algorithms and techniques.
- **Bidirectional learning.** Whether the reviewer or reviewee is more experienced, both improve their skill and learn from each other.
- **Prevent bugs.** A second set of eyes catches more bugs.
- **Prevent outages.** Using a CRS for configuration files catches problems before they hit production.
- **Enforce a style guide.** Code reviewers can give feedback on style violations so they can be fixed.

The time spent on a code review should be proportional to the importance of a file. If a change is temporary and has a small influence on the overall system, the review should be thorough but not overly so. If the file is in the core of an important system with many dependencies, more thought should go into the review.

Members of a healthy team accept criticism well. However, there is a trick to doing code reviews without being mean, or being perceived as mean (which is just as important): criticize the code, not the person. For example, "This algorithm is slow and should be replaced with a faster one" is neutral. "You shouldn't use this algorithm" is blaming the person. This subtle kind of blame undermines team cohesion. The ability for team members to give criticism without being critical should be role-modeled by managers and subtly policed by all. Not doing so risks poisoning the team. Managers who do not follow this advice shouldn't act surprised when members of their team unfairly criticize each other in other forums.

12.7.7 Writing Just Enough Code

Write just enough code to satisfy the requirements of the feature or to fix the bug. No more. No less.

Writing too little code means the feature request is not satisfied. Alternatively, we may have written code that is so terse that it is difficult to understand. Writing too much code creates a maintenance burden, creates more bugs, and wastes time.

Writing too much code is an easy trap to fall into. We may write code that is more flexible, or more configurable, than we currently require, or we may add features that we think might be needed someday. We call this practice "future-proofing" and justify it by suggesting that it will save us time in the future when the feature is needed. It is fun and exciting to go beyond the requirements of what we are creating.

In reality, history teaches us that we are bad at predicting the future. What we think will be needed in the future is wrong 80 percent of the time. Extra code takes time to develop. In an industry where everyone complains there isn't enough time to do their work, we shouldn't be creating extra work. Extra code is a burden for people in the future who will have to maintain the code. A program that is 20 percent larger because of unused code is more than 20 percent more difficult to maintain. Writing less code now saves your entire team time in the future. The vast majority of coding involves maintaining and adding features to existing code; rarely do we start a new project from scratch. Given this fact, making maintenance easier is critical.

Unused code tends to include more bugs because it doesn't get exercised or tested. If it is tested, that means we spent time adding the tests, the automated testing system now has more work to do, and future maintainers will be unsure if they can delete a feature because all the automated testing "must be there for a reason." When the feature finally is needed, possibly months or years in the future, new bugs will be discovered as the requirements and environment will have changed.

That said, there is some reasonable future-proofing to do. Any constant such as a hostname or filename should be settable via a command-line flag or configuration setting. Split out major functions or classes into separate libraries so that they may be reused by future programs.

There are three tips we've found that help us resist the temptation to future-proof. First, use test-driven development and force yourself to stop coding when all tests pass. Second, adding TODO() comments listing features you'd like to add often reduces the emotional need to actually write the code. Third, the style guide should explicitly discourage excessive future-proofing and encourage aggressively deleting unused code or features that have become obsolete. This establishes a high standard that can be applied at code review time.

12.8 Multitenant Systems

Multitenancy is the situation in which one system provides service for multiple groups, each compartmentalized so that it is protected from the actions of the others.

Better than creating automation for just your team is finding a way to automate something in such a way that all other teams can benefit from it. You could provide the software releases internally so that others can run similar systems. Even better, you could create your system such that it can serve other teams at the same time.

When laying out the configuration management aspects of your system, you can achieve greater flexibility and delegate management through **multitenancy**. This simply means setting up the system to allow individual groups, or "tenants," to control their own code base.

Important qualities of a multitenant framework are that it can be used by multiple groups on a self-service basis, where each group's usage is isolated from that of the other groups. Doing so requires a permission model so that each team is protected from changes by the other teams. Each team is its own security domain, even though just one service is providing services to all teams.

Case Study: Multitenant Puppet

Google has one centralized Puppet server system that provides multitenant access to the individual teams that use it. The Mac team, Ubuntu team, Ganeti team, and others are all able to manage their own configurations without interfering with one another.

The system is very sophisticated. Each tenant is provided with a fully source code–controlled area for its files plus separate staging environments for development, testing, and production. Any feature added to the central system benefits everyone. For example, any work the Puppet team does to make the servers handle a larger number of clients benefits all tenants. When the Puppet team made it possible for the Puppet servers to be securely accessed from outside the corporate firewall, all teams gained the ability for all machines to stay updated even when mobile.

While Google's system enables each tenant to work in a self-service manner, protections exist so that no team can modify any other's files. Puppet manifests (programs) run as root and can change any file on the machine being run on. Therefore it is important that (for example) the Ubuntu team cannot make changes to the Mac team's files, and vice versa. Doing so would, essentially, give the Ubuntu team access to all the Macs. This is implemented through a simple but powerful permission system.

12.9 Summary

The majority of a system administrator's job should focus on automating SA tasks. A cloud computing system administrator's goal should be to spend less than half the time doing manual operational work.

Tool building optimizes the work done by a system administrator and is an important step on the way to automation. Automation means replacing a human task with one done by software, often working in partnership with a person. Automation starts by having a documented, well-defined, repeatable process. That document can be used to create scripts that can be used as tools to speed up the process and make it more reliable. Finally, the task can be fully automated by creating a self-service tool or a process that is automatically triggered by changes in a database or configuration file. A self-service tool is particularly useful, as it renders others self-sufficient. When something is automated, the SA's job changes from doing the task to maintaining the automation that does the task. A more enlightened way of thinking of automation is as a partner for operations rather than a replacement.

Many levels of automation exist, from fully manual to systems that work autonomously without human veto or approval. Different levels are appropriate depending on the task type and risk.

SAs can choose between scripting languages and compiled languages for creating automation. Understanding the benefits and disadvantages of each approach enables the SA to choose the right tool for the job. Configuration management systems are also useful for some forms of automation. Configuration management tools use a declarative syntax so that you can specify what the end result should be; the CM tool then figures out how to bring the system to that state.

Best practices dictate that all code for automation and configuration files be kept under revision control or in a database that tracks changes. As is true for the software development environment, automation tools should not be developed or tested in the production environment. Instead, they should be developed in a dedicated development environment, then staged to a testing area for quality assurance tests, before being pushed to the production environment.

Exercises

1. List five benefits of automation. Which ones apply to your own environment and why?
2. Document a process that needs automation in your current environment. Remember that the document should include every step needed to do the process!
3. Describe how to prioritize automation using a decision matrix.
4. When would you use a scripting language instead of a compiled language, and why? In which circumstances would you use a compiled language for automation?

5. Imagine that you are going to implement a configuration management system in your current environment. Which one would you choose and why?

6. What percentage of your time is spent on one-off tasks and operational work that is not automated? What could you do to change this for the better?

7. List three challenges that automation can introduce. For each of them, describe which steps you could take to address that challenge.

Chapter 13

Design Documents

> Be sincere; be brief; be seated.
>
> —Franklin D. Roosevelt

In this chapter we introduce design documents and discuss their uses and the best practices surrounding them. Design documents are written descriptions of proposed and completed projects, big or small. Design documents serve as a roadmap for your projects and documentation of your accomplishments.

13.1 Design Documents Overview

Design documents are descriptions of proposed or completed projects. They record the goals, the design itself, alternatives considered, plus other details such as cost, timeline, and compliance with corporate policies.

Writing out what you are going to do forces you to think through the details. It forces you to plan. Having a written document can make design collaborative when the document becomes a communication vehicle for ideas. Written documents mean fewer surprises for your teammates, and they help you to get consensus among the team before moving forward. After the project is completed, the design document serves as an artifact that documents the work, a reference for the team.

A good design document goes into specific detail about the proposed project or change, including information on why choices were made. For instance, the document might contain detailed descriptions of algorithms, specific packaging parameters, and locations where binary files are to be installed, and explain why the config files are going into /etc instead of elsewhere. A design document about namespace selection, such as the design of a namespace for server/rack names, will not only describe the naming structure, but also give the background on why this namespace was chosen and how it does or does not integrate with existing namespaces.

The document itself is useful for achieving consensus on a project. Sometimes an "obvious" change isn't really so obvious, and people find errors or have questions. As Linus Torvolds said, "Many eyes make all bugs shallow."

Case Study: Working Backward at Amazon

Amazon encourages engineers to start by describing what the customer will see, then work backward to build the design. Engineers start by writing the press release that they would like to see announce the product. They design the marketing materials describing how the customer will benefit from the product, identifying the features, and answering FAQs. This develops the vision of what will be created. Only after this work is finished is the design created that will achieve the vision. The process is fully described in Black (2009).

13.1.1 Documenting Changes and Rationale

Design documents can also be used to describe changes instead of projects. A short design document is a good format to get consensus on a small change such as a new new router configuration, a plan to adopt a new feature of a configuration management system, or a new naming scheme for a file hierarchy.

A design document is created to capture the specifics of the proposed change, and used as a sounding board for team input. If a formal change control process is in place, the same document can be included in the change request.

13.1.2 Documentation as a Repository of Past Decisions

An archive of design documents becomes a reference for anyone needing to understand how things work or how things got the way they are. New team members can come up to speed more quickly if there is documentation they can study. Existing team members find it useful to have a reference when they need a quick refresher on a particular subject. When collaborating with other teams, it is useful, and looks much more professional, to point people to documents rather than to explain things extemporaneously.

When knowledge can be conveyed without requiring personal interaction with an expert, it makes the team more efficient and effective. Teams can grow faster, other people can adopt our service more rapidly, and we have the freedom to transfer between teams because knowledge is not locked to one person.

Design documents convey not just the design, but also goals and inspirations. Since people will refer to design documents for a long time, they are a good place to store background and context.

Often teams retain the history of decisions in their email archive. The problem is that email is, by nature, sequestered in a person's mailbox. New team members cannot find those emails, nor will they appear in a search of a documents archive. Multiply that one simple email by a year's worth of changes and you have an entire set of information that is basically inaccessible to the team.

Don't say it; write it down. Procedures, designs, and wisdom count only when they are written down. People can't refer to your words unless they are in writing. In that regard, email is speech, not writing (Hickstein 2007).

13.2 Design Document Anatomy

A design document has many parts. They start with the highest-level information, getting more detailed as the document proceeds. We aid reader comprehension by standardizing the format, headings, and order of these parts.

Appendix D includes an example of a complete design document in Section D.2. A sample template appears in Section D.1.

The sections are:

Title: The title of the document.

Date: The date of the last revision.

Author(s)/Reviewer(s)/Approver(s): Reviewers are people whose feedback is requested Approvers are people who must approve the document.

Revision Number: Documents should have revisions numbered like software releases.

Status: Status can be draft, in review, approved, or in progress. Some organizations have fewer or more categories.

Executive Summary: A two- to four-sentence summary of the project that contains the major goal of the project and how it is to be achieved.

Goals (Alternatively, "In Scope"): What is to be achieved by the project, typically presented as a bullet list. Include non-tangible, process goals such as standardization or metrics achievements. It is important to look at your goals and cross-check each one to see that your design document addresses each goal. In some organizations, each goal is given a number and the goals are referred to by number throughout the document, with each design description citing the appropriate goals.

Non-goals (Alternatively, "Out of Scope"): A bullet list is typically used to present this information. A list of non-goals should explicitly identify what is not included in the scope for this project. This heads off review comments like "This project doesn't solve XYZ" because we are communicating here that this project is not intended to solve XYZ.

Background: What a typical reader needs to know to be able to understand the design. This section might provide a brief history of how we got here. Identify any acronyms or unusual terminology used. Document any previous decisions made that have placed limitations or constraints on this project, such as "Our company policy of using only open source software when possible precludes commercial solution XYZ in this project."

High-Level Design: A brief overview of the design including how it works at a high level. The design principles should be described but not necessarily the implementation details.

Detailed Design: The full design, including diagrams, sample configuration files, algorithms, and so on. This will be your full and detailed description of what you plan to accomplish on this project.

Alternatives Considered: A list of alternatives that were rejected, along with why they were rejected. Some of this information could have been included in the "Background" section, but including it in a specific location quiets the critics.

Special Constraints: A list of special constraints regarding things like security, auditing controls, privacy, and so on. These are sometimes optional. Document things that are part of the process at your company, such as architectural review, compliance checks, and similar activities. You can lump all of the constraints together in this section or include a section for each of them. Any mandatory process for project review at your company should probably have its own section on your template.

The document may have many more sections, some of which may be optional. Here are some sections that might be useful in a template:

- **Cost Projections:** The cost of the project—both initial capital and operational costs, plus a forecast of the costs to keep the systems running.
- **Support Requirements:** Operational maintenance requirements. This ties into Cost Projections, as support staff have salary and benefit costs, hardware and licensing have costs, and so on.
- **Schedule:** Timeline of which project events happen when, in relation to each other.
- **Security Concerns:** Special mention of issues regarding security related to the project, such as protection of data.
- **Privacy and PII Concerns:** Special mention of issues regarding user privacy or anonymity, including plans for handling personally identifiable information (PII) in accordance with applicable rules and regulations.
- **Compliance Details:** Compliance and audit plans for meeting regulatory obligations under SOX, HIPPA, PCI, FISMA, or similar laws.
- **Launch Details:** Roll-out or launch operational details and requirements.

13.3 Template

Giving someone a template to fill out guides that person through the process of creating his or her own design documents better than a step-by-step guide or a sample document could ever do. The template should include all headings that the final document should have, even optional ones. The template can be annotated with a description of what is expected in each section as well as helpful hints and tips. These annotations should be in a different font or color and are usually deleted as the user fills out the template.

An example template can be found in Section D.1 of Appendix D. Use it as the basis for your organization's template.

The template should be easy to find. When the template is introduced, everyone should be notified that it exists and provided with a link to where the template can be found. The link should appear in other places, such at the table of contents of the design document archive or another place that people frequently see. Make sure the template shows up in intranet searches.

The template should be available in all the formats that users will be using, or any format with which they feel comfortable. If people use MS-Word, HTML, MarkDown (a wiki format), or OpenOffice/LibreOffice, provide the template in all of those formats. Providing it in your favorite format only and assuming everyone else can improvise is not making it easy for others to adopt the system.

It can also be useful to provide a short template and a long template. The short template might be used for initial proposals and small projects. The long template might be used for complex projects or formal proposals.

The template should also be easy to use. Anytime you see someone not using the template is an opportunity to debug the problem. Ask them, in a nonconfrontational way, why the template wasn't used. For example, tell them that you're looking for feedback about how to get more people to adopt the template and ask what you could do to have made it easier for them to use it. If they say they couldn't find the template, ask where they looked for it and make sure all those places are updated to include links.

13.4 Document Archive

There should be a single repository for all design documents. Generally this can be as simple as a list of documents, each linked to the document itself. For the document archive to be useful to readers, it should be easy for people to find the documents that they are looking for. A simple search mechanism can be useful, although people will generally be happy if there is one page that lists the titles of all documents and that page itself can be searched.

It should be easy to add a design document to the document archive. The process of adding to or updating the archive should be self-service. If the process involves emailing a person, then that person will inevitably become a bottleneck. Such an obstacle will discourage people from adding new documents.

The easiest way to create an archive is to use a wiki. With this approach, people add links to their documents on a main page. The actual documents are then stored either in the wiki or elsewhere. People will generally add to whatever structure already exists. Consequently, it is important to put time and thought into making a main page that is simple and easy for others to maintain.

Another way to maintain a repository is to create a location for people to add documents—for example, a source repository or subdirectory on a file server—and write scripts that automatically generate the index. Create a system for file naming so that the document organization happens automatically. The easiest method is for each team to have a unique prefix and to let the teams self-select their prefixes. Generating the index requires either a document format that can be parsed to extract data or a standardized place for people to list the data that is needed for the index—for example, a YAML or JSON file that people include along with the document itself. The scripts then automatically generate an index of all documents that lists the filename, title, and most recent revision number.

13.5 Review Workflows

There should be a defined way for design documents to be approved. An approval process does not need to be a high-overhead activity, but rather can be as simple as replying to an email containing the design document. People need to know that getting approval does not entail a huge workload or they won't seek it.

There are as many approval workflows as there are organizations using design documents. Most styles fall into one of three main groups:

- **Simple:** You create a draft, email it around for comments, and revise it if necessary. No formal approval.
- **Informal:** Similar to the simple workflow, but with review from project approvers or an external review board. This review board exists to give feedback and warn against repeating past mistakes rather than providing a stamp of approval.
- **Formal Workflow:** Multiple approval stages, including project approvers and an external review board. Typical examples include a firewall or security review, a project budget review, and a release schedule review. Each review stage is noted with any comments, and revision numbers or dates track changes.

Different kinds of documents may need different approval workflows. Informational documents may have a very lightweight or no approval process. More extensive approval may be required depending on the scope or impact of the document. Your approval workflow is likely to be determined by your change control or compliance requirements.

13.5.1 Reviewers and Approvers

A design document usually lists authors, reviewers, and approvers. The authors are the people who contributed to the document. Reviewers are the people whose feedback is requested. Approvers are the people whose approval is required to move forward.

Reviewers typically include team members who might end up doing the actual work of the project. They can also include subject-matter experts and anyone whose opinion the author wants to seek. Adding someone as a reviewer is a good way to "FYI" someone in another group that might be impacted by the project work. You should expect meaningful comments from a reviewer, including possibly comments that require you to make changes to the document.

Approvers typically include internal customers who are dependent on the results of the project as well as managers who need to sign off on the resources used for the project. Sometimes approvers include other audit and control processes mandated by the company—for example, a privacy assessment or review of PII used in the project. People who conduct audits of compliance with regulations such as SOX, HIPAA, or PCI are also approvers in the design document process. Approvers are generally a yes-or-no voice, with commentary usually accompanying only a "no" decision. It will be up to your individual process to determine whether approvals must be unanimous, or whether one or more negative approvals can be overridden by a majority of positive approvals.

13.5.2 Achieving Sign-off

The reason to make a distinction between reviewers and approvers is that approvers can block a project. Trying to get consensus from everyone will prevent any progress, especially if one asks for approval from people who are not directly affected by the success of a project. People on the perimeter of a project should not be able to block it. Everyone has a voice, but not everyone has a vote. The reviewer/approver distinction clarifies everyone's role.

Multiple, Highly Specialized Approvals

The design documents approval process used at Google includes sign-off from the group managing various centralized services. For example, if the project will be sending data to the centralized log archive, the design document must include a section called "Logging" that details how many bytes of log data each transaction will generate and justifies the storage and retention policy. Sign-off by the central log team is required. There are similar sections for security, privacy, and other approvers.

Working with a review board can be made easier if the board publishes a checklist of items it is looking for in a document. This permits the author to be better prepared at the review. Publishing the review board checklist is respectful of your colleagues' time as well as your own, as you will see fewer deficient documents once your checklists are made public. A review board may be a group of approvers or of reviewers, or a mix of both—it is in your best interest to determine this ahead of time as you prepare your document.

13.6 Adopting Design Documents

Implementing a design document standard within an organization can be a challenge because it requires a cultural change. People change slowly. Make it easy for people to adopt the new behavior, be a role model, and enlist management support.

Providing a template is the most important thing you can do to drive adoption of such a policy. Make sure the template is easy to access and available in the format people most want to use.

Model the behavior you wish to see in others. Use the design document template everywhere that it is appropriate and strictly adhere to the format.

People emulate the behaviors they see successful people demonstrate. Talk directly with highly respected members of the organization about being early adopters. Their feedback on why they are or are not willing to adopt the design document standard will be enlightening.

Early adopters should be rewarded and their success highlighted. This doesn't need to be a contest with prizes. It can be as simple as saying something positive at a weekly staff meeting. Compliment them even if they didn't use the template perfectly; you are rewarding them for taking the first steps. Save the suggestions on how to use the template more properly for one-on-one feedback.

Enlisting management support is another avenue to adoption. If you are a manager, you have the luxury of making design documents a top-down requirement and insisting that your team use them. Another way to start using design documents is to make them a requirement for certain approval processes, such as budget review, security or firewall review boards, or change control. Avoid requiring blind adherence to the template format as a requirement for approvals. Content is more important than presentation.

When they see that the template is easy to use, team members will start adopting it for other projects.

Use the template yourself. If the template is not benefiting you personally, it is probably not beneficial to others. Using it also helps spot problems that often can be fixed as easily as updating the template. When Tom joined Stack Exchange, one of the first things he did was create a design document template and put it on the department wiki. He used it for two proposals before mentioning it, revising and perfecting the template each time he used it. Only after it had been used a few times did he mention the template to his teammates. Soon others were using it, too.

13.7 Summary

A design document serves as a project roadmap and documentation. Its primary function is to describe a project, but it also communicates key aspects of the project (who, what, why, when, and how) to the team. Design documents are useful for change control as well as for project specifications. Good design documents will capture not only the decisions made but also the reasoning behind the decisions.

Adopting design documents can pose cultural challenges for a team. Start with a good template in an easy-to-find location, made available in the formats your team uses for documents. Create a central repository for design documents, organized in order of most recent updates. Make it easy to add a design document to the repository's main directory page.

Approvals are part of good design document culture. Create a draft document and solicit comments from some portion of the team. For simple workflows, email is sufficient to pass the document for review. For more formal workflows, there may be mandatory review boards or multiple approval steps. In all workflows, the version number of the design document is updated each time review comments are added to the document. Ideally, the document repository's main page will also be updated as revisions occur.

Templates should contain the major points of who, what, why, when, and how. Shorter templates may be used for small or informal projects, with larger, more complete templates being preferred for complex or formal projects. At a minimum, the template should have title, date, author(s), revision number, status, executive summary, goals, high-level design, and detailed design sections. Alternative or optional sections can be added to customize the template based on the needs of your organization.

Exercises

1. What are the primary functions of a design document?
2. List qualities of a good document management system for design documents.
3. Does your organization currently have a standardized design document format? If not, what would be required to implement it in your organization?
4. Which mandatory processes are part of a design review in your organization? Which stakeholders are mandatory reviewers or approvers?
5. Describe your organization's equivalent of design documents, and their strengths and weaknesses when contrasted with the model presented here.
6. Create a design document template for your organization. Show it to coworkers and get feedback about the format and ways that you can make it easier to use.
7. Write the design for a proposed or existing project using the design document format.
8. Take an existing document that your organization uses and rewrite it using the design document format.
9. Use the design document format for something silly or fun—for example, a design for a company picnic or plans to get rich quick.

Chapter 14

Oncall

> Be alert... the world
> needs more lerts.
>
> —Woody Allen

Oncall is the way we handle exceptional situations. Even though we try to automate all operational tasks, there will always be responsibilities and edge cases that cannot be automated away. These exceptional situations can happen at any time of the day; they do not schedule themselves nicely between the hours of 9 AM and 5 PM.

Exceptional situations are, in brief, outages and anything that, if left unattended, would lead to an outage. More specifically, they are situations where the service is, or will become, in violation of the SLA.

An operations team needs a strategy to assure that exceptional situations are attended to promptly and receive appropriate action. The strategy should be designed to reduce future reoccurrence of such exceptions.

The best strategy is to establish a schedule whereby at any given time at least one person is responsible for attending to such issues as his or her top priority. For the duration of the oncall shift, that person should remain contactable and within reach of computers and other facilities required to do his or her job. Between exceptions, the oncall person should be focused on follow-up work related to the exceptions faced during his or her shift.

In this chapter we will discuss this basic strategy plus many variations.

14.1 Designing Oncall

Oncall is the practice of having a group of people take turns being responsible for exceptional situations, more commonly known as emergencies or, less dauntingly, alerts. Oncall schedules typically provide 24×7 coverage. By taking turns, people get a break from such heightened responsibilities, can lead normal lives, and take vacations.

When an alert is received, the person on call responds and resolves the issue, using whatever means necessary to prevent SLA violations, including shortcut solutions that will not solve the problem in the long term. If he or she cannot resolve the issue, there is an escalation system whereby other people become involved. After the issue is managed, any follow-up work should be done during normal business hours—in particular, root causes analysis, postmortems, and working on long-term solutions.

Normally one person is designated the "oncall person" at any given time. If there is an alert from the monitoring system, that individual receives the alert and manages the issue until it is resolved. During business hours this person works as normal, except that he or she always works on projects that can be interrupted easily. After normal business hours, the oncall person should be near enough to a computer so he or she can respond quickly.

There also needs to be a strategy to handle the situation when the oncall person cannot be reached. This can happen due to commuting, network outages, health emergencies, or other issues. Generally a secondary oncall person is designated to respond if the primary person does not respond after a certain amount of time.

14.1.1 Start with the SLA

When designing an oncall scheme for an organization, begin with the SLA for the service. Work backward to create an SLA for oncall that will result in meeting the SLA for the service. Then design the oncall scheme that will meet the oncall SLA.

For example, suppose a service has an SLA that permits 2 hours of downtime before penalties accrue. Suppose also that typical problems can be solved in 30 minutes, and extreme problems take 30 minutes to cause system failover but usually only after 30 minutes of trying other solutions. This would mean that the time between when an outage starts and when the issue is being actively worked on must be less than an hour.

In that hour, the following things must happen. First, the monitoring system must detect the outage. If it polls every 5 minutes and alerts only after three attempts, a maximum of 15 minutes may pass before someone is alerted. This assumes the worst case of the last good poll happening right before the outage. Let's assume that alerts are sent every 5 minutes until someone responds; every third alert results in escalation from primary to secondary or from secondary to the entire team. The worst case (assuming the team isn't alerted) is six alerts, or 30 minutes. From receiving the alert, the oncall person may need 5–10 minutes to log into the system and begin working. So far we have accumulated about 50–55 minutes of outage before "hands on keyboard" has been achieved. Considering we estimated a maximum of 60 minutes to fix a problem, this leaves us with 5 minutes to spare.

Every service is different, so you must do these calculations for each one. If you are managing many services, it can be worthwhile to simplify the process by creating a few classes of service based on the required response time: 5 minutes, 15 minutes, 30 minutes, and longer. Monitoring, alerting, and compensation schemes for each class can be defined and reused for all new services rather than reinventing the wheel each time.

14.1.2 Oncall Roster

The **roster** is the list of people who take turns being oncall. The list is made up of qualified operations staff, developers, and managers. All operations staff should be on the roster. This is generally considered part of any operations staff member's responsibility.

When operations staff are new to the team, their training plan should be focused on getting them up to speed on the skills required to be oncall. They should follow or shadow someone who is oncall as part of their training. In most companies a new hire should be able to handle oncall duties within three to six months, though this time varies.

Some organizations do not require senior operations staff to share oncall responsibilities. This is unwise. The senior staff risk becoming disconnected from the operational realities for which they are responsible.

Developers should be on the roster. This gives them visibility into the operational issues inherent to the system that they have made and helps guide them in future design decisions. In other words, their resistance to add the features listed in Chapter 2 goes away when the lack of such features affects them, too. It creates an incentive to fix operational issues rather than provide workarounds.

For example, if a problem wakes up the oncall person at 3 AM, he or she might use a workaround and file a bug report to request a more permanent fix, one that would prevent the oncall person from being woken up at odd hours in the future. Such a bug is easy to ignore by developers if they do not have oncall shifts themselves. If they are on the oncall roster, they have an incentive to fix such bugs.

It is important that the priorities of operations and developers are aligned, because otherwise operational issues will not get the attention they deserve. In the old days of shrink-wrapped software, people accepted that developers were disconnected from operational needs, but those days are long gone. (If you do not know what shrink-wrapped software is, ask your grandparents.)

Technical managers, team leads, and technical project managers should also share oncall responsibilities. This keeps them in touch with the realities of operations and helps them to be better managers. We also find that oncall playbooks and tools tend to be held to a higher standard for accuracy and efficiency when a wider diversity of talent will be using them. In other words, if your playbook is written well enough that a technical manager can follow it, it's going to be pretty good. (To the managers reading this: we mean that people keep to higher standards when they know you'll see the results of their work.)

14.1.3 Onduty

Onduty is like oncall but focuses on dealing with non-emergency requests from users. Onduty is different from oncall.

Many operations teams also have a queue of requests from users managed similarly to the way IT helpdesks receive and track requests via a helpdesk automation tool. Onduty is a function that assures there is always one person working on these tickets. Otherwise, tickets may be ignored for extended periods of time. Colloquially this function goes by many names: ticket time, ticket week, ticket duty, or simply onduty. Generally the onduty roster is made up of the same people who are on the oncall roster.

The primary responsibility of the onduty person is to respond to tickets within the SLA—for example, 1 business day for initial response; no service at night, weekends, and holidays. Usually the onduty person is responsible for triaging new tickets, prioritizing them, working most of them, and delegating special cases to appropriate people.

Most organizations have different oncall and onduty schedules. In some organizations, whoever is oncall is automatically onduty. This simplifies scheduling but has the disadvantage that if an emergency occurs, tickets will be ignored. That said, for large emergencies tickets will be ignored anyway. Moreover, if there is an emergency that keeps the oncall person awake late at night, the next day that person may not be at his or her best; expecting this individual to respond to tickets under such conditions isn't a good idea. For that reason, you should try to keep a separate oncall schedule unless ticket load is extremely light.

Some organizations do not have onduty at all. They may not be in a situation where there are users who would file tickets with them. Some teams feel that accepting tickets goes against the DevOps philosophy. They are collaborators, they say, not a service desk that people come to with requests. If there is a request to collaborate, it should be handled through the normal business channels. During collaboration, any tasks assigned should be in the work tracking system just like all other project-related tasks.

14.1.4 Oncall Schedule Design

There are many variations on how to structure the oncall schedule. The duration of a person's oncall shift should be structured in a way that makes the most sense for your team. Here are some variations that are commonly used:

- **Weekly:** A person is oncall for one week at a time. The next shift starts the same time each week, such as every Wednesday at noon. Having the change occur mid-week is better than during the weekend. If the change happens on a Wednesday, each onduty person has one complete weekend where travel and other fun are limited. If the transition happens on Saturday, then it ruins the weekend of both oncall people for two weekends in a row. On Mondays, there may be a backlog of follow-up work from the weekend. It is best to let the person who handled the weekend alerts complete the follow-up work, or at least generate the appropriate tickets and documentation, while still oncall. This enables a clean handover and should allow each person to return to project work as quickly as possible after oncall duty ends.

- **Daily:** A person is oncall for one day at a time. This may seem better than a weekly schedule because the shift is not as long, but it means being oncall much more often. A weekly schedule might mean being oncall one week out of every six. With a small team, a daily schedule might mean being oncall every six days, never having a complete week to take a vacation.

- **Split Days:** On a given day multiple people are oncall, each one responsible for a different part of the day or shift. For example, a two-shift schedule might involve two 12-hour shifts per day. One person works 9 AM to 9 PM and another is oncall for the overnight. This way, if an alert happens in each shift, someone is always able to sleep. A three-shift schedule might be 8 hours each: 9 AM to 5 PM, 5 PM to 1 AM, and 1 AM to 9 AM.

- **Follow the Sun:** Members of the operations team live in different time zones, and each is oncall for the hours that he or she would normally be awake (sunlight hours). If the team resides in California and Dublin, a shift change at 10 AM and 10 PM California time means all members have some responsibilities during office hours and sleeping hours, plus there are enough overlap hours for inter-team communication. A team split between many time zones may have three or four shifts per day.

Many variations are also possible. Some teams prefer half-weeks instead of full weeks. Follow the sun can be done with with two, three, or four shifts per day depending on where people are located.

Alert Frequency

With so many variations, it can be difficult to decide which to use. Develop a strategy where the frequency and duration of oncall shifts are determined by how frequent alerts are. People do their best oncall work when they are not overloaded and have not been kept awake for days on end. An oncall system improves operations when each alert receives follow-up work such as causal analysis. Before someone goes oncall again, that person should have had enough time to complete all follow-up work.

For example, if alerts are extremely rare, occurring less than once a week, a single person being oncall for 7 days at a time is reasonable. If there are three alerts each day, two or three shifts gives people time to sleep between alerts and do follow-up tasks. If follow-up work is extensive, half-week rotations of two shifts may be required.

If there is a significantly high alert ratio, more complex schemes are needed. For example, in some schedules, two people are oncall: one receives the alert if the other is busy, plus two secondaries shadow the primaries. Some systems divide the work geographically, with a different rotation scheme and schedule for each major region of the world.

Schedule Coordination

Oncall schedules may be coordinated with other schedules. For example, it may be a guideline that the week before your oncall shift, you are onduty. There may be a dedicated schedule of escalation points. For example, people knowledgeable in a particular service may coordinate to make sure that they aren't all on vacation at the same time. That ensures that if oncall needs to escalate to them, someone is available. Sometimes an escalation schedule is an informal agreement, and sometimes it is a formal schedule with an SLA.

Compensation

Compensation drives some design elements of the schedule. In some countries, being oncall requires compensation if response time is less than a certain interval. The compensation is usually a third of the normal hourly salary for any hour oncall outside of normal business hours. It may be paid in cash or by giving the oncall person time off. Compensation rates may be different if the person is called to action. Your human resources department should be able to provide all the details required. In some countries, there is no legal obligation for oncall compensation but good companies do it anyway because it is unethical otherwise. One benefit of follow-the-sun coverage is that it can be constructed in a way that maximizes time oncall during normal business hours for a location, while minimizing the amount of additional compensation that needs to be budgeted.

14.1.5 The Oncall Calendar

The **oncall calendar** documents who is oncall when. It turns the theory of the schedule and roster into specifics. The monitoring system uses this information to decide who to send alerts to.

Set the calendar far enough ahead to permit all concerned to plan vacations, travel, and other responsibilities in advance. Three to six months is usually sufficient. The details of building the calendar are as varied as there are teams. A team of six that changes the oncall person every Wednesday may simply use the "repeating event" functionality of an online calendar to schedule who is oncall when. Conflicts and other issues can be worked out between members.

A more complex schedule and a larger team require proportionately more complex calendar building strategies. One such system used a shared, online spreadsheet such as Google Drive. The spreadsheet cells represented each time slot for the next three months. Due to the size of the team, everyone was expected to take three time slots. The system was "first come, first served," and there was a lot of back-channel discussion that enabled people to trade time slots. The negotiating continued until a certain cut-off point, at which time the schedule was locked. This system was unfair to people who happened to be out the day the schedule was made.

Some companies take a more algorithmic approach. Google had hundreds of individual calendars to create for any given month due to the existence of many internal and external services. Each team spent a lot of time negotiating and assembling calendars until someone wrote a program that did the task for them. To use the system, a team would create a Google Calendar and everyone inserted events to mark which days they were entirely unavailable, available but not preferred, available, or preferred. The system took a configuration file that described parameters such as how long each shift was, whether there was a required gap of time before someone could have another rotation, and so on. The system then read people's preferences from the Google Calendar and churned on the data until a reasonable oncall calendar was created.

14.1.6 Oncall Frequency

The frequency of how often a person goes oncall needs careful consideration. Each alert has a certain amount of follow-up work that should be completed before the next turn at oncall begins. Each person should also have sufficient time between oncall shifts to work on projects, not just follow-up work.

The follow-up work from an alert can be extensive. Writing a postmortem can be an arduous task. Root cause analysis can involve extensive research that lasts days or weeks.

The longer the oncall shift, the more alerts will be received and the more follow-up projects the person will be trying to do at the same time. This can overload a person.

The more closely the shifts are spaced, the more likely the work will not be completed by the time the next shift starts.

Doing one or two postmortems simultaneously is reasonable, but much more is impossible. Therefore shifts should be long enough that only one or two significant alerts have accumulated. Depending on the service, this may be one day, a week of 8-hour periods, or a week of 24×7 service. The next such segment should be spaced at least three weeks apart if the person is expected to complete both postmortems, do project work, and be able to go on an occasional vacation. If a service receives so many alerts that this is not possible, then the service has deeper issues.

Oncall shifts can be stressful. If the source of stress is that the shift is too busy, consider using shorter shifts or having a second person oncall to handle overflow. If the source of stress is that people do not feel confident in their ability to handle the alerts, additional training is recommended. Ways to train a team to be more comfortable dealing with outage situations are discussed in Chapter 15.

14.1.7 Types of Notifications

There are many levels of urgency at which monitoring and other services need to raise the attention of human operators. Only the most urgent is an alert.

Each level of urgency should have its own communication method. If urgent alerts are simply sent to someone's email inbox, they may not be noticed in time. If non-urgent messages are communicated by sending an SMS to the person oncall, the "Boy Who Cried Wolf" syndrome will develop.

The best option is to build a very high-level classification system:

- **Alert Oncall:** The SLA is in violation, or if a condition is detected that, if left unattended, will result in an SLA violation.
- **Create a Ticket:** The issue needs attention within one business day.
- **Log to a File:** The condition does not require human attention. We do not want to lose the information, but we do not need to be notified.
- **Do Nothing:** There is no useful information; nothing should be sent.

In some organizations, all of these situations are communicated by email to the entire system administration team. Under these conditions, all team members might be compelled to filter all messages to a folder that is ignored. This defeats the purpose of sending the messages in the first place.

Email is, quite possibly, the worst alerting mechanism. Expecting someone to sit and watch an email inbox is silly, and a waste of everyone's time. With this strategy, staff will be unaware of new alerts if they step away or get involved in other projects.

Daily emails that report on the result of a status check are also a bad idea. If the status is fine, log this fact. If a problem was detected, automatically open a ticket. This prevents multiple people from accidentally working on the same issue at the same time. If the problem is urgent enough that someone should be alerted immediately, then why is the check being done only once per day? Instead, report the status to the monitoring system frequently and send alerts normally.

However, it is a good idea to use email as a secondary mechanism. That is, when sending a message to a pager or creating a ticket, also receiving a copy via email is useful. Many systems have mechanisms to subscribe to such messages in a way that permits precise filtering. For example, it is usually possible to configure a ticket system to email notifications of new or updated tickets in a particular queue.

Once an alert is triggered, there are many ways to notify the person who is oncall. The most common alert methods are identified here:

- **One-Way and Two-Way Pagers:** Hand-held devices that receive text messages via terrestrial broadcasts. Two-way pagers permit sending a reply to acknowledge that the message was received.
- **SMS or Text Message to a Mobile Phone:** Sending a text or SMS message to a person's mobile phone is convenient because most people already carry a mobile phone. In some countries, pagers are significantly more reliable than SMS; in others, the reverse is true. If you are creating an alerting system for co-workers in another country, do not assume that what works well for you will be viable elsewhere. Local people should test both.
- **Smart Phone App:** Smart phone apps are able to display additional information beyond a short text message. However, they often depend on Internet connectivity, which may not always be available.
- **Voice Call:** A voice synthesizer and other software is used to call a person's phone and talk to him or her, asking the person to press a button to acknowledge the message (otherwise, the escalation list will be activated).
- **Chat Room Bot:** A chat room bot is a software robot that sits in the team's chat room and announces any alerts. This is a useful way to keep the entire team engaged and ready to help the oncall person if needed.
- **Alerting Dashboard:** The alerting dashboard is a web page that shows the history of alerts sent. It provides useful context information.
- **Email:** Email should never be the only way the oncall person is alerted. Sitting at your computer watching your inbox is a terrible use of your time. Nevertheless, it is useful to have every alert emailed to the oncall person as a backup method. This way the full message is received; SMS truncates messages to 160 characters.

At least two methods should be used to make sure the message gets through. A pager service might have an outage. A sleeping oncall person might require an SMS tone and a voice call to wake him or her. One method should communicate the complete, non-truncated, message to a stable storage medium. Email works well for this. Lastly, chat room bots and other methods should also be deployed, especially given that this strategy enables the entire team to stay aware of issues as they happen. They may seem like novelties at first but they quickly become indispensable.

14.1.8 After-Hours Maintenance Coordination

Sometimes maintenance must be done after hours. For example, another team may do maintenance that requires your participation, such as failing over services so they are not affected by scheduled outages, or being around to verify status, and so on.

It is very common to assign such tasks to whoever will be oncall at the time. For most situations, this is fine. However, it does create the possibility that an oncall person might be dealing with an alert and coordinating an unrelated issue at the same time.

If the oncall person is used for such tasks, the secondary oncall person should take any alerts that happen during the maintenance window. Alternatively, assign the maintenance window coordination to the secondary person.

14.2 Being Oncall

Now that we know how to develop a roster, schedule, and calendar, we can consider the responsibilities associated with being oncall. An oncall person has responsibilities before, during, and after each shift.

14.2.1 Pre-shift Responsibilities

Before a shift begins, you should make sure you are ready. Most teams have an **oncall shift preparedness checklist**. Items on the checklist verify reachability and access. Reachability means that the alert notification system is working. You might send a test alert to yourself to verify that everything is working. Access means that you have access to the resources needed when responding to an alert: your VPN software works, your laptop's batteries are charged, you are sober enough to perform operations, and so on.

Correcting any problems found may take time. Therefore the checklist should be activated appropriately early, or early enough to negotiate extending the current oncall person's shift or finding a replacement. For example, discovering that your two-factor authenticator is not working may require time to set up a new one.

14.2.2 Regular Oncall Responsibilities

Once the shift begins you should do...nothing special. During working hours you should work as normal but take on only tasks that can be interrupted if needed. If you attend a meeting, it is a good idea to warn people at the start that you are oncall and may have to leave at any time. If you are oncall outside of normal working hours, you should sleep as needed and basically live a normal life, other than being accessible. If travel is required, such as to go home from work, establish temporary coverage from your secondary oncall person for the duration of the drive.

What you should not do during oncall is sit at your computer watching your service dashboards and monitoring systems to see if you can spot problems. This is a waste of time and is exactly what monitoring systems are made for. If this kind of activity is a requirement of the oncall shift, then your oncall system has been poorly designed.

Some teams have a list of tasks that are done during each shift. Some example tasks include verifying the monitoring system is working, checking that backups ran, and checking for security alerts related to software used in-house. These tasks should be eliminated through automation. However, until they are automated, assigning responsibility to the current oncall person is a convenient way to spread the work around the team. These tasks are generally ones that can be done between alerts and are assumed to be done sometime during the shift, though it is wise to do them early in the shift so as not to forget them. However, if a shift starts when someone is normally asleep, expecting these tasks to be done at the very start of the shift is unreasonable. Waking people up for non-emergencies is not healthy.

Tasks may be performed daily, weekly, or monthly. In all cases there should be a way to register that the task was completed. Either maintain a shared spreadsheet where people mark things as complete, or automatically open a ticket to be closed when the task is done. All tasks should have an accompanying bug ID that requests the task be eliminated though automation or other means. For example, verifying that the monitoring system is running can be automated by having a system that monitors the monitoring system. (See Section 16.5, "Meta-monitoring.") A task such as emptying the water bucket that collects condensation from a temporary cooling device should be eliminated when the temporary cooling system is finally replaced.

Oncall should be relatively stress-free when there is no active alert.

14.2.3 Alert Responsibilities

Once alerted, your responsibilities change. You are now responsible for verifying the problem, fixing it, and ensuring that follow-up work gets completed. You may not be the person who does all of this work, but you are responsible for making sure it all happens through delegation and handoffs.

You should acknowledge the alert within the SLA described previously. Acknowledging the alert tells the alerting system that it should not try to alert the next contact on the escalation list.

Quick Fixes versus Long-Term Fixes

Now the issue is worked on. Your priority is to come up with the best solution that will resolve the issue within the SLA. Sometimes we have a choice between a long-term fix and a quick fix. The long-term fix will resolve the fundamental problem and prevent the issue in the future. It may involve writing code or releasing new software. Rarely can that be done within the SLA. A quick fix fits within the SLA but may simply push the issue farther down the road. For example, rebooting a machine may fix the problem for now but will require rebooting it again in a few days because the technical problem was not fixed. However, the reboot can be done now and will prevent an SLA violation.

In general, encourage a bias toward long-term fixes over quick fixes: "a stitch in time saves nine." However, oncall is different from normal engineering. Oncall places a higher priority on speed than on long-term perfection. Since solutions that do not fit within the SLA must be eliminated, a quick fix may be the only option.

Asking for Help

It is also the responsibility of the oncall person to ask for help when needed. Escalate to more experienced or knowledgable people, or if the issue was raised long enough ago, find someone who is better rested than you are. You don't have to save the world single-handedly. You are allowed to call other folks for help. Reach out to others especially if the outage is large or if there are multiple alerts at the same time. You don't have to fix the problem yourself necessarily. Rather, it is your responsibility to make sure it gets fixed, which sometimes is best done by looping in the right people and coordinating rather than trying to handle everything yourself.

Follow-up Work

Once the problem has been resolved, the priority shifts to raising the visibility of the issue so that long-term fixes and optimizations will be done. For simple issues, it may be sufficient to file a bug report or add annotations to an existing one. More complex issues require writing a postmortem report that captures what happened and makes recommendations about how it can be prevented in the future. By doing this we build a feedback loop that assures operations get better over time, not worse. If the issue is not given visibility, the core problem will not be fixed. Do not assume that "everyone knows it is broken" means that it will get fixed. Not everyone does know it is broken. You can't expect that managers who prioritize which projects are given resources will know everything or be able to read your mind. Filing bug reports is like picking up litter: you can assume someone else will do it, but if everyone did that nothing would ever be clean.

Once the cause is known, the alert should be categorized so that metrics can be generated. This helps spot trends and the resulting information should be used to determine future project priorities. It is also useful to record which machines were involved in a searchable way. Future alerts can then be related to past ones, and simple trends such as the same machine failing repeatedly can be spotted.

Other follow-up tasks are discussed in Section 14.3.

14.2.4 Observe, Orient, Decide, Act (OODA)

The OODA loop was developed for combat operations by John Boyd. Designed for situations like fighter jet combat, it fits high-stress situations that require quick responses. Kyle Brandt (2014) popularized the idea of applying OODA to system administration.

Suppose the alert relates to indicators that your web site is slow and often timing out. First we **Observe**: checking logs, reading I/O measurements, and so on.

Next we **Orient** ourselves to the situation. Orienting is the act of analyzing and interpreting the data. For example, logs contain many fields, but to turn that data into information the logs need to be queried to find anomalies or patterns. In this process we come up with a hypothesis based on the data and our experience to find the real cause.

Now we **Decide** to do something. Sometimes we decide that more information is needed and begin to collect it. For example, if there are indications that the database is slow, then we collect more specific diagnostics from the database and restart the loop.

The last stage is to **Act** and make changes that will either fix the problem, test a hypothesis, or give us more data to analyze. If you decide that certain queries are making the database server slow, eventually someone has to take action to fix them.

The OODA loop will almost always have many iterations. More experienced system administrators can iterate through the loop logically, rapidly, and smoothly. Also, over time a good team develops tools to make the loop go faster and gets better at working together to tighten the loop.

14.2.5 Oncall Playbook

Ideally, every alert that the system can generate will be matched by documentation that describes what to do in response. An **oncall playbook** is this documentation.

The general format is a checklist of things to check or do. If the end of the list is reached, the issue is escalated to the oncall escalation point (which itself may be a rotation of people). This creates a self-correcting feedback loop. If people feel that there are too many escalations waking up them late at night, they can correct the problem by improving the documentation to make oncall more self-sufficient.

If they feel that writing documentation is unimportant or "someone else's job," they can, by virtue of not creating proper checklists, give oncall permission to wake them up at all hours of the night. It is impressive how someone who feels that writing documentation is below them suddenly learns the joy of writing after being woken up in the middle of the night. The result of this feedback loop is that each checklist becomes as detailed as needed to achieve the right balance.

When writing an oncall playbook, it can be a challenge to determine how detailed each checklist should be. A statement like "Check the status of the database" might be sufficient for an experienced person. The actual steps required to do that, and instructions on what is considered normal, should be included. It is usually too much detail to explain very basic information like how to log in.

Intentionally select a baseline of knowledge that is assumed. There should be documentation that will take a new employee and bring him or her up to that level. The oncall documents, then, can assume that level of knowledge. This also helps prevent the situation where documentation becomes too verbose and repetitive. Requiring authors to include too much detail can become an impediment to writing documentation at all.

14.2.6 Third-Party Escalation

Sometimes escalations must include someone outside the operations team, such as the oncall team of a different service or a vendor. Escalating to a third party has special considerations.

During an outage, one should not have to waste time researching how to contact the third party. All third-party dependencies should be documented. There should be a single globally accessible list that has the oncall information for each internal team. If the oncall numbers change with each shift, this list should be dynamically generated with the current information.

Lists of contact information for vendors usually contain information that should not be shared outside of the team and, therefore, is stored differently. For each dependency, this private list should include the vendor name, contact information, and anything needed to open a support issue. For example, there may be license information or support contract numbers.

Tips for Managing Vendor Escalations

Sometimes support cases opened with a vendor remain open for many days. When this happens:

- One person should interface with the vendor for the duration of the issue. Otherwise, communication and context can become disorganized.
- Trust but verify. Do not let a vendor close the case until you have verified the issue is resolved.
- Report the issue to your sales contact only if you are not getting results. Otherwise, the sales representative may meddle, which is annoying to technical support people.
- Take ownership of the issue. Do not assume the vendor will. Be the person who follows up and makes sure the process keeps moving.
- When possible, make follow-up calls early in the day. This sets up the vendor to spend the day working on your issue.

14.2.7 End-of-Shift Responsibilities

Eventually your shift will end and it will be time to hand off oncall to the next person. Making sure the transition goes well ensures that context is transferred to the next person and open issues are not forgotten.

One strategy is to write an **end-of-shift report** that is emailed to the entire oncall roster. Sending it to just the next person oncall is vulnerable to error. You may pick the wrong person by mistake, or may not know about a substitution that was negotiated. Sending the report to everyone keeps the entire team up-to-date and gives everyone an opportunity to get involved if needed.

The end-of-shift report should include any notable events that happened and anything that the next shift needs to know. For example, it should identify an ongoing outage or behaviors that need manual monitoring.

Another strategy is to have an **explicit handoff** to the next shift. This means the outgoing person must explicitly state that he or she is handing off responsibility to the next person, and the next person must positively acknowledge the handoff. If the next person does not or cannot acknowledge the handoff, then responsibility stays with the original person. This technique is used in situations where availability requirements are very strict.

In this case the end-of-shift report may be verbal or via email. A written report is better because it communicates to the entire team.

If shift change happens when one or both parties may be asleep, a simple email may be sufficient if there are no ongoing issues. If there are ongoing issues, the next oncall person should be alerted. If the outgoing person will be asleep when the shift changes, it is common practice to send out a **provisional end-of-shift report**, noting that unless there are alerts between now and the shift change, this report can be considered final.

14.3 Between Oncall Shifts

The normal working hours between shifts should be spent on project work. That includes follow-up tasks related to oncall alerts. While such work can be done during oncall time, sleep is usually more important.

Projects related to oncall include working on the long-term solutions that weren't possible to implement during oncall and postmortem reports.

14.3.1 Long-Term Fixes

Each alert may generate follow-up work that cannot be done during the oncall period. Large problems may require a causal analysis to determine the root cause of the outage.

In our previous example, a problem was solved by rebooting a machine. Causal analysis might indicate that the software has a memory leak. Working with the developers to find and fix the memory leak is a long-term solution.

Even if you are not the developer who will ultimately fix the code, there is plenty of work that can be done besides hounding the developers who will provide the final solution. You can set up monitoring to collect information about the problem, so that before and after comparisons can be made. You can work with the developers to understand how the issue is affecting business objectives such as availability.

14.3.2 Postmortems

A postmortem is a process that analyzes an outage and documents what happened and why, and makes recommendations about how to prevent that outage in the future.

A good postmortem process communicates up and down the management chain. It communicates to users that action is being taken. It communicates to peer teams so that interactions (good and bad) are learned. It can also communicate to unrelated teams so they can learn from your problems.

The postmortem process should not start until after the outage is complete. It should not be a distraction from fixing the outage.

A postmortem is part of the strategy of continuous improvement. Each user-visible outage or SLA violation should be followed by a postmortem and conclude with implementation of the recommendations in the postmortem report. By doing so we turn outages into learning, and learning into action.

Postmortem Purpose

A postmortem is not a finger-pointing exercise. The goal is to identify what went wrong so the process can be improved in the future, not to determine who is to blame. Nobody should be in fear of getting fired for having their name associated with a technical error. Blame discourages the kind of openness required to have the transparency that enables problems to be identified so that improvements can be made. If a postmortem exercise is a "name and shame" process, then engineers become silent on details about actions and observations in the future. "Cover your ass" (CYA) behavior becomes the norm. Less information flows, so management becomes less informed about how work is performed and other engineers become less knowledgeable about pitfalls within the system. As a result, more outages happen, and the cycle begins again.

The postmortem process records, for any engineers whose actions have contributed to the outage, a detailed account of actions they took at the time, effects they observed, expectations they had, assumptions they had made, and their understanding of the timeline of events as they occurred. They should be able to do this without fear of punishment or retribution.

This is not to say that staff members get off the hook for making mistakes. They are on the hook for many things. They are now the experts responsible for educating the organization on how not to make that mistake in the future. They should drive engineering efforts related to improving the situation.

A culture of accountability, rather than blame, fosters an organization that values innovation. If blame is used to avoid responsibility, the whole team suffers. For more information about this topic, we recommend Allspaw's (2009) article "Blameless Postmortems and a Just Culture."

A Postmortem Report for Every High-Priority Alert

At Google many teams had a policy of writing a postmortem report every time their monitoring system paged the oncall person. This was done to make sure that no issues were ignored or "swept under the rug." As a result there was no back-sliding in Google's high standards for high uptime. It also resulted in the alerting system being highly tuned so that very few false alarms were generated.

Postmortem Report

Postmortem reports include four main components: a description of the outage, a timeline of events, a contributing conditions analysis (CCA), and recommendations to prevent the outage in the future. The outage description should say who was affected (for example, internal customers or external customers) as well as which services were disrupted. The timeline of events may be reconstructed after the fact, but should identify the sequence of what actually happened and when so that it is clear. The CCA should go into detail as to why the outage occurred and include any significant context that may have contributed to the outage (e.g., peak service hours, significant loads). Finally, the recommendations for prevention in the future should include a filed ticket or bug ID for each recommendation in the list.

You will find a sample postmortem template in Section D.3 of Appendix D. If your organization does not have a postmortem template, you can use this as the basis for yours.

The executive summary should include the most basic information of when the incident happened and what the root causes were. It should reiterate any recommendations that will need budget approval so that executives can connect the budget request to the incident in their mind.

Causal analysis or **contributing conditions analysis** finds the conditions that brought about the outage. It is sometimes called **root cause analysis** but that implies that outages have only one cause. If tradition or office politics requires using the word "root," at least call it a root *causes* analysis to emphasize that there are many possible causes.

While emotionally satisfying to be able to point to a single cause, the reality is that there are many factors leading up to an outage. The belief that an outage could have a single cause implies that operations is a series of dominos that topple one by one, leading up to an outage. Reality is much more complex. As Allspaw's (2012a) article "Each Necessary, But Only Jointly Sufficient" points out, finding the root cause of a failure is like finding the root cause of a success.

Postmortem Communication

Once the postmortem report is complete, copies should be sent to the appropriate teams, including the teams involved in fixing the outage and the people affected by the outage. If the users were external to the company, a version with proprietary information removed should be produced. Be careful to abide by your company's policy about external communications. The external version may be streamlined considerably. Publishing postmortems externally builds customer confidence, and it is a best practice.

When communicating externally, the postmortem report should be accompanied by an introduction that is less technical and highlights the important details. Most external customers will not be able to understand a technical postmortem.

Include specific details such as start and end times, who or what was impacted, what went wrong, and what were the lessons learned. Demonstrate that you are using the experience to improve in the future. If possible, include human elements such as heroic efforts, unfortunate coincidences, and effective teamwork. You may also include what others can learn from this experience.

It is important that such communication be authentic, admit failure, and sound like a human, not a press agent. Figure 14.1 is an example of good external communication. Notice that it is written in the first person, and contains real remorse—no hiding here. Avoid the temptation to hide by using the third person or to minimize the full impact of the outage by saying something like "We regret the impact it may have had on our users and customers." Don't regret that there *may* have been impact. There *was* impact—otherwise you wouldn't be sending this message. More advice can be found in the blog post "A Guideline for Postmortem Communication" on the Transparent Uptime blog (Rachitsky 2010).

14.4 Periodic Review of Alerts

The alert log should be reviewed periodically to spot trends and allocate resources to create long-term fixes that ultimately reduce the total number of alerts received. When this strategy is implemented, alerts become more than just a way to be made aware of problems—they become one of your primary vehicles for improving system stability.

Subject: CloudCo Incident Report for February 4, 2014; brief interruption in DNS service

Last week on Tuesday, February 4, CloudCo experienced an outage of our DNS service lasting approximately 4 minutes. As a result of this outage, our customers experienced 4 minutes of downtime as we worked to restore full service. I would like to apologize to our customers for the impact to your daily operations as a result of this outage. Unplanned downtime of any length is unacceptable to us. In this case we fell short of both our customers' expectations and our own. For that, I am truly sorry.

I would like to take a moment and explain what caused the outage, what happened during the outage, and what we are doing to help prevent events like this in the future.

Technical Summary

CloudCo experienced a DNS outage lasting 4 minutes. The issue was the result of accidental input into a DNS rate-limiting tool, which resulted in a rate limit of zero queries per second being set. The problem was recognized by the Network Operations team immediately, the rate limit was identified within 2 minutes, and the configuration was reverted the following minute. DNS service was returned to normal status on a network-wide basis within 4 minutes of the beginning of the incident.

Incident Description

At 17:10 Pacific Standard Time (01:10 UTC), the CloudCo DNS service was not responding to DNS queries. All DNS queries to CloudCo DNS were being dropped during the 4 minutes the rate limit was applied. This affected all DNS queries sent to BIND.

Timeline of Events – February 4, 2014
17:10 PST (01:10 UTC) - An erroneous rate limit was applied to CloudCo DNS service
17:11 PST - Internal automated alerts
17:13 PST - Issue discovered to be with DNS rate limit
17:14 PST - Erroneous DNS rate limit removed
17:14 PST - CloudCo DNS confirmed returned to normal status
17:17 PST - CloudCoStatus tweets status update

Resolution

The erroneous change was made, recognized, and corrected within 4 minutes.

Recommendations

- Internal process revision for applying global DNS rate limits, with peer review.
- Implement additional software controls to validate user input for tools.

Figure 14.1: Example postmortem email sent to customers after an outage

There should be a systematic approach to reduce the number of alerts or entropy is likely to make alerts more frequent over time until the volume of alerts spirals out of control. Alerts should also be analyzed for trends because each alert is a potential indicator of a larger issue. If we aim to improve our system continuously, we must take every opportunity to seek out clues to where improvements are needed.

It's useful to have a weekly meeting to review alerts and issues and look for trends. At this meeting, you can identify projects that would fix more common issues as well as take an overall snapshot of the health of your production environment. Quarterly reviews can be useful to spot even larger trends and can be folded into quarterly project planning cycles.

The alert log should be annotated by the person who received the alert. Most systems permit alerts to be tagged with keywords. The keywords can then be analyzed for trends. Some sample keywords are listed here:

```
cause:network
cause:human
cause:bug
cause:hardware
cause:knownissue
severity:small
severity:medium
severity:large
bug:BUGID
tick:TICKETNUMBER
machine:HOSTNAME
```

These keywords enable you to annotate the general cause of the alert, its severity, and related bug and ticket IDs. Multiple tags can be used. For example, a small outage caused by a hardware failure might be tagged `cause:hardware` and `severity:small`. If the problem was caused by a known bug, the alert might be tagged `cause:knownissue` and `bug:12345`, assuming the known issue has a bug ID 12345. Items marked as such would be reserved for situations where there has been a management decision to not fix a bug *or* the fix is in progress and a workaround is in place until the fix is delivered.

As part of your analysis, produce a report showing the most common causes of alerts. Look for multiple alerts with the same bug ID or ticket numbers. Also look for the most severe outages and give them special scrutiny, examining the postmortem reports and recommendations to see if causes or fixes can be clustered or applied to more than one outage.

14.5 Being Paged Too Much

A small number of alerts is reasonable but if the number grows too much, intervention may be required. What constitutes too many alerts is different for different teams. There should be an agreed-upon threshold that is tolerated.

If the threshold is constantly being violated and things are getting worse, here are some interventions one may consider:

- If a known bug results in frequent pages after a certain amount of time (say, two release cycles), in the future this alert should automatically be directed to the developers' oncall rotation. If there is no developers' oncall rotation, push to start one. This aligns motivations to have problems fixed.

- Any alerts received by pager that are not directly related to maintaining the SLA should be changed from an alert that generates a page to an alert that generates a ticket in your trouble-ticketing system.

- Meet with the developers about this specific problem. Ensure they understand the seriousness of the issue. Create shared goals to fix the most frequent or recurring issues. If it is part of your culture, set up a list of bugs and have bug bash parties or a Fix-It Week.

- Negotiate to temporarily reduce the SLA. Adjust alerts accordingly. If alerting thresholds are already not aligned with SLA (i.e., you receive alerts for low-priority issues), then work to get them into alignment. Get agreement as to the conditions by which the temporary reduction will end. It might be a fixed amount of time, such as a month, or a measurable condition, such as when three successive releases have been pushed without failure or rollback.

- If all else fails, institute a code yellow: allow the team to defer all other work until the situation has improved. Set up a metric to measure success and work toward that goal.

14.6 Summary

As part of our mission to maintain a service, we must have a way to handle exceptional situations. To assure that they are handled properly, an oncall rotation is created.

The people who are in the oncall rotation should include operations people and developers, so as to align operational priorities. There are many ways to design an oncall schedule: weekly, daily, or multiple shifts per day. The goal should be to have no more than a few alerts per shift so that follow-up work can be completed.

An oncall person can be notified many ways. Generally alerts are shared by sending a message to a hand-held device such as a phone plus one other mechanism for redundancy.

Before a shift, an oncall preparedness checklist should be completed. People should be reachable while oncall in case there is an alert; otherwise, they should work and sleep as normal.

Once alerted, the oncall person's top priority is to resolve the situation, even if it means implementing a quick fix and reserving the long-term fix for later.

An oncall playbook documents actions to be taken in response to various alerts. If the documentation is insufficient, the issue should be escalated to the service owner or other escalation rotation.

Alerts should be logged. For major alerts, a postmortem report should be written to record what happened, what was done to fix the problem, and what can be done in the future to prevent the problem.

Alert logs and postmortems should be reviewed periodically to determine trends and select projects that will solve systemic problems and reduce the number of alerts.

Exercises

1. What are the primary design elements of an oncall system?
2. Describe your current oncall policy. Are you part of an oncall rotation?
3. How do priorities change for an oncall staffer when alerted?
4. What are the prerequisites for oncall duty at your organization?
5. Name 10 things that you monitor. For each of them, which type of notification is appropriate and why?
6. Which four elements go into a postmortem, and which details are required with each element?
7. Write a postmortem report for an incident in which you were involved.
8. How should an oncall system improve operations over time?

Chapter 15

Disaster Preparedness

> Failure is not falling down
> but refusing to get back up.
>
> —Theodore Roosevelt

Disasters and major outages happen. Everyone in the company from the top down needs to recognize that fact and adopt a mindset that accepts outages and learns from them. An operations organization needs to be able to handle outages well and avoid repeating past mistakes.

Previously we've examined technology related to being resilient to failures and outages as well as organizational strategies like oncall. In this chapter we discuss disaster preparedness at the individual, team, procedural, and organizational levels. People must be trained so that they know the procedure well enough that they can execute it with confidence. Teams need to practice together to build team cohesion and confidence, and to find and fix procedural problems. Organizations need to practice to find inter-team gaps and to ensure the organization as a whole is ready to handle the unexpected.

Every organization should have a strategy to ensure disaster preparedness at all these levels. At the personnel level, training should be both formal (books, documentation, mentoring) and through game play. Teams and organizations should use fire drills and game day exercises to improve processes and find gaps in coverage. Something like the Incident Command System (ICS) model, described later, should be used to coordinate recovery from outages.

Successful companies operating large distributed systems like Google, Facebook, Etsy, Netflix, and others realize that the right way to handle outages is to be prepared for them, adopt practices that reduce outages in the future, and reduce risk by practicing effective response procedures. In "Built to Win: Deep Inside Obama's Campaign Tech" (Gallagher 2012), we learned that even presidential campaigns have found game day exercises critical to success.

15.1 Mindset

The first step on the road to disaster preparedness is to acknowledge that disasters and major outages happen. They are a normal and expected part of business. Therefore we prepare for them and respond appropriately when they occur.

We want to reduce the number of outages, but eliminating them totally is unrealistic. No technology is perfect. No computer system runs without fail. Eliminating the last 0.00001 percent of downtime is more expensive than mitigating the first 99.9999 percent. Therefore as a tradeoff we tolerate a certain amount of downtime and balance it with preparedness so that the situation is handled well.

Equally, no individual is perfect. Everyone makes mistakes. We strive to make as few as possible, and never the same one twice. We try to hire people who are meticulous, but also innovative. And we develop processes and procedures to try to catch the mistakes before they cause outages, and to handle any outages that do occur as well as possible. As discussed in Section 14.3.2, each outage should be treated as an opportunity to learn from our own and others' mistakes and to improve the system. An outage exposes a weakness and enables us to identify places to make the system more resilient, to add preventive checks, and to educate the entire team so that they do not make the same mistake. In this way we build an organization and a service that is antifragile.

While it is common practice at some companies, it is counterproductive to look for someone to blame and fire when a major incident occurs. When people fear being fired, they will adopt behaviors that are antithetical to good operations. They will hide their mistakes, reducing transparency. When the real root causes are obscured, no one learns from the mistake and additional checks are not put in place, meaning that it is more likely to recur. This is why a part of the DevOps culture is to accept and learn from failure, which exposes problems and thus enables them to be fixed.

Unfortunately, we often see that when a large company or government web site has a highly visible outage, its management scrambles to fire someone to demonstrate to all that the matter was taken seriously. Sometimes the media will inflame the situation, demanding that someone be blamed and fired and questioning why it hasn't happened yet. The media may eventually lay the blame on the CEO or president for not firing someone. The best approach is to release a public version of the postmortem report, as discussed in Section 14.3.2, not naming individuals, but rather focusing on the lessons learned and the additional checks that have been put in place to prevent it from happening again.

15.1.1 Antifragile Systems

We want our distributed computing systems to be **antifragile**. Antifragile systems become stronger the more they are stressed or exposed to random behavior.

Resilient systems survive stress and failure, but only antifragile systems actually become stronger in response to adversity.

Antifragile is not the opposite of fragile. Fragile objects break, or change, when exposed to stress. Therefore the opposite of fragile is the ability to stay unchanged in the face of stress. A tea cup is fragile and breaks if not treated gently. The opposite would be a tea cup that stays the same (does not break) when dropped. Antifragile objects, by comparison, react to stress by getting stronger. For example, the process of making steel involves using heat that would destroy most objects, but the process instead makes steel stronger. The mythical Hydra is antifragile because it grows two heads for each one it loses. The way we learn is antifragile: studying for an exam involves working our brain hard, which strengthens it.

Fragile systems break when the unexpected happens. Therefore, if we want our distributed computing systems to be antifragile, we should introduce randomness, frequently and actively triggering the resiliency features. Every time a malfunction causes a team to failover a database to a replica, the team gets more skilled at executing this procedure. They may also get ideas for improvements. Better execution and procedural improvements make the system stronger.

To accelerate this kind of improvement, we introduce malfunctions artificially. Rather than trying to avoid malfunctions, we instigate them. If a failover process is broken, we want to learn this fact in a controlled way, preferably during normal business hours when the largest number of people are awake and available to respond. If we do not trigger failures in a controlled way, we will learn about such problems only during a real emergency: usually after hours, usually when everyone is asleep.

15.1.2 Reducing Risk

Practicing risky procedures in a controlled fashion enables us to reduce risk. Do not confuse risky behavior with risky procedures. Risky behavior is by definition risky and should be avoided. Procedures that are risky can be improved. For example, being careless is risky behavior that should be avoided. There's no way to make carelessness less risky other than to stop being careless. The risk is built in. However, a procedure such as a web service failover may or may not be risky. If it is a risky procedure, it can be improved and reengineered to make it less risky.

When we confuse risky behavior with risky procedures, we end up applying a good practice to the wrong thing. We make the mistake of avoiding procedures that should, instead, be repeated often until the risk is removed. The technical term for improving something through repetition is called "practice." Practice makes perfect.

The traditional way of thinking is that computer systems are fragile and must be protected. As a consequence, they were surrounded by protection systems, whether they be management policies or technical features. Instead of focusing on building a moat around our operations, we should commit to antifragile practices to improve the strength and confidence of our systems and organizations.

This new attitude toward failure aligns management practices with the reality of complex systems:

- New software releases always have new unexpected bugs.
- Identifying the root cause is not intended to apportion blame, but rather to learn how to improve the system and operational practices.
- Building reliable software on top of unreliable components means that resiliency features are expected, not an undue burden, a "nice to have" feature, or an extravagance.
- At cloud scale, complex failures are inevitable and unpredictable.
- In production, complex systems often interact in ways that aren't explicitly known at first (timeouts, resource contention, handoffs).

Ideally we'd like perfect systems that have perfect uptime. Sadly, such systems don't exist outside of sales presentations. Until such systems do exist, we'd rather have enough failures to ensure confidence in the precautionary measures we put in place. Failover mechanisms need to be exercised whether they are automatic or manual. If they are automatic, the more time that passes without the mechanism being activated, the less confident we can be that it will work properly. The system may have changed in ways that are unexpectedly incompatible and break the failover mechanism. If the failover mechanism is a manual procedure, we not only lose confidence in the procedure, but we also lose confidence in the team's ability to do the procedure. In other words, the team gets out of practice or the knowledge becomes concentrated among a certain few. Ideally, we want services that fail often enough to maintain confidence in the failover procedure but not often enough to be detrimental to the service itself. Therefore, if a component is too perfect, it is better to artificially cause a failure to reestablish confidence.

Case Study: Repeating Risky Behavior to Reduce Risk

At one company everyone knew that the last time a database needed to be failed over, it didn't go well. Therefore the team feared doing the procedure and avoided it, thinking this was good risk management. Instead, it actually increased risk. If the process was needed in an emergency, it was unlikely to work. Realizing this fact, the manager made the team fail the service over every week.

The first few times were rough, but the entire team watched and commented as the person performed the database failover. The procedure book was updated as comments were made. Pre-checks were documented. A team member pointed out that before she did the failover, she verified that the disks had plenty of free disk space because previously that had been a problem. The rest of the team didn't know about this pre-check, but now it could be added to the procedure book and everyone would know to do it.

More importantly, this realization raised an important issue: why wasn't the amount of free disk space always being monitored? What would happen if an emergency failover was needed and disk space was too low? A side project was spawned to monitor the system's available disk space. Many similar issues were discovered and fixed.

Eventually the process got more reliable and soon confidence increased. The team had one less source of stress.

15.2 Individual Training: Wheel of Misfortune

There are many different ways a system can break. People oncall should be able to handle the most common ones, but they need confidence in their ability to do so. We build confidence by providing training in many different ways: documentation, mentoring, shadowing more experienced people, and practice.

Wheel of Misfortune is a game that operational teams play to prepare people for oncall. It is a way to improve an individual's knowledge of how to handle oncall tasks and to share best practices. It can also be used to introduce new procedures to the entire team. This game enables team members to maintain skills, learn new skills as needed, and learn from each other. The game is played as follows.

The entire team meets in a conference room. Each round involves one person volunteering to be the contestant and another volunteering to be the Master of Disaster (MoD). The MoD explains an oncall situation and the contestant explains how they would work the issue. The MoD acts as the system, responding to any actions taken by the contestant. The MoD can give hints about how to fix the problem only after sufficient guessing or if the contestant has reached a dead end. Eventually either the contestant takes the issue to resolution or the MoD explains how it should be solved.

The MoD usually begins by saying an alert has been received from the monitoring system and identifying what the message is. The contestant might respond by saying which dashboard or log should be checked. The MoD explains what is seen on the dashboard or in the logs. This back and forth continues as the contestant first tries to determine what the problem is, then talks through the steps to fix the problem. It can help a lot if the MoD has prepared screenshots (real or fake) that he or she can pull out and show the contestant, if/when the contestant asks the right questions. These might be screenshots from an actual incident or something prepared from scratch. Either way, they add a lot of realism to the exercise.

Some teams have a "no laptops" rule when playing Wheel of Misfortune. Contestants aren't allowed to use a laptop directly to check dashboards and such, but rather must describe what they want to look at or do to one of their teammates, who drives a laptop and projects the result onto the shared screen for everybody else to see. This forces contestants to be explicit about what they're doing and why. It serves to expose the contestants' thought processes to the rest of the audience.

If the contestant is new, basic scenarios should be used: the most common alerts and the most typical solutions. More advanced contestants should get scenarios that involve more nuanced problems so that the audience can learn. The goal should never be to trick the contestant or to provide a no-win, or Kobayashi Maru, situation. The goal of the MoD is to educate workers, not to "win" by defeating the opponent.

To keep it fun, teams can add game show theatrics, starting the session by playing a theme song or spinning a wheel to select the next situation or just for effect.

No score or points are tallied, because Wheel of Misfortune is purely a training exercise. The team leader or manager should observe the game as a way to identify which members should be given additional coaching. There is no need to embarrass individuals; the suggestion that they get more coaching should be made in private. On the positive side, the game is also a way to identify which team members have strong troubleshooting skills that can be nurtured and perhaps used to help others develop their own.

The game should be played more frequently when the group is adding new people or technology, and less frequently when things are static. By turning the educational process into a game, people have an incentive to want to play. The game keeps the process fun and involves the entire team.

15.3 Team Training: Fire Drills

Fire drills exercise a particular disaster preparedness process. In these situations actual failures are triggered to actively test both the technology and the people involved.

The key to building resilient systems is accepting that failure happens and making a commitment to being prepared to respond quickly and effectively to those failures. An untested disaster recovery plan isn't really a plan at all. Fire drills are processes where we preemptively trigger the failure, observe it, fix it, and then repeat until the process is perfected and the people involved are confident in their skills.

Drills work because they give us practice and find bugs in procedures. It's better to prepare for failures by causing them in production while you are watching than to rely on a strategy of hoping the system will behave correctly when you aren't watching. Doing these drills in production does carry the risk that something catastrophic will happen. However, what better time for a catastrophe than when the entire engineering team is ready to respond?

Drills build confidence in the disaster recovery technology because bugs are found and fixed. The less often a failover mechanism is used, the less confidence we have in it. Imagine if a failover mechanism has not been triggered in more than a year. We don't know if seemingly unrelated changes in the environment have made the process obsolete. It is unreasonable to expect it to work seamlessly. Ignorance is not bliss. Being unsure if a failover mechanism will work is a cause of stress.

Drills build confidence within the operations team. If a team is not accustomed to dealing with disaster, they are more likely to react too quickly, react poorly, or feel undue levels of pressure and anxiety. This reduces their ability to handle the situation well. Drills give the team a chance to practice reacting calmly and confidently.

Drills build executive-level confidence in their operations teams. While some executives would rather remain ignorant, smarter executives know that failures happen and that a company that is prepared and rehearsed is the best defense.

Drills can be done to gain confidence in an individual process, in larger tests involving major systems, or even in larger tests that involve the entire company for multiple days. Start small and work your way up to the biggest drills over time. Trying a large-scale exercise is futile and counterproductive, if you haven't first built up capability and confidence through a series of smaller but ever-growing drills.

15.3.1 Service Testing

A very practical place to start is by picking individual failover mechanisms to test. Identify failover mechanisms that are not exercised often and pick one. These tests should be contained such that if an issue is uncovered, only the immediate team members are needed to respond. Typically these tests find broken processes, documentation gaps, knowledge gaps, and configuration problems.

The drill involves causing a failure that will trigger the failover mechanism. It may involve powering off a machine (pulling the power cord), shutting down a virtual machine, killing running software, disconnecting a network connection, or any other way one can disrupt service.

One strategy is to use drills to improve the process. If the process is unreliable or untested, it is worthwhile having the same people run the drill over and over, improving the process documentation and software for each iteration. By having the same people do each iteration, they will learn the system well enough to make big improvements. They may do many iterations in one day, seeking to fine-tune it. Alternatively, doing iterations further apart permits deeper problems to be fixed.

Another strategy is to use drills to improve confidence of the individual team members. Each iteration could be done by a different person until everyone has successfully done the process, possibly more than once.

A hybrid approach uses drills with the same people until the process is solid, then uses an individual team member strategy to verify that everyone on the team can do the process. Once this level of improvement is achieved, the drill is needed less frequently. One may choose to do the drill anytime the process has not been triggered by a real incident for more than a certain amount of time, if the process changes, or if new people join the team.

Picking which day to do such a drill requires serious deliberation. It's best to do it on a day when no major sales demonstrations or new product releases are planned. It should be a day when everyone is available, and probably not the day people return from vacation or the day before people leave for vacation.

Google Chubby Outage Drills

Inside Google is a global lock service called "Chubby." It has such an excellent reputation for reliability that other teams made the mistake of assuming it was perfect. A small outage created big problems for teams that had written code that assumed Chubby could not fail.

Not wanting to encourage bad coding practices, the Chubby team decided that it would be best for the company to create intentional outages. If a month passed without at least a few minutes of downtime, they would intentionally take Chubby down for five minutes. The outage schedule was announced well in advance.

The first planned outage was cancelled shortly before it was intended to begin. Many critical projects had reported that they would not be able to survive the test.

Teams were given 30 days to fix their code, but warned that there would be no further delays. Now the Chubby team was taken seriously. The planned outages have happened ever since.

15.3.2 Random Testing

Another strategy is to test a wide variety of potential failures. Rather than picking a specific failover process to improve, select random machines or other failure domains, cause them to fail, and verify the system is still running. This can be done on a scheduled day or week, or in a continuous fashion.

For example, Netflix created many autonomous agents, each programmed to create different kinds of outages. Each agent is called a monkey. Together they form the Netflix Simian Army.

Chaos Monkey terminates random virtual machines. It is programmed to select different machines with different probabilities, and some machines opt out entirely. Each hour Chaos Monkey wakes up, picks a random machine, and terminates it.

Chaos Gorilla picks an entire datacenter and simulates either a network partition or a total failure. This causes massive damage, such that recovery requires sophisticated control systems to rebalance load. Therefore it is run manually as part of scheduled tests.

The Simian Army is always growing. Newer members include Latency Monkey, which induces artificial delays in API calls to simulate service degradation. An extensive description of the Simian Army can be found in the article "The Antifragile Organization" (Tseitlin 2013).

Drills like this carry a larger risk at the start because they span so many failure domains; consequently, they should be approved by management. Convincing management of the value of this kind of test may be difficult. Most managers want to avoid problems, not induce them. It is important to approach the topic from the point of view of improving the ability to respond to problems that will inevitably happen, and by highlighting that the best time to find problems is in a controlled environment and not late at night when employees are asleep. Tie the process to business goals involving overall service uptime. Doing so also improves the morale and confidence of team members.

15.4 Training for Organizations: Game Day/DiRT

Game Day exercises are multi-day, organization-wide disaster preparedness tests. They involve many teams, often including non-technical teams such as communications, logistics, and finance. Game Day exercises focus on testing complex scenarios, trying out rarely tested interfaces between systems and teams, and identifying unknown organizational dependencies.

Game Day exercises may involve a multi-day outage of a datacenter, a complex week of network and system outages, or verification that secondary coverage personnel can successfully run a service if the primary team disappeared for an extended amount of time. Such exercises can also be used to rehearse for an upcoming event where additional load is expected and the team's ability to handle large outages would be critical. For example, many weeks before the 2012 election day, the Obama campaign performed three all-day sessions where its election-day

"Get Out the Vote" operation was put to the test. This is described in detail in the article "When the Nerds Go Marching in" (Madrigal 2012).

Because of the larger scale and scope, this kind of testing can have more impact and prevent larger outages. Of course, because of the larger scale and scope, this kind of testing also requires more planning, more infrastructure, and a higher level of management approval, buy-in, and support.

The organization needs to believe that the value realized through learning justifies the cost. Game Day exercises might be a sizable engineering effort involving hundreds of staff-days of effort. There is a potential for real accidental outages that result in revenue loss.

Executives need to recognize that all systems will inevitably fail and that confidence is best gained though practice, not avoidance. They should understand that it is best to have these failures happen in a controlled environment when key people are awake. Learning that a failover system does not work at 4 AM when key people are asleep or on vacation is the risk to avoid.

Google's Disaster Recovery Testing (DiRT) is this company's form of Game Day exercises. DiRT is done at a very large scale and focuses on testing interactions between teams. Such interactions are generally less frequently exercised, but when they are required it is due to larger disasters. These exercises are more likely to lead to customer-visible outages and loss of revenue than team-based service testing or random testing. For this reason teams should be doing well at their own particular fire drills before getting involved in DiRT.

15.4.1 Getting Started

While DiRT exercises can be very large, it is best to introduce a company to the concept by starting small. A small project is easier to justify to management. A working small example is easier to approve than a hypothetical big project, which, in all honesty, sounds pretty terrifying to someone who is unfamiliar with the concept. An executive should be very concerned if the people who are supposed to keep their systems up start telling them about how much they want to take those systems down.

Starting small also means simpler tests. Google's DiRT started with only a few teams. Tests were safe and were engineered so they could not create any user-visible disruptions. This was done even if it meant tests weren't very useful. It got teams used to the concept, reassured them that lessons learned would be used for constructive improvements to the system, and let them know that failures would not become blame-fests or hunts for the guilty. It also permitted the DiRT test coordinators to keep the processes simple and try out their methodology and tracking systems.

Google's original Site Reliability Engineering (SRE) teams were located in the company's headquarters in Mountain View, California. Eventually Google added

SRE teams in Dublin, Ireland, to handle oncall at night-time. The first DiRT exercise simply tested whether the Dublin SREs could run the service for an entire week without help. Mountain View pretended to be unavailable. This exposed instances where Dublin SREs were depending on the fact that if they had questions or issues, eventually a Mountain View SRE would wake up and be able to assist.

Another of Google's early, simple tests was to try to work for one day without access to the source code repository. This exercise found areas where production processes were dependent on a system not intended to be always available. In fact, many tests involved verifying that production systems did not rely on systems that were not built to be in the critical path of production systems. The larger an organization grows, the more likely that these dependencies will be found only through active testing.

15.4.2 Increasing Scope

Over time the tests can grow to include more teams. One can raise the bar for testing objectives, including riskier tests, live tests, and the removal of low-value tests.

Today, Google's DiRT process is possibly the largest such exercise in the world. By 2012 the number of teams involved had multiplied by 20, covering all SRE teams and nearly all services.

Growing the process to this size depended on creating a culture where identifying problems is considered a positive way to understand how the system can be improved rather than a cause for alarm, blame, and finger-pointing. Some operations teams could not see the benefit of testing beyond what their service delivery platform's continuous delivery system already provided. The best predictor of a team's willingness to start participating was whether previous failures had resulted in a search for a root cause to be fixed or a person to be blamed. Being able to point to earlier, smaller successes gave new teams and executive management confidence in expanding the program.

An example complex test might involve simulating an earthquake or other disaster that makes the company headquarters unavailable. Forbid anyone at headquarters from talking to the rest of the company. Google DiRT did this and learned that its remote sites could continue, but the approval chain for emergency purchases (such as fuel for backup generators) required the consent of people at the company headquarters. Such key findings are non-technical. Another non-technical finding was that if all the tests leave people at headquarters with nothing to do, they will flood the cafeteria, creating a DoS flood of the food kind.

Corporate emergency communications plans should also be tested. During most outages people can communicate using the usual chat rooms and such. However, an emergency communication mechanism is needed in the event of a total network failure. The first Google DiRT exercise found that exactly one person was able to find the emergency communication plan and show up on the correct phone bridge. Now periodic fire drills spot-check whether everyone has the correct information with them. In a follow-up drill, more than 100 people were able to find and execute the emergency communication plan. At that point, Google learned that the bridge supported only 40 callers. During another drill, one caller put the bridge on hold, making the bridge unusable due to "hold music" flooding the bridge. A requirement to have the ability to kick someone off the bridge was identified. All of these issues were discovered during simulated disasters. Had they been discovered during a real emergency, it would have been a true disaster.

15.4.3 Implementation and Logistics

There are two kinds of tests. Global tests involve major events such as taking down a datacenter and are initiated by the event planners. Team tests are initiated by individual teams.

An event may last multiple days or a single terrible day. Google schedules an entire week but ends DiRT sessions as soon as the tests' goals have been satisfied. To keep everyone on their toes, DiRT doesn't start exactly at the announced start time but rather after a small delay. The length of delay is kept secret.

A large event has many moving parts to coordinate. The coordinator should be someone with both technical and project management experience, who can dedicate a sufficient amount of time to the project. At a very large scale, coordination and planning may require a dedicated, full-time position even though the event happens every 12 months. Much of the year will be spent planning and coordinating the test. The remaining months are spent reviewing outcomes and tracking organization-wide improvement.

Planning

The planning for the event begins many months ahead of time. Teams need time to decide what should be tested, select proctors, and construct test scenarios. Proctors are responsible for designing and executing tests. Long before the big day, they design tests by documenting the goal of the test, a scenario, and a script that will be followed. For example, the script might involve calling the oncall person for a service and having that individual simulate a situation much like a Wheel of Misfortune exercise. Alternatively, the company may plan to actively take down a system or service and observe the team's reaction. During the actual test, the proctor is responsible for the tests execution.

Knowing the event date as early as possible enables teams to schedule project work and vacations. Teams may also use this time to do individual drills so that the event can focus on tests that find the gaps between teams. If the team's individual processes are not well practiced, then DiRT itself will not go well.

Prior to the first Game Day at Amazon, John Allspaw conducted a series of company-wide briefings advising everyone of the upcoming test. He indicated it would be on the scale of destroying a complete datacenter. People did not know which datacenter, which inspired more comprehensive preparation (Robbins, Krishnan, Allspaw & Limoncelli 2012).

Risk is mitigated by having all test plans be submitted in advance for review and approval by a cross-functional team of experts. This team checks for unreasonable risks. Tests never done before are riskier and should be done in a sandbox environment or through simulation. Often it is known ahead of time that certain systems are ill prepared and will not survive the outage. Pre-fail these systems, mark them as failing the test, and do not involve them in the event. There is nothing to be learned by involving them. These machines should be whitelisted so they still receive service during the event. For example, if the outage is simulated using network filtering, these machines can be excluded from the filter.

Organization

Two subteams are needed to make the event a success. The tech team designs the global tests and evaluates team test plans. The tests are graded on quality, impact, and risk. During the event this team is responsible for causing the global outages, monitoring them, and making sure things don't go awry. This team also handles unforeseen issues caused by the tests.

The coordination team is responsible for planning, scheduling, budgets, and execution. It works with the tech team to prevent conflicting tests. Coordination team members verify that all prep work is complete. They also are in charge of communication both with management and corporate-wide.

During the event, both subteams reside in the command center, which operates as a kind of "Mission Control." Due to the nature of the tests, the command center must be a physical location, as relying on virtual meeting spaces is too risky. For large organizations, this involves a considerable amount of travel.

In the command center, individuals call proctors to tell them to start their tests. Test controllers deal with unexpected issues as they come up and communicate globally about the status of the event. They monitor the progress of the tests as well as the effects of the tests on the technical systems that should not be affected. Test controllers can halt all tests if something goes massively wrong.

One of the most valuable roles in the command center is the story teller. One person concocts and narrates the disaster. He or she should create a story that is just unrealistic enough that people know that it is a test. For example, the story might involve a zombie attack, an evil genius who has put everyone at headquarters under hypnosis, or an errant fortune-teller with mystical powers. Daily updates that move the story forward should be distributed by email or old-time radio "broadcasts." The last bulletin should resolve the story and let everyone know that the test is over, the zombies have been defeated, or whatever.

The story teller helps counteract the drudgery of the test. If this person does a good job, people might actually look forward to next year's event.

Suggested Reading

For many years DiRT and related practices were company secrets. However, in 2012 a number of companies and practitioners revealed their disaster testing procedures in a series of articles that were curated by Tom and published in *ACM Queue* magazine:

- "Resilience Engineering: Learning to Embrace Failure" is a group interview Tom conducted with Kripa Krishnan, the coordinator of Google's DiRT program; Jesse Robbins, the architect of Game Day at Amazon; and John Allspaw, senior vice president of technological operations at Etsy (Robbins et al. 2012).
- Krishnan details Google's DiRT program in "Weathering the Unexpected" (Krishnan 2012).
- Allspaw explained the theory and practice of Etsy's program in "Fault Injection in Production" (Allspaw 2012b).
- Tseitlin details the Netflix Simian Army and explains how it has improved resilience and maximized availability in "The Antifragile Organization" (Tseitlin 2013).

Later Steven Levy was allowed to observe Google's annual DiRT process firsthand for an article he wrote for *Wired* magazine titled "Google Throws Open Doors to Its Top-Secret Data Center" (Levy 2012).

After the 2012 U.S. presidential election, an article in *The Atlantic* magazine, "When the Nerds Go Marching in," described the Game Day exercises conducted by the Obama for America campaign in preparation for election day 2012 (Madrigal 2012). Dylan Richard's talk "Gamedays on the Obama Campaign" provided a first-hand account and the disclaimer that technology didn't win the election, but it certainly could have lost it (Richard 2013).

15.4.4 Experiencing a DiRT Test

What follows is a fictionalized account of a Google DiRT exercise as seen from the perspective of the engineers involved in the test. The names, locations, and situations have been changed. This description is adapted from an article Tom wrote for *ACM Queue* magazine titled "Google DiRT: The View from Someone Being Tested" (Limoncelli 2012).

[Phone rings]

Tom: Hello?

Rosanne: Hi, Tom. I'm proctoring a DiRT exercise. You are on call for [name of service], right?

Tom: I am.

Rosanne: In this exercise we pretend the [name of service] database needs to be restored from backups.

Tom: OK. Is this a live exercise?

Rosanne: No, just talk me through it.

Tom: Well, I'd follow the directions in our operational docs.

Rosanne: Can you find the doc?

[A couple of key clicks later]

Tom: Yes, I have it here.

Rosanne: OK, bring up a clone of the service and restore the database to it

Over the next few minutes, I make two discoveries. First, one of the commands in the document now requires additional parameters. Second, the temporary area used to do the restore does not have enough space. It had enough space when the procedure was written, but the database has grown since then.

Rosanne files a bug report to request that the document be updated. She also files a bug report to set up a process to prevent the disk-space situation from happening.

I check my email and see the notifications from our bug database. The notifications are copied to me and the bugs are tagged as being part of DiRT2011. Everything with that tag will be watched by various parties to make sure they get attention over the next few months. I fix the first bug while waiting for the restore to complete.

The second bug will take more time. We'll need to add the restore area to our quarterly resource estimation and allocation process. Plus, we'll add some rules to our monitoring system to detect whether the database size is nearing the size of the restore area.

Tom: OK, the service's backup has been read. I'm running a clone of the service on it, and I'm sending you an instant message with a URL you can use to access it.

[A couple of key clicks later]

Rosanne: OK, I can access the data. It looks good. Congrats!

Tom: Thanks!

Rosanne: Well, I'll leave you to your work. Oh, and maybe I shouldn't tell you this, but the test controllers say at 2 PM there will be some fun.

Tom: You know my oncall shift ends at 3 PM, right? If you happen to be delayed an hour...

Rosanne: No such luck. I'm in California and 3 PM your time is when I'll be leaving for lunch.

A minute after the exercise is over, I receive an email message with a link to a post-exercise document. I update it with what happened and provide links to the bugs that were filed. I also think of a few other ways of improving the process and document them, filing feature requests in our bug database for each of them.

At 2 PM my pager doesn't go off, but I see on my dashboard that there is an outage in Georgia. Everyone in our internal chat room is talking about it. I'm not too concerned. Our service runs out of four datacenters around the world, and the system has automatically redirected web requests to the other three locations.

The transition is flawless, losing only the queries that were "in flight," which is well within our SLA.

A new email appears in my inbox explaining that zombies have invaded Georgia and are trying to eat the brains of the datacenter technicians there. The zombies have severed the network connections to the datacenter. No network traffic is going in or out. Lastly, the email points out that this is part of a DiRT exercise and no actual technicians have had their brains eaten, but the network connections really have been disabled.

[Again, phone rings]

Rosanne: Hi! Having fun yet?

Tom: I'm always having fun. But I guess you mean the Georgia outage?

Rosanne: Yup. Shame about those technicians.

Tom: Well, I know a lot of them and they have big brains. Those zombies will feed for hours.

Rosanne: Is your service still within SLA?

I look at my dashboard and see that with three datacenters doing the work normally distributed to four locations the latency has increased slightly, but it is within SLA. The truth is that I don't need to look at my dashboard because I would have gotten paged if the latency was unacceptable (or growing at a rate that would reach an unacceptable level if left unchecked).

Tom: Everything is fine.

Rosanne: Great, because I'm here to proctor another test.

Tom: Isn't a horde of zombies enough?

Rosanne: Not in my book. You see, your SLA says that your service is supposed to be able to survive two datacenter outages at the same time.

She is correct. Our company standard is to be able to survive two outages at the same time. The reason is simple. Datacenters and services need to be able to be taken down occasionally for planned maintenance. During this window of time, another datacenter might go down for unplanned reasons such as a network or power outage. The ability to survive two simultaneous outages is called $N + 2$ redundancy.

Tom: So what do you want me to do?

Rosanne: Pretend the datacenter in Europe is going down for scheduled preventive maintenance.

I follow our procedure and temporarily shut down the service in Europe. Web traffic from our European customers distributes itself over the remaining two datacenters. Since this is an orderly shutdown, no queries are lost.

Tom: Done!

Rosanne: Are you within the SLA?

I look at the dashboard and see that the latency has increased further. The entire service is running on the two smaller datacenters. Each of the two down datacenters is bigger than the combined, smaller, working datacenters, yet there is enough capacity to handle this situation.

Tom: We're just barely within the SLA.

Rosanne: Congrats. You pass. You may bring the service up in the European datacenter.

I decide to file a bug anyway. We stayed within the SLA, but it was too close for comfort. Certainly we can do better.

I look at my clock and see that it is almost 3 PM. I finish filling out the post-exercise document just as the next oncall person comes online. I send her an instant message to explain what she missed.

I also remind her to keep her office door locked. There's no telling where the zombies might strike next.

15.5 Incident Command System

The public safety arena uses the Incident Command System to manage outages. IT operations can adapt that process for handling operational outages. This idea was first popularized by Brent Chapman in his talk "Incident Command for IT: What We Can Learn from the Fire Department" (Chapman 2005). Brent has extensive experience in both IT operations and public safety.

Outside the system administration arena, teams from different public safety organizations such as fire, police, and paramedics come together to respond to emergencies and disasters. A system called the Incident Command System (ICS) has been developed to allow this to happen productively in a way that can scale up or down as the situation changes.

ICS is designed to create a flexible framework within which people can work together effectively. The key principles of ICS are as follows:

- **Standardized Organizational Structure:** An ICS team is made up of the Incident Commander and subcommand systems: Operations, Logistics, Planning, Admin/Finance, and optionally a Unified Command, a Public Information Officer, and a Liaison Officer.

- **Unambiguous Definition of Who Is in Charge:** There is one and only one Incident Commander. Each person on an ICS team reports to only one supervisor for that ICS incident.

- **Explicit Delegations of Authority:** The Incident Commander sets up certain key branches, such as Logistics and Operations and Planning, and delegates those functions to their commanders.

- **Management by Objective:** Clear objectives and priorities are established for the incident. Tell people what you want to get done, not how to do it; let them figure out the best way to get it done in the current circumstances.

- **Limited Span of Control That Can Scale:** Under ICS, a supervisor should not have more than seven direct reports. Ideally, three to five individuals should report to one supervisor. As the number of people involved grows, the organization expands and new supervisors are created. Through this approach, responsibilities stay limited. Remember that this is a temporary organizational structure created for responding to this specific event. The same group of people might organize differently for a different event.

- **Common Terminology and Organizational Framework:** By using the ICS roles and responsibilities as a common framework, different teams from different organizations can understand clearly who is doing what and where their responsibilities are.

A full description of ICS can be found on the U.S. Federal Emergency Management Administration (FEMA) web site (http://www.fema.gov/incident-command-system). The FEMA Emergency Management Institute publishes free self-study and other training materials (http://training.fema.gov/EMI/). A more approachable introduction is the Wikipedia article on ICS (http://en.wikipedia.org/wiki/Incident_command_system).

15.5.1 How It Works: Public Safety Arena

When a public safety incident begins, the first order of business is to get organized, starting by figuring out who is going to be in charge. In an incident, the first qualified responder to arrive automatically becomes the Incident Commander (IC).

An ICS team is made up of the Incident Commander and the subcommand systems of Operations, Logistics, Planning/Status, and Administration/Finance, as shown in Figure 15.1. A Public Information Officer is also appointed to deal with communication beyond the response team (internal and external) about the incident. A Liaison Officer is the primary contact for outside agencies, such as third-party vendors. A Safety Officer monitors safety conditions.

All incidents have a Command section (the management) and most have an Operations section, which directly provides emergency services such as putting out the fire or providing medical attention. The management structure is a strict hierarchy. In an emergency there is no time for the vagaries and inefficiency of matrix management.

When the IC arrives, he or she is often alone and assumes all roles. As more people arrive, the IC delegates roles as needed. As new people arrive, they check in with Admin/Finance (if it exists) for bookkeeping purposes, but then the IC assigns them to a function. The IC has the global view needed to best determine how to allocate new resources.

The IC role does not transfer to anyone just because they have a higher rank or because a different department arrives. For example, a police chief does not automatically trump a police officer, and a fire fighter does not automatically trump a paramedic. Transfer of control is explicit, implemented by the current IC handing control to someone else who explicitly accepts the role. Role handoffs are disruptive and are done only when needed.

Teams stay small. A team size of three to five people is considered optimal. If a subcommand gains seven direct reports, the team will be split in two when the next person is added.

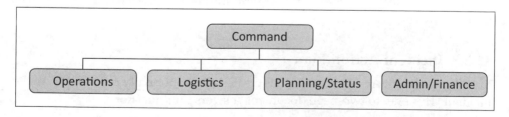

Figure 15.1: The basic ICS organizational structure

15.5.2 How It Works: IT Operations Arena

When adapting this system to an IT operations organization, the Operations team handles the operational aspects of the incident—the actual firefighting, as it were. The Logistics team handles resources, such as people and materials, and makes sure that Operations has what it needs to do its job. The Planning team is responsible for forecasting situation and resource needs, and for collecting and displaying information about the incident. The Admin/Finance team handles general administrative support and budgets.

Initially the IC is whoever is first on site. In IT, that is usually the oncall person who responded to the alert. However, since this person has already been troubleshooting the alert, it usually makes sense for him or her to sound the alarm and handoff the IC role to the next qualified responder, continuing as the Operations (Ops) lead. The IC role is transferred through explicit handoff at shift change or if the IC becomes tired and needs relief. The key point here is that the IC role is always handed off as part of a thoughtful process, not automatically as new people show up. If a better-qualified person arrives on scene, the current IC may decide it's worth the disruption of a handoff to switch ICs.

For small IT incidents, the IC handles all leadership roles on his or her own. However, as an incident grows larger, more people get involved, either because more co-workers notice the outage or because the IC reaches out to them. As people show up, the IC assigns them roles, creating subteams as needed. It's worth noting that the IC and the Ops lead should be made separate individual roles as quickly as possible. The IC has the big-picture view and the Ops lead is down in the trenches dealing with the incident directly. Trying to handle both roles simultaneously often results in doing neither role well.

Outages of long duration require frequent status updates to management and other stakeholders. By designating a single person to be the Public Information Officer, the IC can keep from being distracted by executives demanding updates or users asking, "Is it up yet?" Every status update should end by noting when the next status can be expected. Many organizations standardize on update frequency. Hourly updates balance executives' need to know with technical workers' need to focus on the technical issues at hand. Multi-day outages require less frequent updates to avoid repetition.

15.5.3 Incident Action Plan

In ICS, an Incident Action Plan (IAP) is created and continually refined during the incident. This one- to two-page document answers four questions:

- What do we want to do?
- Who is responsible for doing it?

- How do we communicate with each other?
- What is the procedure if someone becomes unavailable?

In IT operations, we add a fifth question:

- What is the procedure if additional failures are detected?

Create a template that the IC can use to produce this document. Make the template accessible in a standard location so that everyone knows where to find it. An example can be found in Figure 15.2.

15.5.4 Best Practices

To assure success, everyone should get practice using ICS procedures and being the Incident Commander, new hires should be introduced to ICS procedures as part of their onboarding process, and escalation partners should be informed that ICS procedures are in use.

Teams should use ICS procedures for minor incidents to stay in practice so that everyone is comfortable with the process when major situations develop. ICS procedures should be used for non-emergencies such as datacenter moves and major upgrades as well as for security incidents and adversarial terminations.

What do we want to do?
The main web server is down. We must restore it to full functionality.
Who is responsible for doing it?
The IC is Mary. The SRE team is responsible, with help from developers Rosanne, Eddie, and Frances.
How do we communicate with each other?
Video chat room:
`https://plus.google.com/hangouts/_/example.com/outage`
What is the procedure if someone becomes unavailable?
If possible, they should report to the IC for relief via phone (201-555-1212), text message, instant message, or video chat room. If they are unable to, or if someone suspects that someone else has become unavailable, report this information to the IC.
What is the procedure if additional failures are detected?
The IC will be responsible for leading the triage effort, assessing the situation, and deciding how to move forward.

Figure 15.2: A sample Incident Action Plan (IAP)

ICS training should be part of an operation team's new-hire onboarding process. It is important that everyone understand the terminology and processes so that the system works well.

People on a team should rotate through the role of Incident Commander to get an idea of the scope and capabilities of the team as it works together. Selecting the IC in non-emergencies should be done by picking the person who has gone the longest without being in the role.

Escalation partners should be informed about your team's use of ICS procedures and how they will interact with the ICS roles, such as Communications Officer. If they use ICS procedures internally as well, so much the better. Partner teams may have adapted ICS procedures differently for use in IT. This can lead to confusion and conflicts. Therefore multi-team incidents should be practiced to find and fix problems. Both simulated problems and real, but non-emergency issues can be used. A good opportunity for this type of practice is when triaging a major bug that involves both teams.

15.5.5 ICS Example

As an example use of ICS procedures, suppose a major outage is affecting XYZ Company's web operations. Bob, the oncall responder to the outage, activates the ICS process and is the temporary Incident Commander. The first thing Bob does is notify his team about the outage and pass on the role of Incident Commander to his team lead, Janet. Janet starts assembling an ICS team immediately, delegating Operations to Bob. She notifies her manager Sandy about the outage and asks him to be the Public Information Officer.

Bob and Janet start an Incident Action Plan by describing what they believe is going on and what they are doing about it. Bob is taking action and Janet is coordinating efforts. Bob explains that he will need certain resources, such as failover machines, and that the team is likely to end up working late on this one. Janet, as Incident Commander, now reaches out to find someone to take on the Logistics role. She picks Peter and directs him to get the requirements from Bob. The new Logistics Section Chief delegates people to get the machine resources that Operations will need, and arranges for pizza to arrive at 6 PM.

Janet identifies someone from the Monitoring group to ask about getting detailed information on the outage. Jyoti agrees to be the Planning Section Chief and starts working with other members of the Monitoring group to gather the requested information. They are working on forecasting demand, such as knowing that web services are currently coming off daily peak demand in Europe and climbing in North America.

As the outage continues, Janet's manager Sandy (Public Information Officer) interfaces with Janet (Incident Command), Bob (Operations), Jyoti (Planning), and

Peter (Logistics) to keep track of what is going on and notify people about the progress of the outage. Sandy delegates a person on the team to update status pages for XYZ Company's customers as well as an internal status page within the company.

Meanwhile, Bob in Operations has determined that a database needs to be failed over and replicas updated. Managing by objective, he asks Logistics for another resource to do the replica and load balancing work. Logistics finds someone else in the company's IT staff who has experience with the replica system and gets permission for that person to help Bob during this outage. Bob begins the database failover and his new helper begins work on the load balancing and replica work needed.

The new replica completes its initial copy and begins serving requests. Janet confirms with all ICS section chiefs that the service's status has returned to normal. The event is declared resolved and the ICS process is explicitly terminated. Janet takes the action item to lead the postmortem effort.

15.6 Summary

To handle major outages and disasters well, we must prepare and practice. Ignorance may be bliss, but practice makes progress. It is better to learn that a disaster recovery process is broken by testing it in a controlled environment than to be surprised when it breaks during an actual emergency.

To be prepared at every level, a strategy of practicing disaster recovery techniques at the individual, team, and organization levels is required. Each level is dependent on the competency achieved in the previous level.

Wheel of Misfortune is a game that trains individuals by talking through common, and not so common, disaster scenarios. Fire drills are live tests performed to exercise a particular process. Fire drills should first be performed on a process again and again by the same people until the process works and can be performed smoothly. Then the process should be done by each member of the team until everyone is confident in his or her ability to perform the task.

Tests involving shutting down randomly selected machines or servers can find untested failure scenarios. These tests can be done at designated times as a test, or continuously as part of production to ensure that systems that should be resilient to failure have not regressed.

Game Day or DiRT exercises are organization-wide tests that find gaps in processes that involve multiple teams. They often last multiple days and involve cutting off major systems or datacenters.

DiRT events require a large amount of planning and coordination to reduce risk. Tests should be approved by a central planning committee based on quality, impact, and risk. Some tests are initiated by individual teams, whereas tests with company-wide impact are planned by the central committee.

Fire, police, medical, and other public safety organizations use the Incident Command System (ICS) to coordinate efforts during disasters and other emergency situations. The ICS provides standardized organizational structure, processes, and terminology. This system can be adapted for use in coordinating recovery from major IT-related outages. To stay in practice, teams should use ICS procedures for smaller incidents as well.

Exercises

1. What is an antifragile system? How is this different from fragile systems and resilient systems?
2. What are some reasons to do fire drills as part of reliability testing?
3. Draw a graph that represents the ideal frequency of failures as discussed in Section 15.1.1.
4. Describe a critical subsystem in your own environment that could benefit from reliability testing, and explain how you would test it.
5. Compare and contrast the traditional attitude toward failure with the DevOps attitude toward failure. Which lessons can you apply to your own environment?
6. Why not fire people who make mistakes? Wouldn't this result in an organization that employs only perfect people?
7. Which situations have you been part of that might have benefited from using the Incident Command System? Which specific benefits would have occurred?
8. Describe how the ICS process works in emergency services and public safety.
9. Describe how the ICS process could be applied to IT.
10. List the key concepts that go into an Incident Action Plan.
11. How would you attempt to convince your management of the necessity of conducting fire-drill exercises in your environment?

Chapter 16

Monitoring Fundamentals

> You can observe a lot
> by just watching.
>
> —Yogi Berra

Monitoring is the primary way we gain visibility into the systems we run. It is the process of observing information about the state of things for use in both short-term and long-term decision making. The operational goal of monitoring is to detect the precursors of outages so they can be fixed before they become actual outages, to collect information that aids decision making in the future, and to detect actual outages. Monitoring is difficult. Organizations often monitor the wrong things and sometimes do not monitor the important things.

The ideal monitoring system makes the operations team omniscient and omnipresent. Considering that having the root password makes us omnipotent, we are quite the omniarchs.

Distributed systems are complex. Being omniscient, all knowing, means our monitoring system should give us the visibility into the system to find out anything we need to know to do our job. We may not know everything the monitoring system knows, but we can look it up when we need it. Distributed systems are too large for any one person to know everything that is happening.

The large size of distributed systems means we must be omnipresent, existing everywhere at the same time. Monitoring systems permit us to do this even when our systems are distributed around the world. In a traditional system one could imagine a system administrator who knows enough about the system to keep an eye on all the critical components. Whether or not this perception is accurate, we know that in distributed systems it is definitely not true.

Monitoring in distributed computing is different from monitoring in enterprise computing. Monitoring is not just a system that wakes you up at night when a service or site is down. Ideally, that should never happen. Choosing a strategy

---

Terms to Know

Server: Software running to provide a function or API. (Not a piece of hardware.)

Service: A user-visible system or product composed of many servers.

Machine: A virtual or physical machine.

QPS: Queries per second. Usually how many web hits or API calls received per second.

Diurnal Cycles: Metrics that are high during the day and low at night.

---

that involves reacting to outages means that we have selected an operational strategy with outages "baked in." We can improve how fast we respond to an outage but the outage still happened. That's no way to run a reliable system.

Instead, monitoring should be designed to detect the precursors of an outage in time for the problem to be prevented. A system must be instrumented and monitored so as to enable this strategy. This is more difficult than detecting an outage, but much better.

16.1 Overview

To understanding monitoring you must first understand its particular terminology.

A **measurement** refers to a single point of data describing an aspect of a system, usually a value on which numerical operations make sense—for example, 5, −25, 0, or Null. It can also be a string—for example, a version number or a comma-separated list of currently mounted file systems.

A **metric** is a measurement with a name and timestamp. For example:

```
spellcheck:server5.demo.com:request-count@20140214T100000Z = 9566
```

Different monitoring systems use different formats to label the data. In the preceding example, we have a metric from the spellcheck server that was running on server5. The measurement is the request-count, presumably how many requests the server has received since starting. After the @ symbol is the date stamp. The measured value is 9566.

Examples of other metrics include the total RAM in use, the number of outstanding requests in a queue, the build version of the code being run, the number of open bugs, the number of bugs, and the total cost on Amazon AWS.

There is also metadata associated with a metric. In particular, a numeric value usually has a unit associated with it. Knowing the unit permits automatic conversions, chart labeling, and so on. Many monitoring systems do not track the units of a metric, requring people to guess based on the metric name or other context, and perform conversions manually. This process is notably prone to error.

Measurement frequency is the rate at which new measurements are taken. Different metrics are collected at different frequencies. Many pieces of data are collected every 5 minutes, but some metrics are collected many times a second and others once a day or once a week.

Monitoring **perspective** is the location of the monitoring application collecting the measurement. The importance of perspective depends on the metric. The total number of packets sent on an interface is the same no matter the perspective. In contrast, page load times and other timing data depend on the perspective. One might collect the same measurement from different places around the world to see how page load time is affected by distance or to detect problems with a particular country or ISP's connectivity. Alternatively, the measurement may be collected directly on a machine if perspective is less important than consistency.

One way to gather information from many perspectives is **real user monitoring (RUM)**. RUM collects actual application performance measurements from the web browser. Code is inserted into the web page that collects metrics and transmits it back to the site that sent the original web page.

16.1.1 Uses of Monitoring

Monitoring is not just about collecting data. It is also used in various ways, and there is specific terminology for those uses.

Visualization is the assimilation of multiple measurements into a visual representation. These charts and graphs make it possible to find trends and make comparisons between systems and time ranges.

A **trend** is the direction of a series of measurements on a metric. For example, one might use visualization to see that use of a service is growing or shrinking.

Alerting means to bring something to the attention of a person or another system. A sudden drop in QPS might result in alerting the oncall person. Alerts generally need to be acknowledged within a certain amount of time. If the deadline is exceeded, someone else is alerted. This process is called **escalation**.

Visualization is useful for gaining deeper insights into the system. It can help with everything from design to planning to communication. Trends can be used for capacity planning, which is discussed in more detail in Chapter 18. Alerting should be used to warn people about situations that could result in an outage. It is also used as a last resort to warn when an outage has occurred.

16.1.2 Service Management

Lastly, here are some service management terms we will use occasionally. They mostly come from the business world:

- **Service Level Indicator (SLI):** An agreement as to how a measurement will be measured. For example, it might define what is measured, how it is measured, and from what perspective.

- **Service Level Target (SLT):** A target quality of service; in other words, an SLI's expected minimum or maximum. Until ITIL V3, this was called the **Service Level Objective (SLO)**. An example SLT might be a certain level of availability or the maximum permitted latency.

- **Service Level Agreement (SLA):** The contract that states the SLIs, SLTs, and the penalties if the SLTs are not met. For example, there may be a refund or penalty payment for any outage longer than one hour. The term SLA is often overused to mean SLT or any service level requirement.

16.2 Consumers of Monitoring Information

There are many consumers of monitoring information, each of which has different needs. People who monitor operational health need to know state changes immediately for fast response—they need real-time monitoring. Capacity planners, product managers, and others need metrics collected over a long period of time to spot trends—they need historical monitoring data.

A more fine-grained way to differentiate consumers is the Dickson model (Dickson 2013), which uses three characteristics: resolution, latency, and diversity. These characteristics can be rated as high or low.

Resolution describes how frequently the metric is collected. High (R+) is many times a second, minute, or hour. Low (R−) is many times a day.

Latency describes how long a period of time passes before the information is acted upon. Low (L+) is real-time response. High (L−) means data is stored and analyzed later, perhaps used for daily, weekly, or monthly statistics. (Note that the use of + and − are reversed from R and D. Think of + as the case that is more difficult to engineer.)

Diversity describes how many metrics are being collected. High (D+) means many metrics, perhaps many measurements about many different services. Low (D−) means there is a focus on a particular or small set of metrics.

Consumers can be described by a 3-tuple. For example, (R+, L−, D+) describes a high-resolution, high-latency, high-diversity consumer.

Given these axes, we can describe the primary users of monitoring information as follows:

Operational Health/Response (OH)
(R+, L+, D+)   High resolution, low latency, high diversity. System health. The things we get paged about.
Quality Assurance/SLA (QA)
(R+, L−, D+)   High resolution, high latency, high diversity. Longer-term analysis of jitter, latency, and other quality-related factors.
Capacity Planning (CP)
(R−, L−, D+)   Low resolution, high latency, high diversity. Forecasting and purchasing more resources.
Product Management (PM)
(R−, L−, D−)   Low resolution, high latency, low diversity. Determining the number of users, cost, and other resources.

Operational Health is typical monitoring, where exceptional situations are detected and alerts are generated. It is the most demanding use case. The resolution and latency must be sufficient to detect problems and respond to them within an SLA. This usually demands up-to-date access to all metrics, real-time computation for high-speed analysis, and reliable alerting. The storage system must be high speed and high volume at the same time. In fact, this kind of monitoring stresses every part of the monitoring infrastructure.

Quality Assurance usually involves medium- or long-term analysis for specific quality metrics such as variability. For example, some queries should always take approximately the same amount of time with little variation. Quality assurance detects this kind of variability just as an auto assembly line quality assurance team looks for defects and unacceptable variations in the product being built. For this reason, Quality Assurance needs high-resolution data but latency is not critical since the data is often processed in batches after the fact.

Quality Assurance also includes information required when finding and fixing bugs, such as debug logs, process traces, stack traces, coredumps, and profiler output.

Capacity Planning (CP) is the process of predicting resource needs in the future. These predictions require coarse metrics such as the current number of machines, amount of network bandwidth used, cost per user, and machine utilization and efficiency, as well as alerting when resources are running low. CP is also concerned with how resource use changes as the product changes—for example, if a new release requires significantly different resources. CP is the topic of Chapter 18.

Product Management (PM) requires very low-resolution data for calculating key performance indicators (KPIs) such as conversion rates, counts of users, and analysis of user retention (often called 7-day actives or 30-day actives). PM benefits from large amounts of historic data for long-term views and visualizations to help understand trends.

Missing (R, L, D) Combinations

A keen observer will notice that not every combination of R, L, and D appears in the model. Some do describe other operations-related functions. (R+, L+, D−) is what a load balancer requires to determine if it should send traffic to a particular backend. (R+, L−, D−) covers the kind of log analysis that is done in periodically in batches. This leaves (R−, L+, D−) and (R−, L+, D+), which we have not observed in the wild…yet.

16.3 What to Monitor

What should be monitored is different for every organization. The general strategy is to start with the business's KPIs and collect related measurements.

The following are some example KPIs:

- **Availability:** Have a web site that is up 99.99 percent of the time (measured from outside the datacenter).
- **Latency:** The 90th percentile latency for the homepage should not exceed 400 ms (request to render time).
- **Urgent Bug Count:** There should be no more than n outstanding Severity-0 bugs.
- **Urgent Bug Resolution:** All Severity-0 bugs should be closed within 48 hours.
- **Major Bug Resolution:** All Severity-1 bugs should be closed within 10 days.
- **Backend Server Stability:** There should be no more than n percent queries returning HTTP 5xx Server Error.
- **User Satisfaction:** There should be no more than n percent abandoned carts.
- **Cart Size:** The median number of items in a shopping card per order should be n.
- **Finance:** A total of n revenue this month.

If you do not know your organization's KPIs, stop right now and find out what they are. If there aren't any, prepare your resume because your company is a rudderless ship. Alternatively, you can declare yourself the captain and invent the KPIs yourself.

You need to instrument your system enough so that you can see when things are going to fail. To improve on KPIs, we must measure more than just the end result. By measuring things that are deeper in the pipeline, we can make better decisions about how to achieve our KPIs. For example, to improve availability, we need to measure the availability of the component systems that result in the final availability statistic. There may be systems that get overloaded, queues that grow too long, or bottlenecks that start to choke. There may be a search tree that works best when the tree is balanced; by monitoring how balanced it is, we can correlate performance issues with when it becomes imbalanced. To determine why shopping carts are being abandoned, we must know if there are problems with any of the web pages during the shopping experience.

All of the previously mentioned KPIs can be monitored by selecting the right metrics, sometimes in combination with others. For example, determining the 90th percentile requires some calculation. Calculating the average number of items per order might require two metrics, the total number of items and the total number of orders.

A **diagnostic** is a metric collected to aid technical processes such as debugging and performance tuning. These metrics are not necessarily related to a KPI. For example, we might collect a metric that helps us debug an ongoing technical issue that is intermittent but difficult to find. There is generally a minimal set of metrics one collects from all machines: system metrics related to CPU, network bandwidth, disk space, disk access, and so on. Being consistent makes management easier. Hand-crafting a bespoke list for each machine is rarely a good use of your time.

It is conventional wisdom in our industry to "monitor everything" in hopes of preventing the situation where you suddenly realize you wish you had historic data on a particular metric. If this dictate is taken literally, the metrics collection can overwhelm the systems being monitored or the monitoring system itself. Find a balance by focusing on KPIs first and diagnostics as needed.

The Minimum Monitor Problem

A common interview question is "If you could monitor only three aspects of a web server, what would they be?" This is an excellent test of technical knowledge and logical thinking. It requires you to use your technical knowledge to find one metric that can proxy for many possible problems.

For example, much can be learned by performing an HTTPS GET: We learn whether the server is up, if the service is overloaded, and if there is network congestion. TCP timings indicate time to first byte and time to full payload. The SSL transaction can be analyzed to monitor SSL certificate validity and expiration. The other two metrics can be used to differentiate between those issues. Knowing CPU utilization can help differentiate between network congestion and an overloaded system. Monitoring the amount of free disk space can indicate runaway processes, logs filling the disk, and many other problems.

We recommend that you blow the interviewer away by offering to do all that while measuring one metric and one metric only. Assuming it is an e-commerce site, simply measure revenue. If it drops in a way that is uncharacteristic for that time of day, the site is overloaded. If it stops, the site is down (and if it isn't down, there is reason to investigate anyway). If it ramps up, we know we're going to run out of capacity soon. It is the one KPI that ties everything together.

16.4 Retention

Retention is how long collected metric data is stored. After the retention time has elapsed, the old metric data is expired, downsampled, or deleted from the storage system.

How long monitoring data is retained differs for each organization and service. Generally there is a desire or temptation to store all metrics forever. This avoids the problem of suddenly realizing the data you want was deleted. It is also simpler than having to decide on a storage time for each metric.

Unfortunately, storing data forever has a cost—not just in terms of hardware for storage, but also in terms of backups, power, and complexity. Store enough data, and it must be split between multiple storage systems, which is complex. There may also be legal issues around how long the data should be retained.

Creating your retention policy should start with collecting business requirements and goals, and translating them into requirements for the storage system.

Two years is considered to be the minimum storage period because it enables year-over-year comparisons. More is better. It is likely that your next monitoring system will be unable to read the data collected by the previous system, and a conversion process is unlikely to be available. In such a case, if you build a new monitoring system every five or six years, that may be an upper bound. Time-series databases are becoming more standardized and easier to convert, however, making this upper bound likely to disappear.

Having the ability to retain decades of monitoring data at full resolution has benefits we are just beginning to understand. For example, Google's paper "Failure Trends in a Large Disk Drive Population" (Pinheiro, Weber & Barroso 2007) was able to bust many myths about hard disk reliability because the authors had access to high-resolution monitoring data from hundreds of thousands of hard drives' self-monitoring facility (SMART) collected over five years. Of course, not everyone has seemingly infinite data storage facilities. Some kind of consolidation or compaction is needed.

The easiest consolidation is to simply delete data that is no longer needed. While originally many metrics might be collected, many of them will turn out to be irrelevant or unnecessary. It is better to collect too much when setting up the system than to wish you had data that you didn't collect. After you run the service for a while, certain metrics may be deemed unnecessary or may be useful only in the short term. For example, there may be specific CPU-related metrics that are useful when debugging current issues but whose utility expires after a year.

Another way to reduce storage needs is through summarization, or down-sampling. With this technique, recent data is kept at full fidelity but older data is replaced by averages or other form of summarization. For example, metrics might be collected at 1- or 5-minute intervals. When data is more than 13 months old, hourly averages, percentiles, maximums, and minimums are calculated and the raw data is deleted. When the data is even older, perhaps 25–37 months, 4-hour or even daily summaries are calculated, reducing the storage requirements even more. Again, the amount of summarization one can do depends on business needs. If you need to know only the approximate bandwidth utilization, daily values may be sufficient.

16.5 Meta-monitoring

Monitoring the monitoring system is called **meta-monitoring**. How do you know if the reason you haven't been alerted today is because everything is fine or because the monitoring system has failed? Meta-monitoring detects situations where the monitoring system itself is the problem.

The monitoring system needs to be more available and scalable than the services being monitored. Every monitoring system should have some kind of meta-monitoring. Even the smallest system needs a simple check to make sure it is still running. Larger systems should be monitored for the same scale and capacity issues as any other service to prevent disk space, CPU, and network capacity from becoming limiting factors. The accuracy and precision of collected data should be monitored; one should monitor how often an attempt to collect a measurement fails. The display of information must be faster than the average person's attention span. The freshness of the data used to calculate a KPI should be monitored; knowing the age of data used to calculate a KPI may be as important as the KPI itself. Knowing how KPI latency is trending is important to understanding the health of the monitoring system.

One meta-monitoring technique is to deploy a second monitoring system that monitors the primary system. It should have as few common dependencies as possible. If different software is used, it is less likely that the same bug will take down both systems. This technique, however, adds complexity, requires additional training, and necessitates maintenance.

Another technique is to divide the network into two parts, each with its own monitoring system. The two monitoring systems can also monitor each other. For example, a site with two datacenters might deploy a different monitoring system in each one that monitors local machines. This saves on inter-datacenter bandwidth and removes the interconnection as a source of failure.

With more than one datacenter, a similar arrangement can be used, with pairs of datacenters monitoring each other, or each monitoring system monitoring another system in a big circle.

16.6 Logs

Another way of gaining visibility into the system is through analysis of logging data. While not directly related to monitoring, we mention this capability here because of the visibility it brings. There are many kind of logs:

- **Web "Hit" Logs:** Web servers generally log each HTTP access along with statistics about performance, where the access came from, and if the access was a success, error, redirect, and so on. This data can be used for a multitude of business purposes: determining page generation times, analyzing where users come from, tracking the paths users take through the system, and more. Technical operations can use this data to analyze and improve page load time and latency.

- **API Logs:** Logging each API call generally involves storing who made the call, the input parameters, and output results (often summarized as a simple success or error code). API logs can be useful for billing, security forensics, and feature usage patterns. A team that is going to eliminate certain obsolete API calls can use logs to determine which users will be affected, if any.

- **System Logs:** The operating system kernel, devices, and system services contribute to the system log. This is often useful for tracking hardware problems and system changes.

- **Application Logs:** Each service or server generates logs of actions. This is useful for studying errors and debugging problems, as well as providing business information such as which features are used the most.

- **Application Debug Logs:** Applications often generate debugging information in a separate log. This type of log is often more verbose but is retained for a shorter amount of time. Such logs are used for debugging problems by developers and operations staff.

16.6.1 Approach

While logs do not directly fit the Dickson model, if they did they would be (R+, L−, D−) because they are high resolution (generally one log entry per action), high latency (often processed much later in batches), and low diversity (usually collected about a particular topic, such a web server hits).

The architecture of a log processing system is similar to the monitoring architecture discussed in the next chapter. Generally logs are collected from machines and services and kept in a central place for storage and analysis. Retention is often a legal issue, as logging data often contains personal information that is regulated.

The market space for log analysis tools has been growing over the years as new analysis methods are invented. Web logs can be analyzed to determine the path a user takes through the system. As a result one can find user interface "dead ends" that leave users baffled. Application logs can be used to find flaws in sales processes or to identify high-value customers who otherwise would not have been discovered. System logs can be analyzed to find anomalies and even predict hardware failures.

The consolidation of logging data can be rather complex, as different systems generate logs in different formats. It's best to establish a single log format for all systems. By providing a software library that generates logs that conform to the format, you can make the path of least resistance (using the library) be the path that has the desired behavior (conforms to the standard).

16.6.2 Timestamps

Record timestamps the same way in all systems to make it easier to combine and compare logs. In particular, all machines should use NTP or the equivalent to keep clocks synchronized, and timestamps should be stored in UTC rather than local time zones.

This is important because often logs from different systems are compared when debugging or figuring out what went wrong after an outage. For example, when writing a postmortem one builds a timeline of events by collecting logs from various machines and services, including chat room transcripts, instant message sessions, and email discussions. If each of these services records timestamps in its local time zone, just figuring out the order of what happened can be a challenge, especially if such systems do not indicate which time zone was being used.

Consolidating logs on a large scale is generally automated and the consolidation process normalizes all logs to UTC. Unfortunately, configuration mistakes can result in logging data being normalized incorrectly, something that is not noticed until it is too late. This problem can be avoided by using UTC for everything.

Google famously timestamps logs using the U.S./Pacific time zone, which caused no end of frustration for Tom when he worked there. This time zone has a different daylight savings time calendar than Europe, making log normalization extra complex two weeks each year, depending on the year. It also means that software must be written to understand that one day each year is missing an hour, and another day each year has an extra hour. Legend has it that the U.S./Pacific time zone is used simply because the first Google systems administrator did not consider the ramifications of his decision. The time zone is embedded so deeply in Google's many systems that there is little hope it will ever change.

16.7 Summary

Monitoring is the primary way we gain visibility into the systems we run. It includes real-time monitoring, which is used to alert us to exceptional situations that need attention, and long-term or historic data collection, which facilitates trend analysis. Distributed systems are complex and require extensive monitoring. No one person can watch over the system unaided or be expected to intuit what is going on.

The goal of monitoring is to detect problems before they turn into outages, not to detect outages. If we simply detect outages, then our operating process has downtime "baked in."

A measurement is a data point. It refers to a single point of data describing an aspect of a system, usually a numerical value or a string. A metric is a measurement with a name and a timestamp.

Deciding what to monitor should begin with a top-down process. Identify the business's key performance indicators (KPIs) and then determine which metrics can be collected to create those KPIs.

Monitoring is particularly important for distributed systems. By instrumenting systems and servers and automatically collecting the exposed metrics, we can become the omniscient, omnipresent, omnipotent system administrators that stakeholders assume we are.

Exercises

1. What is the goal of monitoring?
2. Why is monitoring important in distributed systems?
3. Why should operations staff be omniscient, omnipresent, and omnipotent? Why are these important characteristics?
4. How is a measurement different from a metric?
5. If you could monitor only three things about a web site, what would they be? Justify your answer.

6. Section 16.2 mentioned that there are no situations where (R−, L+, D−) and (R−, L+, D+) had been observed. Why might this be?

7. Most monitoring systems "ping" devices to determine if they are up. This entire chapter never mentions ping. Based on what you learned in this chapter, why is pinging devices an insufficient or failed operational strategy for monitoring?

Chapter 17

Monitoring Architecture and Practice

What is a cynic? A man who
knows the price of everything
and the value of nothing.

—Oscar Wilde

This chapter discusses the anatomy of a monitoring system. Best practices for each component are described along the way.

A monitoring system has many different parts. Dickson (2013) decomposes monitoring systems into the functional components depicted in Figure 17.1. A measurement flows through a pipeline of steps. Each step receives its configuration from the configuration base and uses the storage system to read and write metrics and results.

The **sensing and measurement system** gathers the measurements. The **collection system** transports them to the **storage system**. From there, one or more **analysis systems** extract meaning from the raw data—for example, detecting problems such as a server being down or anomalies such as a metric for one system being significantly dissimilar from all the others. The **alerting and escalation system** communicates these conditions to interested parties. Visualization systems display the data for human interpretation. Each of these components is told how to do its job via information from the **configuration** base.

Over the years there have been many monitoring products, both commercial and open source. It seems like each one has been very good at two or three components, but left much to be desired with the others. Some systems have done many components well, but none has done them all well.

Interfaces between the components are starting to become standardized in ways that let us mix and match components. This enables faster innovation as new systems can be created without having to reinvent all the parts.

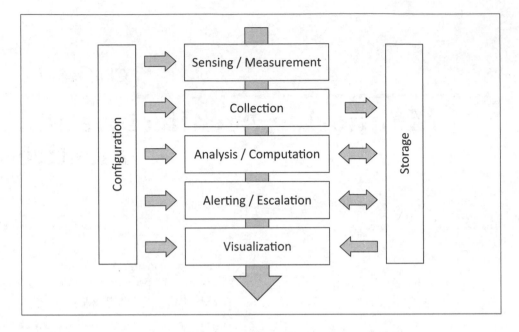

Figure 17.1: The components of a monitoring system

What follows is a deeper discussion of each component, its purpose, and features that we've found to be the most useful.

17.1 Sensing and Measurement

The sensing and measurement component gathers the measurements. Measurements can be categorized as blackbox or whitebox, depending on the amount of knowledge of the internals that is used. Measurements can be direct or synthesized, depending on whether each item is separately counted, or totals are periodically retrieved and averaged. We can monitor the rate at which a particular operation is happening, or the capability of the system to allow that operation to happen. Systems may be instrumented to provide gauges, such as percentage CPU utilization, or counters, such as the number of times that something has occurred.

Let's look at each of those in more detail.

17.1.1 Blackbox versus Whitebox Monitoring

Blackbox monitoring means that measurements try to emulate a user. They treat the system as a blackbox, whose contents are unknown. Users do not know how a system's internals work and can only examine the external properties of the system. They may guess about the internals, but they cannot be sure. In other words, these measurements are done at a high level of abstraction.

Doing an HTTPS GET of a web site's main page is an example of blackbox monitoring. The measurement is unaware of any load balancing infrastructure, internal server architecture, or which technologies are in use. Nevertheless, from this one measurement, we can determine many things: whether the site is up, how fast is it responding, if the SSL certificate has expired, if the system is producing a valid HTML document, and so on. Blackbox testing includes monitoring that attempts to do multi-step processes as a user, such as verifying that the purchasing process is working.

It is tempting to get a particular web page and verify that the HTML received is correct. However, then the monitoring system must be updated anytime the web site changes. An alternative is to verify that the page contains a particular message. For example, a search engine might periodically query for the name of a particular celebrity and verify that the name of the person's fan club is mentioned in the HTML. The measurement communicated to the monitoring system would be 1 or 0, representing whether the string was or wasn't found.

Blackbox monitoring is often highly dependent on perspective. Monitoring might be done from the machine itself, from within the datacenter or other failure domain, or from different places around the world. Each of these tests answers different questions about the system.

A **whitebox** measurement has the benefit of internal knowledge because it is a lower level of abstraction. For example, such a measure might monitor raw counters of the number of times a particular API call was made, the number of outstanding items waiting in a queue, or latency information of internal processes. Such measurements may disappear or change meaning as the system's internals change. In whitebox monitoring, perspective is less important. Usually such measurements are done as directly as possible to be more efficient and to prevent data loss that could occur by adding distance.

17.1.2 Direct versus Synthesized Measurements

Some measurements are direct, whereas others are synthesized. For example, if every time a purchase is made the system sends a metric of the total money collected to the monitoring system, this is a direct measurement. Alternatively, if every 5 minutes the monitoring system tallies the total money collected so far, this is a synthesized metric. If all we have is a synthesized metric, we cannot back-calculate the individual amounts that created it.

Whether direct measurements are available is generally a function of frequency of change. In an e-commerce site where one or two purchases are made each day, direct measurement is possible. By comparison, for a busy e-commerce site such as eBay or Amazon, the monitoring system could not keep up with the number of purchases made if each one resulted in a metric. In this case the synthesized metric of total revenue collected is all that is possible. Exact counts would be the job of the accounting and billing system.

A more obvious example is measuring how much disk space is in use versus being told about every block allocation and deallocation. There can be millions of disk operations each minute. Collecting the details of each operation just to arrive at a metric of how much disk space is in use would be a waste of effort.

17.1.3 Rate versus Capability Monitoring

Event frequency determines what to monitor. One wants to know that a customer *can* make purchases and *is* making purchases. The rate at which purchases happen determines which of these to monitor. If one or two purchases are made each day, monitoring whether customers can make purchases is important because it happens so infrequently that we need to verify that the purchasing flow hasn't somehow broken. If thousands of purchases per minute are made, then we generally know purchases can be made and it is more important to measure the rate and trends.

In short, rate metrics are more important when event frequency is high and there are smooth, predictable trends. When there is low event frequency or an uneven rate, capability metrics are more important.

That said, never collect rates directly. Rates are lossy. Given two *counts* and their time delta, we can compute the rate. Given two *rates* and their time delta, we can only surmise the count—and then only if the two measurements were collected at precise intervals that are in sync with the rate's denominator.

For example, if we are measuring the count of how many API calls have been received, we might collect a metric of 10,000 at 12:10:00 and 16,000 at 12:15:00. We could then calculate the rate by dividing the delta of the counts by the time delta: $(16,000-10,000)/300$, or 20 API calls per second. Suppose that second polling event was skipped, perhaps due to a brief network problem, the next polling event would be at 12:20:00 and might collect the measurement of 21,000. We can still calculate the rate: $(21,000 - 10,000)/600$, or 18.2 API calls per second. However, if we were collecting rates, that network blip would mean we would not be able to estimate what happened during the missing 5 minutes. We could take the average of the two adjacent rates, but if during that time there was a large spike, we would not know.

17.1.4 Gauges versus Counters

Some measurements are gauges, while others are counters.

A **gauge** value is an amount that varies. It is analogous to a real-world gauge like one that indicates barometric pressure. Examples include an indicator of how much unused disk space is available, a temperature reading, and the number of active processes on a system. A gauge's value varies, going up and down as whatever it measures increases or decreases.

High-Speed Network Counters

The frequency and potential rate of change should determine the size of the counter. If the counter that stores the number of bits transmitted on a 10 Gbps interface is 32 bits long, it will roll over to zero after 4,294,967,296 bits have been transmitted. If the interface is running at about 50 percent capacity, the counter will roll over about every 8.5 seconds. It is not possible to correctly synthesize the metric for traffic across this interface unless you collect data faster than the counter rolls over. Therefore a counter that changes this quickly requires a 64-bit counter.

A **counter** is a measurement that only increases—for example, a count of the number of API calls received by a service or the count of the number of packets transmitted on a network interface. A counter does not decrease or run backward. You can't unsend a packet or deny that an API call was received after the fact. However, counters do reset to zero in two circumstances. Unless a counter's value is in persistent storage, the value is reset to zero on reboot or restart. Also, like an automobile odometer that rolls over at 99,999, a counter loops back to zero when it reaches its maximum value. Typically counters are 16-, 32-, or 64-bit integers that have maximum values of 65,535, 4,294,967,295, and 18,446,744,073,709,551,615, respectively (i.e., $2^n - 1$, where n is the number of bits).

Doing math on counter readings is rather complex. In our previous example, we simply subtracted adjacent counter values to learn the delta. However, if the second reading is less than the first, special care must be taken.

If the counter looped around to zero, the actual delta between two readings includes the count up to the maximum value plus the newer counter value: $(\text{maxvalue} - R_n) + R_{n+1}$. However, if the counter was reset to zero due to a restart, then the exact delta value is unobtainable because we do not know the value of the counter when the restart occurred. We can make estimates using a little high school calculus involving the past rate and how long ago the reset occured.

Determining whether the counter reset to zero due to a restart or reaching the maximum value is another heuristic. If the last reading was near the maximum value, we can assume the counter looped around to zero. We can improve the accuracy of this guess, again by applying a little calculus.

Such great complexity still results in a margin of error and risks introducing a loss of accuracy if either heuristic produces incorrect results. A much simpler approach is to ignore the problem. For 64-bit counters, wrap-arounds are rare or nonexistent. For counter resets, if the monitoring frequency is fast enough, the margin of error will be very small. Usually the desired end result is not the count itself, but a rate. The calculation of the rate for the entire interval will not be dramatically affected. For example, if there are 10 counter readings, 9 deltas are produced. If a delta is negative, it indicates there was a counter reset. Simply throw away any negative deltas and calculate the rate with the remaining data.

Java Counters

Systems written in the Java programming language use counters that are signed integers. Signed integers roll over to negative numbers and have a maximum value that is approximately half their signed counterparts.

17.2 Collection

Once we have a measurement, we must transmit it to the storage system. Metrics are collected from many places and brought to a storage system so that they may be analyzed. The metric's identity must be preserved through any and all transmissions.

There are hundreds of ways to collect metrics. Most fall into one of two camps: push or pull. Irrespective of the choice of a push or pull mechanism, there is also a choice of which protocols are used for data collection. Another aspect of data collection is whether the server itself that communicates directly with the collector, or whether an external agent acts as an intermediary between the server and the collector. A monitoring system may have a central collector or regional collectors that consolidate data before passing it back to a central system.

17.2.1 Push versus Pull

Push means the sensor that took the measurement transmits it to the collection mechanism. **Pull** means an agent polls the object being monitored and requests the data and stores it.

Four myths in monitoring are that pull doesn't scale, that push is horrible and shouldn't be used, that pull is horrible and shouldn't be used, and that push doesn't scale. Dispelling these myths is easy.

The ability to scale is a matter of implementation, not push versus pull. Monitoring 10,000 items at least once every 5 minutes requires 33 connections per second if spread evenly. A web server can handle millions of inbound TCP connections. Outbound connections are no different. A monitoring system has the benefit that it can make certain optimizations. It can transmit multiple measurements over each TCP connection. It can simply create a long-lived TCP connection for every machine. Scaling is a concern, but not an insurmountable obstacle.

Whether push or pull is better is a matter of application. Pull is better for synthesized measurements, such as counters. It is also better for direct measurements when change is infrequent. For example, if a change happens a few times per hour, being polled every 5 minutes may be sufficient resolution. Pull is also better if it would be useful to have a variable measurement rate, such as a system that polls at a higher frequency when diagnosing a problem. This approach is analogous to increasing the magnification on a microscope.

Push is better when direct observation is required, such as when we need to know when something happens rather than how many times it has happened. In the event of a failure, it is easier for a push system to store measurements and transmit the backlog when possible. If it is useful to observe each discrete or specific action, then push is more appropriate.

17.2.2 Protocol Selection

Many different protocols are used in monitoring. The Simple Network Management Protocol (SNMP) is horrible and should be avoided. Sadly, if you deal with network equipment, it is likely your only choice. If you manage services and machines, there are many alternatives.

Most of the alternatives are migrating to using JSON transmitted over HTTP. JSON is a text-based standard for human-readable data interchange. HTTP PUT is used for push and HTTP GET is used for pull. Because the same JSON data structure is sent in either case, it simplifies the processing of the data.

> ### SNMP: Simply Not a Management Protocol
>
> We dislike SNMP. Most implementations transmit passwords in clear text and are inefficient because they transmit one measurement per transaction. Version 3 of the protocol can be secure and fast but few vendors implement it. The protocol is complex enough that implementations are a constant source of security-related bugs. The adjective "simple" was intended to describe the protocol, which makes us concerned what the complex protocol, if it had been invented, would look like. Because it scales so badly, we wonder whether "simple" actually describes the kind of network it is good for monitoring. The use of the word "management" in its name has hurt the industry by creating the misperception that managing a network is a matter of collecting measurements.

17.2.3 Server Component versus Agent versus Poller

Collectors can work in several different ways. The cleanest way to implement whitebox monitoring is to have the running server gather its own measurements and handle pushing or pulling the results to the collector. The software that provides these functions can be put into a library for convenient use by any program. For example, every time an API call is received, the software might call `metric.increment('api-calls-count')` to increment the count called `api-calls-count`. To collect how much bandwidth is being used in a video server, after each write to the network the software might call `metric.add('bandwidth-out', x)`, where x is the amount of data sent. The library would maintain a running total under the name `bandwidth-out`. Functions like this are called throughout the program to count, total, or record measurements.

If the collection is done by push, the library spawns a thread that wakes up periodically to push the metrics to the monitoring system. Pull is implemented by the library spawning a thread that listens to a specific TCP port for polling events and replies with some or all of the metrics. If the server already processes HTTP requests, it can simply attach the library to a particular path or route. For example, HTTP requests for `/monitor` would call the library, which would then reply to the request with a JSON representation of the metrics.

Sadly, we can't always modify software to collect metrics this way. In that case we run software on the machine that collects data by reading logs, status APIs, or system parameters and pulls or pushes the information. Such software is called an **agent**. For example, scollector is a software agent that runs on a Linux machine and calls any number of plug-ins to gather metrics, which are then pushed to the Bosun monitoring system. Plug-ins are available that collect performance information about the operating system, disk systems, and many popular open source systems such as MySQL and HBase.

Sometimes we cannot modify software or install software on the machine itself. For example, hardware devices such as network switches, storage area network (SAN) hardware, and uninterruptible power supplies (UPSs) do not permit user-installed software. In these cases software is run on one machine that polls the other devices, collects the information, and transmits it via push or pull to the monitoring system. This type of software is called a **poller** or a **monitoring proxy**.

17.2.4 Central versus Regional Collectors

Some monitoring systems scale to global size by having a collector run in each region and relay the data collected to the main monitoring system. This type of collector is called a **remote monitoring station** or **aggregator**. An aggregator might be placed in each datacenter or geographical region. It may receive metrics by push or pull, and it generally consolidates the information and transmits it to the main system in a more efficient manner. This approach may be used to scale a system globally, saving bandwidth between each datacenter. Alternatively, it may be done to scale a system up; each aggregator may be able to handle a certain number of devices.

17.3 Analysis and Computation

Once the data has been collected, it can be used and interpreted. Analysis extracts meaning from raw data. Analysis is the most important component because it produces the results that justify having a monitoring system in the first place.

Real-time analysis examines the data as it is collected. It is generally the most computationally expensive analysis and is reserved for critical tasks such as determining conditions where someone should be alerted. To do this efficiently, monitoring systems tee the data as it is collected and send one copy to the storage system and another to the real-time analysis system. Alternatively, storage systems may hold copies of recently collected metrics in RAM. For example, by keeping the last hour's worth of metrics in RAM and constructing all alerting rules to refer to only the last hour of history, hundreds or thousands of alert rules can be processed efficiently.

Typically real-time analysis involves dozens or hundreds of **alert rules** that are simultaneously processed to find exceptional situations, called **triggers**. Sample triggers include if a service is down, if HTTP responses from a server exceed n ms for x minutes, or if the amount of free disk space drops below m gigabytes. The real-time analysis includes a language for writing formulas that describe these situations.

This analysis may also detect situations that are not so critical as to require immediate attention, but if left unattended could create a more significant problem. Such situations should generate tickets rather than alerts. See Section 14.1.7 for problem classifications. Alerts should be reserved for problems that do require immediate attention. When an alert is triggered, it prompts the alerting and escalation manager, described later in this chapter, to take action.

Short-term analysis examines data that was collected in the last day, week, or month. Generally dashboards fit into this category. They are updated infrequently, often every few minutes or on demand when someone calls up the specific web page. Short-term analysis usually queries the on-disk copy of the stored metrics. Near-term analysis is also used to generate tickets for problems that are not so urgent as to require immediate attention. See Section 14.1.7.

Dashboard systems generally include a template language that generates HTML pages and a language for describing data graphs. The data graph descriptions are encoded in URLs so they may be included as embedded images in the HTML pages. For example, one URL might specify a graph that compares the ratio of two metrics for the last month for a particular service. It may specify a histogram of latency for the 10 slowest web servers, after calculating latency for hundreds of web servers.

Long-term analysis generally examines data collected over large spans of time, often the entire history of a metric, to produce trend data. In many cases, this involves generating and storing summaries of data (averages, aggregates, and so on) so that navigating the data can be done quickly, although at low resolution. Because this type of analysis requires a large amount of processing, the results are usually stored permanently rather than regenerated as needed. Some systems also handle situations where old data is stored on different media—for example, tape.

Anomaly detection is the determination that a specific measurement is not within expectations. For example, one might examine all web servers of the same type and detect if one is generating metrics that are significantly different from the others. This could imply that the one server is having difficulties that others are not. Anomaly detection finds problems that you didn't think to monitor for.

Anomaly detection can also be predictive. Mathematical models can be created that use last year's data to predict what should be happening this year. One can then detect when this year's data deviates significantly from the prediction. For example, if you can predict how many QPS are expected from each country, identifying a deviation of more than 10 percent from the prediction might be a good way to detect regional outages or just that an entire South American country stops to watch a particular sporting event.

Doing anomaly detection in real time and across many systems can be computationally difficult but systems for doing this are becoming more commonplace.

17.4 Alerting and Escalation Manager

The alerting and escalation component manages the process of communicating to oncall and other people when exceptional situations are detected. If the person cannot be reached in a certain amount of time, this system attempts to contact others. Section 14.1.7 discusses alerting strategy and various communication technologies.

The first job of the alerting component is to get the attention of the person oncall, or his or her substitute. The next job is to communicate specific information. The former is usually done by pager or text message. Since these systems permit only short messages to be sent, there is usually a second method, such as email, to communicate the complete message.

The message should communicate the following information:

- **Failure Condition:** A description of what is wrong in technical terms but in plain English. For example, "QPS too high on service XYZ" is clear. "Error 42" is not.

- **Business Impact:** The size and scope of the issue—for example, how many machines or users this affects, and whether service is reduced or completely unavailable.
- **Escalation Chain:** The escalation chain is who to contact, and who to contact if that person does not respond. Generally, one or two chains are defined for each service or group of services.
- **Suggested Resolution:** Concise instructions of what to do to resolve this issue. This is best done with a link to the playbook entry related to this alert, as described in Section 14.2.5.

The last two items may be difficult to write at the time the alert rule is created. The specific business impact may not be known, but at least you'll know which service is affected, so that information can be used as a placeholder. When the alert rule is triggered, the specifics will become clear. Take time to record your thoughts so as to not lose this critical information.

Update the impact and resolution as part of the postmortem exercise. Bring all the stakeholders together. Ask the affected stakeholders to explain how their business was impacted in their own business terms. Ask the operational stakeholders to evaluate the steps taken, including what went well and what could have been improved. Compare this information with what is in the playbook and update it as necessary.

17.4.1 Alerting, Escalation, and Acknowledgments

The alert system is responsible for delivering the alert to to the right person and escalating to others if they do not respond. As described in Section 14.1.5, this information is encoded in the **oncall calendar**.

In most cases, the workflow involves communicating to the primary oncall person or people. They acknowledge the alert by replying to the text message with the word "ACK" or "YES," clicking on a link, or other means. If there is no acknowledgment after a certain amount of time, the next person on the escalation list is tried.

Having the ability to negatively acknowledge ("NAK") the alert saves time during escalations. A NAK immediately escalates to the next person on the list. For example, if the oncall person receives the alert but is unable to attend to the issue because his or her Internet connection has died, the individual could simply do nothing and in a few minutes the escalation will happen automatically. However, if the escalation schedule involves paging the oncall person every 5 minutes and not escalating until three attempts have been made, this means delaying action for 15 minutes. In this case, the person can NAK and the escalation will happen immediately.

Inevitably, there are alert floods or "pager storms"—situations where dozens or hundreds of alerts are sent at the same time. This is usually due to one network outage that causes many alert rules to trigger. In most cases, there is a mechanism to suppress dependent alerts automatically, but floods may still happen despite the organization's best efforts. For this reason, an alert system should have the ability to acknowledge all alerts at the same time. For example, by replying to the text message with the word "ALL" or "STFU," all pending alerts for that particular person are acknowledged as well as any alerts received in the next 5 minutes. The actual alerts can be seen at the alerting dashboard.

Some alert managers have a two-stage acknowledgment. First the oncall person must acknowledge receiving the alert. This establishes that the person is working on the issue. This disables alerts for that particular issue while personnel are working on it. When the issue is resolved, the oncall person must "resolve" the alert to indicate that the issue is fixed. The benefit of this system is that it makes it easier to generate metrics about how long it took to resolve the issue. But what if the person forgets to mark the issue resolved? The system would need to send out reminder alerts periodically, which defeats the purpose of having two stages.

For this reason, we feel the two-stage acknowledgment provides little actual value. If there is a desire to record how long it takes to resolve an issue, have the system detect when the alert is no longer triggering. It will be more accurate and less annoying than requiring the operator to manually indicate that the issue is resolved.

17.4.2 Silence versus Inhibit

Operationally, there is a need to be able to silence an alert at will. For example, during scheduled maintenance the person doing the maintenance does not need to receive alerts that a system is down. Systems that depend on that system should not generate alerts because, in theory, their operations teams have been made aware of the scheduled maintenance.

The mechanism for handling this is called a **silence** or sometimes a **maintenance**. A silence is specified as a start time, an end time, and a specification of what to silence. When specifying what to silence, it can be useful to accept wildcards or regular expressions.

By implementing silences in the alert and escalation system, the alerts still trigger but no action is taken. This is an important distinction. The alert is still triggering; we're just not receiving notifications. The problem or outage is still really happening and any dashboards or displays will reflect that fact.

Alternatively, one can implement silences in the real-time analysis system. This approach is called an **inhibit**. In this case the alert does not trigger and as a result no alerts are sent. An inhibit can be implemented by a mechanism where an alert rule specifies it should not be evaluated (calculated) if one or more prerequisite alert rules are currently triggering. Alternatively, the formula language could include a Boolean function that returns true or false depending on whether the alert is triggering. This function would be used to short-circuit the evaluation of the rule.

For example, an alert rule to warn of a high error rate might be inhibited if the database in use is offline. There is no sense in getting alerted for something you can't do anything about. Monitoring the database is handled by another rule, or by another team. The alert rule might look like:

```
IF http-500-rate > 1% THEN
    ALERT(error-rate-too-high)
        UNLESS ACTIVE_ALERT(database-offline)
```

Silence Creation UI Advice

We learned the hard way that people are bad at doing math related to dates, times, and time zones, especially when stress is high and alerts are blaring. It is also easy to make mistakes when wildcards or regular expressions can be used to specify what to silence. Therefore we recommend the following UI features:

- The default start time should be "now."
- It should be possible to enter the end time as a duration in minutes, hours, or days, as well as a specific time and date in any time zone.
- So that the user may check his or her work, the UI should display what will be silenced and require confirmation before it is activated.

Inhibits can cause confusion if an outage is happening and, due to inhibits, the monitoring system says that everything is fine. Teams that depend on the service will be confused when their dashboards show it being up, yet their service is malfunctioning due to the outage. Therefore we recommend using inhibits sparingly and carefully.

The difference between a silence and an inhibit is very subtle. You silence an alert when you know it would be erroneous to page someone based on some condition such as a planned outage or upgrade. You inhibit alerts to conditionally cause one alert to not fire when another condition is active.

17.5 Visualization

Visualization is the creation of a visual representation of one or more metrics. It is more than just creating the pretty graphs that will impress management. Visualization helps find meaning in large amounts of data.

A well-designed monitoring system does not collect data twice, once for real-time alerting and yet again for visualization. If you collect it for visualization, be able to alert on it. If you alert on it, store it so that you can visualize it.

Simple graphs can display raw data, summarized data, or a comparison of two more metrics. Visualization also involves synthesizing new metrics from others. For example, a rate can be calculated as the function of a counter and time.

Raw data graphed over time, either as a single point or as an aggregate of similar metrics, is useful for metrics that change slowly. For example, if the memory use of a server over time, which usually remains nearly constant, changes after a particular software release, it is something to investigate. If the usage went up and developers did not expect it to, there may be a memory leak. If usage went down and developers did not expect it to, there may be a bug.

Counters are best viewed as rates. A counter, visualized in its raw form, looks like a line going up and to the right. If the rate over time is calculated, we will see either acceleration, deceleration, or an equilibrium.

Some visualizations are less useful and, in fact, can be misleading. A pie chart of disk space used and unused is a common dashboard fixture that we find rather pretty but pointless. Knowing that a disk has 30 percent space remaining isn't useful without knowing the size of the disk. Seeing two such pie charts, side by side, of two different-sized disks, is rarely a useful comparison.

In contrast, calculating the rate at which the disk is filling and displaying the derivative of that rate becomes an actionable metric. It helps predict when the disk space will be exhausted. Graph this derivative against the derivative of other resource consumption rates, such as the number of new accounts created, and you can see how resources are consumed in proportion to each other.

The only thing we dislike more than pie charts are averages, or the mathematical mean. Averages can be misleading in ways that encourage you to make bad decisions. If half of your customers like hot tea and the other half like cold tea, none of them will be happy if you serve them all lukewarm tea even though you have served them the same average temperature. A network link that is overloaded during the day and barely used at night will be, on average, half used. It would be a bad idea to make a decision based on the average utilization. Averages lie. If billionaire Bill Gates walks into a homeless shelter, the average person in the building is a multimillionaire but it doesn't take a genius to realize that the homeless problem hasn't been eliminated.

That said, averages aren't inherently misleading and have a place in your statistical toolbox. Like other statistical functions they need to be used wisely.

17.5.1 Percentiles

Percentiles and medians are useful when analyzing utilization or quality. These terms are often misunderstood. Here's a simple way to understand them.

Imagine a school has 400 students. Stand those students up along a 100-meter line in order of lowest GPA to highest. Stretch out the line evenly so that the student with the lowest GPA is at 0 and the one with the highest GPA is at 100. The student standing at the 90-meter mark is the 90th percentile. This means that 90 percent of the student body did worse than this person. The student at the 50-meter mark, exactly in the middle, is known as the median.

If there are more students, if there are fewer students, or if the grading standard changed, there will always be a student at (or closest to) the 90-meter mark. The GPA of the 90th percentile student could be a C- or an A+. It all depends on the makeup of the entire student body's GPAs. The entire school could have excellent grades but someone is still going to be at the 90th percentile. Trends can be analyzed by, for example, graphing the GPA of the 50th and 90th percentile students each year.

It is common for colocation facilities to charge based on the 90th percentile of bandwidth used. This means they take measurements every 5 minutes of how much bandwidth is being used at that moment. All these measurements are sorted, but duplicates are not removed. If you wrote all these measurements, distributed evenly, along a 100-meter football field, the measurement at the 90-meter mark would be the bandwidth rate you will be billed for. This is a more fair billing method than charging for the maximum or average rate.

It is very smart of your colocation facility to charge you this way. If it charged based on the average bandwidth used, the company would take the total amount of bytes transmitted in the day, divide by the number of seconds in a day, and use that rate. That rate would be misleadingly low for customers that consume very little bandwidth at night and a lot during the day, what is known as a **diurnal** usage pattern. In contrast, the 90th percentile represents how heavily you use bandwidth without penalizing you for huge bursts that happen from time to time. In fact, it forgives you for your 30 most extreme 5-minute periods of utilization, nearly 2.5 hours each day. More importantly for the colocation facility, it best represents the cost of the bandwidth used.

Percentiles are also commonly used when discussing latency or delay per unit. For example, a site that is trying to improve its page-load time might set a goal of having the 80th percentile page load time be 300 ms or less. A particular API call might have a lot of variation in how long it takes to execute due to caching, type of request, and so on. One might set a goal of having its 99th percentile be less than some amount, such as 100 ms.

17.5.2 Stack Ranking

Stack ranking makes it easy to compare data by sorting the elements by value. Figure 17.2 is an example of **stack ranking**. If the cities had been sorted alphabetically, it would not be clear how, for example, Atlanta compares to New York. With the stack rank we can clearly see the difference.

Stack ranking is best used when data is apples-to-apples comparable. One way to achieve this is to normalize the data to be per unit (e.g., per capita, per machine, per service, per thousand queries). Figure 17.2 would mean something very different if the y-axis was thousands of tacos eaten in total by all people in that city versus being normalized to be a per-person metric. The latter is a more comparable number.

If you do not have a base-line, a stack rank can help establish one. You might not know if "55" is a lot or a little, a bad or good amount, but you know only two cities were bigger. Managers who are unskilled at determining whether an employee is effective can instead rely on peer stack ranking rather than making the decision themselves.

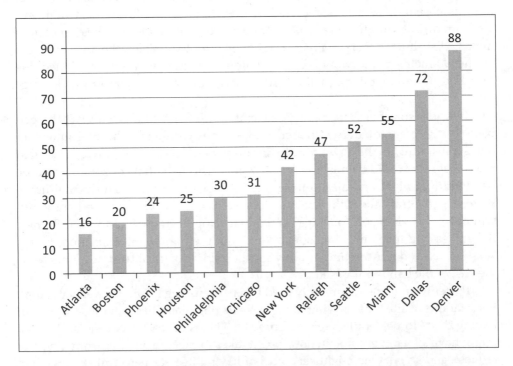

Figure 17.2: Cities stack ranked by number of tacos consumed

17.5.3 Histograms

Histograms can reveal a lot about datasets and are particularly useful when analyzing latency. A histogram is a graph of the count of values in a dataset, possibly after rounding. For example, if we take a set of data and round all the values to the nearest multiple of 5, we would graph the number of 0s, 5s, 10s, 15s, and so on. We might simply round to the nearest integer. These ranges are often called **buckets**. Each data point is put in its most appropriate bucket and the graph visualizes how many items are in each bucket.

Figure 17.3a shows the page load measurements collected on a fictional web site. Graphing them as a line plot does not reveal much except that there is a lot of variation. The average is 27, which is also not very actionable.

However, if we take each measurement, round it to the nearest multiple of 5, and graph the number of 0s, 5s, 10s, and so on, we end up with the graph in Figure 17.3b. This reveals that the majority of the data points are in the 10, 15, 35, and 40 buckets. The graph has two humps, like a camel. This pattern is called bimodal. Knowing that the data has this shape gives us a basis for investigation. We can separate the data points out into the two humps and look for similarities. We might find that most of the site's pages load very quickly, but most of the data points in the first hump are from a particular page. Investigation shows that every time this page is generated, a large amount of data must be sorted. By pre-sorting that data, we can reduce the load time of that page. The other hump might be from a web page that requires a database lookup that is larger than the cache and therefore performs badly. We can adjust the cache so as to improve performance of that page.

There are many other ways to visualize data. More sophisticated visualizations can draw out different trends or consolidate more information into a picture. Color can be used to add an additional dimension. There are many fine books on

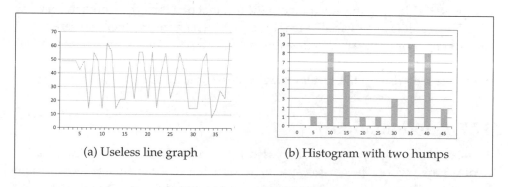

(a) Useless line graph   (b) Histogram with two humps

Figure 17.3: Page load time recorded from a fictional web site

this subject. We highly recommend *The Visual Display of Quantitative Information* by Tufte (1986).

17.6 Storage

The storage system holds the metrics collected and makes them accessible by the other modules.

Storage is one of the most architecturally demanding parts of the monitoring system. New metrics arrive in a constant flood, at high speed. Alerting requires fast, real-time, read access for recent data. At the same time, other analysis requires iterations over large ranges, which makes caching difficult. Typical SQL databases are bad at all of these things.

Medium-sized systems often collect 25–200 metrics for each server. There are multiple servers on each machine. A medium-sized system may need to store 400 new metrics each second. Larger systems typically store thousands of metrics per second. Globally distributed systems may store tens or hundreds of thousands of metrics every second.

As a result, many storage systems handle either real-time data or long-term storage but not both, or can't do both at large scale. Recently a number of time-series databases such as OpenTSDB have sprung up that are specifically designed to be good at both real-time and long-term storage. They achieve this by keeping recent data in RAM, often up to an hour's worth, as well as by using a highly tuned storage format.

On-disk storage of time-series data is usually done one of two ways. One method achieves fast high-speed random access by using fixed-size records. For example, each metric might be stored in a 20-byte record. The system can efficiently find a metric at a particular time by using a modified binary search. This approach is most effective when real-time visualization is required. Another method is to compress the data, taking advantage of the fact that deltas can be stored in very few bits. The result is often variable-length records, which means the time-series data must be read from the start to find the metric at a particular time. These systems permit much greater storage density. Some systems achieve a balance by storing fixed-size records on a file system with built-in compression.

17.7 Configuration

The six monitoring components discussed so far all need configuration information to direct their work. The sensing system needs to know which data to measure and how often. The collection system needs to know what to collect and where to send it. The analysis system has a base of formulas to process. The alerting system needs to know who to alert, how, and who to escalate to. The visualization system needs to know which graphs to generate and how to do so. The storage system needs to know how to store and access the data.

These configurations should be treated like any other software source code: kept under revision control, tested using both unit tests and system tests, and so on. Revision control tracks changes of a file over time, enabling one to see what a file looked like at any point in its history. A unit test framework would take as input time-series data for one or more metrics and output whether the alert would trigger. This permits one to validate alert formulas.

In distributed monitoring systems, each component may be separated out and perhaps replicated or sharded. Each piece needs a way to access the configuration. A system like ZooKeeper, discussed in Section 11.7, can be used to distribute a pointer to where the full configuration can be found, which is often a source code or package repository.

Some monitoring systems are multitenant. This is where a monitoring system permits many teams to independently control metric collection, alert rules, and so on. By centralizing the service but decentralizing the ability to use it, we empower service owners, developers, and others to do their own monitoring and benefit from the ability to automatically collect and analyze data. Other monitoring systems achieve the same goal by making it easy for individuals to install their own instance of the monitoring system, or just their own sensing and collection components while centralizing storage and other components.

17.8 Summary

Monitoring systems are complex, with many components working together.

The sensing and measurement component takes measurements. Whitebox monitoring monitors the systems internals. Blackbox monitoring collects data from the perspective of a user. Gauges measure an amount that varies. Counters are non-decreasing indicators of how many times something has happened.

The collection system gathers the metrics. Metrics may be pushed (sent) to the collection system or the collection system may pull (query) systems to gather the metrics.

The storage system stores the metrics. Usually custom databases are used to handle the large volume of incoming data and take advantage of the unique qualities of time-series data.

The analysis system extracts meaning from the data. There may be many different analysis systems, each providing services such as anomaly detection, forecasting, or data mining. Some analysis occurs in real time, happening as the data is gathered. Short-term analysis focuses on recent data or provides the random access needed by specific applications such as dashboards. Long-term analysis examines large spans of data to detect trends over many years. It is often done in batch mode, storing intermediate results for later use.

Alerting and escalation systems reach out to find people when manual intervention is needed, finding a substitute when a person doesn't respond within a certain amount of time.

Visualization systems provide graphs and dashboards. They can combine and transform data and do operations such as calculating percentiles, building histograms, and determining stack ranks.

All of this is tied together by a configuration manager that directs all of the other components in their work. Changes to configurations can be distributed in many ways, often by distributing configuration files or more dynamic systems such as ZooKeeper.

When monitoring systems are multitenant, we empower individual service teams to control their own monitoring configurations. They benefit from centralized components, freeing them from having to worry about capacity planning and other operational duties.

When all the components work together, we have a monitoring system that is scalable, reliable, and functional.

Exercises

1. What are the components of the monitoring system?
2. Pick three components of the monitoring system and describe them in detail.
3. Do all monitoring systems have all the components described in this chapter? Give examples of why components may be optional.
4. What is a pager storm, and what are the ways to deal with one?
5. Research the JSON format for representing data. Design a JSON format for the collection of metrics.
6. Describe the monitoring system in use in your organization or one you've had experience with in the past. How is it used? What does it monitor? Which problems does it solve?
7. Create one or more methods of calculating a rate for a counter metric. The method should work even if there is a counter reset. Can your method also calculate a margin of error?
8. Design a better monitoring system for your current environment.
9. Why are averages discouraged? Present a metric misleadingly as an average, and non-misleadingly some other way.

Chapter 18

Capacity Planning

> Plans are nothing,
> planning is everything.
>
> —Philip Kotler

Capacity planning means ensuring that there will be enough resources when they are needed. Optimally this is done such that the system is neither under capacity nor over capacity. Resources include CPUs, memory, storage, server instances, network bandwidth, switch ports, console connections, power, cooling, datacenter space, and any other infrastructure components that are required to run a service.

There are two major objectives of capacity planning. First, we want to prevent service interruptions due to lack of capacity. Second, we want to preserve capital investment by adding only the capacity required at any given time. Good capacity planning provides a demonstrable return on investment (ROI) by showing the need for resources and capping resource usage at a level that ensures good service.

Capacity planning should be a data-driven process, using data collected about the running system to forecast trends. It also should be informed by future business plans for growth. This chapter explains which data you need to collect and how to use it to forecast your future capacity requirements.

Capacity planning in large, fast-growing services becomes highly complex and relies on sophisticated mathematical models. Organizations often hire a full-time statistician to develop and maintain these models. A statistician with a technical background may be difficult to find, but such a person is worth his or her weight in gold. This chapter introduces some mathematical models that were developed for trading on the financial markets, and shows how you can apply them to capacity planning in a rapidly changing environment.

This chapter does not look at the enterprise-style capacity planning required to meet the day-to-day needs of the people who work for the service provider. Instead, this chapter focuses on capacity planning for the service itself.

Terms to Know

QPS: Queries per second. Usually how many web hits or API calls received per second.

Active Users: The number of users who have accessed the service in the specified timeframe.

MAU: Monthly active users. The number of users who have accessed the service in the last month.

Engagement: How many times on average an active user performs a particular transaction.

Primary Resource: The one system-level resource that is the main limiting factor for the service.

Capacity Limit: The point at which performance starts to degrade rapidly or become unpredictable.

Core Driver: A factor that strongly drives demand for a primary resource.

Time Series: A sequence of data points measured at equally spaced time intervals. For example, data from monitoring systems.

18.1 Standard Capacity Planning

Capacity planning needs to provide answers to two questions: What are you going to need to buy in the coming year? and When are you going to need to buy it? To answer those questions, you need to know the following information:

- **Current Usage:** Which components can influence service capacity? How much of each do you use at the moment?

- **Normal Growth:** What is the expected growth rate of the service, without the influence of any specific business or marketing events? Sometimes this is called **organic growth**.

- **Planned Growth:** Which business or marketing events are planned, when will they occur, and what is the anticipated growth due to each of these events?

- **Headroom:** Which kind of short-term usage spikes does your service encounter? Are there any particular events in the coming year, such as the Olympics or an election, that are expected to cause a usage spike? How much spare capacity do you need to handle these spikes gracefully? Headroom is usually specified as a percentage of current capacity.

- **Timetable:** For each component, what is the lead time from ordering to delivery, and from delivery until it is in service? Are there specific constraints for bringing new capacity into service, such as change windows?

Math Terms

Correlation Coefficient: Describes how strongly measurements for different data sources resemble each other.

Moving Average: A series of averages, each of which is taken across a short time interval (window), rather than across the whole data set.

Regression Analysis: A statistical method for analyzing relationships between different data sources to determine how well they correlate, and to predict changes in one based on changes in another.

EMA: Exponential moving average. It applies a weight to each data point in the window, with the weight decreasing exponentially for older data points.

MACD: Moving average convergence/divergence. An indicator used to spot changes in strength, direction, and momentum of a metric. It measures the difference between an EMA with a short window and an EMA with a long window.

Zero Line Crossover: A crossing of the MACD line through zero happens when there is no difference between the short and long EMAs. A move from positive to negative shows a downward trend in the data, and a move from negative to positive shows an upward trend.

MACD Signal Line: An EMA of the MACD measurement.

Signal Line Crossover: The MACD line crossing over the signal line indicates that the trend in the data is about to accelerate in the direction of the crossover. It is an indicator of momentum.

From that information, you can calculate the amount of capacity you expect to need for each resource by the end of the following year with a simple formula:

$$\text{Future Resources} = \text{Current Usage} \times (1 + \text{Normal Growth} + \text{Planned Growth}) + \text{Headroom}$$

You can then calculate for each resource the additional capacity that you need to purchase:

$$\text{Additional Resources} = \text{Future Resources} - \text{Current Resources}$$

Perform this calculation for each resource, whether or not you think you will need more capacity. It is okay to reach the conclusion that you don't need any more network bandwidth in the coming year. It is not okay to be taken by surprise and run out of network bandwidth because you didn't consider it in your capacity planning. For shared resources, the data from many teams will need to be combined to determine whether more capacity is needed.

18.1.1 Current Usage

Before you can consider buying additional equipment, you need to understand what you currently have available and how much of it you are using. Before you can assess what you have, you need a complete list of all the things that are required to provide the service. If you forget something, it won't be included in your capacity planning, and you may run out of that one thing later, and as a result be unable to grow the service as quickly as you need.

What to Track

The two most obvious things that the provider of an Internet-based service needs are some machines to provide the service and a connection to the Internet. Some machines may be generic machines that are later customized to perform given tasks, whereas others may be specialized appliances. Going deeper into these items, machines have CPUs, caches, RAM, storage, and network. Connecting to the Internet requires a local network, routers, switches, and a connection to at least one ISP. Going deeper still, network cards, routers, switches, cables, and storage devices all have bandwidth limitations. Some appliances may have higher-end network cards that need special cabling and interfaces on the network gear. All networked devices need IP addresses. These are all resources that need to be tracked.

Taking one step back, all devices run some sort of operating system, and some run additional software. The operating systems and software may require licenses and maintenance contracts. Data and configuration information on the devices may need backing up to yet more systems. Stepping even farther back, machines need to be installed in a datacenter that meets their power and environment needs. The number and type of racks in the datacenter, the power and cooling capacity, and the available floor space all need to be tracked. Datacenters may provide additional per-machine services, such as console service. For companies that have multiple datacenters and points of presence, there may be links between those sites that also have capacity limits. These are all additional resources to track.

Outside vendors may provide some services. The contracts covering those services specify cost or capacity limits. To make sure that you have covered a very possible aspect, talk to people in every department, and find out what they do and how it relates to the service. For everything that relates to the services, you need to understand what the limits are, how you can track them, and how you can measure how much of the available capacity is used.

How Much Do You Have

There is no substitute for a good up-to-date inventory database for keeping track of your assets. The inventory database should be kept up-to-date by making it a core component in the ordering, provisioning, and decommissioning processes. An up-to-date inventory system gives you the data you need to find out how much of each resource you have. It should also be used to track the software license and maintenance contract inventory, and the contracted amount of resources that are available from third parties.

Using a limited number of standard machine configurations and having a set of standard appliances, storage systems, routers, and switches makes it easier to map the number of devices to the lower-level resources, such as CPU and RAM, that they provide.

How Much Are You Using Now

Identify the limiting resources for each service. Your monitoring system is likely already collecting resource use data for CPU, RAM, storage, and bandwidth. Typically it collects this data at a higher frequency than required for capacity planning. A summarization or statistical sample may be sufficient for planning purposes and will generally simplify calculations. Combining this data with the data from the inventory system will show how much spare capacity you currently have.

Tracking everything in the inventory database and using a limited set of standard hardware configurations also makes it easy to specify how much space, power, cooling, and other datacenter resources are used per device. With all of that data entered into the inventory system, you can automatically generate the datacenter utilization rate.

18.1.2 Normal Growth

The monitoring system directly provides data on current usage and current capacity. It can also supply the normal growth rate for the preceding years. Look for any noticeable step changes in usage, and see if these correspond to a particular event, such as the roll-out of a new product or a special marketing drive. If the offset due to that event persists for the rest of the year, calculate the change and subtract it from subsequent data to avoid including this event-driven change in the normal growth calculation. Plot the data from as many years as possible on a graph, to determine if the normal growth rate is linear or follows some other trend.

18.1.3 Planned Growth

The second step is estimating additional growth due to marketing and business events, such as new product launches or new features. For example, the marketing department may be planning a major campaign in May that it predicts will increase the customer base by 20 to 25 percent. Or perhaps a new product is scheduled to launch in August that relies on three existing services and is expected to increase the load on each of those by 10 percent at launch, increasing to 30 percent by the end of the year. Use the data from any changes detected in the first step to validate the assumptions about expected growth.

18.1.4 Headroom

Headroom is the amount of excess capacity that is considered routine. Any service will have usage spikes or edge conditions that require extended resource usage occasionally. To prevent these edge conditions from triggering outages, spare resources must be routinely available. How much headroom is needed for any given service is a business decision. Since excess capacity is largely unused capacity, by its very nature it represents potentially wasted investment. Thus a financially responsible company wants to balance the potential for service interruption with the desire to conserve financial resources.

Your monitoring data should be picking up these resource spikes and providing hard statistical data on when, where, and how often they occur. Data on outages and postmortem reports are also key in determining reasonable headroom.

Another component in determining how much headroom is needed is the amount of time it takes to have additional resources deployed into production from the moment that someone realizes that additional resources are required. If it takes three months to make new resources available, then you need to have more headroom available than if it takes two weeks or one month. At a minimum, you need sufficient headroom to allow for the expected growth during that time period.

18.1.5 Resiliency

Reliable services also need additional capacity to meet their SLAs. The additional capacity allows for some components to fail, without the end users experiencing an outage or service degradation. As discussed in Chapter 6, the additional capacity needs to be in a different failure domain; otherwise, a single outage could take down both the primary machines and the spare capacity that should be available to take over the load.

Failure domains also should be considered at a large scale, typically at the datacenter level. For example, facility-wide maintenance work on the power systems requires the entire building to be shut down. If an entire datacenter is offline, the service must be able to smoothly run from the other datacenters with no capacity problems. Spreading the service capacity across many failure domains reduces the additional capacity required for handling the resiliency requirements, which is the most cost-effective way to provide this extra capacity. For example, if a service runs in one datacenter, a second datacenter is required to provide the additional capacity, about 50 percent. If a service runs in nine datacenters, a tenth is required to provide the additional capacity; this configuration requires only 10 percent additional capacity.

As discussed in Section 6.6.5, the gold standard is to provide enough capacity for two datacenters to be down at the same time. This permits one to be down for planned maintenance while the organization remains prepared for another datacenter going down unexpectedly. Appendix B discusses the history of such resilient architectures.

18.1.6 Timetable

Most companies plan their budgets annually, with expenditures split into quarters. Based on your expected normal growth and planned growth bursts, you can map out when you need the resources to be available. Working backward from that date, you need to figure out how long it takes from "go" until the resources are available.

How long does it take for purchase orders to be approved and sent to the vendor? How long does it take from receipt of a purchase order until the vendor has delivered the goods? How long does it take from delivery until the resources are available? Are there specific tests that need to be performed before the equipment can be installed? Are there specific change windows that you need to aim for to turn on the extra capacity? Once the additional capacity is turned on, how long does it take to reconfigure the services to make use of it? Using this information, you can provide an expenditures timetable.

Physical services generally have a longer lead time than virtual services. Part of the popularity of IaaS and PaaS offerings such as Amazon's EC2 and Elastic Storage are that newly requested resources have virtually instant delivery time.

It is always cost-effective to reduce resource delivery time because it means we are paying for less excess capacity to cover resource delivery time. This is a place where automation that prepares newly acquired resources for use has immediate value.

18.2 Advanced Capacity Planning

Large, high-growth environments such as popular internet services require a different approach to capacity planning. Standard enterprise-style capacity planning techniques are often insufficient. The customer base may change rapidly in ways that are hard to predict, requiring deeper and more frequent statistical analysis of the service monitoring data to detect significant changes in usage trends more quickly. This kind of capacity planning requires deeper technical knowledge. Capacity planners will need to be familiar with concepts such as QPS, active users, engagement, primary resources, capacity limit, and core drivers. The techniques described in this section of the book were covered by Yan and Kejariwal (2013), whose work inspired this section.

18.2.1 Identifying Your Primary Resources

Each service has one **primary resource**, such as CPU utilization, memory footprint or bandwidth, storage footprint or bandwidth, or network bandwidth, that is the dominant resource consumed by the service. For example, a service that does a lot of computation is usually limited by the available CPU resources—that is, it is CPU-bound. Capacity planning focuses on the primary resource.

Services also have **secondary resource** needs. For example, a service that is CPU-bound may, to a lesser extent, use memory, storage, and network bandwidth. The secondary resources are not interesting from a capacity planning point of view, with the current software version and hardware models, but one of them may become the primary resource later as the code or hardware changes. Consequently, these secondary resources should also be monitored and the usage trends tracked. Detecting a change in which resource is the primary resource for a given service is done by tracking the constraint ratio (disk:CPU:memory:network) between the primary and secondary resources. Whenever a new software version is released or a new hardware model is introduced, this ratio should be recalculated.

Primary and secondary resources are low-level resource units that drive the need for **ancillary resources** such as server instances, switch ports, load balancers, power, and other datacenter infrastructure.

The first step in capacity planning is to identify your primary resources, as these are the resources that you will focus on for capacity planning. You must also define a relationship between your primary and ancillary usage. When your capacity planning indicates that you need more of your primary resources, you need to be able to determine how much of the ancillary resources are required as a result. As the hardware that you use changes, these mappings need to be updated.

18.2.2 Knowing Your Capacity Limits

The **capacity limit** of any resource is the point at which performance starts to degrade rapidly or become unpredictable, as shown in Figure 18.1. Capacity limits should be determined by load testing. Load testing is normally performed in an isolated lab environment. It can be performed by synthetically generating traffic or by replaying production traffic.

For each primary and secondary resource, you need to know the capacity limit. To generate such data for each resource in isolation, your lab setup should be equipped with lots of excess capacity for all but one low-level resource. That resource will then be the limiting factor for the service, and response times can be graphed against the percentage utilization of that resource and separately against the absolute amount of that resource that is available. For completeness, it is best to repeat this test several times, each time scaling up the whole environment uniformly. This approach will enable you to determine if the limit is more closely related to percentage utilization or to quantity of remaining resources.

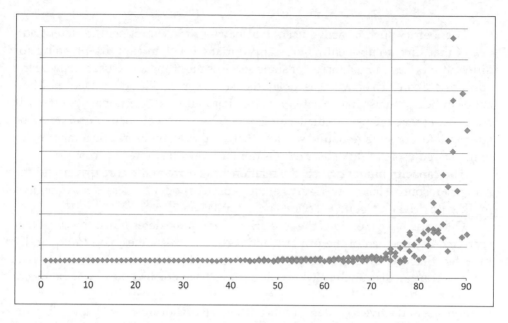

Figure 18.1: Response time starts to degrade beyond a certain percent utilization.

18.2.3 Identifying Your Core Drivers

Core drivers are factors that strongly drive demand for a primary resource. They typically include values such as MAU, QPS, the size of the corpus, or other high-level metrics that represent well the factors that generate traffic or load on the service. These metrics also often have meaningful business implications, with links to sources of revenue, for example.

A site may have millions of registered users, but it will typically have many fewer users who are active. For example, many people sign up for accounts and use the service a few times, but never return. Counting these users in your planning can be misleading. Many people register with social networking sites, but rarely use their accounts. Some people who are registered with online shopping sites may use the service only before birthdays and gift-buying holidays. A more accurate representation of users may be how many were active in the last 7 or 30 days. The number of users in the last 7 days is often called **7-day actives (7DA)**, while the term **weekly active users (WAU)** is used to indicate how many were active in a specific calendar week. Likewise, **30-day actives (30DA)** measures the number of users in the last 30 days, with the term **monthly active users (MAU)** used if the measurement was bounded by a specific calendar month. These measurements often reflect usage much more accurately than the number of registered users.

For metrics such as active users that have a time component, different values of that time component may be appropriate to use in capacity planning for different services. For example, for some services monthly active users may be the appropriate core driver, whereas for another service minutely active users may be a better indicator to use in capacity planning. For highly transactional systems that are driven by active users, smaller time scales like minutely active users may be appropriate. For storage-bound services that are driven by users, the total number of registered users (or total user corpus number) may be more appropriate.

The **capacity model** depicts the relationship between the core driver and the primary resource. For a given service, the capacity model expresses how changes in the core driver affect that service's need for its core driver.

Once you have identified the core drivers, and have determined the effect that each one has on each of the primary and secondary resources, you can quantify the effect that each will have on your requirements for ancillary resources, such as servers. You can also analyze whether your ancillary resources are well balanced. If servers run out of CPU cycles long before they run out of RAM, then it may be more cost-effective to order servers with less RAM or more or faster CPUs, for example. Or it may be possible to rework the service by taking advantage of the extra RAM or making it less CPU-intensive. Similarly, if your switches run out of ports long before backplane bandwidth, perhaps a different switch model would be more appropriate.

18.2.4 Measuring Engagement

If the number of active users is growing rapidly, it might seem as if this number is the only core driver that needs to be taken into consideration. However, that works on the assumption that this growth will continue. Another factor can, and should, be tracked separately—user engagement. **Engagement** is the number of times that the average active user accesses the particular service in a given period of time. In other words, it is a measure of the popularity of a particular feature. For example, a site might find that when it first introduces a video-sharing functionality, not many people are interested, and only about 1 percent of the monthly active users access that feature. However, as time goes on, this feature may become more popular, and six months later 25 percent of the monthly active users may be accessing that feature.

If the number of active users stays static but engagement increases, then the load on your service will also increase. Taken in combination, these two numbers indicate how often a service is accessed.

The engagement graph for each service will be different, and an increase in engagement for one service will have a different effect on resource requirements than a change in engagement for another service. For example, an increase in engagement for video uploads will have more of an impact on disk space and I/O bandwidth than an increase in engagement for the chat service will.

18.2.5 Analyzing the Data

Once you have decided which metrics to collect and started gathering data, you need to be able to process that data and generate useful inputs for your capacity planning process. Standard capacity planning looks at year-to-year statistics and makes projections based on those data. This approach is still necessary, but in a large-scale, rapidly changing environment, we need to augment it so that we are able to react more quickly to changes in demand.

In a large-scale environment, one of the goals is to be able to simply but accurately specify how many resources you need to have based on a measured core driver. One way to meet this goal is to simplify the metrics down to blocks of users based on the serving capacity of one rack or cluster of machines. With this approach, capacity planning is simplified into a more cookie-cutter approach. One application might serve 100,000 active users per rack. Another application might serve 1000 active users per cluster, where each cluster is a standardized combination of machines that act as an independent unit. Engineering can produce new ratios as newer, faster hardware becomes available or new software designs are created. Now capacity planning is simplified and resources can be managed based on blocks of active users. While this approach is less granular, it is sufficient because it matches the deployment granularity. You can't buy half a machine, so capacity planning doesn't need to be super precise.

To identify such a relationship between a core driver and resource consumption, you first need to understand which core drivers influence which resources and how strongly. The way to do so is to correlate the resource usage metrics with the core driver metrics.

Correlation

Correlation measures how closely data sources resemble each other. Visually, you might see on a monitoring graph that an increase in CPU usage on a server matches up with a corresponding increase in network traffic to the same server, which also matches up with a spike in QPS. From these observations you might conclude that these three measurements are related, although you cannot necessarily say that the changes in one caused the changes in another.

Regression analysis mathematically calculates how well time-series data sources match up. Regression analysis of your metrics can indicate how strongly changes in a core driver affect the usage of a primary resource. It can also indicate how strongly two core drivers are related.

To perform a regression analysis on time-series data, you first need to define a time interval, such as 1 day or 4 weeks. The number of data samples in that time period is n. If your core driver metric is x and your primary resource metric is y, you first calculate the sum of the last n values for x, x^2, y, y^2, and x times y, giving $\sum x$, $\sum x^2$, $\sum y$, $\sum y^2$, and $\sum xy$. Then calculate SS_{xy}, SS_{xx}, SS_{yy}, and R as follows:

$$SS_{xy} = \sum xy - \frac{(\sum x)(\sum y)}{n}$$

$$SS_{xx} = \sum x^2 - \frac{(\sum x)^2}{n}$$

$$SS_{yy} = \sum y^2 - \frac{(\sum y)^2}{n}$$

$$r = \frac{SS_{xy}}{\sqrt{SS_{xx}SS_{yy}}}$$

Regression analysis results in a correlation coefficient R, which is a number between -1 and 1. Squaring this number and then multiplying by 100 gives the percentage match between the two data sources. For example, for the MAU and network utilization figures shown in Figure 18.2, this calculation gives a very high correlation, between 96 percent and 100 percent, as shown in Figure 18.3, where R^2 is graphed.

When changes in a core driver correlate well with changes in usage of a primary resource, you can derive an equation of the form $y = a + bx$, which describes the relationship between the two, known as the **regression line**. This equation enables you to calculate your primary resource requirements based on core driver

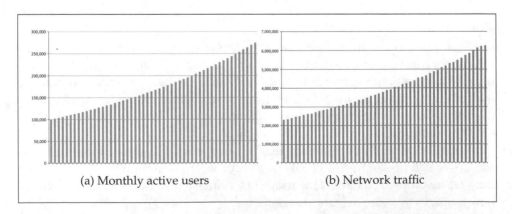

(a) Monthly active users   (b) Network traffic

Figure 18.2: The number of users correlates well with network traffic.

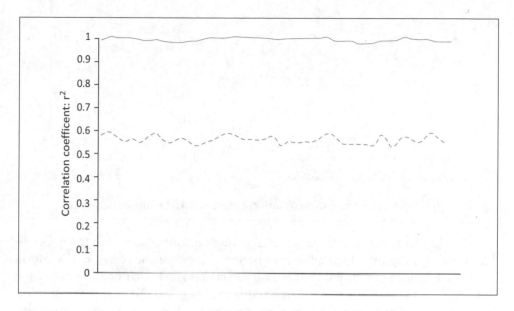

Figure 18.3: The upper line shows a high correlation of over 96% between two data sources. The lower line shows low correlation—less than 60%.

measurements. In other words, given a value for your core driver x, you can calculate how much of your primary resource y you think you will need, with a confidence of R^2. To calculate a and b, first calculate the *moving* average of the last n data points for x and y, giving x and y. Then:

$$b = \frac{SS_{xx}}{SS_{yy}}$$

$$a = \bar{y} - b\bar{x}$$

Correlation between metrics changes over time, and should therefore be graphed and tracked with a rolling correlation analysis, rather than assessed once and assumed to be constant. Changes in the service can have a significant impact on correlation. Changes in the end-user demographic are usually slower, but can also affect correlation by changing how the average customer uses the service.

Figure 18.4a shows a sharp drop in correlation corresponding to a change in resource usage patterns between one software release and the next. The change in correlation in the graph actually corresponds to a step-change in resource usage patterns from one release to the next. After the time interval chosen for the rolling correlation measurement elapses, correlation returns to normal.

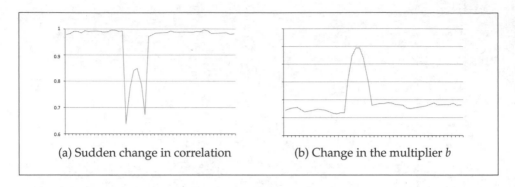

(a) Sudden change in correlation   (b) Change in the multiplier b

Figure 18.4: Change in correlation between MAU and bandwidth

Figure 18.4b shows b for the same time interval. Notice that after the upgrade b changes significantly during the time period chosen for the correlation analysis and then becomes stable again but at a higher value. The large fluctuations in b for the length of the correlation window are due to significant changes in the moving averages from day to day, as the moving average has both pre- and post-upgrade data. When sufficient time has passed so that only post-upgrade data is used in the moving average, b becomes stable and the correlation coefficient returns to its previous high levels.

The value of b corresponds to the slope of the line, or the multiplier in the equation linking the core driver and the usage of the primary resource. When correlation returns to normal, b is at a higher level. This result indicates that the primary resource will be consumed more rapidly with this software release than with the previous one. Any marked change in correlation should trigger a reevaluation of the multiplier b and corresponding resource usage predictions.

Forecasting

Forecasting attempts to predict future needs based on current and past measurements. The most basic forecasting technique is to graph the 90th percentile of the historical usage and then find an equation that best fits this data. You can then use that equation to predict future usage. Calculating percentiles was discussed in Section 17.5.1.

Of course, growth rates change, usage patterns change, and application resource needs change. We need to be able to detect these changes and alter our resource planning accordingly. To detect changes in a trend, we use the moving average convergence/divergence (MACD) metric. MACD measures the difference between a long-period (e.g., 3 months) and a short-period (e.g., 1 month) moving average. However, a standard moving average tends to mask recent changes in metrics. Since forecasting aims to provide early detection for such changes, MACD uses an exponential moving average (EMA), which gives an average with a much heavier weighting for recent data and a very low weighting for old data. An EMA is calculated as follows, where n is the number of samples:

$$k = \frac{2}{n+1}$$

$$EMA_x = \text{Value}_x \times k + EMA_{x-1} \times (1 - k)$$

To get started, the first EMA_{x-1} value (actually EMA_n) is just a straight average of the first n data points.

To use MACD to give early warning of changes in behavior, you need to calculate and plot some additional data, called the MACD signal line, on the same graph. The MACD signal is an EMA of the MACD. When the MACD line crosses the MACD signal line, that is an indication that the trend is changing. When the MACD line crosses from below the signal line to above the signal line, it indicates an increase. For example, for an engagement metric, it would indicate an unexpected increase in engagement for a particular feature. When the MACD line crosses from above the signal line to below it, it indicates a downward trend. For example, in a memory usage graph, it might indicate that the most recent release is more memory efficient than the previous one. This may cause you to reassess the number of users a cluster can support.

The challenge in measuring and graphing MACD is to define the time scales to use for the long and short periods. If the periods are too short, the MACD will indicate changes in trends too frequently to be useful, as in Figure 18.5. The bar chart in the background of this figure is the 90th percentile data. The smoother graph line is the MACD signal line, and the other line is the MACD.

However, increasing the short period, in particular, will tend to delay triggering a change in trend event. In Figure 18.6, the downward trend is triggered 2 days earlier with a 2-week short period (Figure 18.6a) than with the 4-week short period (Figure 18.6b), keeping the long period constant at 3 months. However, the 2-week short period also has a little extra noise, with a downward trigger followed 2 days later by an upward trigger, followed a week later by the final downward trigger.

When choosing your long and short periods, you can validate the model by seeing if older data predicts more recent data. If it does, it is reasonable to conclude that the model will be a good predictor in the near-term future. Start with existing data, as far back as you have available. Try several different combinations of short and long periods, and see which combination best predicts trends observed in your historical datasets.

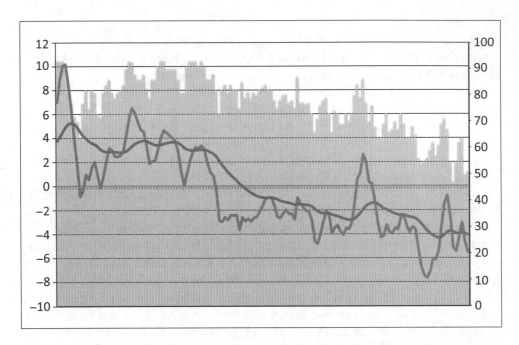

Figure 18.5: Noisy data from a 1-week short period and a 4-week long period

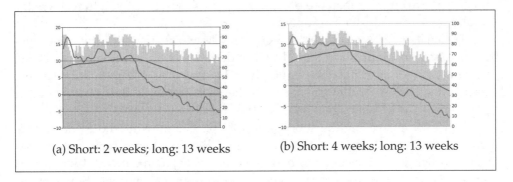

(a) Short: 2 weeks; long: 13 weeks   (b) Short: 4 weeks; long: 13 weeks

Figure 18.6: Effect of changing only the short period

18.2.6 Monitoring the Key Indicators

The correlation coefficients between core drivers and resources should be graphed and monitored. If there is a significant change in correlation, the relationship between the core driver and resource consumption should be reassessed, and any changes fed back into the capacity planning process.

Similarly, the MACD and MACD signal for each core driver and resource should be monitored. Since these metrics can be used for early detection in changes in trends, they are key elements in capacity management. Alerts generated by the MACD line and MACD signal line crossing should go straight to the team responsible for capacity planning. If the core drivers and relationships to the primary resources are well defined, theoretically it should be necessary to monitor only the core drivers and the correlation coefficients. In reality, it is prudent to monitor everything to minimize the chance of surprises.

18.2.7 Delegating Capacity Planning

Capacity planning is often done by the technical staff. However, with good metrics and a clear understanding of how core drivers affect your resource requirements, you can decouple the capacity planning from the deployment. A program manager can do the capacity planning and ordering, while technical staff take care of deployment.

You can enable non-technical staff to do the capacity planning by building a capacity planning dashboard as part of your monitoring system. Create one or more web pages with capacity data in a specialized view, ideally with the ability to create graphs automatically. Make this dashboard accessible within the organization separately from the main monitoring dashboard. This way anyone in the organization can access the data in a reasonable form to justify capital expenditure on additional capacity.

Sometimes the decision is not to buy more resources but rather to make more efficient use of existing resources. Examples might include compressing data rather than buying more storage or bandwidth, or using better algorithms rather than increasing memory or CPU. Testing such scenarios relies on resource regression, which we will examine next.

18.3 Resource Regression

A resource regression is a calculation of the difference in resource usage between one release or version and another. It is expected that each software release will have slightly different resource needs. If a new software release uses significantly more resources, that discrepancy is often unintended; in other words, it is a bug that should be reported. If it is intended, it means capacity planners need to adjust their models and purchasing plans.

To perform a resource regression, do workflow analysis based on the user transactions associated with a release. This is simply a fancy way of saying that you make lists of which capabilities are possible with the new release and which kind of resource usage goes with each capability. Then, for each capability, you multiply by the number of projected transactions per customer and the number of customers active. This will give you a resource projection for the new release.

For example, suppose you have a photo sharing site. There are three main transactions that your site has with a customer. First, the user can log in and edit their profile data. Second, the user can upload a picture. Third, the user can view a picture. Each of these transactions has a resource cost that can be measured. How would you measure it? The easiest way would be by analyzing data from a staging system with sample users whom you control.

By using automated testing scripts to simulate user login and transactions, you can have a known number of users, each involved in a particular transaction. The monitoring data you gather from that system can then be compared with data from the baseline (no simulated users) system. It is reasonable to assume that the differences in memory, disk, CPU, and network usage are due to the user transactions. Subtract the baseline footprint of each of those resources from the loaded footprint. The difference can then be divided by the number of user transactions, allowing you to get a sense of the per-transaction resource usage. Be sure to load test your predictions to see whether the resource usage scales linearly or whether inflection points appear as you add more transactions.

When calculating workflow analysis, be sure to include infrastructure resource costs as well. How many DNS lookups are required for this end-to-end transaction? How many database calls? A single transaction may touch many services within your system infrastructure, and those service resources must be assessed as well and scaled appropriately along with the transaction server scaling.

18.4 Launching New Services

Now that we understand how to plan for capacity on an existing system, let's talk about launching new services. Launching a new service is difficult and risky because you have no prior experience or service metrics to plan the initial capacity required. For large services, testing may be unreliable, as there may be insufficient capacity on a staging environment for a true test.

Adding to this risk, launch day is often when the service will have the most media scrutiny. If the system runs out of capacity and becomes unreliable, the media will have nothing to write about except what a terrible launch it was. This makes a bad first impression on customers.

One way to mitigate this risk is to find a way to have a slow ramp-up in the number of active users. For example, enabling a product but not announcing it (a **soft launch**) gives engineers time to find and fix problems as they happen. However, if additional resources are needed and will require weeks of lead time, only the slowest of ramp-ups will help.

Relying on a slow ramp-up is not an option for well-known companies. Google and Facebook haven't had a slow ramp-up on a new service, even with a soft launch, for years. Any new service is immediately flooded with new users.

Therefore the ability to do accurate capacity planning on new services has become a highly desired skill.

Fortunately, there is a technique that can be used to bridge the knowledge gap, and that technique is the **dark launch**. Facebook used a dark launch of its chat messaging system to ensure that the company would bring a reliable system to its user base.

In a dark launch, the new feature is released into production with simulated traffic, in effect treating the production environment as a well-controlled testbed for the new feature's resource needs. No user-visible information is created—service agents exercise a feature silently from the user perspective, but employ real user activity to trigger simulated activity for the new feature.

For example, suppose we wanted to add a photo editing capability to our photo sharing site from the earlier example. To do a dark launch, we might do the following:

- Create a software toggle for the photo editing feature: on or off. (Software toggles were described in Section 2.1.9.)
- Create a dark launch toggle for the photo editing feature: on or off.
- Create a sample photo editing transaction that is saved to a dummy area. The customer's photo is not changed, but behind the scenes the photo is edited and a modified version saved elsewhere.
- Modify an existing transaction to behave differently when the dark launch toggle is "on." In this case, photo upload will be modified to run the sample photo editing transaction 25 percent of the time that uploads occur, feeding the uploaded photo into the editing transaction.

The 25 percent value is only an example—it could be any percentage. It simply represents a known quantity that can be calculated at a later time based on transaction data. Starting with a more conservative number such as 5 percent is likely to be a good idea with an actual complex service. Use the resource regression analysis technique to see which kind of resource costs are associated with the new launch feature. This will give you a first pass at capacity planning for the new feature launch, based on actual production environment usage. Adjust your capacity accordingly, and then continue the dark launch, fixing any bugs that are found and adjusting capacity as needed. Gradually increase the percentage of sample dark launch transactions until you reach a level where real usage is likely to occur. Be sure to go beyond that by some percentage to give yourself headroom.

Finally the dark launch is turned off and the feature is turned on for the customers. With the appropriate toggles, this can all be done without rolling a new release. In practice, enough bug fixing happens during a dark launch that you will almost certainly upgrade new releases during the dark launch period. However, all of these bugs should be invisible to your customer community, and your actual launch will be the better for having done a dark launch.

> **Case Study: Facebook Chat's Dark Launch**
>
> The term "dark launch" was coined in 2008 when Facebook revealed the technique was used to launch Facebook Chat. The launch raised an important issue: how to go from zero to 70 million users overnight without scaling issues. An outage would be highly visible. Long before the feature was visible to users, Facebook pages were programmed to make connections to the chat servers, query for presence information, and simulate message sends without a single UI element drawn on the page (Letuchy 2008). This gave Facebook an opportunity to find and fix any issues ahead of time. If you were a Facebook user back then, you had no idea your web browser was sending simulated chat messages but the testing you provided was greatly appreciated. (Section 11.7 has a related case study.)

18.5 Reduce Provisioning Time

As discussed in Section 18.1.4, one of the factors influencing your headroom requirement is resource acquisition and provisioning time. If you can reduce the acquisition and provisioning time, you can reduce your headroom, which in turn reduces the amount of capital investment that is idle. In addition, faster acquisition and provisioning enables faster response to changing demands and can be a significant competitive advantage.

However, idle excess capacity also can be a result of being unable to reduce the available resources quickly. Being able to jettison increased capacity, and its associated costs, at will is also a competitive advantage. There are a number of approaches to reducing idle excess capacity, and they can often be combined to have greater effect:

- **Lease computers rather than purchase them.** There may be a shorter acquisition time depending on what is in stock, and the ability to terminate a lease and return the hardware may be useful. Leasing can be used to shift capacity costs from capital expenditures into operational costs.
- **Use virtual resources** that are allocated quickly and have little or no startup costs associated with them. These resources can also be quickly terminated, and billing reflects only actual usage of the resources.

- **Improve the ordering process for new hardware resources.** Preapprove budget decisions and create standardized ordering.
- **Improve installation time.** Part of the provisioning time is the time from when hardware hits the loading dock to when it is actually in use. Find ways to streamline the actual rack and burn-in.
- **Manage your time.** Make it a priority to install new equipment the moment it arrives. Have no idle hardware. Alternatively, dedicate staff to doing this. Hire non-system administrators ("technicians") to unbox and rack mount systems.
- **Work with vendors** (supply chain management) to reduce ordering time.
- **Place many smaller orders rather than one huge order.** This improves parallelism of the system. Vendors may be able to chop up one big order into periodic deliveries and monthly billing. A transition from one huge order every 6 months to 6 monthly orders and deliveries may have billing, capital cost, and labor benefits.
- **Automate configuration** so that once new hardware is racked, it is soon available for use.

18.6 Summary

Capacity planning is the process that ensures services have enough resources when they are needed. It is challenging to prevent service interruptions due to lack of capacity and, simultaneously, preserve capital by adding only the capacity required at any given time.

Standard capacity planning is based on current usage and simple rates of change. It assumes future resource needs will be similar to current usage plus two kinds of growth. Normal or organic growth is what is expected based on current trends. Planned growth is what is expected due to new initiatives such as marketing plans. Additional capacity, called headroom, is added to handle short-term spikes. Based on the timetable showing lead time (i.e., how long it takes to acquire and configure new resources), capacity schedules can be determined. By reducing lead time, capacity planning can be more agile.

Standard capacity planing is sufficient for small sites, sites that grow slowly, and sites with simple needs. It is insufficient for large, rapidly growing sites. They require more advanced techniques.

Advanced capacity planning is based on core drivers, capacity limits of individual resources, and sophisticated data analysis such as correlation, regression analysis, and statistical models for forecasting. Regression analysis finds correlations between core drivers and resources. Forecasting uses past data to predict future needs.

With sufficiently large sites, capacity planning is a full-time job, often done by project managers with technical backgrounds. Some organizations employ full-time statisticians to build complex models and dashboards that provide the information required by a project manager.

Good capacity planning models can also detect unexpected changes in resource needs—for example, a new software release that unexpectedly requires more resources.

Capacity planning is highly data-driven and uses past data to predict future needs. Launching a brand-new service, therefore, poses a special challenge. Dark launches and other techniques permit services to gather accurate data before the service is visible to users.

To improve cost-effectiveness, reduce the time it takes to provision new resources. Provisioning involves acquiring, configuring, and putting new resources into production. Total provisioning time is called lead time. Long lead times tie up capital. Reducing lead time reduces idle capacity and improves financial efficiency.

Capacity planning is a complex and important part of reliable operations.

Exercises

1. Describe how standard capacity planning works.
2. Describe how advanced capacity planning works.
3. Compare and contrast standard and advanced capacity planning. When is each best used?
4. What are the challenges of launching a new service?
5. List the resources used by your main application.
6. Use regression analysis to determine the correlation between two resources.
7. Create a forecasting model for a service's capacity needs.
8. Describe how you would implement a dark launch of a new feature in your main application.
9. What is a resource regression and why is it important?
10. Perform a resource regression between your current application release and a previous release. Discuss what you find and its implications for your capacity planning.
11. There are many ways to reduce provisioning time. Which three ways would have the most impact in your environment? (Alternatively, group the methods listed in this chapter by categories of your choosing.)
12. Why is it desirable to reduce provisioning time?

Chapter 19

Creating KPIs

> The only man I know who
> behaves sensibly is my tailor;
> he takes my measurements anew
> each time he sees me. The rest go on
> with their old measurements and
> expect me to fit them.
>
> —George Bernard Shaw

A startup decides that web site speed is important to the success of its business. Management decides that page load time will be the **key performance indicator (KPI)** that determines employee pay raises at the end of the year. Soon services that shared machines are given dedicated resources to avoid any possibility of inter-process interference. Only the fastest machines are purchased. Many features are delayed as time is dedicated to code optimization. By the end of the year, the KPI measurements confirm the web pages have extremely fast load times. The goal has been reached. Sadly, the company has no money for raises because it has spent its way out of business.

Measurement affects behavior. People change their behavior when they know they are being measured. People tend to find the shortest path to meeting a goal. This creates unintended side effects.

In this chapter we talk about smart ways to set goals and create KPIs. Managers need to set goals that drive desired behavior to achieve desired results while minimizing the unintended consequences. Done correctly, this enables us to manage operations in a way that is more efficient, is fairer, and produces better results.

Setting KPIs is quite possibly the most important thing that a manager does. It is often said that a manager has two responsibilities: setting priorities and providing the resources to get those priorities done. Setting KPIs is an important way to verify that those priorities are being met.

The effectiveness of the KPI itself must be evaluated by making measurements before and after introducing it and then observing the differences. This changes management from a loose set of guesses into a set of scientific methods. We measure the quality of our system, set or change policies, and then measure again to see their effect. This is more difficult than it sounds.

19.1 What Is a KPI?

A key performance indicator is a type of performance measurement used to evaluate the success of an organization or a particular activity. Generally KPIs are used to encourage an organization or team to reach a particular goal.

KPIs should be directly tied to the organization's strategy, vision, or mission. Generally they come from executive management but often other levels of management create KPIs for their own purposes, usually as a way of furthering the KPIs relevant to them.

A well-defined KPI follows the SMART criteria: **S**pecific, **M**easurable, **A**chievable, **R**elevant, and **T**ime-phrased. It is specific, unambiguously defined and not overly broad. It is measurable so that success or failure can be objectively quantified. It is achievable under reasonable circumstances. It is relevant to the success of the organization as a whole, or the project as a whole. It is time-phrased, which means the relevant time period is specified.

Goals should be measurable so that one can unambiguously determine what fraction of the goal was achieved, or if it was achieved at all. Things you can count, such as uptime, disk space, and the number of major features released this month, are all measurable. Example measurable goals include the following:

- Provide 10T of disk space to each user.
- Page load time less than 300 ms.
- Fewer than 10 "severity 1" open bugs.
- Launch 10 major features this month.
- 99.99 percent service uptime.

Non-measurable goals cannot be quantified or do not include a specific numerical goal. Some examples are shown here:

- Get better at writing Python code.
- Get better at failing over to DR systems.
- Provide more free disk space.
- Make pages load faster.

These are all good things, of course. They could all be turned into measurable goals. However, as stated, they are not measurable.

KPIs go by many different names. Sometimes they are informally called "metrics," which is true in the sense that a KPI is a kind of metric—the kind used to drive organizational behavior. However, that would be like calling oranges "fruit" and expecting people to know you mean a specific kind of fruit.

Intel's OKR System

Intel uses a related term called OKRs, which stands for "objectives and key results." OKRs are often used to set goals at the personal, team, division, and company levels. The key results are often measured via KPIs. The acronym OKR was popularized by venture capitalist John Doerr, who brought the concept to Google. Rick Klau's video "IIow Google Sets Goals: OKRs" is an excellent explanation of OKRs and serves as a tutorial on how to adopt Google's OKR system to your team or business (Klau 2012).

19.2   Creating KPIs

Creating good KPIs requires serious time and effort. This process has many steps. First we envision what the world would look like if the goal was met. Next we determine ways to quantify how close we are to that ideal. This leads to one or more potential KPIs. Then we consider all the ways that people could behave but still match the incentive. Based on that information, we revise the potential KPIs. Now we repeat these steps until we have our final KPI.

When defined correctly, KPIs can improve a team's performance by 10 to 30 percent. The total cost of a typical engineer, including salary, benefits, and other expenses, can be $200,000 or more per year. For an organization with 50 engineers, such an improvement is worth $1 million to $3 million per year. Most managers facing a $3 million project would dedicate days or weeks of planning to assure its proper execution. In terms of return on investment, spending 10 hours to create such an improvement has a 1:1000 or 1:3000 payoff. Who would turn down such a return? Yet KPIs are often created with little forethought and the unintended side effects negate any benefit.

These numbers should be your personal incentive to develop the skills required to create effective KPIs. Better KPIs are, quite possibly, more important than anything else you say or do.

19.2.1 Step 1: Envision the Ideal

Pause to imagine what the world would be like if this goal was met perfectly. How would it be different from what it is today? Think in terms of the end result, not how we get there. Exercise your creativity. How would you describe the company, project, or service? How would resources be used?

One place to look for inspiration is subteams that are doing well in this area. Generally they won't have a KPI you can use, but they often have qualities you want to reproduce. Sometimes the quality may be their culture, not a particular tangible outcome.

The most common mistake we see is managers skipping this first step and going directly to creating a KPI formula. Taking this shortcut is a bad idea. If you don't first decide on the destination, it isn't likely you'll get there.

19.2.2 Step 2: Quantify Distance to the Ideal

Ask yourself, how can we measure how far we are now from this ideal? We create many candidate KPIs that might measure this distance. The measurement might be a time duration, a count, the number of times something happens or doesn't happen, a quantity, or any other numerical quantification. The measurement should be real and repeatable.

For example, if the ideal is users having a web experience that is faster than with native software applications on a PC, the way to measure our distance to the ideal would involve measuring page load time. If the ideal envisions a world with no security breaches, the way to measure how far we are from that ideal would be the count of known security breaches detected each month. The ideal might also be that all detected intrusions are investigated within a certain time frame, in which case we would quantify both the time from detection to start of investigation and the duration of the investigation.

19.2.3 Step 3: Imagine How Behavior Will Change

For each potential KPI, try to defeat it. What are all the ways that people could behave but still match the incentive? How could a person maximize his or her personal gain?

Set aside hope that employees will "just behave." If they are following your formula, they're behaving. You can't expect them to read your mind and understand your intention.

Salespeople make a good example. If they are selling many products, they will immediately analyze the commission structure and figure out which product to focus on to maximize the use of their time. If they sell two products with the same price and same commission rate but one is easier to sell, the other product will be starved for attention. If they sell 10 products, each with a different price, commission, and likelihood of a successful sale, they will do the math and figure out which products to actively sell; the others will be ignored. This is not cheating, but rather following the rules they've been given. This is why some companies have separate sales teams for big customers and small customers. Who would spend time trying to make $1,000 deals with small customers when they can make million-dollar deals with big companies? The sales cycle would have to be 1000 times longer for the big deals to be less efficient. Without dedicated sales teams, the company would miss out on any sales to small companies.

Similarly, engineers will examine the KPIs given and follow them as stated. Again, this is not "gaming the system," but simply following the rules. This is doing what the engineers were told to do. Gaming the system would be falsifying logs or going around the KPIs to benefit themselves. Do not be upset or surprised when people conform to what you wrote, rather than what you intended.

Returning to our earlier security example, the easiest way to achieve the goals as stated is to turn off any mechanisms that detect such breaches. This is probably not the intended reaction. Thus, it should be revised.

19.2.4 Step 4: Revise and Select

Based on what we've learned in Step 3, we revise the KPI. We may select one KPI over another or loop back to Step 1 and start over.

Seek confirming and non-confirming data. For example, calculate the KPI based on past or current metrics. If such metrics are not available, test against simulated data.

Seek the opinions of others. Ask how they would behave under such KPIs. You will get different answers depending on whether the person has a vested interest in the KPI. If the person's work will be judged by the KPI, filter what he or she says based on the individual's potential bias toward personal gain or preferring to be judged less harshly. If the person would benefit from the KPI's goal succeeding, he or she will have the opposite bias but may not be in tune with the internal processes that can be used to subvert the KPI.

Asking for feedback on KPIs that have not been announced creates the potential that rumors will spread about the new KPI. Like the children's game "Telephone," where the message becomes more and more misconstrued as it gets passed along, the rumor of the new KPI will invariably portray it as harsher as it moves from person to person. This will hurt morale and will result in misinformation that confuses people when the real KPI is announced. The worst situation is where the draft KPI is tossed out but the rumors persist. Therefore discussing potential KPIs should be done with an understanding of who they can be shared with.

It is sometimes possible to test the KPI on one team or one project before applying it to all the others. This gives us real-world experience with how people react.

Alternatively, it can be employed during a trial period so that people expect some revision before it becomes policy.

We don't have many chances to revise the KPI after it becomes policy. If a KPI is announced and has unintended negative side effects, you should modify the KPI to fix any bugs. However, if the KPI changes again and again, management looks like they don't know what they are doing. Employees lose trust. Morale will suffer greatly if the rules keep changing. People will feel like the rug is being pulled out from under their feet if they have just finished adjusting their behavior to align with one KPI when it changes and requires opposite adjustments.

Because of this, great effort should be put into getting it right the first time. Because of the benefits of a well-structured KPI, and the potential damage of a badly engineered KPI, this effort should be given high priority and be taken seriously. The final KPI doesn't have to be simple, but it has to be easy to understand. If it is easy to understand, it will be easy to follow.

Returning to our security breach example, our last draft contained a bug in that it did not include both the coverage of the intrusion detection system and the number of intrusions detected. Thus, we revise it to be three KPIs: one that reflects the percentage of subnets that are covered by the intrusion detection system, one that reflects the total number of intrusions, and one that reflects the duration of investigations.

19.2.5 Step 5: Deploy the KPI

The next step is to deploy the KPI, or institute it as policy. This is mostly a communication function. The new KPI must be communicated to the team that is responsible for the KPI, plus key stakeholders, management, and so on.

Deploying the KPI means making people aware of it as well as putting into place mechanisms to measure the KPI. The KPI should be deployed with the assumption that it may require revision in the future, but this should not be an excuse to do a bad job in creating it.

If at all possible, the metrics that are used to calculate KPIs should be collected automatically. This might occur via the monitoring system, or it might be done by extracting the information from logs. Either way, the process should not require human intervention. Even if you forget about them, the metrics you need should automatically accumulate for you.

If the metrics cannot be collected automatically, there are two actions to take. One is to find a way to ensure that the metrics are collected manually. This could be an automated email reminder or a repeating calendar entry. The other is to develop a mechanism so that the collection will be automated. There are no metrics that can't be collected automatically, only metrics whose collection has not yet been automated.

Once the data is collected, a dashboard should be created. A dashboard is a web page that shows a visualization of the KPI. It may have related metrics and information useful for drilling down into the data.

Important KPIs should have a second dashboard, one that is appropriate for large displays. Install a large monitor in a hallway or other common area and display this dashboard continuously. Such displays should use large fonts and have graphics that are easy to view from a distance. Such displays serve as an important reminder of the KPIs' status and can become a point of pride when the KPIs are met.

19.3 Example KPI: Machine Allocation

Suppose we are developing a KPI to assess the quality of the process by which virtual machines (VMs) are created. This KPI may apply to a public cloud service provider, it may be geared toward a team that creates VMs for an internal cloud service within a large company, or perhaps it is intended just to assess the process that a team uses for creating its own VMs.

19.3.1 The First Pass

We begin with Step 1, Envision the Ideal. In an ideal world, people would get the VMs they want as soon as they request them. There would be no delay.

In Step 2, Quantify Distance to the Ideal, we simply measure the duration of time from the request to when the VM is created.

In Step 3, Imagine How Behavior Will Change, we brainstorm all the ways that people could behave but still match the incentive. We foresee many challenges.

One challenge is that people could get very creative about the definition of "start time." It could be the time when the request is received from the user, or it could be when the creation process actually begins. If requests are made by creating tickets in a helpdesk request system, the delay before someone processes the ticket could be very large. If the requests come in via a web portal or API, they may be queued up and processed sequentially. If that wait time is not included in the metric, it would make the team look good, but would not truly reflect the service users receive.

A more realistic indication comes from measuring the end-to-end result from the customer's perspective. Doing so might inspire the team to move from a ticket-based request system to a self-service portal or API. This would not only replace the human process of re-entering data from a ticket, but also ensure that all the information needed to complete the process is collected at the very beginning. Thus it avoids the back-and-forth communication that might be required to collect information the user forgot or didn't know to include in the ticket.

People could also demonstrate creativity in how they define when the request is "complete." The incentive is to interpret completion time as soon as possible. Is the VM created when the VM Manager allocates RAM, disk, and other resources to create the empty virtual machine, or when that virtual machine has loaded its operating system? If a different team is responsible for the OS installation mechanism, can we be "complete" once the OS installation starts, whether or not it finishes successfully? To the user, a failed, half-installed VM is worthless, but a mistated KPI might permit it.

The team could rationalize any of these end points to be the end time. Thus, we go back to Step 1 and use what we have learned to do better.

19.3.2 The Second Pass

Our original definition was a very narrow definition of the end result. Let's broaden the definition and focus on what the user sees as the desired result.

To the user, the end result is that the VM is ready for use for the purpose the user intended.

Ideally, the user always receives the VM that has been requested: it has the right name, size (amount of RAM, disk, and vCPU), operating system, and so on. Thus, our ideal world implies that the right information is gathered from the user and the user receives a VM that works as requested.

Perhaps some roadblocks might prevent the customer from using the machine right away. These should be included in the metric. For example, to use the machine requires DNS changes to be propagated, access controls to be implemented, and so on.

Also consider the use of company resources. Can users request an infinite number of VMs? Who pays for them? Billing for resources is often an effective way to lead users to restrain their use of a resource. We'll use that.

Therefore we revise our ideal-world definition as follows: Users get a usable VM, as they requested, as quickly as possible, with billing arrangements established.

Continuing our example into Step 2, we define the start time as when the request is initially received from the user. The end time is when the VM is usable by the requester. We can define "usable" as the user being able to log into the machine. This automatically includes DNS propagation and access control as well as issues we are unaware of.

The draft KPI becomes:

The 90th percentile creation time, which starts when the request is created, and ends when the user is able to log into the machine.

We use a percentile instead of an average because, as discussed in Section 17.5, averages can be misleading. A single long-delayed creation would unfairly ruin an average.

An ideal world has no resource shortages. Anytime a new VM is needed, there would be capacity to allocate one. New capacity would come online just in time to fulfill any request. We could add a metric related to capacity planning but it is better to keep the KPI at a high level of abstraction, rather than micro-managing how the service is run. We are concerned with the end result. If capacity planning is not done right, that fact will surface due to the KPI we have constructed as requests are held while waiting for new capacity to come on line. That said, if capacity planning becomes an issue, we can later establish KPIs specifically related to capacity planning efficiency.

In Step 3, we imagine how behavior will change. If a cancelled request does not count toward the KPI, we could simply cancel any request that takes too long. For example, if requests are made via a helpdesk ticket, if the user doesn't supply all the information required to complete the task, we could cancel the request and let the user know what information we need when the user creates the new ticket. This would be terrible behavior but would improve the KPI.

If the OS installation step is unreliable and requires multiple restarts, this would delay the total creation time. To improve our KPI numbers, the operators could simply cancel jobs that fail rather than retry them. Again, this would benefit the KPI but not the user.

We could work around this loophole by adding significant complexity to the KPI. However, often it is easier to prevent bad behavior by letting people know they are being watched. First, we can publish the number of customer-initiated cancellation requests. This permits management to quietly watch for shenanigans. Second, we can privately agree with the team's manager that such behavior will be discouraged. Executive management can assist by creating an environment with high standards, including only hiring managers who wouldn't tolerate such behavior. Such managers would, for example, notice that the system doesn't log who cancelled a request, and require that this be changed so that the KPI can properly measure customer-initiated cancellations versus cancellations from operational staff.

Step 4, Revise and Select, results in the following KPI:

The 90th percentile creation time, measured from when the request is received from the user until the user is able to log into the machine. Manual and automatic retries after a failure are counted as part of the original request, not as separate requests. Requests that are outright canceled will be logged and investigated if within a week there are more than 5 operator-initiated cancellations or if more than 1 percent of all requests end in customer-initiated cancellation.

Step 5 deploys the KPI. The KPI is communicated to key stakeholders. Measurements required to calculate the KPI plus the computation itself should be automated and presented in a dashboard. In our example, the system might generate the metric we require or it might timestamp the request and completion times, requiring some post-processing to correlate the two and calculate the duration. However the metric is gathered, it should then be stored and made available to whatever data visualization system is in use so that a graphical dashboard can be created.

19.3.3 Evaluating the KPI

A few weeks after deployment, the initial results should be audited for unintended negative side effects.

In our example, depending on how often VMs are created, the resulting KPI measurements might be reviewed daily, weekly, or monthly. These results might inspire additional metrics to isolate problem areas. The VM creation process is made up of many steps. By measuring the wait time before each step, as well as the duration of each step, opportunities for improvement can be easily found.

For example, measuring lead time might reveal a long span of time between when a ticket is filed and when the actual creation begins, indicating that a self-service request system would have a large benefit. Lead time might reveal that requests are often delayed for weeks waiting for new resources to be installed, indicating that capacity planning needs improvement. Collecting data on how many times a task fails and is retried might indicate that the OS installation process is unstable and should be improved. Perhaps DNS propagation delays can be tightened or the OS installation process can be made faster using image-based installations. Monitoring network utilization might find an overloaded link that, if improved, could result in faster installation time in general. By analyzing the types of requests, it may be determined that a few standard-size VMs can be pre-created and simply handed out as needed.

All these changes are viable. By taking measurements, we can predict how each one might improve the KPI. By collecting KPI measurements before and after changes, we can measure the actual improvement.

19.4 Case Study: Error Budget

Benjamin Treynor Sloss, Vice President of Engineering at Google, revealed a highly successful KPI called Google Error Budget. The goal was to encourage high uptime without stifling innovation, and to encourage innovation without encouraging undue risk.

19.4.1 Conflicting Goals

There is a historic conflict between developers and operations teams. Developers want to launch new features; operations teams want stability.

Developers are in the business of making change. They are rewarded for new features, especially ones that are highly visible to the end customers. They would prefer to have each feature they create pushed into production as fast as possible so as not to delay gratification. The question they get the most from management is likely to be, "When will it ship?"

Operations people are in the business of stability. They want nothing to break so they don't get paged or otherwise have a bad day. This makes them risk averse. If they could, they would reject a developer's request to push new releases into production. If it ain't broke, don't fix it. The question they get the most from management is likely to be, "Why was the system down?"

Once a system is stable, operations would prefer to reject new software releases. However, it is culturally unacceptable to do so. Instead, rules are created to prevent problems. They start as simple rules: no upgrades on Friday; if something goes wrong, we shouldn't have to spend the weekend debugging it. Then Mondays are eliminated because human errors are perceived to increase then. Then early mornings are eliminated, as are late nights. More and more safeguards are added prior to release: 1 percent tests go from being optional to required. Basically operations never says "no" directly but enough rules accumulate that "no" is virtually enforced.

Not to be locked out of shipping code, developers work around these rules. They hide large amounts of untested code releases behind flag flips; they encode major features in configuration files so that software upgrades aren't required, just new configurations. Workarounds like these circumvent operations' approvals and do so at great risk.

This situation is not the fault of the developers or the operations teams. It is the fault of the manager who decreed that any outage is bad. One hundred percent uptime is for pacemakers, not web sites. The typical user is connecting to the web site via WiFi, which has an availability of 99 percent, possibly less. This dwarfs any goal of perfection demanded from on high.

19.4.2 A Unified Goal

Typically four 9s (99.99 percent) availability is sufficient for a web site. That leaves a "budget" of 0.01 percent downtime, a bit less than an hour each year (52.56 minutes). Thus the Google Error Budget was created. Rather than seeking perfect uptime, a certain amount of imperfection is budgeted for each quarter. Without permission to fail, innovation is stifled. The Error Budget encourages risk taking without encouraging carelessness.

At the start of each quarter, the budget is reset to 13 minutes, which is about 0.01 percent of 90 days. Any unavailability subtracts from the budget. If the budget has not been exhausted, developers may release as often as they want. When the budget is exhausted, all launches stop. An exception is made for high-priority security fixes. The releases begin again when the counter resets and there is once again a 13-minute budget in place.

As a result, operations is no longer put into the position of having to decide whether to permit a launch. Being in such a position makes them "the bad guys" every time they say no, and leads developers to think of them as "the enemy to be defeated." More importantly, it is unfair to put operations in this position because of the information asymmetry inherent in this relationship. Developers know the code better than operations and therefore are in a better position to perform testing and judge the quality of the release. Operations staff, though they are unlikely to admit it, are not mind readers.

19.4.3 Everyone Benefits

For developers, the Error Budget creates incentives to improve reliability by offering them something they value highly: the opportunity to do more releases. This encourages them to test releases more thoroughly, to adopt better release practices, and to invest effort in building frameworks that improve operations and reliability. Previously these tasks might have been considered distractions from creating new features. Now these tasks create the ability to push more features.

For example, developers may create a framework that permits new code to be tested better, or to perform 1 percent experiments with less effort. They are encouraged to take advantage of existing frameworks they may not have considered before. For example, implementation of lame-duck mode, as described in Section 2.1.3, may be built into the web framework they use, but they have simply not taken advantage of it.

More importantly, the budget creates peer pressure between developer teams to have high standards. Development for a given service is usually the result of many subteams. Each team wants to launch frequently. Yet one team can blow the budget for all teams if they are not careful. Nobody wants to be the last team to adopt a technology or framework that improves launch success. Also, there is less information asymmetry between developer teams. Therefore teams can set high standards for code reviews and other such processes. (Code reviews are discussed in Section 12.7.6.)

This does not mean that Google considers it okay to be down for an hour each year. If you recall from Section 1.3, user-visible services are often composed of the output of many other services. If one of those services is not responding, the composition can still succeed by replacing the missing part with generic filler, by showing blank space, or by using other graceful degradation techniques as described in Section 2.1.10.

This one KPI has succeeded in improving availability at Google and at the same time has aligned developer and operations priorities, helping them work together. It removes operations from the "bad guy" role of having to refuse releases, and it gives developers an incentive to balance time between adding new features and improving operational processes. It is simple to explain and, since availability is already tightly monitored, easy to implement. As a result, all of Google's services benefit.

19.5 Summary

Managing by using KPIs is a radical departure from traditional IT management. It is effective because it sets goals and permits the smart people whom you hired to work out how to achieve them. Those people are closer to the task and more knowledgable about the technical details at hand, making them better suited to inventing ways to achieve the goal.

Creating effective KPIs is difficult—and it should be. It yields a huge return on investment when done right. Something that has a 1:1000 payoff is not going to be easy. KPIs should be specific, measurable, achievable, relevant, and time-phrased. Poorly written KPIs have unintended consequences when people follow the rules as written rather than what you intended. It is important to think through all the ways that the KPI may be interpreted, and the actions that people might take to improve their performance on this metric.

Spend time up front examining and amending the KPI to make sure that the KPI will most likely give the result you want. Do not over-complicate the KPI. If you suspect that the KPI might trigger an adverse behavior, measure and publish that behavior as well, and make sure that your managers know to watch out for and discourage it.

Remember that the KPI should be achievable. One hundred percent availability is not achievable, unless the definition of "availability" is adjusted to cover more than you intended. However four 9s (99.99 percent) is achievable. Google's Error Budget KPI successfully uses that target to achieve the desired result: a stable service with innovative new features deployed frequently. It is an excellent example of how a good KPI can benefit everyone.

Exercises

1. What is a KPI?
2. What are the SMART criteria? Briefly describe each one.
3. Give examples of unintended side effects of KPIs.

4. What are the steps for creating KPIs? Evaluate which steps are the most difficult and provide justification as to why they are difficult.

5. Which KPIs do you track in your environment and why?

6. Create an effective KPI for assessing a service in your environment. After creating it, have three other people tell you how they would maximize their personal gain. Revise the KPI. Report on the ideal (Step 1), the initial KPI(s), people's reactions, and the final KPI.

7. How does the KPI you created address each of the SMART criteria?

8. When managed through KPIs, why do people follow what is written rather than what was intended? Is this good or bad?

9. The example in Section 19.3 always discusses measuring the end-to-end time based on the customer's perspective. Would there be value in measuring the time from when the VM creation starts to when it is usable?

10. How would you modify the KPI created in Section 19.3 if after the request was made, the requester's manager had to approve the request?

Chapter 20

Operational Excellence

> A company can seize
> extraordinary opportunities
> only if it is very good at
> the ordinary operations.

—Marcel Telles

This chapter is about measuring or assessing the quality of service operations. It proposes an assessment tool and gives examples of how to use it to evaluate an individual service, a team, or multiple teams.

In Chapter 19, we discussed how to create KPIs that drive desired behavior to achieve specific goals. This chapter describes an assessment system that evaluates the degree of formality and optimization of processes—that is, whether processes are ad hoc, or formal, or actively optimized. This assessment is different than KPIs in that it gauges teams on a more generic level, one that is more comparable across teams or across services within a team.

Such assessments help identify areas of improvement. We can then make changes, reassess, and measure the improvement. If we do this periodically, we create an environment of continuous improvement.

20.1 What Does Operational Excellence Look Like?

What does great system administration look like? Like art and literature, it is difficult to define other than to say you know it when you see it. This ambiguity makes it difficult to quantitatively measure how well or poorly a system administration team is performing.

High-performing organizations have smooth operations, well-designed policies and practices, and discipline in what they do. They meet or exceed the needs of their customers and delight them with innovations that meet future needs often before such needs ever surface. The organization is transparent about how it plans, operates, provides services, and handles costs or charge-backs to customers. The vast majority of customers are happy customers. Even dissatisfied customers feel they have a voice, are heard, and have a channel to escalate their issues. Everyone feels the operations organization moves the company forward. Its funding reflects a reasonable budget for the work the organization does. The organization makes its successes visible and, more importantly, is honest and forthright when it comes to discussing its own faults. The organization is constantly improving. Outages and escalated issues result in action plans that reduce future occurrences of that problem. The world is constantly changing, and the organization incorporates new technologies and techniques to improve its inner workings as well as the services it provides.

Operations organizations seem to fall into three broad categories or strata: the great ones, the ones that want to be great, and the ones that don't even know what great is.

We estimate that 5 to 10 percent of all operations teams fall into this first category. They know and use the best practices of our industry. Some even invent new ones. The next 25 to 30 percent know that the best practices exist but are struggling to adopt them. The remaining super-majority do not even know these best practices exist.

Science fiction writer William Gibson famously said, "The future is already here—it's just not very evenly distributed." Likewise, the knowledge of how to be a great system administration team is here—it's just not very evenly distributed.

20.2 How to Measure Greatness

Measuring the quality of an operations team is extremely difficult. Other aspects of operations are easy to measure. For example, size can be measured by counting the number of team members, the number of services provided, or the dollars spent per year. Scale can be measured by counting the number of machines, the amount of storage, the total bandwidth used, and so on. We can measure efficiency using cost ratios.

Alas, quality is not so easy to measure.

Imagine for a moment that we could measure quality. Imagine we had a standard way to rate the quality of an operations team with a simple value on a scale of 0 to 1000. Also imagine that we could, possibly by some feat of magic, rank every operations organization in the world.

If we could do that, we could line all of these organizations up from "best" to "worst." The potential for learning would be incredible. We could observe what the top 50 percent do differently from the bottom 50 percent. Alternatively, a single organization could study the organizations ranked higher for inspiration on how to improve.

Alas, there is no such single measurement. Operations is just too complex. Therefore the measurement, or **assessment**, must reflect that complexity.

Assessments sound a lot like the grades we received in school, but the concept is very different. A student assessment evaluates an individual student's learning and performance. Grades assess learning, but they also incorporate attendance, participation, and effort. An assessment is more focused.

An assessment of a service is an evaluation based on specific criteria related to process maturity. It is not an evaluation of whether the service is popular, has high availability, or is fast. Not all services need to be popular, highly available, or fast. In contrast, all services need good processes to achieve whatever goals they do have. Therefore we assess process because good processes are a roadmap to success.

20.3 Assessment Methodology

This assessment methodology is a bottom-up assessment. A service is evaluated on eight attributes, called **operational responsibilities (OR)**. Each OR is assessed to be at one of five levels, with 5 being best. If assessment is done periodically, one can see progress over time. A weighted average can be used to roll up the eight individual assessments to arrive at a single number representing the service.

A team performs this assessment on each service. A team can be assessed using the weighted average of the services it provides. Teams can then be compared by stack rank. Teams can seek to improve their rank by identifying problem areas to work on. Best practices of high-ranking teams can be identified and shared.

The eight core ORs are geared toward service management and do not fit well for transactional IT services such as a helpdesk or other front-of-house, tier 1, or other customer-facing service center.

20.3.1 Operational Responsibilities

We have identified eight broad categories of operational responsibilities that most services have. Some may be more or less important for a particular service. Your team may emphasize or de-emphasize certain ORs by using a weighted average when performing roll-ups. Teams may also choose to add more ORs if need be.

The eight common operational responsibilities are as follows:

- **Regular Tasks (RT):** How normal, non-emergency, operational duties are handled; that is, how work is received, queued, distributed, processed, and verified, plus how periodic tasks are scheduled and performed.
- **Emergency Response (ER):** How outages and disasters are handled. This includes technical and non-technical processes performed during and after outages (response and remediation). This is the stuff of Chapters 6, 14, and 15.

- **Monitoring and Metrics (MM):** Collecting and using data to make decisions. Monitoring collects data about a system. A metric uses that data to measure a quantifiable component of performance. This is the stuff of Chapters 16, 17, and 19.

- **Capacity Planning (CP):** Determining future resource needs. Capacity planning involves the technical work of understanding how many resources are needed per unit of growth, plus non-technical aspects such as budgeting, forecasting, and supply chain management. This is the stuff of Chapter 18.

- **Change Management (CM):** Managing how services are purposefully changed over time. This includes the service delivery platform and how it is used to create, deliver, and push into production new application and infrastructure software. This includes firmware upgrades, network changes, and OS configuration management.

- **New Product Introduction and Removal (NPI/NPR):** Determining how new products and services are introduced into the environment and how they are deprecated and removed. This is a coordination function. Introducing and removing a service or product from an environment touches on multiple teams. Removing it involves tracking down the current users and managing the migration away from the service so it can be eliminated. For example, it may involve coordinating all teams that are touched by introducing a new brand of hardware into an ecosystem, launching an entirely new service, or decommissioning all instances of an old hardware platform.

- **Service Deploy and Decommission (SDD):** Determining how instances of an existing service are created and how they are turned off (decommissioned). After a service is introduced to an environment, it is deployed many times. After serving their purpose, these deployments are decommissioned. Examples include turning up a new datacenter, adding a replica of a service, or adding a replica of a database.

- **Performance and Efficiency (PE):** Measuring how well a service performs and how cost-effectively resources are used. A running service needs to have good performance without wasting resources. Examples include managing utilization or power efficiency and related costs.

The difference between NPI, SDD, and CM is subtle. NPI is how something is launched for the first time. It is the non-technical coordinating function for all related processes, many of which are technical. SDD is the technical process of deploying new instances of an existing item, whether it is a machine, a server, or a service. It may include non-technical processes such as budget approval, but these are in support of the technical goal. CM is how upgrades and changes are managed, either using a software deployment platform or an enterprise-style change management review board.

See Appendix A for more detailed descriptions of these, plus additional ORs specific to certain chapters of this book.

20.3.2 Assessment Levels

The rating, or assessment, uses a scale of 1 to 5, based on the **Capability Maturity Model (CMM)**. The CMM is a tool designed to measure the maturity of a capability or responsibility.

The term "maturity" indicates how formally or informally an operational aspect is practiced. The formality ranges from ad hoc and improvised, to having a documented process, to measuring the results of the process, to actively improving the system based on those measurements.

The CMM defines five levels:

- **Level 1, Initial:** Sometimes called Chaotic. This is the starting point for a new or undocumented process. Processes are ad hoc and rely on individual heroics.
- **Level 2, Repeatable:** The process is at least documented sufficiently such that it can be repeated with the same results.
- **Level 3, Defined:** Roles and responsibilities of the process are defined and confirmed.
- **Level 4, Managed:** The process is quantitatively managed in accordance with agreed-upon metrics.
- **Level 5, Optimizing:** Process management includes deliberate process optimization/improvement.

Level 1: Initial

At this level, the process is ad hoc. Results are inconsistent. Different people do tasks in different ways, usually with slightly different results. Processes are not documented. Work is untracked and requests are often lost. The team is unable to accurately estimate how long a task will take. Customers and partners may be happy with the service they receive, but there is no evidence-based determination at this time.

Level 2: Repeatable

At this level, the process has gone from being ad hoc to repeatable. The steps are defined in such a way that two different people can follow them and get the same results. The process is documented with no missing steps. The end results are relatively consistent. This is not to say that errors don't happen; after all, nothing is perfect. Because there is little measurement at this level, we may not know how often work is defective.

Level 3: Defined

At this level, the roles and responsibilities of the process are defined and confirmed. At the previous level, we learned what needed to be done. At this level, we know who is responsible for doing it, and we have definitions of how to measure correctness. The correctness measurements might not be collected, but at least the people involved know what they are. Each step has a series of checks to find errors as they happen rather than waiting until the end of the process to find out what went wrong. Duplication of effort is minimized. If we need to increase the rate of production, we can duplicate the process or add more capacity.

Level 4: Managed

At this level, aspects of the process are measured. How long each step takes is measured, including what portion of that time involved waiting to begin the process itself. Measurements include how often the process is done each month, how often it is performed without error, and how many times an exceptional case arises that requires special treatment and ad hoc processes. Variation is measured. These measurements are collected automatically. There is a dashboard that shows all of these measurements. It is easy to spot bottlenecks. Postmortems are published within a specific amount of time after an exception. Exceptions are cataloged and periodically reviewed. Requests to change a process are justified using measurement data to show that there is a problem. Capacity needs are predicted ahead of time.

Level 5: Optimizing

At this level, the measurements and metrics are being used to optimize the entire system. Improvements have been made at all the previous levels but the improvements made here are prompted by measurements and, after the change is made, the success is evaluated based on new measurements. Analyzing the duration of each step exposes bottlenecks and delays. Measurements indicate month-over-month improvements. We can stress-test the system to see what breaks, fix it, and then run the system at the new level.

Defined versus Managed

People often have a difficult time conceptualizing the subtle difference between Levels 3 and 4. Consider the example of assessing the load balancer aspect of a service. Load balancers can be used to improve capacity or resiliency, or both. Resiliency requires the system to run with enough spare capacity to withstand a failed backend. (See Section 6.3.)

   If there is a written policy that the load balancer is used for resiliency, this is a Level 3 behavior. If there exists monitoring that determines the current level of redundancy ($N + 0$, $N + 1$, and so on), this is Level 4 behavior. In this case, Level 4 is significantly more difficult to achieve because it requires a lot of effort to accurately determine the maximum capacity of a backend, which is required to know how much spare capacity is available.

Somewhat surprisingly, we have found many situations where there is no clear sense of how a load balancer is being used, or there is disagreement among team members about whether the role of a load balancer is to improve capacity or to improve resiliency. This demonstrates Level 1 behavior.

20.3.3 Assessment Questions and Look-For's

To perform an assessment for an operational responsibility, describe the current practices in that area. Based on this description, evaluate which level describes the current practices.

To help this process, we have developed a standard set of questions to ask to help form your description.

We've also developed a set of **look-for's** for each level. A look-for is a behavior, indicator, or outcome common to a service or organization at a particular level. In other words, it is "what a level looks like." If you read a description and it "sounds like you're talking about where I work," then that's a good indication that your organization is at that level for that service.

For example, in Regular Tasks, at Level 1 there is no playbook of common operational duties, nor is there a list of what those duties are. At Level 3 those duties have been defined and documented.

Look-for's are not checklists. One does not have to demonstrate every look-for to be assessed at that level. Some look-for's are appropriate only for certain situations or services. Look-for's are simply signals and indicators, not steps to follow or achievements to seek out.

Appendix A lists operational responsibilities, questions, and look-for's for each level. Take a moment to flip there and review some of them. We'll wait.

20.4 Service Assessments

To put this evaluation process into action, staff must periodically perform an assessment on each major service or group of related services they provide. The assessment is used to expose areas for improvement. The team brainstorms ways to fix these problems and chooses a certain number of projects to fix the highest-priority issues. These become projects for the new quarter.

The team then repeats the process. Services are assessed. The assessment inspires new projects. The projects are worked on. The services are assessed. The process then begins again. Teams that work this way benefit from having a structure in place that determines projects. They always know what they should be working on.

20.4.1 Identifying What to Assess

First, identify the major services that your organization provides. A web-based service might identify the major components of the service (major feature groups served by software components) and infrastructure services such as networks, power, cooling, and Internet access. An enterprise IT organization might identify the major applications provided to the company (e.g., email, file storage, centralized compute farm, desktop/laptop fleet management), plus infrastructure services such as DNS, DHCP, ActiveDirectory/LDAP, NTP, and so on. Smaller sites may group services together (DNS, DHCP, and ActiveDirectory/LDAP might be "name services"), and larger sites may consider each individual component its own service. Either way, construct your list of major services.

For each service, assess the service's eight operational responsibilities. Each section in Appendix A lists questions that will help in this assessment. These questions are generic and should apply to most services. You may wish to add additional questions that are appropriate for your organization or for a particular service. It is important to use the same questions for each assessment so that the numbers are comparable. Make a reference document that lists which questions are used.

20.4.2 Assessing Each Service

During each assessment period, record the assessment number (1 through 5) along with notes that justify the assessment. Generally these notes are in the form of answers to the questions.

Figure 20.1 shows an example spreadsheet that could be used to track the assessment of a service. The first column lists the eight operational responsibilities. The other columns each represent an assessment period. Use a different sub-sheet for each service. Use the spreadsheet's "insert comment" feature to record notes that justify the assessment value.

It is a good idea to list the responsibilities in an order that indicates their importance to that service. For example, a service that does not grow frequently is less concerned with capacity planning, so that responsibility might be listed last.

Color the squares red, orange, yellow, green, and blue for the values 1 through 5, respectively. This gives a visual indication and creates a "heat map" showing progress over time as the colors change.

For the person responsible for a service, this tool is a good way to help evaluate the service as well as track progress.

Service A	12/2014	1/2015	2/2015	3/2015	4/2015
Regular Response	1	2	2	2	3
Emergency Response	3	3	4	4	4
Monitoring and Metrics	1	1	2	2	2
Capacity Planning	1	1	1	1	2
Life-Cycle Management	2	2	2	3	2
New Service Introduction and Removal	1	2	2	3	3
Service Deployment and Decommissioning	2	2	3	3	4
Resource Efficiency	1	1	1	2	2

Figure 20.1: Assessment of a service

Team 1	2014Q1	2015Q1	2015Q2	2015Q3	2015Q4
Service A	1	2	2	2	1
Service B	3	4	4	4	5
Service C	1	2	2	3	3

Figure 20.2: Roll-up to assess a team

20.4.3 Comparing Results across Services

Figure 20.2 shows an example spreadsheet being used to roll up the assessments to compare the services. The services should be listed by order of importance. Each number represents all eight assessments for that service. The number may be a weighted average or simply the mathematical "mode" (the most common number). Whatever method you use, be consistent.

Both of these spreadsheets should be filled out by the team as a group exercise. The manager's role is to hold everyone to high standards for accuracy. The manager should not do this assessment on his or her own and surprise the team with the result. A self-assessment has an inherent motivational factor; being graded by a manager is demotivating at best.

20.4.4 Acting on the Results

We can now determine which services need the most improvement and, within each service, identify the problem areas.

Determine which projects will fix the areas that are both low assessment and for which improvements would have a large impact. That is, focus on the most needed improvements for the most important services.

Level 3 is often good enough for most services. Unless it is directly revenue generating or has highly demanding requirements, generally one should achieve "a solid 3" across most responsibilities before expending effort on projects that would result in achieving Level 4 or 5.

Work on the selected projects during the next quarter. At the start of the next quarter, repeat the assessment, update the spreadsheet, and repeat the process.

20.4.5 Assessment and Project Planning Frequencies

The frequencies of assessments and project planning cycles do not have to be the same. Plan for monthly assessments and quarterly project cycles. Monthly assessment is a good frequency to track progress. More-frequent assessments become a waste of time if very little measurable progress will have happened in that interval. Less-frequent assessments may make it difficult to spot new problems quickly.

The project cycle may be quarterly to sync up with performance review cycles or simply because three months is a reasonable amount of time for a project to be completed and show results. If the project selection occurs too infrequently, it may slow the cadence of change. If the project cycle is too frequent, it may discourage large, meaningful projects.

The longer the gap between assessments, the larger a burden they become. If the cycle is monthly, a meeting that lasts an hour or two can generally complete the assessment. A yearly cycle makes assessment "a big deal" and there is a temptation to stop all work for a week to prepare for day-long assessment meetings that analyze every aspect of the team. Such annual assessments become scary, unhelpful, and boring, and they usually turn into a bureaucratic waste of time. This is another case of small batches being better.

20.5 Organizational Assessments

As an executive or manager responsible for many services, this assessment system is a good way to guide the team's direction and track progress. These assessments also clearly communicate expectations to team members.

The people responsible for the service should do the assessments as a group. When people are allowed to do their own assessments, it motivates them to take on related improvement projects. You will be surprised at how often someone, seeing a low assessment, jumps at the chance to start a project that fixes related problems, even before you suggest it.

Your role as manager is to hold the team to high standards for accuracy and consistency as they complete the assessment. The rubric used should be consistent across all services and across all teams. If you use the assessment questions and look-for's in Appendix A, revise them to be better suited to your organization.

Larger organizations have many operational teams. Use this assessment tool with all teams to spot problem areas needing resources and attention, track progress, and motivate healthy competition. Senior managers responsible for multiple teams should work together to assure that rubrics are used consistently.

Figure 20.3 shows an example spreadsheet that could be used to roll up the assessments of many teams so they can be compared. Notice that teams 1, 4, and 5 have consistently improved over time; team 4's progress has been slower. Team 3 had a bad year and is just starting to make progress. This team may need extra attention to assure the progress continues. Team 2's progress is erratic, flipping between Levels 3 and 4 with a small trend upward.

	2014Q1	2015Q1	2015Q2	2015Q3	2015Q4
Team 1	1	2	2	3	3
Team 2	3	4	3	4	5
Team 3	1	1	1	1	2
Team 4	1	1	2	2	2
Team 5	2	3	3	3	4

Figure 20.3: Roll-up to compare teams

High-performing employees will see such comparisons as a source of pride or inspiration to do better. Teams with high assessments should be encouraged to share their knowledge and best practices.

20.6 Levels of Improvement

Each CMM level builds on the next. Level 2 contains the seeds that enable Level 3; Level 3 contains the seeds that enable Level 4. For this reason organizations pass through the levels in order and levels cannot be skipped.

It is not important to get to Level 5 for all operational responsibilities of all services. It would be a waste of resources to achieve Level 5 for a service that is little used and has low priority. In fact, it would be professionally negligent to expend the resources required to achieve a Level 5 assessment on a low-priority service when more important services need improvement.

Level 3 assessment is designed to be good enough for most services. Going above that level should be reserved for high-priority services such as revenue-generating services or services that are particularly demanding.

When setting organizational goals, focus on fixing a problem, rather than achieving a particular assessment level. That is, never set a goal of improving the assessment of an operational responsibility for the sake of improving the assessment. That is putting the cart before the horse. Instead, identify a problem, engineer a solution, and measure the success or failure by whether the assessment improves. This is a subtle but important difference.

Setting the goal of an improved assessment drives the wrong behavior. It encourages people to create spot fixes that do not solve the larger problem or to fix unimportant-but-easy issues just to get a better assessment. It would be like paying teachers based on the grades their students receive; such a system would simply lead to all students receiving A+'s as exams become easier and easier.

For this reason it is equally wrong to set a goal of raising the assessment level of all services to a certain level. An engineer's time is scarce. A push to have a high assessment for every organizational responsibility results in expending those scarce resources on low-priority services in the name of raising an average. Such a pursuit creates bureaucratic handcuffs that strangle an organization. It is something you should never do; indeed, it is a trap that you should only hope your competition falls into.

This point cannot be overstated. If your management ever sets a corporate, division, or organizational goal of achieving a certain assessment level on all organizational responsibilities of all services, you are to show them this section of the book and tell them that such a plan is a recipe for disaster.

Likewise, one should never make raises and bonuses contingent on the results of an assessment. This discourages people from joining the projects that need the most help. Instead, encourage your best people to join projects where they can do the most good. Engineers are highly motivated by the opportunity to do good work. The best reward for an improved assessment is not money, but the opportunity to work on the most interesting project, or to receive notoriety by sharing their knowledge with other teams. Rewards based on rising assessment levels are also not recommended because often it is a major achievement to simply retain a particular level in the face of challenging times.

20.7 Getting Started

Introducing this assessment system to a team can be a challenge. Most teams are not used to working in such a data-driven assessment environment. It should be introduced and used as a self-improvement tool—a way to help teams aspire to do their very best.

To begin, the team should enumerate the major services it provides. For example, a team that is responsible for a large web site might determine that each web property is a service, each internal API is a service, and the common platform used to provide the services is a service. There may be multiple platforms, in which case each is considered a service. Finally, the infrastructure itself is often counted as a service as far as assessment is concerned.

Assessments should be done on a periodic and repeatable schedule. The first Monday of each month is a common choice for frequency. The team meets and conducts a self-assessment of each service. Management's role is to maintain high standards and to ensure consistency across the services and teams. Management may set global standards for how certain ORs are evaluated. For example, there may be a corporate change management policy; compliance with that policy should be evaluated the same way for all services by all teams.

Eight core ORs should be used to assess all services. Appendix A includes details about these eight operational responsibilities, along with questions to ask during assessment to aid the team's understanding of the OR. The questions are followed by look-for's describing behaviors typically seen at various levels. Look-for's are indicators that the service is operating at a particular level. They are not checklists of behaviors to emulate. Do not attempt to achieve every look-for. They are indicators, not requirements or checklists. Not every look-for is appropriate for every service.

In addition to the eight core ORs, Appendix A lists other ORs that are particular to specific services. They are optional and serve as examples of service-specific ORs that an organization may choose to add to the core eight. Organizations may also choose to invent ORs for their own special needs.

As the monthly assessments progress, the changes over time should be apparent. The results of the assessments will help teams determine project priorities.

Over time, the roll-ups described in this chapter can be used to compare services or teams.

20.8 Summary

In this chapter we discussed how to assess the quality of operations and how to use this assessment to drive improvements.

Measuring the quality of system administration is complex. Therefore for each service we assess eight different qualities, called operational responsibilities: regular tasks (how normal, nonemergency tasks are performed), emergency response (how outages and other emergencies are handled), monitoring and metrics (collecting data used to make decisions), capacity planning (determining future resource needs), change management (how services are purposefully changed from birth to end), new service introduction and removal (how new products, hardware, or services are introduced into the environment and how they are removed), service deployment and decommissioning (how instances of an existing service are created and decommissioned), and performance and efficiency (how cost-effectively resources are used).

Each operational responsibility is assessed as being at one of five levels, reflecting the Capability Maturity Model (CMM) levels used in software engineering. The CMM is a set of maturity levels for assessing processes: Initial (ad hoc), Repeatable (documented, automated), Defined (roles and responsibilities are agreed upon), Managed (decisions are data-driven), and Optimizing (improvements are made and the results measured). The first three levels of the CMM are the most important; the other levels are often attempted only for high-value services.

The eight responsibilities of a service are individually assessed. These numbers are rolled up to create a single assessment of the service. Teams are typically responsible for many services. The individual service assessments are rolled up to assess the team, usually via a weighted average since not all services are equally important. These assessments can be used to rank teams.

By doing assessments periodically, progress can be tracked on the service, team, or organization level. High-ranking teams should be encouraged to share their best practices so others may adopt them.

The goal is to make improvements and measure their effectiveness by seeing if the assessment changes. The goal should not be to improve the assessment or to achieve an average assessment across a set of services.

Using assessments to drive decisions in IT brings us closer to a system of scientific management for system administration and moves us away from "gut feelings" and intuition. The importance of the first three levels of the CMM is that they take us away from ad hoc processes and individual heroics and create repeatable processes that are more efficient and of higher quality.

Exercises

1. Why is it difficult to assess the quality of operations work, or to compare two different operations teams?

2. Describe the five Capability Maturity Model (CMM) levels.

3. Rank the eight "operational responsibilities" from most important to least important. Justify your ranking.

4. In what ways could assessments become too bureaucratic and how might one prevent this?

5. Why is the mathematical mode recommended when rolling up a service's assessments, and a weighted average used when rolling up a team's assessments?

6. In which other ways could one roll up assessments? Discuss their pros and cons.

7. Select a service you are responsible for. Assess it based on the CMM levels for each of the operational responsibilities

8. Perform an assessment on a service you are not responsible for but for which you are familiar with its IT staff. Interview those personnel to assess the service based on the CMM levels for each of the operational responsibilities.

9. Compare your experience doing Exercises 7 and 8.

10. The eight operational responsibilities may not be appropriate for all services in all companies. Which modifications, additions, or subtractions would you propose for a service you are involved in? Justify your answer.

11. There are disadvantages to repeating the assessment cycle too frequently or not frequently enough. What would be the advantages and disadvantages of using a weekly cycle? A yearly cycle?

12. This chapter advises against setting goals that specify achieving a particular CMM level. Relate the reason given to a personal experience (inside or outside of IT).

Epilogue

> We look for things.
> Things that make us go.
>
> —Pakled Captain Grebnedlog

We want a better world.

We want a world where food is safer and tastes better.

We want a world where deliveries happen on time.

We want a world where visiting the Department of Motor Vehicles is a fast and efficient process.

We want a world where relationships are stronger, more meaningful, and more loving.

We want a world where we are happier in our jobs.

We want a world where the gloriously fanciful ideas of visionary science fiction become the real-life products and experiences available to everyone.

We want a world without war, hunger, poverty, and hate.

We want a world where optimism, science, and truth win out over pessimism, ignorance, and lies.

We want a world where everyone works together for the betterment of all.

We, the authors of this book, were born when computers could not fit on a desktop, let alone in a pocket. As youths, we saw the rise of computers and felt deep in our hearts that technology would save the world. As adults, we've seen technology transform the world, make it smaller, and enable us to do things that our parents would never have dreamed of.

Now we realize that computers and software are just a small piece of the picture. To make the world a better place requires operational practices that bring all the parts together, that bring all the people together, to run it and maintain it and keep it going.

People say that software "eats" one industry at a time, disrupting and revolutionizing it. When that happens, it is the operational practices that determine success or failure.

The logistics of producing and distributing food is now a software function. From the farm to the dinner table, better software makes it possible to grow more with fewer resources, harvest it at the right time, and transport it. Because the operational practices are successful, we eat a wider variety of food that is fresher and less expensive than ever before.

What looks like the simple act of buying something online requires a chain of organizations working together: raw material suppliers, factories, distribution, sales, marketing, purchasing, logistics, and delivery. Each of these is embodied in software and works well, or not, because of the operational practices involved.

The creation of new products is accelerated by the improved cycle time that brings new ideas and technologies to market faster. New ideas breed new ideas. Who would have imagined that someday we'd use our phone to run apps that enable us to deposit checks by taking their picture, reserve a car by pressing a button, or toss disgruntled birds at unstable structures?

When operations is done right, we are happier in our jobs. We eliminate the terror and uncertainty of major upgrades. We end the practice of requiring certain tasks to be done at odd hours that steal our sleep and distract us from pleasure. The stress from our jobs that hurts our nonwork relationships goes away. We live happier lives. We have more time for living and loving. We have more freedom to use our time to help others. Happiness multiplies love and it overflows us, leading us to share it with others.

These are the early years of all this stuff whose names and definitions are still evolving: cloud computing, distributed computing, DevOps, SRE, the web, the internet of things. We are standing at the base of the mountain, looking up, wondering what the future holds.

If you follow every bit of advice in this book, it will not cure all the world's ills. It will not end poverty or make food taste better. The advice in this book is obsolete as we write it.

But it is a start.

We hope this book gave you good things to think about. Interesting ideas to try. A starting place. We are merely collectors of the good ideas we've learned from others, read and heard about, and often been lucky enough to have experienced. We are scribes. We hope we have translated these ideas and experiences into words that convey their essence without misrepresenting them or leaving out the important bits. Where we haven't, we apologize in advance.

These are the early years. This book is just one voice. The rest is up to you. Take what you've learned here and build a better world.

Part III

Appendices

Assessments

This appendix contains assessment questions and look-for's for various operational responsibilities (ORs). Chapter 20, "Operational Excellence," is the instruction manual for this appendix. Advice on getting started is in Section 20.7.

Assessment Levels

Level 1	Initial/Chaotic	Ad hoc and relying on individual heroics
Level 2	Repeatable	Repeatable results
Level 3	Defined	Responsibilities defined/confirmed
Level 4	Managed	Quantitatively managed metrics
Level 5	Optimizing	Deliberate optimization/improvement

Core Operational Responsibilities

Additional Operational Responsibilities

A.1 Regular Tasks (RT)

Regular Tasks include how normal, non-emergency, operational duties are handled—that is, how work is received, queued, distributed, processed, and verified, plus how periodic tasks are scheduled and performed. All services have some kind of normal, scheduled or unscheduled work that needs to be done. Often web operations teams do not perform direct customer support but there are interteam requests, requests from stakeholders, and escalations from direct customer support teams. These topics are covered in Chapters 12 and 14.

Sample Assessment Questions

- What are the common and periodic operational tasks and duties?
- Is there a playbook for common operational duties?
- What is the SLA for regular requests?
- How is the need for new playbook entries identified? Who may write new entries? Edit existing ones?
- How are requests from users received and tracked?
- Is there a playbook for common user requests?
- How often are user requests not covered by the playbook?
- How do users engage us for support? (online and physical locations)
- How do users know how to engage us for support?
- How do users know what is supported and what isn't?
- How do we respond to requests for support of the unsupported?
- What are the limits of regular support (hours of operation, remote or on-site)? How do users know these limits?
- Are different size categories handled differently? How is size determined?
- If there is a corporate standard practice for this OR, what is it and how does this service comply with the practice?

Level 1: Initial

- There is no playbook, or it is out of date and unused.
- Results are inconsistent.
- Different people do tasks differently.
- Two users requesting the same thing usually get different results.
- Processes aren't documented.
- The team can't enumerate all the processes a team does (even at a high level).
- Requests get lost or stalled indefinitely.

- The organization cannot predict how long common tasks will take to complete.
- Operational problems, if reported, don't get attention.

Level 2: Repeatable

- There is a finite list of which services are supported by the team.
- Each end-to-end process has each step enumerated, with dependencies.
- Each end-to-end process has each step's process documented.
- Different people do the tasks the same way.
- Sadly, there is some duplication of effort seen in the flow.
- Sadly, some information needed by multiple tasks may be re-created by each step that needs it.

Level 3: Defined

- The team has an SLA defined for most requests, though it may not be adhered to.
- Each step has a QA checklist to be completed before handing off to next step.
- Teams learn of process changes by other teams ahead of time.
- Information or processing needed by multiple steps is created once.
- There is no (or minimal) duplication of effort.
- The ability to turn up new capacity is a repeatable process.

Level 4: Managed

- The defined SLA is measured.
- There are feedback mechanisms for all steps.
- There is periodic (weekly?) review of defects and reworks.
- Postmortems are published for all to see, with a draft report available within x hours and a final report completed within y days.
- There is periodic review of alerts by the affected team. There is periodic review of alerts by a cross-functional team.
- Process change requests require data to measure the problem being fixed.
- Dashboards report data in business terms (i.e., not just technical terms).
- Every "failover procedure" has a "date of last use" dashboard.
- Capacity needs are predicted ahead of need.

Level 5: Optimizing

- After process changes are made, before/after data are compared to determine success.
- Process changes are reverted if before/after data shows no improvement.
- Process changes that have been acted on come from a variety of sources.
- At least one process change has come from every step (in recent history).
- Cycle time enjoys month-over-month improvements.
- Decisions are supported by modeling "what if" scenarios using extracted actual data.

A.2 Emergency Response (ER)

Emergency Response covers how outages and disasters are handled. This includes engineering resilient systems that prevent outages plus technical and non-technical processes performed during and after outages (response and remediation). These topics are covered in Chapters 6, 14, and 15.

Sample Assessment Questions

- How are outages detected? (automatic monitoring? user complaints?)
- Is there a playbook for common failover scenarios and outage-related duties?
- Is there an oncall calendar?
- How is the oncall calendar created?
- Can the system withstand failures on the local level (component failure)?
- Can the system withstand failures on the geographic level (alternative data-centers)?
- Are staff geographically distributed (i.e., can other regions cover for each other for extended periods of time)?
- Do you write postmortems? Is there a deadline for when a postmortem must be completed?
- Is there a standard template for postmortems?
- Are postmortems reviewed to assure action items are completed?
- If there is a corporate standard practice for this OR, what is it and how does this service comply with the practice?

Level 1: Initial

- Outages are reported by users rather than a monitoring system.
- No one is ever oncall, a single person is always oncall, or everyone is always oncall.
- There is no oncall schedule.
- There is no oncall calendar.
- There is no playbook of what to do for various alerts.

Level 2: Repeatable

- A monitoring system contacts the oncall person.
- There is an oncall schedule with escalation plan.
- There is a repeatable process for creating the next month's oncall calendar.
- A playbook item exists for any possible alert.
- A postmortem template exists.

- Postmortems are written occasionally but not consistently.
- Oncall coverage is geographically diverse (multiple time zones).

Level 3: Defined

- Outages are classified by size (i.e., minor, major, catastrophic).
- Limits (and minimums) for how often people should be oncall are defined.
- Postmortems are written for all major outages.
- There is an SLA defined for alert response: initial, hands-on-keyboard, issue resolved, postmortem complete.

Level 4: Managed

- The oncall pain is shared by the people most able to fix problems.
- How often people are oncall is verified against the policy.
- Postmortems are reviewed.
- There is a mechanism to triage recommendations in postmortems and assure they are completed.
- The SLA is actively measured.

Level 5: Optimizing

- Stress testing and failover testing are done frequently (quarterly or monthly).
- "Game Day" exercises (intensive, system-wide tests) are done periodically.
- The monitoring system alerts before outages occur (indications of "sick" systems rather than "down" systems).
- Mechanisms exist so that any failover procedure not utilized in recent history is activated artificially.
- Experiments are performed to improve SLA compliance.

A.3 Monitoring and Metrics (MM)

Monitoring and Metrics covers collecting and using data to make decisions. Monitoring collects data about a system. Metrics uses that data to measure a quantifiable component of performance. This includes technical metrics such as bandwidth, speed, or latency; derived metrics such as ratios, sums, averages, and percentiles; and business goals such as the efficient use of resources or compliance with a service level agreement (SLA). These topics are covered in Chapters 16, 17, and 19.

Sample Assessment Questions

- Is the service level objective (SLO) documented? How do you know your SLO matches customer needs?
- Do you have a dashboard? Is it in technical or business terms?
- How accurate are the collected data and the predictions? How do you know?
- How efficient is the service? Are machines over- or under-utilized? How is utilization measured?
- How is latency measured?
- How is availability measured?
- How do you know if the monitoring system itself is down?
- How do you know if the data used to calculate key performance indicators (KPIs) is fresh? Is there a dashboard that shows measurement freshness and accuracy?
- If there is a corporate standard practice for this OR, what is it and how does this service comply with the practice?

Level 1: Initial

- No SLOs are documented.
- If there is monitoring, not everything is monitored, and there is no way to check completeness.
- Systems and services are manually added to the monitoring system, if at all: there is no process.
- There are no dashboards.
- Little or no measurement or metrics.
- You think customers are happy but they aren't.
- It is common (and rewarded) to enact optimizations that benefit a person or small group to the detriment of the larger organization or system.
- Departmental goals emphasize departmental performance to the detriment of organizational performance.

Level 2: Repeatable

- The process for creating machines/server instances assures they will be monitored.

Level 3: Defined

- SLOs are documented.
- Business KPIs are defined.
- The freshness of business KPI data is defined.
- A system exists to verify that all services are monitored.
- The monitoring system itself is monitored (meta-monitoring).

Level 4: Managed

- SLOs are documented and monitored.
- Defined KPIs are measured.
- Dashboards exist showing each step's completion time; the lag time of each step is identified.
- Dashboards exist showing current bottlenecks, backlogs, and idle steps.
- Dashboards show defect and rework counts.
- Capacity planning is performed for the monitoring system and all analysis systems.
- The freshness of the data used to calculate KPIs is measured.

Level 5: Optimizing

- The accuracy of collected data is verified through active testing.
- KPIs are calculated using data that is less than a minute old.
- Dashboards and other analysis displays are based on fresh data.
- Dashboards and other displays load quickly.
- Capacity planning for storage, CPU, and network of the monitoring system is done with the same sophistication as any major service.

The Unexpectedly Slow Cache

Stack Exchange purchased a product that would accelerate web page delivery to customers using a globally distributed cache. Most customers deploy this product and assume it has a "can't lose" benefit.

Before deploying it, Stack Exchange engineer Nick Craver created a framework for measuring end-to-end page load times. The goal was to precisely know how much improvement was gained both globally and for customers in various geographic regions.

We were quite surprised to discover that the product degraded performance. It improved certain aspects but only at the detriment of others, resulting in a net performance loss.

Stack Exchange worked with the vendor to identify the problem. As a result, a major design error was found and fixed.

If care hadn't been taken to measure performance before and after the change, Stack Exchange's efforts would have unknowingly made its service slower. One wonders how many other customers of this product did no such measurements and simply assumed performance was improved while in reality it was made worse.

A.4 Capacity Planning (CP)

Capacity Planning covers determining future resource needs. All services require some kind of planning for future resources. Services tend to grow. Capacity planning involves the technical work of understanding how many resources are needed per unit of growth, plus non-technical aspects such as budgeting, forecasting, and supply chain management. These topics are covered in Chapter 18.

Sample Assessment Questions

- How much capacity do you have now?
- How much capacity do you expect to need three months from now? Twelve months from now?
- Which statistical models do you use for determining future needs?
- How do you load-test?
- How much time does capacity planning take? What could be done to make it easier?
- Are metrics collected automatically?
- Are metrics available always or does their need initiate a process that collects them?
- Is capacity planning the job of no one, everyone, a specific person, or a team of capacity planners?
- If there is a corporate standard practice for this OR, what is it and how does this service comply with the practice?

Level 1: Initial

- No inventory is kept.
- The system runs out of capacity from time to time.
- Determining how much capacity to add is done by tradition, guessing, or luck.
- Operations is reactive about capacity planning, often not being able to fulfill the demand for capacity in time.
- Capacity planning is everyone's job, and therefore no one's job.
- No one is specifically assigned to handle CP duties.
- A large amount of headroom exists rather than knowing precisely how much slack is needed.

Level 2: Repeatable

- CP metrics are collected on demand, or only when needed.
- The process for collecting CP metrics is written and repeatable.

- Load testing is done occasionally, perhaps when a service is new.
- Inventory of all systems is accurate, possibly due to manual effort.

Level 3: Defined

- CP metrics are automatically collected.
- Capacity required for a certain amount of growth is well defined.
- There is a dedicated CP person on the team.
- CP requirements are defined at a subsystem level.
- Load testing is triggered by major software and hardware changes.
- Inventory is updated as part of capacity changes.
- The amount of headroom needed to survive typical surges is defined.

Level 4: Managed

- CP metrics are collected continuously (daily/weekly instead of monthly or quarterly).
- Additional capacity is gained automatically, with human approval.
- Performance regressions are detected during testing, involving CP if performance regression will survive into production (i.e., it is not a bug).
- Dashboards include CP information.
- Changes in correlation are automatically detected and raise a ticket for CP to verify and adjust relationships between core drivers and resource units.
- Unexpected increases in demand are automatically detected using MACD metrics or similar technique, which generates a ticket for the CP person or team.
- The amount of headroom in the system is monitored.

Level 5: Optimizing

- Past CP projections are compared with actual results.
- Load testing is done as part of a continuous test environment.
- The team employs a statistician.
- Additional capacity is gained automatically.
- The amount of headroom is systematically optimized to reduce waste.

A.5 Change Management (CM)

Change Management covers how services are deliberately changed over time. This includes the software delivery platform—the steps involved in a software release: develop, build, test, and push into production. For hardware, this includes firmware upgrades and minor hardware revisions. These topics are covered in Chapters 9, 10, and 11.

Sample Assessment Questions

- How often are deployments (releases pushed into production)?
- How much human labor does it take?
- When a release is received, does the operations team need to change anything in it before it is pushed?
- How does operations know if a release is major or minor, a big or small change? How are these types of releases handled differently?
- How does operations know if a release is successful?
- How often have releases failed?
- How does operations know that new releases are available?
- Are there change-freeze windows?
- If there is a corporate standard practice for this OR, what is it and how does this service comply with the practice?

Level 1: Initial

- Deployments are done sparingly, as they are very risky.
- The deployment process is ad hoc and laborious.
- Developers notify operations of new releases when a release is ready for deployment.
- Releases are not deployed until weeks or months after they are available.
- Operations and developers bicker over when to deploy releases.

Level 2: Repeatable

- The deployment is no longer ad hoc.
- Deployment is manual but consistent.
- Releases are deployed as delivered.
- Deployments fail often.

Level 3: Defined

- What constitutes a successful deployment is defined.
- Minor and major releases are handled differently.
- The expected time gap between release availability and deployment is defined.

Level 4: Managed

- Deployment success/failure is measured against definitions.
- Deployments fail rarely.
- The expected time gap between release availability and deployment is measured.

Level 5: Optimizing

- Continuous deployment is in use.
- Failed deployments are extremely rare.
- New releases are deployed with little delay.

A.6 New Product Introduction and Removal (NPI/NPR)

New Product Introduction and Removal covers how new products and services are introduced into the environment and how they are removed. This is a coordination function: introducing a new product or service requires a support infrastructure that may touch multiple teams.

For example, before a new model of computer hardware is introduced into the datacenter environment, certain teams must have access to sample hardware for testing and qualification, the purchasing department must have a process to purchase the machines, and datacenter technicians need documentation. For introducing software and services, there should be tasks such as requirements gathering, evaluation and procurement, licensing, and creation of playbooks for the helpdesk and operations.

Product removal might involve finding all machines with a particularly old release of an operating system and seeing that all of them get upgraded. Product removal requires identifying current users, agreeing on timelines for migrating them away, updating documentation, and eventually decommissioning the product, any associated licenses, maintenance contracts, monitoring, and playbooks. The majority of the work consists of communication and coordination between teams.

Sample Assessment Questions

- How is new hardware introduced into the environment? Which teams are involved and how do they communicate? How long does the process take?
- How is old hardware or software eliminated from the system?
- What is the process for disposing of old hardware?
- Which steps are taken to ensure disks and other storage are erased when disposed?
- How is new software or a new service brought into being? Which teams are involved and how do they communicate? How long does the process take?
- What is the process for handoff between teams?
- Which tools are used?
- Is documentation current?
- Which steps involve human interaction? How could it be eliminated?
- If there is a corporate standard practice for this OR, what is it and how does this service comply with the practice?

Level 1: Initial

- New products are introduced through ad hoc measures and individual heroics.
- Teams are surprised by NPI, often learning they must deploy something into production with little notice.
- NPI is delayed due to lack of capacity, miscommunication, or errors.
- Deprecating old products is rarely done, resulting in operations having to support an "infinite" number of hardware or software versions.

Level 2: Repeatable

- The process used for NPI/NPR is repeatable.
- The handoff between teams is written and agreed upon.
- Each team has a playbook for tasks related to its involvement with NPR/NPI.
- Equipment erasure and disposal is documented and verified.

Level 3: Defined

- Expectations for how long NPI/NPR will take are defined.
- The handoff between teams is encoded in a machine-readable format.
- Members of all teams understand their role as it fits into the larger, overall process.
- The maximum number of products supported by each team is defined.
- The list of each team's currently supported products is available to all teams.

Level 4: Managed

- There are dashboards for observing NPI and NPR progress.
- The handoff between teams is actively revised and improved.
- The number of no-longer-supported products is tracked.
- Decommissioning no-longer-supported products is a high priority.

Level 5: Optimizing

- NPI/NPR tasks have become API calls between teams.
- NPI/NPR processes are self-service by the team responsible.
- The handoff between teams is a linear flow (or for very complex systems, joining multiple linear flows).

A.7 Service Deployment and Decommissioning (SDD)

Service Deployment and Decommissioning covers how instances of an existing service are created and how they are turned off (decommissioned). After a service is designed, it is usually deployed repeatedly. Deployment may involve turning up satellite replicas in new datacenters or creating a development environment of an existing service. Decommissioning could be part of turning down a datacenter, reducing excess capacity, or turning down a particular service instance such as a demo environment.

Sample Assessment Questions

- What is the process for turning up a service instance?
- What is the process for turning down a service instance?
- How is new capacity added? How is unused capacity turned down?
- Which steps involve human interaction? How could it be eliminated?
- How many teams touch these processes?
- Do all teams know how they fit into the over all picture?
- What is the workflow from team to team?
- Which tools are used?
- Is documentation current?
- If there is a corporate standard practice for this OR, what is it and how does this service comply with the practice?

Level 1: Initial

- The process is undocumented and haphazard. Results are inconsistent.
- The process is defined by who does something, not what is done.
- Requests get delayed due to miscommunication, lack of resources, or other avoidable reasons.
- Different people do the tasks differently.

Level 2: Repeatable

- The processes required to deploy or decommission a service are understood and documented.
- The process for each step is documented and verified.
- Each step has a QA checklist to be completed before handing off to the next step.
- Teams learn of process changes by other teams ahead of time.

- Information or processing needed by multiple steps is created once.
- There is no (or minimal) duplication of effort.
- The ability to turn up new capacity is a repeatable process.
- Equipment erasure and disposal is documented and verified.

Level 3: Defined

- The SLA for how long each step should take is defined.
- For physical deployments, standards for removal of waste material (boxes, wrappers, containers) are based on local environmental standards.
- For physical decommissions, standards for disposing of old hardware are based on local environmental standards as well as the organization's own standards for data erasure.
- Tools exist to implement many of the steps and processes.

Level 4: Managed

- The defined SLA for each step is measured.
- There are feedback mechanisms for all steps.
- There is periodic review of defects and reworks.
- Capacity needs are predicted ahead of need.
- Equipment disposal compliance is measured against organization standards as well as local environmental law.
- Waste material (boxes, wrappers, containers) involved in deployment is measured.
- Quantity of equipment disposal is measured.

Level 5: Optimizing

- After process changes are made, before/after data is compared to determine success.
- Process changes are reverted if before/after data shows no improvement.
- Process changes that have been acted on come from a variety of sources.
- Cycle time enjoys month-over-month improvements.
- Decisions are supported by modeling "what if" scenarios using extracts from actual data.
- Equipment disposal is optimized by the reduction of equipment deployment.

A.8 Performance and Efficiency (PE)

Performance and Efficiency covers how cost-effectively resources are used and how well the service performs. A running service needs to have good performance without wasting resources. We can generally improve performance by using more resources, or we may be able to improve efficiency to the detriment of performance. Achieving both requires a large effort to bring about equilibrium. Cost-efficiency is cost of resources divided by quantity of use. Resource efficiency is quantity of resources divided by quantity of use. To calculate these statistics, one must know how many resources exist; thus some kind of inventory is required.

Sample Assessment Questions

- What is the formula used to measure performance?
- What is the formula used to determine utilization?
- What is the formula used to determine resource efficiency?
- What is the formula used to determine cost efficiency?
- How is performance variation measured?
- Are performance, utilization, and resource efficiency monitored automatically? Is there a dashboard for each?
- Is there an inventory of the machines and servers used in this service?
- How is the inventory kept up-to-date?
- How would you know if something was missing from the inventory?
- If there is a corporate standard practice for this OR, what is it and how does this service comply with the practice?

Level 1: Initial

- Performance and utilization are not consistently measured.
- What is measured depends on who set up the systems and services.
- Resource efficiency is not measured.
- Performance problems often come as a surprise and are hard to diagnose and resolve because there is insufficient data.
- Inventory is not up-to-date.
- Inventory may or may not be updated, depending on who is involved in receiving or disposing of items.

Level 2: Repeatable

- All metrics relevant to performance and utilization are collected across all systems and services.
- The process for bringing up new systems and services is documented and everyone follows the process.
- Systems are associated with services when configured for use by a service, and disassociated when released.
- Inventory is up-to-date. The inventory process is well documented and everyone follows the process.

Level 3: Defined

- Performance and utilization monitoring is automatically configured for all systems and services during installation and removed during decommission.
- Performance targets for each service are defined.
- Resource usage targets for each service are defined.
- Formulas for service-oriented performance and utilization metrics are defined.
- Performance of each service is monitored continuously.
- Resource utilization of each service is monitored continuously.
- Idle capacity that is not currently used by any service is monitored.
- The desired amount of headroom is defined.
- The roles and responsibilities for keeping the inventory up-to-date are defined.
- Systems for tracking the devices that are connected to the network and their hardware configurations are in place.

Level 4: Managed

- Dashboards track performance, utilization, and resource efficiency.
- Minimum, maximum, and 90th percentile headroom are tracked and compared to the desired headroom and are visible on a dashboard.
- Goals for performance and efficiency are set and tracked.
- There are periodic reviews of performance and efficiency goals and status for each service.
- KPIs are used to set performance, utilization, and resource efficiency goals that drive optimal behavior.
- Automated systems track the devices that are on the network and their configurations and compare them with the inventory system, flagging problems when they are found.

Level 5: Optimizing

- Bottlenecks are identified using the performance dashboard. Changes are made as a result.
- Services that use large amounts of resources are identified and changes are made.
- Changes are reverted if the changes do not have a positive effect.
- Computer hardware models are regularly evaluated to find models where utilization of the different resources is better balanced.
- Other sources of hardware and other hardware models are regularly evaluated to determine if cost efficiency can improved.

A.9 Service Delivery: The Build Phase

Service delivery is the technical process of how a service is created. It starts with source code created by developers and ends with a service running in production.

Sample Assessment Questions

- How is software built from source code to packages?
- Is the final package built from source or do developers deliver precompiled elements?
- What percentage of code is covered by unit tests?
- Which tests are fully automated?
- Are metrics collected about bug lead time, code lead time, and patch lead time?
- To build the software, do all raw source files come from version control repositories?
- To build the software, how many places (repositories or other sources) are accessed to attain all raw source files?
- Is the resulting software delivered as a package or a set of files?
- Is everything required for deployment delivered in the package?
- Which package repository is used to hand off the results to the deployment phase?
- Is there a single build console for status and control of all steps?
- If there is a corporate standard practice for this OR, what is it and how does this service comply with the practice?

Level 1: Initial

- Each person builds in his or her own environment.
- People check in code without checking that it builds.
- Developers deliver precompiled elements to be packaged.
- Little or no unit testing is performed.
- No metrics are collected.
- Version control systems are not used to store source files.
- Building the software is a manual process or has manual steps.
- The master copies of some source files are kept in personal home directories or computers.

Level 2: Repeatable

- The build environment is defined; everyone uses the same system for consistent results.
- Building the software is still done manually.

- Testing is done manually.
- Some unit tests exist.
- Source files are kept in version-controlled repositories.
- Software packages are used as the means of delivering the end result.
- If multiple platforms are supported, each is repeatable, though possibly independently.

Level 3: Defined

- Building the software is automated.
- Triggers for automated builds are defined.
- Expectations around unit test coverage are defined; they are less than 100 percent.
- Metrics for bug lead time, code lead time, and patch lead time are defined.
- Inputs and outputs of each step are defined.

Level 4: Managed

- Success/fail build ratios are measured and tracked on a dashboard.
- Metrics for bug lead time, code lead time, and patch lead time are collected automatically.
- Metrics are presented on a dashboard.
- Unit test coverage is measured and tracked.

Level 5: Optimizing

- Metrics are used to select optimization projects.
- Attempts to optimize the process involve collecting before and after metrics.
- Each developer can perform the end-to-end build process in his or her own sandbox before committing changes to a centralized repository.
- Insufficient unit test code coverage stops production.
- If multiple platforms are supported, building for one is as easy as building for them all.
- The software delivery platform is used for building infrastructure as well as applications.

A.10 Service Delivery: The Deployment Phase

The goal of the deployment phase is to create a running environment. The deployment phase creates the service in one or more testing and production environments. This environment will then be used for testing or for live production services.

Sample Assessment Questions

- How are packages deployed in production?
- How much downtime is required to deploy the service in production?
- Are metrics collected about frequency of deployment, mean time to restore service, and change success rate?
- How is the decision made to promote a package from testing to production?
- Which kind of testing is done (system, performance, load, user acceptance)?
- How is deployment handled differently for small, medium, and large releases?
- If there is a corporate standard practice for this OR, what is it and how does this service comply?

Level 1: Initial

- Deployment involves or requires manual steps.
- Deployments into the testing and production environments are different processes, each with its own tools and procedures.
- Different people on the team perform deployments differently.
- Deployment requires downtime, and sometimes significant downtime.
- How a release is promoted to production is ad hoc or ill defined.
- Testing is manual, ill defined, or not done.

Level 2: Repeatable

- Deployment is performed in a documented, repeatable process.
- If deployment requires downtime, it is a predictable.
- Testing procedures are documented and repeatable.

Level 3: Defined

- Metrics for frequency of deployment, mean time to restore service, and change success rate are defined.
- How downtime due to deployments is to be measured is defined; limits and expectations are defined.

- How a release is promoted to production is defined.
- Testing results are clearly communicated to all stakeholders.

Level 4: Managed

- Metrics for frequency of deployment, mean time to restore service, and change success rate are collected automatically.
- Metrics are presented on a dashboard.
- Downtime due to deployments is measured automatically.
- Reduced production capacity during deployment is measured.
- Tests are fully automated.

Level 5: Optimizing

- Metrics are used to select optimization projects.
- Attempts to optimize the process involve collecting before and after metrics.
- Deployment is fully automated.
- Promotion decisions are fully automated, perhaps with a few specific exceptions.
- Deployment requires no downtime.

A.11 Toil Reduction

Toil Reduction is the process by which we improve the use of people within our system. When we reduce toil (i.e., exhausting physical labor), we create a more sustainable working environment for operational staff. While reducing toil is not a service per se, this OR can be used to assess the amount of toil and determine whether practices are in place to limit the amount of toil.

Sample Assessment Questions

- How many hours each week are spent on coding versus non-coding projects?
- What percent of time is spent on project work versus manual labor that could be automated?
- What percentage of time spent on manual labor should raise a red flag?
- What is the process for detecting that the percentage of manual labor has exceeded the red flag threshold?
- What is the process for raising a red flag? Whose responsibility is it?
- What happens after a red flag is raised? When is it lowered?
- How are projects for reducing toil identified? How are they prioritized?
- How is the effectiveness of those projects measured?
- If there is a corporate standard practice for this OR, what is it and how does this service comply with the practice?

Level 1: Initial

- Toil is not measured and grows until no project work, or almost no project work, can be accomplished.
- There is no process for raising a red flag.
- Some individuals recognize when toil is becoming a problem and look for solutions, but others are unaware of the problem.
- Individuals choose to work on the projects that are the most interesting to them, without looking at which projects will have the biggest impact.

Level 2: Repeatable

- The amount of time spent on toil versus on projects is measured.
- The percentage of time spent on toil that constitutes a problem is defined and communicated.
- The process for raising a red flag is documented and communicated.
- Individuals track their own toil to project work ratio, and are individually responsible for raising a red flag.
- Red flags may not always be raised when they should be.

- The process for identifying which projects will have the greatest impact on toil reduction is defined.
- The method for prioritizing projects is documented.

Level 3: Defined

- For each team, the person responsible for tracking toil and raising a red flag is identified.
- The people involved in identifying and prioritizing toil-reduction projects are known.
- Both a red flag level of toil and a target level are defined. The red flag is lowered when toil reaches the target level.
- During the red flag period, the team works on only the highest-impact toil-reduction projects.
- During the red flag period, the team has management support for putting other projects on hold until toil is reduced to a target level.
- After each step in a project, statistics on toil are closely monitored, providing feedback on any positive or negative changes.

Level 4: Managed

- Project time versus toil is tracked on a dashboard, and the amount of time spent on each individual project or manual task is also tracked.
- Red flags are raised automatically, and the dashboard gives an overview of where the problems lie.
- The time-tracking data is monitored for trends that give an early alert for teams that are showing an increase in toil in one or more areas.
- KPIs are defined and tracked to keep toil within the desired range and minimize the red flag periods.

Level 5: Optimizing

- The target and red flag levels are adjusted and the results are monitored to the effect on overall flow, performance, and innovation.
- Changes to the main project prioritization process are introduced and evaluated for positive or negative impact, including the impact on toil.
- Changes to the red flag toil-reduction task prioritization process are introduced and evaluated.

A.12 Disaster Preparedness

An operations organization needs to be able to handle outages well, and it must have practices that reduce the chance of repeating past mistakes. Disasters and major outages happen. Everyone in the company from the top down needs to recognize that fact, and adopt a mind-set that accepts outages and learns from them. Systems should be designed to be resilient to failure.

Sample Assessment Questions

- What is the SLA? Which tools and processes are in place to ensure that the SLA is met?
- How complete are the playbooks?
- When was each scenario in the playbooks last exercised?
- What is the mechanism for exercising different failure modes?
- How are new team members trained to be prepared to handle disasters?
- Which roles and responsibilities apply during a disaster?
- How do you prepare for disasters?
- How are disasters used to improve future operations and disaster response?
- If there is a corporate standard practice for this OR, what is it and how does this service comply with the practice?

Level 1: Initial

- Disasters are handled in an ad hoc manner, requiring individual heroics.
- Playbooks do not exist, or do not cover all scenarios.
- Little or no training exists.
- Service resiliency and different failure scenarios are never tested.

Level 2: Repeatable

- Playbooks exist for all failure modes, including large-scale disasters.
- New team members receive on-the-job training.
- Disasters are handled consistently, independent of who is responding.
- If multiple team members respond, their roles, responsibilities, and handoffs are not clearly defined, leading to some duplication of effort.

Level 3: Defined

- The SLA is defined, including dates for postmortem reports.
- Handoff procedures are defined, including checks to be performed and documented.

- How to scale the responding team to make efficient use of more team members is defined.
- The roles and responsibilities of team members in a disaster are defined.
- Specific disaster preparedness training for new team members is defined and implemented.
- The team has regular disaster preparedness exercises.
- The exercises include fire drills performed on the live service.
- After every disaster, a postmortem report is produced and circulated.

Level 4: Managed

- The SLA is tracked using dashboards.
- The timing for every step in the process from the moment the event occurred is tracked on the dashboard.
- A program for disaster preparedness training ensures that all aspects are covered.
- The disaster preparedness program measures the results of disaster preparedness training.
- As teams become better at handling disasters, the training expands to cover more complex scenarios.
- Teams are involved in cross-functional fire drills that involve multiple teams and services.
- Dates for publishing initial and final postmortem reports are tracked and measured against the SLA.

Level 5: Optimizing

- Areas for improvement are identified from the dashboards.
- New techniques and processes are tested and the results measured and used for further decision making.
- Automated systems ensure that every failure mode is exercised within a certain period, by artificially causing a failure if one has not occurred naturally.

The Origins and Future of Distributed Computing and Clouds

To me it seems quite clear
that it's all just a little bit of
history repeating

—Propellerheads

Modern, large datacenters typically consist of rack after rack of pizza box–sized computers. This is a typical design pattern for any large cloud-scale, distributed computing environment. Why is this? How did so many companies arrive at the same design pattern?

The answer is that this design pattern was inevitable. To manage enormous datacenters, hardware and processes must be highly organized. Repeating the same rack structure within a datacenter reduces complexity, which reduces management and administrative overhead. Many other factors led to the choice of hardware to fit into those racks.

However, nothing is truly inevitable. Thus the appearance of massive datacenters full of machines built from commodity hardware, distributed computing replacing large computers, and the popularity of cloud computing were inevitable only in the sense that necessity is the mother of invention.

Earlier approaches to large web and e-commerce sites did not have the right economies of scale. In fact, scaling became more expensive per user. This caused the first dot-com bubble to be unsustainable. What drove the distributed computing revolution was the need to create the right economies of scale, where addtional users become cheaper to support.

Every order of magnitude improvement in the cost of computing enables a new era of applications, each of which was unimaginable just a few years before.

Each requires new supporting infrastructure technology and operational method-ologies. These technologies and methodologies do not always arrive in time, and sometimes they are ahead of their time.

Understanding the historical context of all these changes gives context to the tools and techniques described in this book. If this doesn't interest you, feel free to skip this appendix.

The history of the computer industry is quite long, starting with the abacus. This appendix will skip ahead a few years and focus on a few specific periods:

- *The pre-web era:* The years immediately prior to the web, from 1985 to 1994
- *The first web era:* "The dot-com bubble" from 1995 to 2000
- *The dot-bomb era:* The economic downturn from 2000 to 2003
- *The second web era:* The resurgence from 2003 to 2010
- *The cloud computing era:* Where we are today

Each period had different needs that drove the technology decisions of the day, pushing evolution forward step by step. These needs changed over time due to the ebb and flow of economic prosperity, the march of technological improvement, and increasing expectations of reliability and speed. This appendix provides our interpretation of how it happened.

B.1 The Pre-Web Era (1985–1994)

Computing was different prior to the web. Reliability and scale were important but not in the same way they are today. The Internet was used only by a small group of technologists, and most people were unaware of its existence.

Availability Requirements

For most businesses, their internal operations were reliant on computers, but outages were largely invisible to external customers. The exceptions were com-panies whose customers included a large segment of the population and accessed the services from outside the business premises—for example, telephone compa-nies whose customers were making phone calls and banks that provided ATMs. Customers expect those services to be available on a 24 × 7 basis.

In this era most large businesses were already heavily reliant on computers for the bulk of their work. Some employees had remote access from home, over a telephony-based modem, sometimes with a dumb terminal, sometimes with a PC or Mac.

Most businesses could schedule outages for maintenance—by looking at prod-uct release schedules and avoiding the end-of-quarter period. The customers of the computer systems were internal to the company, and there were easy, defined ways of contacting them to schedule downtime.

The Internet was largely text-based, with email, Internet news, bulletin boards, and file transfer programs. Outages of an Internet service might cause a backlog of email or news, but went largely unnoticed by most people. For most people, Internet access was a perk, but it was not business-critical. Some companies offered anonymous-ftp drop-boxes for third parties, such as customers needing support. Little other commercial business was carried out over the Internet. It was far from clear in the early days whether it was a potential acceptable use policy violation to use the Internet for commercial purposes.

During this era, 24 × 7 operation was important for some internal corporate systems, but not for Internet services. Maintenance outages of internal systems could be scheduled, because the user population was known and could be easily informed.

Downtime Used to Be Normal

Tom's first computer experience was in 1980. Tom was in sixth grade and his school gave a small group of students access to a terminal connected to a main-frame. When someone logged into the system, it would display a message that "the system will be down every day after 6 PM for taping." Neither Tom nor his teacher knew what that meant, but years later Tom realized that "taping" must have meant "doing backups." The system was down for hours each day to do backups and that was normal.

Technology

Business applications and services ran on mainframes and minicomputers. These devices often had megabytes of storage and could execute less than 1 million instructions per second (MIPS). They were server-class machines, which were built with high-quality components, high-speed technologies, and expansion capabilities.

Home computers were a new thing. There was no Internet access and common applications (stand-alone games, word processing, spreadsheets, and tax packages) came on floppy disk. The hardware components were "consumer grade," which meant cheap, underpowered, and unreliable. The computers often relied on 8-bit and later 16-bit processors, with RAM and disk storage measured in kilobytes and megabytes, not gigabytes and terabytes. CPU speed was measured in MHz, and GHz was science fiction. Data was stored on slow floppy disks.

A 10MB hard drive was a luxury item, even though it was fragile and being dropped would destroy it.

Scaling

A company's computer systems served internal customers, applications, and business processes. They needed to scale with the growth of the company. As the company's business grew, so would the number of employees and the computing requirements. Even for fast-growing companies, this growth was relatively predictable and often bounded by the much slower rate at which new employees were hired.

Business-critical applications ran on a small number of large, high-end computers. If a computer system ran out of capacity, it could be upgraded with additional disks, memory, and CPUs. Upgrading further meant buying a bigger machine, so machines that were to be servers were typically purchased with plenty of spare upgrade capacity. Sometimes services were also scaled by deploying servers for the application into several geographic regions, or business units, each of which would then use its local server. For example, when Tom first worked at AT&T, there was a different payroll processing center for each division of the company.

High Availability

Applications requiring high availability required "fault-tolerant" computers. These computers had multiple CPUs, error-correcting RAM, and other technologies that were extremely expensive at the time. Fault-tolerant systems were niche products. Generally only the military and Wall Street needed such systems. As a result they were usually priced out of the reach of typical companies.

Costs

During this era the Internet was not business-critical, and outages for internal business-critical systems could be scheduled because the customer base was a limited, known set of people. When necessary, advanced reliability and scaling needs were addressed with very expensive specialized hardware. However, businesses could easily calculate the costs of any outages, do a risk analysis to understand what the budget for providing higher reliability was, and make an informed decision about how to proceed. These costs were under control.

Scaling was handled through hardware upgrades, but compute requirements scaled in predictable ways with the company's business. As the business grew, the budget for the compute infrastructure grew, and upgrades could be planned and scheduled.

B.2 The First Web Era: The Bubble (1995–2000)

In the beginning of the first web era, web sites were relatively static reposito-ries of linked documents. The first corporate web sites were largely marketing literature—information about the company and its products, press releases, job listings, and contact information for various customer-facing groups, such as sales and customer support. But many businesses quickly realized the potential for conducting business over the Internet, and e-commerce was born.

Availability Requirements

For most companies, their Internet presence was initially treated in much the same way as their key internal systems. They used server-grade hardware with some high-availability options and additional capacity for scaling. For most companies, their Internet presence was just another part of the infrastructure, and not a par-ticularly business-critical part at that. Under normal conditions the site should remain up, but system administrators could schedule outages for maintenance as needed. Usually a scheduled outage for the web service involved configuring another machine to respond with a static page letting people know that the site was down for maintenance and to try again later.

Then new startup companies appeared with business models that revolved around conducting business entirely on the web. These companies did not have existing products, channels, and customers. They were not adapting existing busi-ness processes to include the web. For these companies, their Internet presence was the entire business. If their web sales channel failed, everything came to a standstill. They did not have the luxury of contacting their customers to schedule a mainte-nance window, as they had no way to know who their customers might be during that time period. Anyone with Internet access was a potential customer. These com-panies needed a highly reliable Internet presence in a way that no other companies had before. Companies wanted 24 × 7 operations with no maintenance windows.

Technology

During this era, home computers became more common, as did faster connections to the home with xDSL and Internet service from cable TV companies. Better graph-ics and more powerful computers resulted in better games, many of which were networked, multi-user games. Voice over IP (VoIP) emerged, with associated new products and services. Disks became larger and cheaper, so people started digitiz-ing and storing new types of data, such as music and videos. Inevitably companies built products and Internet services around that data as well.

On the server side, companies looking to provide a more reliable Internet pres-ence started buying RAID subsystems instead of plain disks, multiple high-end processors, and so on. While these technologies are common today, they were extremely expensive then. Vendors that previously sold to the very small set of customers who needed either very large or very reliable computers had an entirely new group of customers who wanted machines that were both large and reliable. Sun Microsystems' E4500 server was the normative hardware of the dot-com era.

Load balancers also appeared on the market during this era. A load balancer sits in front of a group of machines that are all providing the same service. It continually tests to see if the service is available on each of the machines. Load balancers can be configured in a primary/secondary setup—sending all traffic to the primary device until it fails, and then automatically switching to the secondary device. They can also be configured to load-share between machines that all provide the same service. In this latter mode, when a machine stops responding correctly, the load balancer stops directing queries to it until it resumes responding correctly. Load balancers provide automatic failover in case a machine is down, making them a useful tool for a service that needs high availability.

Scaling

Businesses needed servers to power their web sites. System administrators applied their old methods to the new requirements: one machine for each web site. As the site got more popular, larger machines were used to meet the demand. To achieve better performance, custom CPUs and new internal architectures were developed, but these machines were expensive. Software was also expensive. A typical web server required an OS license, a web server license, and a database server license. Each was priced proportionately to the hardware.

With the web the requirements for scaling are not bound to the number of employees in the company. The web introduces an environment where the users of the service can be anyone with an Internet connection. That is a very large and rapidly growing number. When a site introduces or successfully markets a web-based service, the number of people accessing the servers can increase very rapidly over a short period of time. Scaling for sudden, unpredictable fluctuations in service usage was a new challenge that was not well understood in this era, although it was something for which Internet startups tried to prepare. Internet startups planned for success and purchased the biggest, most reliable systems available. These were expensive times.

However, the practice of growing web sites through bigger, more reliable, more expensive hardware was not economically viable. Normally as a company grows, economies of scale result in lower cost per unit. The dot-coms, however, required computers that were more expensive per unit of capacity as the company grew larger. A computer that is 10 times more powerful than an average computer is more than 10 times as expensive. These larger, more reliable systems used custom hardware and had a smaller market—two factors that drove up prices. For linear increases in performance, the cost per unit of capacity was growing super-linearly. The more users the web site gained, the more expensive it was to provide the service. This model is the opposite of what you want. Additional costs came from the techniques used to ensure high availability, which are covered in the next section.

Oddly enough, these high costs were acceptable at the time. The dot-coms were flush with cash. Spending it on expensive machines was common, because it showed how optimistic you were about your company's success. Also, the economics of scaling sites in this way was not well understood—the traditional model of increased sales yielding a lower cost per unit was assumed to still hold true. In addition, startup valuations were made in a rather strange manner in those days. If a startup was achieving a small profit, it got a low valuation. However, if it was showing a loss, it got a high valuation. Moreover, the larger the loss, the higher the valuation. When these startups were floated on the stock market, their stock prices went through the roof, and the investors made substantial profits, even if the business model made no sense.

The saying at the time was "We may lose money on every sale, but we'll make it up in volume." Behind the scenes was the thought that if the company could corner the market, it could raise prices later. However, that assumption failed to take into account that the next startup would immediately undercut the higher prices with its own loss-making corner-the-market scheme.

This gold rush mentality kept the economy buzzing for quite a while. Then in 2000 the bubble burst. The house of cards collapsed. This approach to scaling web-based services was unsustainable. If the bubble had not burst due to issues of investment and cash flow, it would have failed due to the bad economics of the technology being used.

High Availability

With the advent of the web, the user base changed from known internal company employees with predictable, cyclic availability (the 9-to-5 business day) requirements and access schedules, to unknown external Internet users who required constant access. This change created the need for higher reliability. The first approach to meeting these availability goals was to buy more expensive hardware with built-in higher availability—for example, RAID and multiple CPUs.

But even the most reliable system fails occasionally. Traditional options for critical systems were to have a service contract with a four-hour turnaround for replacement parts, or to purchase spare parts to be stored near the machine. Either way, some downtime would be required in the event of a hardware failure.

There was also the issue of downtime to perform software upgrades. Applying the internal corporate approach of notifying the user base, it became common practice for web sites to pre-announce such downtime. There would be a warning that "This site will be down Saturday from noon to 5 PM PST for an upgrade." Regular users could plan around this, but new or occasional customers would be caught unaware, as there was no other way to notify them. Advertising upgrades in advance could also lead to adverse headlines if the upgrade went poorly, as some people would watch to see how the upgrade went and to report on the new service.

N + 1 Configurations

Using two machines became the best practice. One would run the service and the other was idle but configured and ready to take over if the first machine failed. Unless the site had a load balancer the "failover" usually required manual intervention but a good systems administrator could do the switch fast enough that the web site would be down for less than an hour. This is called an N + 1 configuration since there is one more device than required to provide the service. This technique is very expensive considering that at any given time 50 percent of your investment is sitting idle.

Software upgrades could be done by upgrading the spare server and switching to it when it was time to unveil the new features. The downtime would only be minutes or seconds to perform the failover. Users might not even notice!

N + 2 Configurations

What if the primary machine failed while the spare was being upgraded? The half-configured machine would not be in a usable state. As software releases increased in frequency, the likelihood that the spare would not be in a usable state also increased.

Thus, the best practice became having three machines, or an N + 2 configuration. Now systems administrators could safely perform upgrades but 66 percent of the hardware investment was idle at any given time. Imagine paying for three houses but only living in one. Imagine being the person who had to tell the CEO how much money was used on idle equipment!

Some companies tried to optimize by load sharing between the machines. Extra software development or a load balancer was required to make this work but it was possible. In an N + 1 configuration, systems administrators could perform software upgrades by taking one machine out of service and upgrading it while the other remained running. However, if both machines were at 80 percent utilization, the site now had a single machine that was 160 percent utilized, which would make it unacceptably slow for the end users. The web site might as well be down. The easy solution to that problem is to never let either machine get more than 50 percent utilized—but that simply returns us to the situation where half the capacity we paid for is idle. The idle capacity is just split between two machines!

Some companies tried to do such upgrades only late at night when fewer users meant that utilization had dipped below 50 percent. That left very little time to do the upgrade, making large or complex upgrades extremely risky. Changes that required an operating system upgrade or extensive testing were not possible. If the site became popular internationally and was busy during every time zone, this option disappeared. Also, no one can schedule hardware failures to happen only at night! Neither of these approaches was a viable option for better utilization of the available resources.

For high availability, sites still needed three machines and the resulting 66 percent idle capacity.

Costs

The cost of providing a highly available and popular web service during this era was very high. It was run on expensive high-end hardware, with expensive reliability features such as RAID and multiple CPUs, in an $N + 1$ or $N + 2$ configuration. That architecture meant that 50 to 66 percent of this expensive hardware was always idle. To reduce downtime to next to nothing, sites might also use expensive load balancers.

The OS costs and support costs for this high-end hardware were also very high, as were the costs for the application software, such as the web server software and database software.

Scaling a site built in this way meant that the cost per unit of performance increased as the site got bigger. Rather than more customers resulting in economies of scale, more customers meant a higher cost per unit. The cost model was the reverse of what a business would normally expect.

B.3 The Dot-Bomb Era (2000–2003)

The dot-com bubble collapse started in 2000. By 2001, the bubble was deflating as fast as it could. Most of the dot-coms burned through their venture capital and their stock ceased trading, often never having reached profitability.

After the collapse came a period of calm. Things slowed down a bit. It was possible to pause and consider what had been learned from the past. Without all the hype, marketing, and easy money, the better technologies survived. Without pressure from investors wanting their cash spent quickly so that they would get a quick return on their investment, people could take enough time to think and invent new solutions. Silicon Valley is, for the most part, a meritocracy. Working technology rules; hype and self-promotion are filtered out.

Availability Requirements

During the dot-bomb era, there were no significant changes in availability requirements. The Internet-based companies that had survived the crash developed a better understanding of their availability requirements and figured out how to meet them without breaking the bank.

Technology

Three trends enabled the next phase: surplus capacity left over from the previous boom years, the commoditization of hardware, and the maturation of open source software.

The first trend was short-lived but significant. A lot of capacity had been built up in the previous boom years and suppliers were slashing prices. Millions of miles of fiber had been laid in the ground and in the oceans to meet the predicted bandwidth needs of the world. With relatively few customers, telecommunications providers were desperate to make deals. Similarly, huge datacenter "colocation facilities" had been built. A colocation facility is a highly reliable datacenter facility that rents space to other companies. Many colocation providers went bankrupt after building some of the world's largest facilities. That space could now be rented very inexpensively. While these surpluses would eventually be exhausted, the temporarily depressed prices helped kickstart the era.

The second trend was the commoditization of hardware components used in home computers, such as Intel x86 CPUs, low-end hard drives, and RAM. Before the advent of the web, the average home did not have a computer. The popularity of the Internet created more demand for home computers, resulting in components being manufactured at a scale never before seen. In addition, the popularity of games that required high-end graphics, lots of memory, and fast CPUs was one of the major drivers toward making increasingly higher-end devices available in the consumer market. This mass production led to commoditization and, in turn, lower prices. The price of home PCs came down, but servers still used different components and remained expensive.

The third trend was the maturity of open source projects such as Linux, Apache, MySQL, and Perl. The rise of Linux brought a UNIX-like server operating system to the Intel x86 platform. Previously systems that used the Intel x86 chips could not run server-class, UNIX and UNIX-like operating systems. SGI, IBM, Sun, and others did not make their operating systems available for the x86. Intel x86 computers ran Windows 95 and variants that were not designed as server operating systems. Even Windows NT, which was designed as a server operating system, did not achieve success as a web service platform.

There were also free versions of BSD UNIX available for x86-based computers at the same time. Eventually, however, Linux became the dominant x86 UNIX because various companies like RedHat offered versions of Linux with support. Corporations had typically shied away from free open source software, because it was not supported. These companies were slowly persuaded that commercial versions of Linux were acceptable for servers, because they could still buy support. Even though they were still paying for the OS and support for the OS, they realized significant cost savings through the use of cheaper x86 hardware and reduced OS costs.

Although Linux was available during the first web era, it was not mature enough for production use. In fact, tools like Linux, Apache, MySQL, and Perl were considered toys compared to a Solaris OS, Netscape web server, Oracle database, Java "stack" or a Microsoft NT Server, IIS (web server), and SQL Server database and .NET environment. Even so, those open source projects were now creating software that was reliable enough for production use. Linux matured. Apache proved to be faster, more stable, more feature rich, and easier to configure than commercial platforms. MySQL was easier to install and manage than Oracle. Oracle's price tag was so high that the moment a free SQL database was available, the floodgates opened. Perl matured, added object oriented features, and gained acceptance outside of its initial niche as a system administration language. All of this was unimaginable just a few years earlier. One combination of open source software was so common that the acronym "LAMP" was coined, referring to the quartet of Linux, Apache, MySQL, and Perl. The ability to use commodity servers running a free operating system was revolutionary.

High Availability

While a LAMP system was less expensive, it was slower and less reliable. It would take many such servers to equal the aggregate processing capacity of the larger machine being replaced. Reliability was more complex.

Researchers started experimenting with using low-cost components to build servers. Research such as Recovery-Oriented Computing (ROC) at University of California–Berkeley (Patterson et al. 2002) discovered that many small servers could work better and be cheaper than individual large servers. This was previously unheard of. How could that underpowered CPU designed for desktops compete with a custom-designed Sun SPARC chip? How could a cheap consumer-grade hard disk compete with a fancy SCSI drive?

The conventional engineering wisdom is that more components means more failures. If one computer is likely to fail every 100 days, then it is likely that a system with two computers will have a failure every 50 days. If you had enough computers, you were likely to experience failures every day.

Research projects like ROC at UC-Berkeley and others reversed that logic. More computers could be more reliable when "distributed computing" techniques were employed. Rather than design a system where any one machine's failure prevented the system from providing service, these researchers developed distributed computing techniques that let many machines share the workload and have enough spare capacity that a certain percentage of the machines could be down and service would be unaffected.

ROC also observed that companies were paying for reliability at every level. The load balancer provided reliability, sending traffic to only the "up" server(s). The servers provided reliability by using expensive custom CPUs. The storage systems provided reliability by using expensive RAID controllers and high-end hard drives. Yet, to avoid downtime due to applications that required manual failover, companies still had to write software to survive outages. Why pay for many layers of reliability and also pay to develop software that survives outages? ROC reasoned that if the software already survived outages, why pay for extra quality at every level? Using the cheaper commodity components might result in less reliable servers, but software techniques would result in a system that was more reliable as a whole. Since the software had to be developed anyway, this made a lot of sense.

Digital electronics either work or they don't. The ability to provide service is binary: the computer is on or off. This is called the "run run run dead" problem. Digital electronics typically run and run and run until they fail. At that point, they fail completely. The system stops working. Compare this to an analog system such as an old tube-based radio. When it is new, it works fine. Over time components start to wear out, reducing audio quality. The user hears more static, but the radio is usable. The amount of static increases slowly, giving the user months of warning before the radio is unusable. Instead of "run run run dead," analog systems degrade slowly.

With distributed computing techniques, each individual machine is still digital: it is either running or not. However, the collection of machines is more like the analog radio: the system works but performance drops as more and more machines fail. A single machine being down is not a cause for alarm but rather a signal that it must be repaired before too many other machines have also failed.

Scaling

ROC researchers demonstrated that distributed computing could be reliable enough to provide a service requiring high availability. But could it be fast enough? The answer to this question was also "yes." The computing power of a fully loaded Sun E10K could be achieved with enough small, pizza box–sized machines based on commodity hardware.

Web applications were particularly well suited for distributed computing. Imagine a simple case where the contents of a web site can be stored on one machine. A large server might be able to deliver 4000 queries per second (QPS) of service. Suppose a commodity server could provide only 100 QPS. It would take 40 such servers to equal the aggregate capacity of the larger machine. Distributed computing algorithms for load balancing can easily scale to 40 machines.

Data Scaling

For some applications, all the data for the service might not fit on a single commodity server. These commodity servers were too small to store a very large dataset. Applications such as web search have a dataset, or "corpus," that could be quite large. Researchers found that they could resolve this issue by dividing the corpus into many "fractions," each stored on a different machine, or "leaf." Other machines (called "the root") would receive requests and forward each one to the appropriate leaf.

To make the system more resilient to failures, each fraction could be stored on two different leaves. If there were 10 fractions, there would be 20 leaves. The root would divide the traffic for a particular fraction among the two leaves as long as both were up. If one failed, the root would send all requests related to that fraction to the remaining leaf. The chance of a simultaneous failure by two leaves holding the same data was unlikely. Even if it did happen, users might not notice that their web searches returned slightly fewer results until the replacement algorithms loaded the missing data onto a spare machine.

Scaling was also achieved through replication. If the system did not process requests fast enough, it could be scaled by adding leaves. A particular fraction might be stored in three or more places.

The algorithms got more sophisticated over time. For example, rather than splitting the corpus into 10 fractions, one for each machine, the corpus could be split into 100 fractions and each machine would store 10. If a particular fraction was receiving a particularly large number of hits (it was "hot"), that fraction could be placed on more machines, bumping out less popular fractions. Better algorithms resulted in better placement, diversity, and dynamically updatable corpus data.

Applicability

These algorithms were particularly well suited for web search and similar applications where the data was mostly static (did not change) except for wholesale replacements when a new corpus was produced. In contrast, they were inappropriate for traditional applications. After all, you wouldn't want your payroll system built on a database that dealt with machine failures by returning partial results. Also, these systems lacked many of the features of traditional databases related to consistency and availability.

New distributed computing algorithms enabled new applications one by one. For example, the desire to provide email as a massive web-based service led to better storage systems. Over time more edge cases were conquered so that distributed computing techniques could be applied to more applications.

Costs

If distributed computing could be more reliable and faster, could it be more cost effective, too? The cost of one highly reliable and expensive machine compared very well to the cost of enough commodity machines to provide equivalent capacity. In fact, the cost per unit of capacity was often 3 to 50 times less expensive using distributed computing. Remember that previously we saw 50 to 66 percent idle capacity with the large servers when used in $N + 1$ and $N + 2$ configurations. Suppose an entire rack of machines was required to provide the equivalent capacity. That would typically be 40 machines, with two held as spares. ($N + 2$ redundancy). The "waste" now drops from 66 percent to 5 percent. That shrinking of idle capacity gives the distributed computing design a head start. Factoring in the power of a commodity market to drive down the cost of components improves the situation further. Moreover, one gets a volume discount when purchasing many computers—something you can't do when buying one or two large machines.

In the 2003 article "Web Search for a Planet: The Google Cluster Architecture," Barroso et al. wrote:

> The cost advantages of using inexpensive, PC-based clusters over high-end multiprocessor servers can be quite substantial, at least for a highly parallelizable application like ours. The example $278,000 rack contains 176 2-GHz Xeon CPUs, 176 Gbytes of RAM, and 7 Tbytes of disk space. In comparison, a typical x86-based server contains eight 2-GHz Xeon CPUs, 64 Gbytes of RAM, and 8 Tbytes of disk space; it costs about $758,000. In other words, the multiprocessor server is about three times more expensive but has 22 times fewer CPUs, three times less RAM, and slightly more disk space. (Barroso, Dean & Hölzle 2003)

Further cost reductions came by stripping the machines down to the exact components needed. These machines did not need video cards, audio cards, speakers, keyboards, USB ports, or a fancy plastic bezel with a cool logo on the front. Even if eliminating an item saved just a few dollars, when buying thousands of machines it added up. Some companies (Yahoo!) worked with vendors to build custom computers to their exact specifications, while others grew large enough to design their own computers from scratch (Google).

All these changes altered the economics of computing. In fact, they are what enabled the second web era.

Under the old economics, the larger the scale, the more disproportionately expensive the system became. In the new economics, the larger the scale, the more opportunity for the economics to improve. Instead of super-linear cost curves, cost growth was closer to linear.

B.4 The Second Web Era (2003–2010)

In the history of computing, every jump in improved cost led to a wave of new applications. Distributed computing's better economics was one such leap. Web services that had previously failed, unable to make a profit, were now cheaper to operate and got a second chance.

Availability Requirements

As before, companies that conducted business entirely over the Internet typically aimed at a global audience of Internet users. That meant that they required 24 × 7 availability with no scheduled downtime, and as close to no unscheduled downtime as possible. Companies started applying the newly developed distributed computing techniques to their service offerings to meet these availability requirements in a more cost-effective way.

Technology

Many companies embraced distributed computing techniques. Google adopted the techniques to provide web search that was faster than ever seen before. Previously web searches took many seconds and sometimes minutes or hours to show search results. Google was so proud of its ability to return results in less than half a second that it listed the number of milliseconds your request took to process at the bottom of every page.

New advertising systems like Google AdSense, which collects pennies per click, could be profitable now that the cost of computing was significantly cheaper. Earlier business models that involved selling advertising on a web site required huge sales forces to get advertisers to buy ads on their web site. AdSense and similar systems were fully automated. Potential advertisers would bid in a huge, online auction for ad placement. This reduced and often eliminated the need for a sales force. All the company needed to do was add some JavaScript code to its site. Soon the advertisements would start appearing and money would start rolling in. Such advertising systems created a new business model that enabled the development of entire new industries.

Web hosting became much cheaper. The software got much easier to use. This led to the invention of "blogs" (originally from the term "web-log"), which required very little technical knowledge to operate. Rather than needing a sales force and a large IT department, a single person could run a successful blog. Bloggers could focus on creating content and the advertising network would send them checks.

High Availability

With distributed computing techniques, high availability and scaling became closely coupled. Techniques used to ensure high availability also aided scaling, and vice versa. Google published many of the distributed computing techniques it invented. Some of the earliest of these were the Google File System (GFS) and MapReduce.

GFS was a file system that scaled to multiple terabytes of data. Files were stored as 64-megabyte chunks. Each chunk was stored on three or more commodity servers. Accessing the data was done by talking directly to the machine with the desired data rather than going through a mediator machine that could be a bottleneck. GFS operations often happened in parallel. For example, copying a file was not done one block at a time. Instead, each machine that stored a part of the source file would be paired with another machine and all blocks would be transmitted in parallel. Resiliency could be improved by configuring GFS to keep more than three replicas of each block, decreasing the chance that all copies of the file would be on a down machine at any given time. If one machine did fail, the GFS master would use the remaining copies to populate the data elsewhere until the replication factor was achieved. Increasing the replication level also improved performance. Data access was load balanced among all the replicas. More replicas meant more aggregate read performance.

Case Study: MapReduce

MapReduce is a system for processing large batches of data in parallel. Suppose you needed to process 100 terabytes of data. Reading that much data from start to finish would take a long time. Instead, dozens (or thousands) of machines could be set up to process a portion of the data each in parallel. The data they read would be processed (mapped) to create an intermediate result. These intermediates would be processed and then summarized (reduced) to gain the final result. MapReduce did all the difficult work of dividing up the data and delegating work to various machines. As a software developer using MapReduce, you just needed to write the "map" function and the "reduce" function. Everything else was taken care of.

Because MapReduce was a centralized service, it could be improved and all users would benefit from the changes. For example, there was a good probability that a machine would fail during a MapReduce run that takes days and involves thousands of machines. The logic for detecting a failed machine and sending its portion of data to another working machine is incorporated in the MapReduce system. The developer does not need to worry about it. Suppose a better way to detect and replace a failed machine is developed. This improvement would be made to the central MapReduce system and all users would benefit.

One such improvement involved predicting which machines would fail. If one machine was taking considerably longer to process its share of the data, that slow performance could be a sign that it had a hard disk that was starting to fail or that some other problem was present. MapReduce could direct another machine to process the same portion of data. Whichever machine finished first would "win" and its results would be kept. The other machine's processing would be aborted. This kind of preemptive redundancy could save hours of processing, especially since a MapReduce run is only as fast as the slowest machine. Many such optimizations were developed over the years.

Open source versions of MapReduce soon appeared. Now it was easy for other companies to adopt MapReduce's techniques. The most popular implementation is Hadoop. It includes a data storage system similar to GFS called HBase.

Scaling

If you've spent money to invent ways to create highly available distributed computing systems that scale well, the best way to improve your return on investment (ROI) is to use that technology on as many datacenters as possible.

Once you are maintaining hundreds of racks of similarly configured computers, it makes sense to manage them centrally. Centralized operations have economic benefits. For example, standardization makes it possible to automate operational tasks and therefore requires less labor. When labor is manual, larger systems require more labor. When operations are automated, the cost of developing the software is spread across all the machines, so the cost per machine decreases as the number of machines increases.

To gain further efficiencies of scale, companies like Google and Facebook take this one step further. Why not treat the entire datacenter as one giant computer? A computer has memory, disks, and CPUs that are connected by a communication "bus." A datacenter has a network that acts like a bus connecting units of compute and storage. Why not design and operate datacenters as one large, warehouse-sized computer? Barroso, Clidaras, and Hölzle (2013) coined the phrase "warehouse-scale computing" to capture this idea of treating the entire datacenter as one giant computer.

Costs

In this era companies also competed to develop better and less expensive datacenters. The open source movement was reducing the cost of software. Moore's law was reducing the cost of hardware. The remaining costs were electricity and operations itself. Companies saw that improvements in these areas would give them a competitive edge.

Prior to the second web era, datacenters wasted electricity at unbelievable rates. According to the Uptime Institute, the typical datacenter has an average power usage effectiveness (PUE) of 2.5. This means that for every 2.5 watts in at the utility meter, only 1 watt is used for the IT. By using the most efficient equipment and best practices, most facilities could achieve 1.6 PUE. The lack of efficiency primarily comes from two places. First, some efficiency is lost every time there is a power conversion. A UPS converts the power from alternating current (A/C) to direct current (D/C), and back to A/C—two conversions. Power is converted from high-voltage lines to 110 VAC used in power outlets to 12 V and other voltage levels required by the components and chips in computers—four or five more conversions. In addition, cooling is a major factor. If 1 watt of power makes a computer generate a certain amount of heat, it takes at least 1 watt of power to remove that heat. You don't actually "cool" a datacenter; you extract the heat. Companies seeking to reduce their operational costs like Google, Microsoft, and Facebook achieved closer to 1.2 PUE. In 2011, Google reported one datacenter achieved 1.08 PUE during winter months (Google 2012). Every decimal improvement in PUE means a big competitive edge.

Other things are even more important than power efficiency. Using less power—for example, by shutting off unused machines—is an improvement no matter your PUE rating. Smart companies work toward achieving the best price per unit of computation. For example, for internet search, true efficiency comes from getting the most QPS for your money. This may mean skipping a certain generation of Intel CPU because, while faster, the CPU uses a disproportionate amount of power.

The new economics also made it more feasible to give away a service because advertising revenue was sufficient to make the business viable. Many sites were free for most features but offered "premium" services at an additional cost. This "freemium" (free + premium) business model was a great way to attract large numbers of customers. Being free meant there was very little barrier to entry. Once the user was accustomed to using the service, selling the premium features was easier. If advertising revenue was sufficient, the free users were no burden.

Software, hardware, and power costs were all significantly lower with this new approach, enabling the emergence of new business models. Could the price drop to the point that computing becomes cost free? The answer will surprise you.

B.5 The Cloud Computing Era (2010–present)

The trend so far as been that each era has computing capacity that is more economical than the previous era. Increases in capacity and reliability went from having super-linear cost growth to linear and sub-linear cost growth. Can it get any better? Could it become free?

Many landlords live "rent free" by simply having enough profitable tenants to cover the cost of the apartment they live in. This is the economic thinking that enables cloud computing: build more computing resources than you need and rent the surplus.

Availability Requirements

Around this time, mobile computing became more affordable and, in turn, more accessible. Cell phones became smartphones running operating systems as sophisticated as those found on PCs. Mobile applications created demand for even better latency and reliability.

Mobile applications create demand for lower-latency services—that is, services that respond faster. A mobile map application would not be useful if it took an hour to calculate the best driving route to a location. It has to be fast enough to be usable in a real-world context, responding in a second or two. If such calculations can be done hundreds of times a second, it opens the door to new applications: the ability to drag points in the map and see the route recalculated in real time. Now instead of one request, dozens are sent. Because the application is so much more usable this way, the number of users increases. Thus capacity demands increase by multiple orders of magnitude, which requires quantum leaps in support infrastructure.

Mobile applications demand new levels of reliability. A map application is not very useful if the map service it relies on is down when you need it. Yes, map tiles can be cached but real-time traffic reports less so. As mobile apps become more and more life-critical, the reliability of their supporting services becomes more important. As reliability improvements leap forward, more life-critical applications become possible.

Costs

As computing was done at even larger scales, new economics present themselves. If computing becomes cheaper at larger scales, then it becomes advantageous to build a larger infrastructure. If you build an infrastructure larger than you need, you simply have to develop the technology that lets you "rent" the spare capacity to others. The part you use is cheaper than it would have been otherwise; the part you don't use turns a profit. If the profit is small, it offsets the cost of your infrastructure. If the profit is large enough, it could pay for all of your infrastructure. At that point your computing infrastructure becomes "free" for you. Do things right and you could have an infrastructure with a negative cost. Imagine running all of Amazon's infrastructure and having someone else pay for it. Now imagine trying to start a new web site that sells books when your competition gets its infrastructure "for free." These are the economic aspirations that drive the supplier side of cloud computing.

In the cloud computing era, the scale provides economics that make the cost a new order less expensive. This frees up enough headroom to price the service at less than customers could do it themselves and delivers additional profit that subsidizes the provider's infrastructure. Anything done to improve the efficiency of operations either adds to the service provider's profitability or enables it to offer services at a lower cost than the competition.

To understand the consumer demand for cloud computing, we need to look at the costs associated with small-scale computing systems. At a small scale one cannot take advantage of the economics of distributed computing. Instead, one must achieve reliability through more expensive hardware. Automation makes less sense when doing things at a small scale, which drives up the operational cost. When automation is created, it is more expensive because the cost is not amortized over as many uses. Many distributed computing technologies require people with specialized knowledge that a small company does not possess, since at a small scale one must hire generalists and can't afford a full-time person (or team) to oversee just one aspect of the system. The use of external consultants when such expertise is needed can be expensive.

Many of these problems are mitigated when small-scale computing is done by renting space on a cloud infrastructure. Customers get to take advantage of the lower cost and greater power efficiency. Difficult-to-maintain services such as specialized storage and networking technology can be offered in a way that hides the difficult behind-the-scenes management such systems require.

There are also non-cost advantages for the customers. Elasticity is the ability to increase and decrease the amount of resources consumed dynamically. With many applications, being able to spin up many servers for a short amount of time is valuable. Suppose you have an advertising campaign that will last for just one week. While the ads are running, you may need hundreds of web servers to handle the traffic. Being able to acquire so many servers in hours is invaluable. Most companies would need months or a year to set up so many servers.

An advertising agency previously would not have the ability to do so. Now, without even the knowledge of how to build a datacenter, an ad agency can have all the systems it needs. Possibly more important is that at the end of the campaign, the servers can be "given back" to the cloud provider. Doing that the old way with physical hardware would be impractical.

Another non-cost advantage for many companies is that cloud computing enabled other departments to make an end-run around IT departments that had become recalcitrant or difficult to deal with. The ability to get the computing resources they need by clicking a mouse, instead of spending months of arguing with an uncooperative and underfunded IT department, is appealing. We are ashamed to admit that this is true but it is often cited as a reason people adopt cloud computing services.

Scaling and High Availability

Meeting the new requirements of scaling and high availability in the cloud computing era requires new paradigms. Lower latency is achieved primarily through faster storage technology and faster ways to move information around.

In this era SSDs have replaced disks. SSDs are faster because there are no moving parts. There is no wait for a read head to move to the right part of a disk platter, no wait for the platter to rotate to the right position. SSDs are more expensive per gigabyte but the total cost of ownership is lower. Suppose you require 10 database server replicas to provide enough horsepower to provide a service at the latency required. While using SSDs would be more expensive, the same latency can be provided with fewer machines, often just two or three machines in total. The SSDs are more expensive, it is true—but not as expensive as needing seven additional machines.

Service latency is also reduced by reducing the latency of internal communication. In the past, information sent between two machines went through many layers of technology. The information was converted to a "wire format," which meant making a copy read for transmission and putting it in a packet. The packet then went through the operating system's TCP/IP layer and device layer, through the network, and then reached the other machine, where the process was reversed. Each of these steps added latency. Most or all of this latency has now been removed through technologies that permit direct memory access between machines. Sometimes these technologies even bypass the CPU of the source or destination machine. The result is the ability to pass information between machines nearly as fast as reading local RAM. The latency is so low that it has caused underlying RPC mechanisms to be redesigned from scratch to fully take advantage of the new capabilities.

Technology

The technology that drives cloud computing itself is the ability to segment infrastructure such that one "tenant" cannot interfere with another. This requires networking technologies that allow segmenting computers from each other at a very fine granularity such as programmable VLANs and software-defined networks. It requires the ability to partition one large machine into many smaller ones—that is, virtualization technology. It requires control panels, APIs, and various self-service administration capabilities so that customers support themselves and do not add considerable labor cost to datacenter operations. It requires storage and other services to attract customers.

Amazon was the first company to develop such a system. Amazon Elastic Compute Cloud (Amazon EC2) was the first major company to rent virtual machines on its infrastructure to subsidize its cost. The term "elastic" comes from the fact that this approach makes it so fast to expand and contract the amount of resources being used. One of the most attractive features is how quickly one can spin up new machines. Even more attractive is how quickly one can dispose of machines when they aren't needed. Suppose you needed 1000 machines for a month-long web advertising campaign. It would be an arduous task to set up that many machines yourself and difficult to get rid of them a month later. With EC2, you can spin them all up with a mouse click or a few API calls. When the campaign is over, releasing the machines is just as simple.

Such "tenant" systems are just getting started. We are just now beginning to understand these new economics and their ramifications.

B.6 Conclusion

The goal of this appendix was to explain the history of technologies used for providing web services. The techniques described here form the basis for the platform options introduced in Chapter 3, the web architectures presented in Chapter 4, and the scaling and resiliency techniques described in Chapters 5 and 6. The other chapters in this book reflect the operational practices that make all of the above work.

The economics of computing change over time. Faster and more reliable computing technology had a super-linear cost curve in the pre-web and first web eras. The second web era was enabled by linear cost curves. Cloud computing gives us sub-linear cost curves. These changes happened by taking advantage of commoditization and standardization, shifting to open source software, building more reliability through software instead of hardware, and replacing labor-intensive operations with more software.

Every order-of-magnitude improvement in the cost of computing enables a new era of applications, each of which was unimaginable just a few years before.

Could the person who used an 8-bit computer to balance his or her checkbook in 1983 ever have imagined Facebook or Google Glass?

What will follow cloud computing is anyone's guess. The applications of tomorrow will demand computing resources that are orders-of-magnitude faster, have lower latency, and are less expensive. It will be very exciting to see what develops.

Exercises

1. This appendix provides a history of five eras of computing technology: pre-web era, first web era, dot-bomb era, second web era, and cloud computing era. For each era, describe the level of economic prosperity, the technological improvements, and the expectations for reliability and computing power.

2. The practice of owning the entire process instead of using external providers for certain steps or parts is called "vertical integration." Which examples of vertical integration were described in this appendix? What were the benefits?

3. What role did open source software play in the maturation of the second web era?

4. Describe the redundant reliability levels replaced by ROC-style distributed computing.

5. The history discussed in this appendix is described as inevitable. Do you agree or disagree? Support your case.

6. What era will follow cloud computing? Identify the trends described in this appendix and extrapolate them to predict the future based on past performance.

Scaling Terminology and Concepts

> The essence of life is statistical
> improbability on a colossal scale.
>
> —Richard Dawkins

You've probably experienced software that works well with a small amount of data but gets slower and slower as more data is added. Some systems get a little slower with more data. With others, the slow-down is much bigger, often dramatically so.

When discussing scalability, there is terminology that describes this phenomenon. This enables us to communicate with each other with great specificity.

This appendix describes some basic terminology, a more mathematical way of describing the same concepts, and finally some caveats for how modern systems do or do not act as one would expect.

C.1 Constant, Linear, and Exponential Scaling

There is a lot of terminology related to describing how systems perform and scale. Three terms are used so commonly that to be a professional system administrator you should be able to use these terms conversationally. They describe how a system performs as data size grows: the system is unaffected, gets slower, or gets much slower.

- **Constant Scaling:** No matter the scale of the input, performance does not change. For example, a hash-table lookup in RAM can always be done in constant time whether the table contains 100 items or 100 million items. It would be nice if all systems were so fast, but such algorithms are rare. In fact, even a hash-table lookup is limited to situations where the data fits in RAM.

- **Linear Scaling:** As input size grows, the system slows down proportionately. For example, twice as much data will require twice as much processing time. Suppose an authentication system for a service with 10,000 users takes 10 ms to authenticate each request. When there are 20,000 users, the system might take 60 ms. With 30,000 users, the system might take 110 ms. Each unit of growth resulted in a slowdown that was the same size (50 ms slower per 10,000 users added). Therefore we can classify this as a system with linear performance with respect to the size of the user database.

- **Exponential Scaling:** As input size grows, the system slows down disproportionately. Continuing our authentication system example, if adding more users resulted in response times of 10 ms, 100 ms, and 1000 ms, this would be exponential scaling. A system that slows down at such a rate, if it interacts with all parts of our system, would be a disaster! It might be fine if the input size is not expected to change and, at the current size, the system is fast enough. This assumption carries a high risk.

C.2 Big O Notation

$O()$ or "Big O notation" is used to classify a system based on how it responds to changes in input size. It is the more mathematical way of describing a system's behavior. $O()$ notation comes from computer science. The letter "O" is used because the growth rate of an algorithm's run-time is known as its "order."

Here is a list of common Big O terms that a system administrator should be familiar with. The first three we've already described:

- $O(1)$: **Constant Scaling:** No change in performance no matter the size of the input.
- $O(n)$: **Linear Scaling:** Gets slower in proportion to the size of the input.
- $O(n^m)$: **Exponential Scaling:** Performance worsens exponentially.
- $O(n^2)$: **Quadratic Scaling:** Performance worsens relative to the square of the size of input. Quadratic scaling is a special case of exponential scaling, where m is 2. People tend to refer to systems as scaling "exponentially" when they actually mean "quadratically." This is so common that one rarely hears the term "quadratic" anymore except when someone is being very specific (or pedantic) about the performance curve.
- $O(\log n)$: **Logarithmic Scaling:** Performance worsens proportional to the $\log_2$ of the size of input. Performance asymptotically levels off as input size grows. For example, a binary search grows slower as the size of the corpus being searched grows, but less than linearly.
- $O(n \log n)$: **Loglinear Scaling:** Performance worsens more than linearly, with the "more than" component being proportional to $\log_2$ of the size of input. Think of this as linear scaling with a small but ever-growing performance

surcharge added as the input size grows. People often incorrectly use the term "logarithmic scaling" when they actually mean "loglinear scaling." You can use the term "loglinear" when you want to sound like a true expert.

- $O(n!)$: **Factorial Scaling:** Performance worsens proportional to the factorial of the size of input. In other words, performance gets bad so quickly that each additional unit of size worsens performance by a leap as big as all previous leaps put together plus some more! $O(n!)$ algorithms are usually a worst-case scenario. For example, the breakthrough that permits Google PageRank and Facebook SocialRank to work so well came from computer science research that invented replacements for $O(n!)$ algorithms.

The term **sub-linear** refers to anything that grows less than linearly, such as constant and logarithmic scaling. **Super-linear** refers to anything that grows faster, such as exponential and factorial scaling.

In addition to being used to describe scaling, these terms are often used to describe growth. One might describe the increase in customers being attracted to your business as growing linearly or exponentially. The run-time of a system might be described as growing in similar terms.

Super-linear systems sound awful compared to sub-linear systems. Why not always use algorithms that are constant or linear? The simplest reason is that often algorithms of that order don't exist. Sorting algorithms have to touch every item at least once, eliminating the possibility of $O(1)$ algorithms. There is one $O(n)$ sort algorithm but it works on only certain kinds of data.

Another reason is that faster algorithms often require additional work ahead of time: for example, building an index makes future searches faster but requires the overhead and complexity of building and maintaining the index. That effort of developing, testing, and maintaining such indexing code may not be worth it if the system's performance is sufficient as is.

At small values, systems of different order may be equivalent. What's bigger, x or x^2? Your gut reaction may be that the square of something will be bigger than the original number. However, if x is 0.5, then this is not true. $0.5^2 = 0.25$, which is smaller than 0.5. Likewise, an $O(n)$ algorithm may be slower than an $O(n^2)$ algorithm for very small inputs. Also an $O(n^2)$ algorithm may be the easiest to implement, even though it wouldn't be the most efficient for larger-sized input. Thus the more complex algorithm would be a waste of time to develop. It would also be riskier. More complex code is more likely to have bugs.

It is important to remember that the concept of $O()$ is a gross generalization that focuses on the trend as its input grows, not the specific run-time. For example, two systems that are both $O(n^2)$ will not to have the exact same performance. The shared order simply indicates that both scale worse than, say, an $O(n)$ system.

$O()$ notation is an indicator of the biggest factor, not all factors. A real system may be dominated by an $O(n)$ lookup, but might also involve many $O(1)$

operations and possibly even some $O(n^2)$ operations, albeit ones that are inconsequential for other reasons.

For example, an API call might perform an $O(n)$ lookup on a small list of authorized users and then spend the majority of its time doing an $O(1)$ lookup in a large database. If the list of authorized users is tiny (say, it verifies the user is one of three people permitted to use the system) and done in RAM, it is inconsequential compared to the database lookup. Therefore this API call would be considered $O(1)$, not $O(n)$. Such a system may run at acceptable speed for years but then the number of authorized users surges, possibly due to a management change that authorizes thousands of additional users. Suddenly this $O(n)$ lookup starts to dominate the run-time of the API call. Surprises like this happen all the time in production systems.

While the "O" in Big O notation stands for "order," conversationally you may hear the word "order" used as shorthand for **order of magnitude**. Order of magnitude is related but different. Order of magnitude means, essentially, how many digits are in a number that describes a size (the magnitude of a digit literally means if it is in the 1s, 10s, 100s, or some other place). If you work for a company with 100 employees and your friend works at a company with 1000 employees, then your friend works at a company that is an order of magnitude larger. You may hear phrases like an algorithm working for situations "for 1 million users but breaks down on larger order of magnitude." You might hear references to a system processing "on the order of 2000 queries per second," which is a fancy way of saying "approximately 2000" with the implication that this is a very coarse estimate.

C.3 Limitations of Big O Notation

$O()$ notation relates to the number of operations an algorithm will perform. However, not all operations take the same amount of time. Reading two adjacent records from a database, if both fit into the same disk block, is essentially one disk read followed by two reads from the RAM that caches the entire block. Two algorithms with the same $O()$ order, one that takes advantage of this fact and one that does not, will have extremely different performance.

In Kamp's (2010) description of the Varnish HTTP accelerator, he explains that by taking advantage of a deep understanding of how a modern OS handles disk I/O, significantly better performance can be achieved than with naive $O()$ comparisons. Varnish was able to replace 12 overloaded machines running a competing software package with three machines that were 90 percent idle. He writes:

> What good is an $O(\log_2 n)$ algorithm if those operations cause page faults and slow disk operations? For most relevant datasets an $O(n)$ or even an $O(n^2)$ algorithm, which avoids page faults, will run circles around it.

The improvement came from structuring his heap in such a way that nodes would avoid generating virtual memory page faults. Kamp arranged data structures such that parent and child nodes tended to be on the same page in virtual memory.

A page fault occurs when a program accesses virtual memory that is not currently in the computer's RAM. The operating system pauses the process, reads the data from disk, and unpauses the process when the read is complete. Since memory is handled in 4KB blocks, the first access to a block may cause a page fault but later accesses within that same 4KB area do not.

A page fault takes about as long as 10 million instructions could run. In other words, spending 10,000 instructions to avoid a page fault has a 1000-to-1 payback. By carefully organizing where in memory objects are stored, Kamp was able to eliminate many page faults.

His message to the industry, titled "You're Doing It Wrong," details in very technical terms how most computer science education is still teaching algorithm design as appropriate for computer systems that have not existed for 30 years.

Modern CPUs have many complexities that make performance non-intuitive. Linear access is significantly faster than random access. Instructions execute in parallel when they are provably independent. The performance of a CPU drops when multiple CPUs are accessing the same part of memory.

For example, reading every element in an array in row order is significantly faster than reading the elements in column order. If the rows are bigger than the CPU's memory cache, the latter is essentially going to be a cache "miss" for every read. The former would be linear memory reads, which CPUs are optimized to do quickly. Even though either way reads the same number of bytes from memory, the former is faster.

More surprisingly, a loop that reads every element of an array takes approximately the same amount of time to execute as a loop that reads every 16th element of the same array. Even though the former does 1/16th of the number of operations, the number of RAM cache misses is the same for both loops. Reading blocks of memory from RAM to the CPU's L1 (Level 1) cache is slow and dominates the run-time of either algorithm. The fact that the former runs faster is due to the fact that there are special instructions for sequentially reading memory.

Above and beyond RAM, virtual memory, and disk issues, we also have to consider the effect of threads, multiple CPUs trying to access the same data, locks, and mutexes. All of these cloud the issue. You can't really tell how fast an algorithm will be without benchmarking. O() notation becomes a general guide, not an absolute.

That said, O() notation is still useful when conversationally describing systems and communicating with other system administrators. Therefore understanding the nomenclature is essential to being a system administrator today.

Templates and Examples

D.1 Design Document Template

Below is a simple design document template as described in Section 13.2.

Title:
Date:
Author(s): *(add authors, please link to their email addresses)*
Reviewers(s): *(add reviewers, please link to their email addresses)*
Approvers(s): *(add approvers, please link to their email addresses)*
Revision Number:
Status: *(draft, in review, approved, in progress)*

Executive Summary:
(2–4 sentences explaining the project)

Goals:
(bullet list describing the problem being solved)

Non-goals:
(bullet list describing the limits of the project)

Background:
(terminology and history one needs to know to understand the design)

High-Level Design:
(a brief, high-level description of the design; diagrams are helpful)

Detailed Design:
(the design in detail; usually a top-down description)

Alternatives Considered:
(alternatives considered and rejected; include pros and cons of each)

Security Concerns:
(security/privacy ramifications and how those concerns are mitigated)

D.2 Design Document Example

Below is an example design document as described in Section 13.2.

To illustrate the principle of design documents, we have created a sample design document with most of the parts included:

Title: New Monitoring System
Date: 2014-07-19
Author(s): Strata Chalup <src@example.com>
and Tom Limoncelli <tal@example.com>
Reviewers: Joe, Mary, Jane
Approvers: Security Operations 2014-08-03, Chris (Build System Tech Lead) 2014-08-04, Sara (Director of Ops) 2014-08-10
Revision Number: 1.0
Status: Approved

Executive Summary:
Create a monitoring system for devices that will support real-time alerting via pagers and deploy to production cluster.

Goals:
A monitoring system for our network:

- Be able to monitor at least 10,000 devices, 500 attributes each, collected each minute.

- Must support real-time alerting via SMS.
- Must retain data for 30 years.

Non-goals:

- Monitoring external systems.
- Building chat functionality into the system.

Background:
Historically we have used home-brew monitoring scripts, but we keep having to adjust them based on changing platforms. We want to have a standardized way of monitoring that doesn't require development time on our part as we add platforms.

High-Level Design:
The plan is to use Bosun with remote collectors. The server will be the current corporate standard configuration for server hardware and Linux. The server will be named bosun01.example.com. It will be in the Phoenix and Toronto datacenters. Monitoring configuration will be kept in the Git "sysadmin configs" repo, in the top-level directory /monitor.

Detailed Design:

Server configuration:
Dell 720XD with 64G RAM, 8 disks in RAID6 configuration
Debian Linux (standard corporate "server configuration")
Bosun package name is "bosun-server."

- Any system being monitored will have the "bosun-client" package installed.
- Backups will be performed nightly using the standard corporate backup mechanism.
- (The full document would include a description of operational tasks such as adding new monitoring collectors, and alerting rules.)

Cost Projections:

- Initial cost [cost of server].
- Software is open source.
- One half-time FTE for 3 weeks to set up monitoring and launch.

Schedule after approval:

1. 1 week to procure hardware.
2. 2 days of installation and testing.
3. "Go live" on week 3.

Alternatives Considered:
Zappix and SkunkStorm were both considered, but the feature set of Bosun is more closely aligned with the project goals. [link to comparison charts]

Special Constraints:
Bosun stores SNMP "community strings," which are essentially passwords, in a password vault. The storage method has been reviewed and approved by Security Operations.

D.3 Sample Postmortem Template

Below is a simple postmortem template as described in Section 14.3.2.

Title:
Report Status:
Executive Summary:
  List what happened, who was affected, and what are the key recommendations for prevention in the future (especially any that will require budget or executive approval).
Outage Description:
  A general description of the outage, from a technical perspective of what happened.
Affected users:
  Who was affected.
Start Date/Time:
End Date/Time:
Duration:
Timeline:
  A minute-by-minute timeline assembled from system logs, chat logs, emails, and whatever other resources are available.
Contributing Conditions Analysis:
  What were the contributing causes that led to the outage?

What went well?

    A bullet list of what went well. This is a good opportunity to thank anyone who went above and beyond expectations to help out.

What could have gone better?

    A bullet list of which actions could have been taken that would have improved how fast we were back in service, the techniques used, and so on.

Recommendations:

    A bullet list of recommendations that would prevent this outage in the future. Each should be actionable and measurable. Good example: "Monitor disk space for database server and alert if less than 20 percent is available." Bad example: "Improve monitoring." File a bug/feature request for each recommendation; list bug IDs here.

Names of people involved:

    List of the people involved in the resolution of the outage.

Recommended Reading

> To achieve great things, two things
> are needed; a plan, and
> not quite enough time.

— Leonard Bernstein

DevOps:

- *The Phoenix Project: A Novel about IT, DevOps, and Helping Your Business Win* (Kim et al. 2013)
  A fictional story that teaches the Three Ways of DevOps.
- *Building a DevOps Culture* (Walls 2013)
  Strategies for building a DevOps culture, including aligning incentives, defining meaningful and achievable goals, and creating a supportive team environment.
- *Continuous Delivery: Reliable Software Releases through Build, Test, and Deployment Automation* (Humble & Farley 2010)
  The canonical book about service delivery platforms.
- *Release It!: Design and Deploy Production-Ready Software* (Nygard 2007)
  Detailed coverage and examples of how to implement many of the ideas in Chapter 11.
- *Blameless PostMortems and a Just Culture* (Allspaw 2009)
  Theory and practice of postmortems.
- *A Mature Role for Automation* (Allspaw 2012c)
  Why "Automate Everything!" is bad, and what to do instead.
- *Each Necessary, But Only Jointly Sufficient* (Allspaw 2012a)
  Myths and limits of "root cause analysis" and "The Five Why's."

ITIL:

- *Owning ITIL: A Skeptical Guide for Decision-Makers* (England 2009)
  A gentle introduction to ITIL with honest advice about how to make it work.

Theory:

- *In Search of Certainty: The Science of Our Information Infrastructure* (Burgess 2013)
  The physics of distributed systems.
- *Promise Theory: Principles and Applications* (Burgess & Bergstra 2014)
  The theory of configuration management and change management.

Classic Google Papers:

- "The Anatomy of a Large-Scale Hypertextual Web Search Engine" (Brin & Page 1998)
  The first paper describing the Google search engine.
- "Web Search for a Planet: The Google Cluster Architecture" (Barroso, Dean & Hölzle 2003)
  Google's first paper revealing how clusters are designed using commodity class PCs with fault-tolerant software.
- "The Google File System" (Ghemawat, Gobioff & Leung 2003)
- "MapReduce: Simplified Data Processing on Large Clusters" (Dean & Ghemawat 2004)
- "Bigtable: A Distributed Storage System for Structured Data" (Chang et al. 2006)
- "The Chubby Lock Service for Loosely-Coupled Distributed Systems" (Burrows 2006)
- "Spanner: Google's Globally-Distributed Database" (Corbett et al. 2012)
- "The Tail at Scale" (Dean & Barroso 2013)
  Improving latency means fixing the last percentile.
- "Failure Trends in a Large Disk Drive Population" (Pinheiro, Weber & Barroso 2007)
  Longitudinal study of hard drive failures.
- "DRAM Errors in the Wild: A Large-Scale Field Study" (Schroeder, Pinheiro & Weber 2009)
  Longitudinal study of DRAM failures.

Classic Facebook Papers:

- "Cassandra: A Decentralized Structured Storage System" (Lakshman & Malik 2010)

Scalability:

- *The Art of Scalability: Scalable Web Architecture, Processes, and Organizations for the Modern Enterprise* (Abbott & Fisher 2009)
    An extensive catalog of techniques and discussion of scalability of people, process, and technology.
- *Scalability Rules: 50 Principles for Scaling Web Sites* (Abbott & Fisher 2011)
    A slimmer volume, focused on technical strategy and techniques.

UNIX Internals:

- *The Design and Implementation of the FreeBSD Operating System* (McKusick, Neville-Neil & Watson 2014)
    This is the best deep-dive into how UNIX-like operating systems work. While the examples are all FreeBSD, Linux users will benefit from the theory and technical details the book provides.

UNIX Systems Programming:

- *The UNIX Programming Environment* (Kernighan & Pike 1984)
- *Advanced Programming in the UNIX Environment* (Stevens & Rago 2013)
- *UNIX Network Programming* (Stevens 1998)

Network Protocols:

- *TCP/IP Illustrated, Volume 1: The Protocols* (Stevens & Fall 2011)
- *TCP/IP Illustrated, Volume 2: The Implementation* (Wright & Stevens 1995)
- *TCP/IP Illustrated, Volume 3: TCP for Transactions, HTTP, NNTP, and the UNIX Domain Protocols* (Stevens & Wright 1996)

Bibliography

Abbott, M., & Fisher, M. (2009). *The Art of Scalability: Scalable Web Architecture, Processes, and Organizations for the Modern Enterprise,* Pearson Education.

Abbott, M., & Fisher, M. (2011). *Scalability Rules: 50 Principles for Scaling Web Sites,* Pearson Education.

Abts, D., & Felderman, B. (2012). A guided tour through data-center networking, *Queue* **10**(5): 10:10–10:23.
http://queue.acm.org/detail.cfm?id=2208919

Adya, A., Cooper, G., Myers, D., & Piatek, M. (2011). Thialfi: A client notification service for internet-scale applications, *Proceedings of the 23rd ACM Symposium on Operating Systems Principles (SOSP),* pp. 129–142.
http://research.google.com/pubs/pub37474.html

Allspaw, J. (2009). Blameless postmortems and a just culture.
http://codeascraft.com/2012/05/22/blameless-postmortems.

Allspaw, J. (2012a). Each necessary, but only jointly sufficient.
http://www.kitchensoap.com/2012/02/10/each-necessary-but-only-jointly-sufficient.

Allspaw, J. (2012b). Fault injection in production, *Queue* **10**(8): 30:30–30:35.
http://queue.acm.org/detail.cfm?id=2353017

Allspaw, J. (2012c). A mature role for automation.
http://www.kitchensoap.com/2012/09/21/a-mature-role-for-automation-part-i

Anderson, C. (2012). Idea five: Software will eat the world, *Wired.*
http://www.wired.com/business/2012/04/ff_andreessen/5

Armbrust, M., Fox, A., Griffith, R., Joseph, A. D., Katz, R., Konwinski, A., Lee, G., Patterson, D., Rabkin, A., Stoica, I., & Zaharia, M. (2010). A view of cloud computing, *Communications of the ACM* **53**(4): 50–58.
http://cacm.acm.org/magazines/2010/4/81493-a-view-of-cloud-computing

Barroso, L. A., Dean, J., & Hölzle, U. (2003). Web search for a planet: The Google cluster architecture, *IEEE Micro* **23**(2): 22–28.
http://research.google.com/archive/googlecluster.html

Barroso, L. A., Clidaras, J., & Hölzle, U. (2013). *The Datacenter as a Computer: An Introduction to the Design of Warehouse-Scale Machines*, 2nd ed., Morgan and Claypool Publishers.
`http://research.google.com/pubs/pub41606.html`

Beck, K., Beedle, M., van Bennekum, A., Cockburn, A., Cunningham, W., Fowler, M., Grenning, J., Highsmith, J., Hunt, A., Jeffries, R., Kern, J., Marick, B., Martin, R. C., Mellor, S., Schwaber, K., Sutherland, J., & Thomas, D. (2001). Manifesto for agile software development.
`http://agilemanifesto.org`

Black, B. (2009). EC2 origins.
`http://blog.b3k.us/2009/01/25/ec2-origins.html`

Brandt, K. (2014). OODA for sysadmins.
`http://blog.serverfault.com/2012/07/18/ooda-for-sysadmins`

Brin, S., & Page, L. (1998). The anatomy of a large-scale hypertextual web search engine, *Proceedings of the Seventh International Conference on World Wide Web 7*, WWW7, Elsevier Science Publishers, Amsterdam, Netherlands, pp. 107–117.
`http://dl.acm.org/citation.cfm?id=297805.297827`

Burgess, M. (2013). *In Search of Certainty: The Science of Our Information Infrastructure*, Createspace Independent Publishing.

Burgess, M., & Bergstra, J. (2014). *Promise Theory: Principles and Applications*, On Demand Publishing, Create Space.

Burrows, M. (2006). The Chubby lock service for loosely-coupled distributed systems, *Proceedings of the 7th Symposium on Operating Systems Design and Implementation*, OSDI '06, USENIX Association, Berkeley, CA, pp. 335–350.
`http://research.google.com/archive/chubby.html`

Candea, G., & Fox, A. (2003). Crash-only software, *HotOS*, pp. 67–72.
`https://www.usenix.org/conference/hotos-ix/crash-only-software`

Chang, F., Dean, J., Ghemawat, S., Hsieh, W. C., Wallach, D. A., Burrows, M., Chandra, T., Fikes, A., & Gruber, R. E. (2006). Bigtable: A distributed storage system for structured data, *Proceedings of the 7th USENIX Symposium on Operating Systems Design and Implementation*, pp. 205–218.

Chapman, B. (2005). Incident command for IT: What we can learn from the fire department., *LISA*, USENIX.
`http://www.greatcircle.com/presentations`

Cheswick, W. R., Bellovin, S. M., & Rubin, A. D. (2003). *Firewalls and Internet Security: Repelling the Wiley Hacker*, Addison-Wesley.
`http://books.google.com/books?id=_ZqIh0IbcrgC`

Clos, C. (1953). A study of non-blocking switching networks, *The Bell System Technical Journal* **32**(2): 406–424.
`http://www.alcatel-lucent.com/bstj/vol32-1953/articles/bstj32-2-406.pdf`

Corbett, J. C., Dean, J., Epstein, M., Fikes, A., Frost, C., Furman, J. J., Ghemawat, S., Gubarev, A., Heiser, C., Hochschild, P., Hsieh, W., Kanthak, S., Kogan, E., Li, H., Lloyd, A., Melnik, S., Mwaura, D., Nagle, D., Quinlan, S., Rao, R., Rolig, L., Saito, Y.,

Szymaniak, M., Taylor, C., Wang, R., & Woodford, D. (2012). Spanner: Google's globally-distributed database, *Proceedings of the 10th USENIX Conference on Operating Systems Design and Implementation*, OSDI'12, USENIX Association, Berkeley, CA, pp. 251–264.
http://research.google.com/archive/spanner.html

Dean, J. (2009). Designs, lessons and advice from building large distributed systems.
http://www.cs.cornell.edu/projects/ladis2009/talks/dean-keynote-ladis2009.pdf

Dean, J., & Barroso, L. A. (2013). The tail at scale, *Communications of the ACM* **56**(2): 74–80.
http://cacm.acm.org/magazines/2013/2/160173-the-tail-at-scale

Dean, J., & Ghemawat, S. (2004). MapReduce: Simplified data processing on large clusters, *OSDI'04: Proceedings of the 6th USENIX Symposium on Operating Systems Design and Implementation*, USENIX Association.

Debois, P. (2010a). Jedi4Ever blog.
http://www.jedi.be/blog

Debois, P. (2010b). DevOps is a verb. Slideshare of talk.
http://www.slideshare.net/jedi4ever/devops-is-a-verb-its-all-about-feedback-13174519

Deming, W. (2000). *Out of the Crisis*, Massachusetts Institute of Technology, Center for Advanced Engineering Study.

DevOps-Toolchain. (2010). A set of best practices useful to those practicing DevOps methodology.
http://code.google.com/p/devops-toolchain/wiki/BestPractices

Dickson, C. (2013). A working theory of monitoring, presented as part of the 27th Large Installation System Administration Conference, USENIX, Berkeley, CA.
https://www.usenix.org/conference/lisa13/working-theory-monitoring

Edwards, D. (2010). DevOps is not a technology problem.
http://dev2ops.org/2010/11/devops-is-not-a-technology-problem-devops-is-a-business-problem

Edwards, D. (2012). Use DevOps to turn IT into a strategic weapon.
http://dev2ops.org/2012/09/use-devops-to-turn-it-into-a-strategic-weapon

Edwards, D., & Shortland, A. (2012). Integrating DevOps tools into a service delivery platform.
http://dev2ops.org/2012/07/integrating-devops-tools-into-a-service-delivery-platform-video

England, R. (2009). *Owning ITIL: A Skeptical Guide for Decision-Makers*, Two Hills.

Fitts, P. (1951). Human engineering for an effective air navigation and traffic-control system, *Technical Report ATI-133954*, Ohio State Research Foundation.
http://www.skybrary.aero/bookshelf/books/355.pdf

Flack, M., & Wiese, K. (1977). *The Story about Ping*, Picture Puffin Books, Puffin Books.

Gallagher, S. (2012). Built to win: Deep inside Obama's campaign tech.
http://arstechnica.com/information-technology/2012/11/built-to-win-deep-inside-obamas-campaign-tech

Ghemawat, S., Gobioff, H., & Leung, S.-T. (2003). The Google file system, *Proceedings of the Nineteenth ACM Symposium on Operating Systems Principles*, SOSP '03, ACM, New York, NY, pp. 29–43.
http://doi.acm.org/10.1145/945445.945450

Gilbert, S., & Lynch, N. (2002). Brewer's conjecture and the feasibility of consistent, available, partition-tolerant web services, *SIGACT News* **33**(2): 51–59.
http://doi.acm.org/10.1145/564585.564601

Google. (2012). Efficiency: How we do it.
http://www.google.com/about/datacenters/efficiency/internal

Gruver, G., Young, M., & Fulghum, P. (2012). *A Practical Approach to Large-Scale Agile Development: How HP Transformed HP LaserJet FutureSmart Firmware*, Addison-Wesley.

Haynes, D. (2013). Understanding CPU steal time: When should you be worried.
http://blog.scoutapp.com/articles/2013/07/25/understanding-cpu-steal-time-when-should-you-be-worried.

Hickstein, J. (2007). Sysadmin slogans.
http://www.jxh.com/slogans.html

Hohpe, G., & Woolf, B. (2003). *Enterprise Integration Patterns: Designing, Building, and Deploying Messaging Solutions*, Addison-Wesley Longman, Boston, MA.

Humble, J., & Farley, D. (2010). *Continuous Delivery: Reliable Software Releases through Build, Test, and Deployment Automation*, Addison-Wesley Professional.

Jacob, A. (2010). Choose your own adventure: Adam Jacob on DevOps.
http://www.youtube.com/watch?v=Fx8OBeNmaWw

Kamp, P.-H. (2010). You're doing it wrong, *Communications of the ACM* **53**(7): 55–59.
http://queue.acm.org/detail.cfm?id=1814327

Kartar, J. (2010). What DevOps means to me.
http://www.kartar.net/2010/02/what-devops-means-to-me

Kernighan, B., & Pike, R. (1984). *The UNIX Programming Environment*, Prentice Hall.

Kernighan, B., & Plauger, P. (1978). *The Elements of Programming Style*, McGraw-Hill.

Kim, G., Behr, K., & Spafford, G. (2013). *The Phoenix Project: A Novel about IT, DevOps, and Helping Your Business Win*, IT Revolution Press.
http://books.google.com/books?id=mqXomAEACAAJ

Klau, R. (2012). How Google sets goals: OKRs.
http://gv.com/1322

Krishnan, K. (2012). Weathering the unexpected, *Queue* **10**(9): 30:30–30:37.
http://queue.acm.org/detail.cfm?id=2371516

Lakshman, A., & Malik, P. (2010). Cassandra: A decentralized structured storage system, *SIGOPS Operating Systems Review* **44**(2): 35–40.
http://doi.acm.org/10.1145/1773912.1773922

Lamport, L. (2001). Paxos made simple, *SIGACT News* **32**(4): 51–58.
http://research.microsoft.com/users/lamport/pubs/paxos-simple.pdf

Lamport, L., & Marzullo, K. (1998). The part-time parliament, *ACM Transactions on Computer Systems* **16**: 133–169.

Lee, J. D., & See, K. A. (2004). Trust in automation: Designing for appropriate reliance, *Human Factors* **46**(1): 50–80.

Letuchy, E. (2008). Facebook Chat.
https://www.facebook.com/note.php?note_id=14218138919

Levinson, M. (2008). *The Box: How the Shipping Container Made the World Smaller and the World Economy Bigger*, Princeton University Press.

Levy, S. (2012). Google throws open doors to its top-secret data center, *Wired* **20**(11).
http://www.wired.com/wiredenterprise/2012/10/ff-inside-google-data-center/all

Limoncelli, T. A. (2005). *Time Management for System Administrators*, O'Reilly and Associates.

Limoncelli, T. (2012). Google DiRT: The view from someone being tested, *Queue* **10**(9): 35:35–35:37.
http://queue.acm.org/detail.cfm?id=2371516#sidebar

Limoncelli, T. A., Hogan, C., & Chalup, S. R. (2015). *The Practice of System and Network Administration*, 3rd ed., Pearson Education.

Link, D. (2013). Netflix and stolen time.
http://blog.sciencelogic.com/netflix-steals-time-in-the-cloud-and-from-users/03/2011

Madrigal, A. C. (2012). When the nerds go marching in: How a dream team of engineers from Facebook, Twitter, and Google built the software that drove Barack Obama's reelection.
http://www.theatlantic.com/technology/archive/2012/11/when-the-nerds-go-marching-in/265325

McKinley, D. (2012). Why MongoDB never worked out at Etsy.
http://mcfunley.com/why-mongodb-never-worked-out-at-etsy

McKusick, M. K., Neville-Neil, G., & Watson, R. N. (2014). *The Design and Implementation of the FreeBSD Operating System*, Prentice Hall.

Megiddo, N., & Modha, D. S. (2003). ARC: A self-tuning, low overhead replacement cache, *Proceedings of the 2nd USENIX Conference on File and Storage Technologies*, FAST '03, USENIX Association, Berkeley, CA, pp. 115–130.
https://www.usenix.org/conference/fast-03/arc-self-tuning-low-overhead-replacement-cache

Metz, C. (2013). Return of the Borg: How Twitter rebuilt Google's secret weapon, *Wired*.
http://www.wired.com/wiredenterprise/2013/03/google-borg-twitter-mesos/all

Nygard, M. T. (2007). *Release It!: Design and Deploy Production-Ready Software*, Pragmatic Bookshelf.

Oppenheimer, D. L., Ganapathi, A., & Patterson, D. A. (2003). Why do Internet services fail, and what can be done about it?, *USENIX Symposium on Internet Technologies and Systems*.

Parasuraman, R., Sheridan, T. B., & Wickens, C. D. (2000). A model for types and levels of human interaction with automation, *Transactions on Systems, Man, and Cybernetics Part A* **30**(3): 286–297.
http://dx.doi.org/10.1109/3468.844354

Patterson, D., Brown, A., Broadwell, P., Candea, G., Chen, M., Cutler, J., Enriquez, P., Fox, A., Kiciman, E., Merzbacher, M., Oppenheimer, D., Sastry, N., Tetzlaff, W., Traupman, J., & Treuhaft, N. (2002). Recovery Oriented Computing (ROC): Motivation, definition, techniques, and case studies, *Technical Report UCB/CSD-02-1175*, EECS Department, University of California, Berkeley, CA.
http://www.eecs.berkeley.edu/Pubs/TechRpts/2002/5574.html

Pfeiffer, T. (2012). Why waterfall was a big misunderstanding from the beginning: Reading the original paper.
http://pragtob.wordpress.com/2012/03/02/why-waterfall-was-a-big-misunderstanding-from-the-beginning-reading-the-original-paper

Pinheiro, E., Weber, W.-D., & Barroso, L. A. (2007). Failure trends in a large disk drive population, *5th USENIX Conference on File and Storage Technologies (FAST 2007)*, pp. 17–29.

Rachitsky, L. (2010). A guideline for postmortem communication.
http://www.transparentuptime.com/2010/03/guideline-for-postmortem-communication.html

Richard, D. (2013). Gamedays on the Obama campaign.
http://velocityconf.com/velocity2013/public/schedule/detail/28444;
http://www.youtube.com/watch?v=LCZT_Q3z520

Robbins, J., Krishnan, K., Allspaw, J., & Limoncelli, T. (2012). Resilience engineering: Learning to embrace failure, *Queue* **10**(9): 20:20–20:28.
http://queue.acm.org/detail.cfm?id=2371297

Rockwood, B. (2013). Why SysAdmin's can't code.
http://cuddletech.com/?p=817

Rossi, C. (2011). Facebook: Pushing millions of lines of code five days a week.
https://www.facebook.com/video/video.php?v=10100259101684977

Royce, D. W. W. (1970). Managing the development of large software systems: Concepts and techniques.

Schlossnagle, T. (2011). Career development.
http://www.youtube.com/watch?v=y0mHo7SMCQk

Schroeder, B., Pinheiro, E., & Weber, W.-D. (2009). DRAM errors in the wild: A large-scale field study, *SIGMETRICS*.

Schwarzkopf, M., Konwinski, A., Abd-El-Malek, M., & Wilkes, J. (2013). Omega: Flexible, scalable schedulers for large compute clusters, *SIGOPS European Conference on Computer Systems (EuroSys)*, Prague, Czech Republic, pp. 351–364.
http://research.google.com/pubs/pub41684.html

Seven, D. (2014). Knightmare: A DevOps cautionary tale.
    `http://dougseven.com/2014/04/17/knightmare-a-devops-cautionary-tale`

Siegler, M. (2011). The next 6 months worth of features are in Facebook's code right now (but we can't see).
    `http://techcrunch.com/2011/05/30/facebook-source-code`

Spear, S., & Bowen, H. K. (1999). Decoding the DNA of the Toyota production system, *Harvard Business Review*.

Spolsky, J. (2004). Things you should never do, Part I, *Joel on Software*, Apress.
    `http://www.joelonsoftware.com/articles/fog0000000069.html`

Stevens, W. (1998). *UNIX Network Programming: Interprocess Communications, UNIX Networking Reference Series, Vol. 2*, Prentice Hall.

Stevens, W. R., & Fall, K. (2011). *TCP/IP Illustrated, Volume 1: The Protocols*, Pearson Education.
    `http://books.google.com/books?id=a230An5i8R0C`

Stevens, W., & Rago, S. (2013). *Advanced Programming in the UNIX Environment*, Pearson Education.

Stevens, W., & Wright, G. (1996). *TCP/IP Illustrated, Volume 3: TCP for Transactions, HTTP, NNTP, and the UNIX Domain Protocols*, Addison-Wesley.

Tseitlin, A. (2013). The antifragile organization, *Queue* **11**(6): 20:20–20:26.
    `http://queue.acm.org/detail.cfm?id=2499552`

Tufte, E. R. (1986). *The Visual Display of Quantitative Information*, Graphics Press, Cheshire, CT.

Walls, M. (2013). *Building a DevOps Culture*, O'Reilly Media.

Willis, J., & Edwards, D. (2011). Interview with Jesse Robbins.
    `http://www.opscode.com/blog/2011/09/22/jesse-robbins-interview-on-devops-cafe-19-w-full-transcript`

Willis, J., Edwards, D., & Humble, J. (2012). DevOps Cafe Episode 33: Finally it's Jez.
    `http://devopscafe.org/show/2012/9/26/devops-cafe-episode-33.html`

Wright, G., & Stevens, W. (1995). *TCP/IP Illustrated, Volume 2: The Implementations*, Pearson Education.

Yan, B., & Kejariwal, A. (2013). A systematic approach to capacity planning in the real world.
    `http://www.slideshare.net/arunkejariwal/a-systematic-approach-to-capacity-planning-in-the-real-world`

Index